No, Minister

No, Minister

Navigating Power, Politics and Bureaucracy with a Steely Resolve

Subhash Chandra Garg

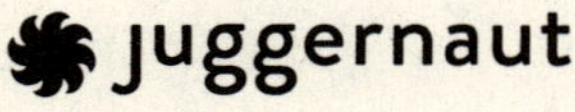

JUGGERNAUT BOOKS
C-I-128, First Floor, Sangam Vihar, Near Holi Chowk,
New Delhi 110080, India

First published by Juggernaut Books 2025

10 9 8 7 6 5 4 3 2 1

P-ISBN: 9789353454531
E-ISBN: 9789353459338

Typeset in Adobe Caslon Pro by R. Ajith Kumar, Noida

Printed at Thomson Press India Ltd

To my wife, soulmate and strength, Anjali.

To my sons Shrey and Dhruv,
who, having seen nothing extraordinary in my life,
decided not to pursue a career in the IAS.

Contents

Prologue: 'I Will Finish Him Off' 1

PART A: ADMINISTRATION IN RAJASTHAN

1. Fixing Land Unsettlement and Other Chaos 17
2. A Collector Complains Against His SDO! 29
3. Dysfunctional Rural Benefits Delivery 39
4. 'Why Do We Need Interviews to Recruit Teachers?' 52
5. Making the White Elephant Dance 58
6. 'Sell Off Before It Is Too Late' 70
7. 'You Are Working Well but It Does Not Suit Us' 83
8. Challenges of Transfers and Short Tenures 98
9. Personnel Battles in Agriculture Development 107
10. Getting Waylaid by the Wheels of Corruption 122
11. In the Den of Union Leaders 128
12. Conducting Board Exams Without Teachers 140
13. A University Student's Tragic Suicide 158
14. Rajasthan Begins Its Journey on the Renewable Energy Path 166

PART B: BUDGET AND FINANCE IN RAJASTHAN

15. In and Out of Helming Finance in Rajasthan 183
16. State-Level Finance and Budgets 194
17. Bhamashah Got Stalled Just Before Elections 202
18. Two Budgets in Six Months 214
19. 'I Don't Want to See Him in the Cabinet Today' 224

PART C: AT THE WORLD BANK AND THE CENTRE

20. 'You Must Be a Dummy Candidate' 241
21. Resetting India's Relationship with the World Bank and IMF 252
22. Dabhol Power Plant For $1 and Other Matters 264
23. Pulling States Out of the Debt Trap 275
24. A 'Smiling Assassin' 286
25. Detour to Implementing Agriculture Programmes 299
26. 'Officers Do What They Are Told to Do' 314
27. Serving Global Development at the World Bank Group 325
28. Bringing Indus Waters Arbitration Back from the Brink 342
29. 'You Are Arun Jaitley and Piyush Goyal for Me' 358
30. 'Stay Away from the PM KISAN Scheme' 376
31. 'Has the Government Approved Your Dissent Note?' 389
32. 'You Are Not in Tune with the Government's Thinking' 403

Epilogue 414

Notes 421

Acknowledgements 422

Prologue

'I Will Finish Him Off'

Sometime in late September 1987, V.S. Singh, an officer of the 1978 batch of the Indian Administrative Service (IAS), five years my senior, working as a deputy secretary to the government of Rajasthan, summoned me to his office in the secretariat. I had no functional relationship with him as I was serving as additional collector, Development, and project director of the District Rural Development Agency (DRDA), Jaipur.

'Why did you do this to M.P. Rajan?' he asked with a stern face and in a somewhat threatening tone.

For a few moments, I was a little lost. Quickly collecting my thoughts, I asked him whether he was referring to the then collector of Seoni in Madhya Pradesh, whom I had met in December 1983 when I was part of a group of probationers undergoing our 'tribal attachment' in Seoni district.

V.S. Singh nodded and then told me that Rajan was extremely upset and agitated. He further informed me that Rajan spoke to him of me and had vowed that he would make my life difficult. 'I will finish him off,' were the exact words he used, V.S. Singh informed me. I related the entire story to him. He seemed to be understanding but not satisfied.

Though I was not quite worried, it seemed my career in the IAS was going to witness a baptism by fire.

Fourth position in IAS despite challenges

My father, a telegraphist in the Post and Telegraph (P&T) department, had developed significant health issues since 1972, and by 1978 he had virtually stopped going to work. With no family assets to fall back on and his salary practically amounting to almost nothing, I, the eldest brother amongst six siblings, started giving tuition classes and doing some manual jobs in my senior school days to help the family.

I did have an excellent academic record, securing third position in Rajasthan Board in the secondary and sixth in the higher secondary examinations. When I was in the first year of my BCom degree course in the Government College, Ajmer (college education practically cost nothing, and I was able to earn some income from debates, essay competitions and so on), I had made up my mind that I would try and build a career in the IAS. I was quite aware of the fact that getting into the IAS was not only super-competitive but a matter of enormous luck as well with only about 150 persons making it every year from amongst the lakhs who competed.

Believing that there should always be an alternative to fall back on, I had decided to also get the professional membership of the Institute of Cost and Works Accountants of India (ICWAI), as it was known then. (Today, it is known as the Institute of Cost Accountants of India or ICAI). I decided not to do the chartered accountancy course – a better alternative, but beyond my financial capacity. I secured the first position in India in the ICWAI's intermediate examination. Later, I completed the company secretaries' course as well securing the first position in the final examination.

My first possible go at the civil services examination was in 1982. Our family of eight lived in small Type-2 government quarter with two small rooms, a tiny kitchen and a short veranda. As the space and atmosphere in the home were not conducive to studying, I decided to share a 5 ft × 8 ft room in a dharmshala attached to a Jain temple, at a rent of ₹5 per month, with a friend, Om Prakash Dadhich, who later joined Indian Customs and Excise Service and remains one of my closest friends.

There was no separate charge for electricity and a lone 40-watt bulb was adequate to light up the room. The manager of the temple's affairs was, however, quite unhappy with our 'excessive' use of electricity as I would study late into the night and Om early in the morning.

One day in late September 1982, the manager pulled out the wire that connected the bulb to the line and asked us to vacate the room within 24 hours. The plea that I had Union Public Service Commission (UPSC) examinations in two weeks later made no difference to him. In these circumstances, I decided to go to Jaipur, which was the examination centre as well.

The small room that I rented on the third floor leaked heavily when a cyclonic disturbance brought a deluge of rain in the first week of October. This disturbance, along with the absence of a workable arrangement for meals, made me fall ill. I had to shift to a friend's one-room tenement nearby, which also took care of my meals. I still was running high fever.

When I told the doctor that I had to appear for my civil services examination four days later and asked him to do something to bring my fever down, he prescribed me very strong medicines. The medicines did bring my fever down though it had its side-effects. Though physically quite weak, I took the Indian Civil Service (ICS) exam that had six main papers: two for general studies and two each for two elective subjects. I had chosen generally considered tougher subjects of law and commerce and accountancy, based on the simple logic that I knew these subjects the best, having studied them for my graduate degrees.

When the drill was over, I believed I had performed quite well and was confident of securing good marks and entry into IAS. I also decided to go for a job as I had offers from quite a few public sector undertakings like Oil India Ltd (OIL), Steel Authority of India and Bharat Heavy Electricals Ltd.

On 31 May 1983, the results for 1982 were published in the newspapers. However, I was in Duliajan in Assam, employed with OIL, where the newspapers reached only in the evening. On my request, a colleague in the finance wing of OIL in the Calcutta (now Kolkata) office looked at the newspapers and teleprinted the news by noon. I had secured the fourth position in the country. I was indeed happy.

Later, on receiving the marksheet, I discovered that, in the interview, I had secured only 120 marks out of 250, lower than the average. My performance in the written examination, though, turned out to be excellent. I secured the highest marks in the country in both law and accountancy. While the final ranking in civil services merit list is based on a total of written and interview marks, my marks in the written examination alone would have secured me fifty-first rank in the IAS that year.

I joined the Lal Bahadur Shastri National Academy of Administration (LBSNAA), the IAS Academy, on 29 August 1983.

'Tribal attachment' in Seoni

The IAS officers were put through a training-cum-probation period of two years, comprising a three-month Foundation Course (FC) that officers of Indian Foreign Service (IFS), Indian Police Service (IPS) and other central services recruited through the common civil services examination also joined;

a five-month Phase 1, exclusively for the IAS, with state and district training of about a year in their respective cadres; and, finally, a Phase 2 of about two-and-a-half months.

The FC, Phase 1 and Phase 2 took place at the Academy. As part of the FC, the officers would go for a village visit – for familiarization with rural life and administration – and a trekking tour in the Himalayas. Phase 1 included a long tour (also called Bharat Darshan) of the country, with officers divided into groups. A mandatory part of Bharat Darshan was a visit to tribal areas, which was termed 'tribal attachment'. It was meant to expose officers to the tribal way of life and the government programmes under implementation for their betterment.

Our FC concluded at the end of November and the first phase of the professional training programme began immediately thereafter. As December and January are the coldest months of the year, not very suitable for academic studies in Mussoorie, the Academy sent out the officers, called probationers, for Bharat Darshan in batches of 25–30 each. For the two weeks of tribal attachment, the groups of probationers were further broken down into smaller groups of four or five officers each.

Thus, I landed, with four other probationers, in a forest guesthouse amid the jungles inhabited by Gond tribals in the Seoni district of Madhya Pradesh. The other smaller groups were likewise sent out to other forest guesthouses in the district.

M.P. Rajan was the district magistrate and collector of Seoni district.

The forest guesthouses where we were staying fell in the Pench Wildlife Sanctuary (later elevated to a national park and a tiger reserve). One evening, M.P. Rajan decided to organize a large party in a guesthouse in the middle of Pench National Park and take the probationers and other guests for a night safari in the jungles.

He had already hosted a party at his official residence in Seoni for us probationers when we had first landed at the district headquarters. During these two parties, the liquor flowed freely, with his son, just seven or eight years old, also joining in and consuming liquor without any inhibitions. When the liquor got to M.P. Rajan, he related with a lot of relish the stories of his (mis)adventures in the Academy when he was a probationer; this included a dance performance with a liquor bottle placed on the head of the statue of Lal Bahadur Shastri at the Academy entrance. He also shared stories ridiculing the director of the Academy during his time, Rajeshwar Dayal, who had initiated the enactment of the Ramayana by the probationers during their Phase-1 training in 1977. M.P. Rajan also used searchlights mounted on top of jeeps to locate tigers in the sanctuary in the dead of night.

During the tribal attachment, probationers were expected to study tribal life by interacting with tribal families. Each probationer was supposed to interview about 50 tribal families and fill in a questionnaire for each family. As probationers were housed in guesthouses in deep forests that were sparsely inhabited, there were not enough families to interact with and interview. Not surprisingly, the questionnaires were filled in with imaginary families.

Probationers' reports were required to be presented to the collector as well as the Academy. A man with little faith in the utility of the tribal attachment exercise, M.P. Rajan disposed this minor matter by declaring, during the dinner he hosted, that the reports were taken as presented.

The dinner and jungle safari were attended by several senior forest officers, who also appeared quite unconcerned. They were happy to enjoy the party and night safari.

As I was interested in learning about the Gond tribals, their way of life and the division of these otherwise cohesive tribals in the three states of Madhya Pradesh, Gujarat and Rajasthan, I did visit a few Gond tribal families in the area. However, by and large, the tribal attachment turned out to be a big sham.

A case study causes a storm

The Academy ran a programme to encourage probationers to write case studies. The accepted studies were published in the academy's journal, *The Administrator*, and the author earned a reward of ₹250.

My financial position was tight. The Academy paid ₹1,600 a month as an advance against the monthly salary that would be drawn later in the cadres when probationers reached their respective cadre states for district training. The mess charges took away about ₹800 per month. As my family back home in Ajmer was dependent on me, I would send ₹700 per month to them. In such a precarious financial state, a reward of ₹250 was good enough motivation to write a case study.

Dr D.C. Tiwari, a respected professor at the Academy and in charge of case study work, was the counsellor of my group of probationers. When he mentioned writing case studies in one of our conversations, I decided to write one on my experience of the tribal attachment.

Within the next two months, I completed the case study and handed it to Dr Tiwari. He informed me that it would go to a committee, which would take some time, and the remuneration would be paid by the Academy thereafter. As the examination of the case study was not completed by the time we left for our district training at the end of May 1984, I departed for Rajasthan without receiving the reward.

I checked with him a few times when I was undergoing my district training in Jodhpur and when we were back in the Academy for Phase 2 of our probation, which ran from June to mid-August 1985. He would always say that the case study was very well done but the committee still had to take a final view.

R.N. Chopra of the Madhya Pradesh cadre joined the Academy as the director, the top boss, in June 1985, around the time when we, the probationers of the 1983 batch, joined the Academy for our Phase-2 training. One day, he called me to his office in the presence of D.C. Tiwari. He asked me whether the incidents I had described in the case study were all true. I confirmed they were.

Unknown to me, he sent my case study with a semi-official (DO) letter to the chief secretary of Madhya Pradesh, asking for action to be taken against M.P. Rajan for not organizing and conducting the right kind of tribal attachment training to probationers. I discovered later, after M.P. Rajan had complained to V.S. Singh, that Rajan had once caused some harm to R.N. Chopra, and the latter was carrying a grudge. My case study came in handy for Chopra to settle old scores.

M.P. Rajan was quite a controversial officer. Later, in the 1990s, he got involved in one of the largest financial scandals in Madhya Pradesh, borrowing hundreds of crores of money from markets for the Madhya Pradesh State Industrial Development Corporation (MPSIDC) when he was its managing director (MD) and 'investing' these funds in phony and weak companies of some industrialists as loans without any collaterals except a promissory note. The MPSIDC lost a good deal of money on these investments.

My case study did get some traction in the corridors of power in Madhya Pradesh and led to Rajan having to offer an explanation. That's what led to his threat that he would 'finish me off'.

I wasn't unduly concerned. For my part, I had truthfully recorded his shenanigans, with no personal malice, to earn a ₹250 reward for writing a case study and, to some extent, to express my disgust at the way the tribal attachment was reduced to a farce. Unfortunately, that princely ₹250 never came through.

M.P. Rajan did not do anything to me. I never heard anything from him or any other officer about the matter. I did learn from the newspapers of the scandal at the MPSIDC. Instead of being punished, Rajan was, however, allowed to take voluntary retirement from IAS.

My probation otherwise turned out to be quite interesting and educative.

'He came in sneakers'

Rajasthan had a system of state counsellors at that time, with one senior officer appointed as a state guide for a IAS probationer for the district training. V.B.L. Mathur, a very senior IAS officer, who later served for six years as chief secretary of Rajasthan (1986–92), was my state counsellor.

One forenoon in 1984, I called on him at his residence, in line with the usual practice. At that time, in 1984, he was handling a lighter assignment as secretary, Regional Development. Having served in several commercial organizations in the Government of India, including the Delhi Super Bazaar, he had a thorough commercial and economic orientation. He was very considerate and explained to me the great opportunities IAS officers would be getting in public-sector organizations.

On the day of his retirement in 1992, he was given a very warm send-off in true Rajasthani tradition. During his speech, his eyes were suddenly fixed on me and he said, 'What a fine officer Subhash has become from the day he came to call on me as a probationer wearing sneakers to someone who could turn around the ailing soybean plant in Kota.' He was certainly a keen observer! For my part, I had evidently not realized that calling on a senior officer in sneakers was not good manners.

First brush with corruption

A kind-hearted and affable S.D. Srivastava, an officer promoted to the IAS from the Rajasthan Administrative Service (RAS), was the collector and district magistrate of Jodhpur under whom I did my district training. He also strongly believed in on-the-job training. As part of this training, I was appointed *tehsildar* (the officer in charge of revenue administration in a tehsil) of Phalodi, Rajasthan, when Gautam Mehta, the incumbent, went on a two-week leave.

A day after I took charge, a registry clerk (who prepares papers for registering property documents) came to me. In the tehsils, where there was no independent sub registrar (very few tehsils in Rajasthan had an independent sub registrar in

1984), the tehsildar also functioned as sub registrar for registering sale deeds and other documents. He nonchalantly informed me that ₹25 was collected for the tehsildar for every registry made, which would be paid to me as I was the tehsildar in the absence of Gautam Mehta.

This came as a huge shock to me, steeped as I was in the idealism of public service without corruption. Three to five registries were done every day. In two days, the Phalodi tehsildar would collect ₹ 250, the princely amount for which I had written a comprehensive case study and for which I was still awaiting payment!

Though I had an inkling that the revenue machinery was corrupt, the blatant and systemic nature of it shocked me – the registry clerk did not bat an eyelid when he informed me that I would receive ₹100–125 per day. Determined to make an example of how to eradicate this malpractice, I decided to announce in the open court of the tehsildar, in the presence of tens of lawyers, that no amount would be collected for registering documents. I got a notice made to this effect and pasted it outside my office. I also wrote a confidential letter to the collector about rampant and systemic corruption in Phalodi and the measure I had taken to deal with it. The message spread across the town in no time. Some senior lawyers even hailed the decision.

I don't know whether the collection of money stopped (nothing was offered to me) or whether the registration expenditure of buyers reduced. The number of registrations did increase significantly during that period. Probably, people wanted to use the opportunity to get registries done without bribes, or fewer bribes at any rate.

When I returned to district headquarters after two weeks, Shyam Agarwal, an officer of the 1980 batch, who retired as secretary, Tribal Development, Government of India, and was serving as additional collector, Development (Jodhpur), at that time, informed me that Gautam Mehta was a relatively clean and competent officer. He further informed me that the responsibility of taking care of ministers and senior officers when they visited and meeting their stay and other expenditures, for which there were no official provision, fell upon the tehsildars. In Shyam's judgement, Gautam Mehta was possibly collecting ₹25 per registry to cater to these expenditures, while other tehsildars took more money and pocketed it for themselves.

One of the lessons I learnt from this first brush with corruption was that I would never accept the hospitality of tehsildars and would always pay my bills and collect the receipts.

'You will face enquiries for decisions'

The responsibility of managing law and order in the city limits of Jodhpur and granting permissions – holding public rallies, licences for new arms, renewal of old arms licences, opening cinema halls and so on – was assigned to the city magistrate. Rajhans Upadhyay, an officer of the 1981 batch, an alumnus of the Indian Institute of Technology (IIT) and one of the youngest officers in his batch in the country, was city magistrate Jodhpur. As in the case of Phalodi, when Upadhyay went on a leave, Collector S.D. Shrivastava decided to make me the city magistrate.

A few cases would come up every day in the city magistrate's court concerning Section 107 and other provisions of the Code of Criminal Procedure (CrPC). These sections deal with the applications of people, made either on their own or through the police, who felt threatened by others and requested the latter to be 'bound down' with bonds, so that if they indulge in any violence thereafter, they could be punished by encashing their bonds. I would try to understand the real cause of apprehension/trouble and, if appropriate, would issue orders for binding down the arraigned person or discharge him if the case appeared to be based on false grounds. These cases were not 'judicial' matters per se and the most important element was the assessment by the magistrate of the reality of the threat. Moreover, as the perception had to be of an imminent threat, the matter, in my opinion, needed to be decided quickly. Therefore, I disposed of several such matters when I was holding charge. The pendency of 'court cases' came down substantially by the time Rajhans Upadhyay returned.

Likewise, in non-court matters – renewal of gun licences etc. – I felt that renewal should be a routine process unless there was a real likelihood of misuse. In all cases of such applications, the office of the city magistrate would seek a report from the police about the conduct and character of the licensee. I called for all the pending files. There were many. These files were also dealt with like court matters. Applicants would be asked to come on a certain date, which they would comply with, sometimes accompanied by a lawyer although there was no need for a lawyer for such an administrative matter. If the city magistrate was not in the office for any reason, another date would be fixed and the applicants sent back. I found this process inefficient, causing undue hardship to people. I asked the clerk to classify the files in three categories: those where the applications were complete, due police reports had been received and there was no apparent reason to deny renewal; those where the application was complete, due reports had been received and there was reason to suspect misuse; and the remaining ones. In the first category, I decided to grant renewal in one day and got the office to send the renewal permissions by post. The applications in the second category were rejected and orders despatched by post. The office suddenly felt light with more than 50 per cent of pending applications disposed of.

There was one matter that had attracted considerable media attention. In early 1980s, cinema halls were the biggest source of entertainment for people. Jodhpur was witnessing construction of new cinema halls. There was one cinema hall, Kohinoor, which had been constructed, and its licence was pending in the city magistrate's office. Certain compliances were required before a cinema hall was licensed. As this was one of the most lucrative businesses at the time, there was also a possibility of corruption. Some news item or the other report would routinely appear in the local newspapers about the pending licence of Kohinoor cinema. I decided to take the bull by the horns and made a visit to the cinema hall to conduct an inspection required by the law. I reviewed all safety, electrical and other arrangements in the presence of all concerned officials and found everything in order. I, therefore, decided to issue the licence. This made headlines in Jodhpur. The cinema hall was inaugurated with fanfare a few days later by Collector Srivastava.

When Rajhans Upadhyay returned from leave, he found his office load considerably lighter. While he appreciated my efforts to expedite things, he had a word of advice for me. He felt it was risky to decide matters in a hurry – people could question one's motives, which might lead to enquiries if anything was found amiss later. I decided to take his advice in my stride and duly ignored it.

That said, an explanation was, indeed, sought later from the collector, Srivastava, on a complaint against him in the matter of the Kohinoor cinema licence. No one asked me anything about this or any other matter. It appeared to me later that my order recorded on the file, giving the factual state of affairs, noting completion of all requisite compliances and the necessity of deciding the matter quickly in public interest, held good, and the allegation of corruption against Collector Srivastava also received no credence.

The matter of the giant peepal tree

The Sojati Gate crossing was one of the busiest in Jodhpur in 1984. It connected new Jodhpur, including the High Court, district magistrate offices and other frequently visited places with the old city as well as the business district. On one corner of the crossing stood a very large and old peepal tree. The government wanted to construct a slip lane to allow the traffic from the old city side to pass seamlessly to the collectorate side. The tree was in the way.

The traffic police recommended removal of the tree. Many people agreed. However, many others simply didn't want the sacred tree to be touched. There was a big file on the matter that must have weighed over 2 kg and even a case pending in the city magistrate's court.

My study of the bulky file and a visit to the site convinced me that removal of the tree was indeed in the larger public interest. Ashok Patni, the deputy superintendent of police (DSP), accompanied me during this inspection, and we discussed the matter thoroughly. A jovial and carefree character otherwise, Patni was against touching the tree on account of the prevailing sentiment. I tried to convince him, telling him that the municipal personnel would cut and remove the tree in the dead of the night when there would be no traffic and the likelihood of people assembling would be remote. At the end of the discussion, he relented and agreed to provide a posse of police and come himself for some time.

The collector and the superintendent of police (SP) were informed, and on the appointed date, the municipal force reached with the necessary equipment. However, at 11 p.m., when the operation was scheduled to start, there was no sign of the police force or Ashok Patni! I tried to contact him but he would not pick up the phone.

I tried to reach him until midnight without success and then reached out to Collector Srivastava. Despite his own reluctance, he was convinced the job was necessary. After making certain enquiries, he gave me permission to go ahead without police presence. What's more, an hour later, at around 1.30 a.m., he came to the site personally. By that time, we had cut down about one-third of the tree. He stayed for over two hours. By 5 a.m., the giant tree was gone and the debris substantially removed. I left at about 6 a.m.

I was told later that there was some commotion initially in the morning, but people accepted the fact of the tree was removed for the city's good, and that was that.

Troubled elections of 1984 provided good training

The assassination of Prime Minister Indira Gandhi on 31 October 1984 triggered massive anti-Sikh riots in Delhi and elsewhere. There was an undercurrent of anti-Sikh feeling in Jodhpur as well. The administration was on edge. The massive gas leak in Bhopal on 2 December 1984 could not have come at a worse time. Amid these tragedies, the Lok Sabha elections took place in the last week of December 1984.

For me, the Lok Sabha elections of 1984 and the Vidhan Sabha elections of March 1985 provided a major opportunity to participate in the organization of elections and view the entire process at close quarters. As I was attached to the collector, I had access to all aspects of the election process.

The new prime minister, Rajiv Gandhi, visited Jodhpur a few days after the Bhopal gas tragedy. There was no Special Protection Group (SPG) at the time and district authorities made all the security arrangements. I stood behind him on the rostrum when he addressed an election rally. I was decidedly impressed by his well-meaning address, pleasant demeanour and cool disposition. The Congress had a landslide victory with over 400 seats. Jodhpur returned Ashok Gehlot to Parliament; he became a minister of state in the union government.

The Vidhan Sabha elections in March 1985 were not a clean sweep. Paras Ram Maderna, an influential Congressman and chief ministerial candidate, lost in the Bhopalgarh constituency of Jodhpur.

I was appointed assistant returning officer (ARO) for a constituency in the Vidhan Sabha elections. The ARO is second in command to the returning officer of the constituency for the segment entrusted to him. Those were the days of ballot papers. The process of counting was slow and fraught with lot of difficulties.

One of the most contentious aspects was dealing with disputed votes. Some voters would affix the seal on the band between the spaces provided for the candidates, some would do so in more than one candidate's box. Some votes would have a clear seal in the box of one candidate but a smudge or some other mark in another candidate's box. Some seals would be very faint, some would carry a reverse image on another candidate's box. It was a Herculean task to take a decision on such votes without the representative of one candidate or the other objecting. I went by the principle of assessing whether the voter's intent was clearly determinable. If some part of the seal was in one candidate's box, with the rest in the middle band, which did not belong to any candidate, I allotted the vote to that candidate. Where there were two images – one right and the other a mirror – I allocated the vote to the candidate with the right image. Anyway, as the margin of victory in the constituency I was a part of was substantial, there were no vehement protests, and the counting got completed quickly.

In the 1980s, the counting for all Vidhan Sabha constituencies in Jodhpur would take place in the Government Polytechnic College. Once I was finished with my constituency, I donned the probationer's hat and went to the hall where the counting for Bhopalgarh constituency was underway. Tension there was palpable. Paras Ram Maderna was losing, though not very heavily. He was there in person and was making the life difficult for the district supply officer (DSO), who was the returning officer for the constituency. He questioned every ballot paper with the slightest issue, which was not awarded to him. He held up the declaration of the result for hours. I tried to help DSO in making the right judgements, which led to Maderna looking at me askance. By the time the returning officer signed the certificate declaring his opponent the winner, Maderna had left, cursing many people, including the administration.

My ranking improved to third

The UPSC had placed me at no. 4 in the country. The final ranking of the officers of a batch considered the assessment marks earned during their probation as well performance in Phase 1, examinations in the state and performance during district training. After taking this into account, my overall rank was improved to no. 3 in the batch.

I was confirmed in the IAS. Life in the IAS to serve the public interest began.

Part A

Administration in Rajasthan

1

Fixing Land Settlement and Other Chaos

In 1985, the districts were divided into tehsils in Rajasthan, on the civil side, with a subdivisional officer (SDO) usually supervising two or more tehsils. The SDO had independent jurisdiction over specified land and revenue matters under the tenancy and land revenue laws of the state. The SDO also acted as a subdivisional magistrate (SDM) for maintenance of law and order, exercising authority under the CrPC. Over the years, the SDOs' jurisdiction has also been reduced to one tehsil mostly. The CrPC has been replaced with Bharatiya Nagarik Suraksha Sanhita (BNSS) in 2024.

Land revenue collected from the produce of agricultural lands was the primary source of government revenue for ages and lasted until the end of British rule. All agricultural lands were periodically 'settled' (once in 20–25 years) under an elaborate field measurement and survey system, called settlement, to decide what land revenue/rent the parcels of lands (called *khasra*s) needed to pay to the government, directly or through landlords. Besides settling annually payable rents, the settlement updated the status of the land parcels on many parameters including current agricultural status and ownership.

With land revenue becoming an increasingly insignificant source of government revenues (Rajasthan government had abolished it for a large section of farmers), the 'settlement' process had lost its primary driver and rigour.

The posting as an SDO and SDM is the first time a newly minted young IAS officer is thrown into the ring of land, civil and law-and-order administration. The involvement of the SDO in development schemes was relatively small in those days but the court work, law and order, and administration of relief and rehabilitation in the event of natural calamities (floods and droughts were very common) were major responsibilities which SDOs had to shoulder.

While Chittorgarh was a relatively small subdivision with two tehsils in its jurisdiction (Nimbaheda in Chittorgarh district had four where a 1982 batch officer, Bharat Lal Meena, was posted as the SDO), I was eagerly looking forward to assuming my first real independent job. I reported for duty in the middle of August 1985 and assumed charge of the office of the SDO and SDM, Chittorgarh. Being a bachelor with few possessions, I decided to live in a room in the Circuit House.

An unsettling 'settlement'

With the necessity of determining assessment of land parcels for government revenue becoming quite insignificant (land revenue has been completely abolished in most states), the settlement process had become more of an exercise in updating land holding records to reflect the latest ground situation of every *khasra* (in terms of the map, its placement relative to others in its neighbourhood and the ownership position in the record of rights or the *jamabandi*). For individual farmers, this was an all-important matter.

The settlement process was carried out by the settlement department, which functioned independently under the settlement commissioner and the Board of Revenue. It had taken more than seven years to complete the settlement process. At the end of the process, the settlement *jamabandi* was notified as the new record of rights and superseded the earlier *jamabandi*. Once the notification for conclusion of the settlement is issued, the settlement record, including the record of rights, is handed over to the concerned tehsil. When I assumed responsibility of Chittorgarh sub-division, the settlement of Gangrar (another tehsil in my charge in addition to Chittorgarh) was going on. It was completed about three months after I arrived, and the record was handed over to the tehsil office. With this handover, the settlement *jamabandi* and *khasra girdawari* (the record of all khasras in a village) became the official record of rights and land record documents for the people of Gangrar tehsil.

All hell broke loose as soon as the people of the tehsil started receiving copies of their *khata* (tenancy ownership account in the record of rights). All kinds of anomalies were observed by hundreds of farmers. In many cases, the names of some co-owners in the *khata* were missing. In others, some of the *khasra*s were missing from a person's *jamabandi* record, while in some, people were made owners of *khasra*s they did not actually own. The field position of many *khasra*s were different on revenue maps than the actual state on ground. Although over 80–85 per cent accounts were perhaps fully accurate, errors in 10–15 per cent *khata*s – which affected about 5,000 farming families, and had been caused due to the inefficiency and corruption of settlement staff – were significant enough to cause an uproar. The people attributed this to corruption and inefficiency of settlement staff.

Gangrar tehsildar Narendra Singh, a veteran of many years in the land revenue system, having risen from a patwari (a grassroot worker in the revenue system who maintains all revenue records and assists in the fieldwork of an area designated as a *patwar* circle) to a tehsildar, was quite sceptical of the settlement department's abilities and motivation. He concluded that like many other settlements, the settlement of Gangrar tehsil had unsettled everything. His considered advice was that the notification for conclusion of the settlement should be rescinded, all the records returned to the settlement department and the old *jamabandi* and other land records should continue to be legally valid until all grievances of the people are addressed.

I did not find the solution appealing or practical. There was not a good chance that the state government would agree to rescind the settlement. Moreover, if it were to go back to the same demotivated and clueless officers and patwaris in the settlement department, there was no guarantee they would do a better job the next time. It would have taken a long time as well. In the interim, people would have continued to suffer as many normal and routine operations like mutations in the record of rights remained suspended. There had to be a quicker and more effective solution to the problem, I concluded.

The land revenue/records machinery in a tehsil typically comprised the tehsildar, inspectors of land records (ILRs) and patwaris, with a deputy (*naib*) tehsildar thrown in between. I asked the tehsil machinery to bring the old land records and the new settlement records of a patwar circle and explain to me the errors evident in the settlement. In addition, I asked them to explain how those wrongs could be righted following a due process of law.

It was an eye-opener. Taking a simple case of one of two brothers' names missing in the record of rights/*jamabandi*, the concerned farmer would have to take an official copy of his account in both the old and new settlement *jamabandi*s and copies of the old and new maps of the *khasra*s concerned from the patwari concerned or from the tehsil, as most old records had been deposited in the tehsil. Thereafter, he would have to hire an advocate to file a declaratory suit in the court of the SDO to declare him co-owner of the land parcel concerned. Copies of the suit would have to be served on the tehsildar, as the representative of the state, and on the other brother. In turn, both the tehsildar and the other brother would have to file their replies, contesting or accepting the pleadings in the suit. The SDO would have to take the evidence from all concerned after settling the issues in the case. If there were no disagreements and all parties and their lawyers agreed, the SDO's court would pronounce a judgement and write out a decree.

The party concerned would have to apply for and take an official copy of the decree from the court and produce it with the relevant application form and fees to the concerned patwari to record a mutation. After the patwari recorded the change in the mutation book, he would make the alterations in the *jamabandi* and *khasra girdawari*, respectively, after obtaining the approval of the tehsildar or panchayat, depending upon where the power to approve mutation lay. Finally, the applicant would receive an official copy of the amended *jamabandi* and *khasra girdawari* as evidence of the correction of the wrong committed by the settlement.

It didn't take a rocket scientist to understand that this process would easily take years and set the concerned farmer back by a few thousand rupees at least, while wasting considerable time in attending court and visiting revenue and advocate offices. There had to be a simpler solution. On reflection, I figured out that the entire machinery involved in correcting the wrong was sitting right in front of me. Further, there was no real dispute involved, and the parties concerned would, in most cases, be willing to cooperate to right the wrong.

I proposed that we complete the entire process in one sitting by holding a camp court in the village concerned. As the patwari and the tehsil staff would be available there with the records, the farmer concerned could be given the copies of records on site. We could design a simple and common declaratory suit format, in which necessary pleadings would be made in the names of the parties concerned on a stencilled paper. The tehsildar and other parties concerned could also file their replies in a similar manner. I would hold the court, pass the judgment, record the decree and issue it on the spot. The patwari could make the change in the concerned land records and provide an official copy of the amended land records then and there.

Narendra Singh could not believe his eyes and ears for the incredibly simple solution offered. He became an avid supporter of the process. After refining the process in a few camps, it became ridiculously simple and efficient. I must have held such camps in about 50 villages. Most camps took about 10–12 hours a day, sometimes stretching to well beyond midnight. The tehsil team led by the well-meaning tehsildar Narendra Singh worked long hours and enabled thousands of declaratory suits being decided in a period of about three months. It was a pleasure to see the smiles on the faces of harassed farmers. I derived enormous satisfaction from undoing the pangs caused by the unsettling settlement of Gangrar tehsil.

An out-of-the-box solution for land allotments

The Rajasthan government ran a major programme allotting land parcels to the poor and landless. The allottable land came from three sources: government-owned land (called *siwaichak*) available for allotment; land acquired in ceiling operations (land owned in excess of the limits set by the state, usually referred to as ceiling surplus land); and land in *bhoodan* villages (lands gifted away by people under the influence of the voluntary Bhoodan Movement launched by Vinoba Bhave). Allotment of land to the poor and the landless was a priority programme of the government and was closely monitored as part of the 20-Point Programme (though launched by Indira Gandhi during Emergency, the programme remained a major national and state level monitorable programme even then).

Unfortunately in field, while a good part of the *siwaichak* land available for allotment was free from encroachment, most of the ceiling surplus land and *bhoodan* land parcels were encroached upon by someone or the other – in most cases by people whose land had gone in ceiling or who had gifted it away, or their henchmen or the farmers whose land parcels were adjacent to the allottable land. Earlier, tehsildars had the power to allot land, but by the time I joined as SDO, with available land for allotment becoming increasingly smaller, the allotment power had been given to the SDOs.

When I scheduled meetings in villages for allotment of land, I noted a very peculiar phenomenon: There was no great enthusiasm or interest in getting land among the poor and landless. Another notable feature was that there were several proposals for allotting 'strips' of land. A little digging revealed that most of the land proposed for allotment, though government land on paper, had already been encroached upon. The government rules permitted the allotment of a small 'strip of land' adjoining somebody's land parcel(s) to that person. Encroachers were quite keen to get such lands allotted to them.

Further enquiries revealed that in cases where the encroached land was allotted to a poor or landless person, the encroacher would invariably file a case in the court of the district collector. The poor or landless person, not having any means of defence, would generally end up losing the allotment as well as his labour income for the days he appeared in court.

There was another iniquitous aspect to the entire process. There was no difference in terms of the price charged between the land allotted to the encroacher and the land parcels allotted to the landless poor – both were free. Thus, the encroacher was a clear winner in such allotments. The land allotment machinery tacitly sided with encroachers, as it meant fewer cases in the court of the district collector as well as for making some income on the side.

My assessment of the situation suggested that there was no real benefit in allotting such disputed and encroached lands to the poor. I also judged that allotting encroached lands as strips of land to encroachers was not serving any public interest either. The rules had no provision for auctioning government land and selling the same to the highest bidder at market price.

I designed a solution that was not strictly within the four walls of the law and rules but appeared fair and in the larger public interest. I proposed to the revenue machinery (tehsildar, patwari and others) and development machinery (panchayat sarpanch, members and village-level panchayat workers) that encroached land be allotted to the encroacher at market price and the proceeds of the sale be deposited in the panchayat as donation. There were initial doubts and opposition – some officials thought this was not lawful while encroachers saw their 'lawful' advantage slipping away. However, in the face of my decision not to make any allotment otherwise, soon all concerned accepted the solution as pragmatic and fair without breaking any law or rule.

I supervised the allotment of encroached land in several villages/panchayats under this template. The tehsil representatives would work out the market price based on registered documents and after taking a poll of the people. The encroacher would deposit the price of the land in the panchayat and produce a copy of the receipt as evidence. The strip would be allotted free of cost in accordance with the applicable land allotment rules. I had the satisfaction of not creating any further dispute and subjecting the poor to unmitigated litigation. The larger public interest was also well served as the money collected got utilized in financing development works in the villages.

Some people complained to the collector and my boss Dharam Singh Sagar about the 'irregular' land allotments. The collector did not ask me anything. Nor did he stop me from continuing with the allotments. Subsequently, however, he would use it against me. More on that in next chapter.

Unconventional solution for land acquisition by the railways

Chittorgarh was a small town of about 50,000 people, though the district was quite large, with about 14 tehsils and five subdivisions. Chittorgarh subdivision last had a direct recruit IAS officer as an SDO about 15 years before I arrived in 1985 (Jhumki Satish Kumar in 1970).

Indian Railways was constructing a new broad-gauge line between Chittorgarh and Kota. The SDO worked as the land acquisition officer for his sub-division as well. The office of the SDO had issued what was known as a Section 4 notification listing the land parcels of each *khasra* to be acquired for constructing the railway line. As this was considered an urgent land acquisition, another notification published under Section 17 of the Land Acquisition Act (then prevailing) allowed the Railways to take immediate possession of land without first paying the compensation. The Railways had done that and were in the midst of constructing the railway line, though hundreds of farmers had not received their compensation.

The process of paying compensation was tedious and complicated. It involved determining the rights of each owner of the land parcels under acquisition, determining the price of the land and other on-land assets (such as house, trees, etc.), taking into account all relevant factors, and issuing an award of compensation to be paid to each *jamabandi* account-holder.

The compensation payment process had made the lives of farmers, who had lost their land, more miserable. The compensation amount was determined by the SDO's office, but the amount was paid by a cheque issued by the Railways. The payment system required all the farmer/owners to have a bank account with exactly the same names as recorded in the *jamabandi*. As bank branches were few and far between, to open a bank account, it required all the *khatedar*s (the people named in the *jamabandi* for a land parcel) to come to the district headquarters with at least one person who had an account in the bank (there were no Aadhaar identifications or Jan Dhan accounts at that time, and ration cards were not viewed as legitimate identifications). The Railways would issue a combined single cheque in the names of all the account holders, which would have to be deposited in the bank account. This required all the account holders to come to the bank at the time of withdrawing the cash as well.

There were more complications. In those days, the government prescribed heavy targets for small savings collections. The collectors passed these on to all subordinate offices. Banks and the Railways, though not subject to the control of the state government, were also advised to 'encourage' the collection of funds for small savings. The land acquisition awards came in handy for this purpose. An unwritten rule had become a practice that 10 per cent of the award amount had to be deposited by the farmers concerned into small savings. The encashment of cheques was linked to the purchase of small savings certificates and deposits in other eligible accounts or instruments.

The farmers were trapped in this maze. If even one person in the combined landholding account had died or was not available for any reason, the entire process just stopped in its tracks. The inconvenience of getting disputes resolved, award issued, cheques issued, accounts opened, cash withdrawn and investment made in small savings instruments had become a nightmare for most farm families.

Every day, many farmers would come to my office with their litany of woes. I tried to help by speaking to the Railway officers, including an executive engineer from the Indian Railway Services of Engineers, Mukesh Gupta, who became a friend for life, and two other executive engineers. They were very helpful, but it was not sufficient to take care of the major structural and procedural issues bogging down the entire process. I reached out to bankers, but they also had their limitations. The real challenge was the number of governmental agencies involved with everyone working in silos. Some discussion with all the concerned stakeholders led to a solution, along the lines of court camps held to undo the damage done by the settlement in Gangrar district, though the villages involved in the acquisition of land for the Railways were all in Chittorgarh tehsil.

I decided to take all the concerned departments, including the post office for small savings, to the field to complete the entire compensation determination and payment process as a one-stop shop. In these camps, the concerned executive engineer from the Railways would participate, and the banks would be present, besides the tehsil, the field staff and other concerned agencies.

After listening to what the farmers had to say and the viewpoint of the Railways, I would determine the minimum extent of land to be acquired, fix the compensation and pass the award. An account would be opened in the bank for all account holders. And if they authorized one or two of them in writing to receive the compensation cheque on behalf of all the account holders, the bank account was opened in the names of only such authorized representatives.

The railway officers would issue the cheque of the award amount on the spot, which would be deposited in the newly opened bank account. The farmers would deposit 10 per cent willingly in small savings and the post office would issue them national savings certificates or Kisan Vikas Patras, or make a deposit in their savings/recurring/fixed deposit accounts, as per their preference. If the compensation was very small or there were other overwhelming reasons, I waived the small savings condition as well. The bankers would come with adequate cash to these camps. If farmers wanted to withdraw their amount, they could do so.

All the stakeholders, especially the farmers, were very happy. My office and tehsil staff were also quite cooperative. One clerk did make a bit of a show in one of the early camps, arguing that it was difficult to prepare awards and type them out with so many people milling around. He was relieved of his responsibilities.

The camps, more than 10 in all, proved quite productive. What could not be accomplished in months earlier was done in a few days with full transparency and no disputes or corruption. The word spread. The Rao of Bassi, the second biggest town in Chittorgarh tehsil, a respected figure and a former panchayat samiti pradhan, spoke to the local press on the evening of a camp in Bassi (without informing me). The next morning, there was a front-page lead story in the local newspaper about the land acquisition and compensation camp, showering high praise on the public-spirited approach the administration exhibited. The administration earned enormous goodwill by holding such camps. That was the first ever coverage I received in the media.

Dealing with lawyers in their own game

It was unfortunate but true – almost no lawyer was interested in quick disposal of revenue cases. To decide the cases quickly, while I started hearing quite regularly, usually, their juniors or clerks would come and ask for the next date. I decided to be quite strict about this and stopped giving the next date routinely. If any advocate was not present on time – at most within half an hour of the case being called – I would either dismiss the case in default or impose fines. As a result, most advocates started taking the court seriously. Their preparation standards also improved. The president of the Chittorgarh Bar Association, who had cases in my court as well, did not do so on two occasions within a short span of time. Once, I imposed a fine; the next time, I dismissed his case on account of non-appearance.

A few minutes after the case was dismissed, the gentleman in question barged into my court and started shouting. I told him he was not conducting himself in the manner expected of an advocate and possibly committing contempt of court. This infuriated him more and he announced a strike by lawyers and a boycott of my court. With that, all other advocates also walked out and court work got disrupted.

I had to find an unconventional but effective solution. From the next day, I decided to hold court in the villages and started listing the cases in villages where parties to the cases came. This was permissible in accordance with the revenue courts manual. While the advocates boycotted the court and sat in dharna, I held my court in the field every alternate day.

M.L. Mehta, director of the Officers' Training School (OTS), who had trained me, in the meanwhile, had been posted as commissioner, Udaipur, under whose jurisdiction Chittorgarh fell. He also belonged to a village in Chittorgarh district, though in another subdivision. Most people in the area knew him. M.L. Mehta, an illustrious officer of Rajasthan, would retire as chief secretary later.

Some advocates complained to him about my 'high-handedness'. When the lawyers' strike was on, he came to Chittorgarh on an official visit. During an evening get-together, he told me, 'Subhash, *vakil bhir jaise hote hain aur tumne unke chatte mein hath dal diya hai*!' (Advocates are like hornets and you have disturbed their nest by thrusting your hand in it.) I told him about the camp courts I was holding and the excellent response from the people. He did not question me further or give me any directions, leaving me to my devices.

The response to the camp courts was phenomenal. Most revenue cases were lodged out of actual misunderstanding about the rights of the two parties and remained pending on account of neglect by both the court and the advocates. I used the opportunity of the field camp court to explain to both the parties their case, the position of the law and what would finally emerge after they had spent many years and much money fighting the case. It was a real Lok Adalat, court of the people. Not surprisingly, when they heard *bado hukum* (Rajasthan's way of addressing authorities) explaining facts and likely outcome, many parties agreed to enter into a *rajinama* (voluntary agreement). When they agreed to settle the case, I would ask for a consent decree to be drawn up with their agreement duly noted on the paper and the court file. Thereafter, like the settlement camp courts of Gangrar, the judgment and decree were issued on the spot. Not only that, the necessary changes were made in the land records and certified copies of the current status of their land and rights given to the parties concerned.

Soon, the advocates started getting news of the disposal of cases in camp courts. By the second week of their boycott and dharna, they began to realize that their boycott had no impact on my working or that of the court. Moreover, they were losing out on the income they earned from litigation. I got some feelers seeking a compromise, which I dismissed. On the fourteenth day, the advocates called off their boycott unilaterally.

Normalcy resumed. The rate of disposal of cases improved with no advocate asking for unnecessary extension or failing to appear in court on the due date.

Settling Gadi Luhars

The Gadi Luhars, ironsmiths (*luhar*s) who lived and worked out of carts (*gadi*), were a tribe who proudly traced their nomadic origins to a vow taken at the time of the fall of the giant fort of Chittorgarh in the sixteenth century, when their king, Maharana Pratap, was defeated after a prolonged siege by the Mughal emperor Akbar. The Gadi Luhars, whose ancestors worked as ironsmiths in the fort, vowed not to settle anywhere until the fort was recaptured and Maharana Pratap reinstated to the throne.

The Chittorgarh Fort was not recaptured during Maharana Pratap's lifetime. For their part, the Gadi Luhars adopted the nomadic life, carrying their families and tools in bullock carts, temporarily camping near villages, repairing and making iron objects, and moving on. This became their way of life as decades and centuries rolled by.

After Independence, successive governments endeavoured to resettle the Gadi Luhars. The Congress party organized a great gathering of Gadi Luhars in 1955 – Prime Minister Jawaharlal Nehru stood at the gate of the Chittorgarh Fort and welcomed them in. I was told that Nehru invited the Gadi Luhars to attack the fort in a mock fight; he, as the representative ruler of India, lost the fort to them, symbolically releasing them from their bond of nomadic life. Each family was promised a plot of 250 yards as well as agricultural land. A large school was constructed in Chittorgarh to bring the children of Gadi Luhars to the mainstream.

The pleasant and energetic Havildar Ram Singh, an ex-serviceman belonging to the community, would drop in sometimes to my office in Chittorgarh. I admired his effortless positivity and desire to do something for his community. My assessment was that while the Gadi Luhars were promised urban land to settle down, agricultural land to raise crops and schools for their children, and government and community leaders had made sincere efforts to deliver on these promises, the combination of their way of life and difficulty in assimilating into mainstream society had made them reluctant partners in the settlement project. As a result, when I was SDO Chittorgarh, there were very few and patchy settlements of Gadi Luhars in the subdivision.

One day in late 1986, an excited Havildar Ram Singh asked me to come and see a plot of land in the Senthi area of Chittorgarh municipality. He wanted that piece of real estate, about a hectare or so, allotted to the Gadi Luhar families who were camping there. I made some enquiries and met the families. When I came to know that they had been camping in that area for over two years and the families showed a sincere interest in settling down, I felt this was a service worth doing.

After I spoke to the executive officer of Chittorgarh municipality, despite some initial reluctance, the municipality undertook measurement of the land (which was the government *siwaichak* land) and plotting for some 55 families. The whole process took about four months. We found a rule, of 1955 origin, which allowed urban land to be allotted (250 yards per family) to the Gadi Luhars. It was a very happy moment when the *patta*s (land title documents) were distributed to the Gadi Luhar families.

One day in February 1987, the Gadi Luhars invited my wife Anjali and me to come to their newly established colony. The women took Anjali inside a tent and helped her change into their traditional attire. I went to another tent and happily donned the white dhoti-kurta dress of the community. We sat on their carts; I tried my hand at some ironsmith work, though the *hathoda* (hammer) they used was quite heavy for me! We also had lunch with them. I felt doubly blessed with the satisfaction that even as I was settling down in my own family life with Anjali, 50 Gadi Luhar families had made the transition to a settled life, which their forefathers had abandoned 400 years earlier.

2

A Collector Complains Against His SDO!

Dharam Singh Sagar, an IAS officer of the 1976 batch, joined as district collector of Chittorgarh a few days before I reported for duty as SDO, Chittorgarh in August 1985. Sagar had entered the service at a relatively late age of 30. He was more a politician than a civil servant, though quite jovial and affable. He had no ego or airs.

Sagar received me with a lot of warmth when I called on him the first time. He made it a point to enquire about my background, education, professional career, family and more. He signalled in the first meeting itself that I was expected to work on my own, being a direct recruit who 'would be a collector soon'.

In a departure from tradition, Sagar gave me charge of the revenue section of the collectorate along with the land records section, which the SDO (headquarters), i.e., the SDO posted at the district headquarters, traditionally held. The revenue section of the collector dealt with land conversion, allotment and related matters for industry and other parties for the entire district.

I settled into my job, working largely on my own without Collector Sagar interfering or even supervising much. It was as if I was the collector of the subdivision of Chittorgarh. Sagar never asked me to do anything wrong or grant undue favours to anyone; he would not interfere in my work in any manner. While he was not intellectually strong and one did not look to learn much from him, he was a good person and boss.

New year arrives with bad publicity

A little after four months on the job in Chittorgarh, the new year, 1986, arrived. Collector Sagar organized a big bash in the district club on 31 December 1985. No contributions were solicited from individual officers, nor were they expected to foot any bill in their official capacity. I attended the party, though I did not drink or eat non-vegetarian food. The party went on for hours and concluded well after midnight. I walked back to my room in the Circuit House, which was next to the district club. I did not notice anything unusual.

The next morning, a local paper ran a front-page story with the headline, '*Sharab, kabab aur naach gaana, yon hua afsaron ka naya sal manana!*' (Officers celebrated the new year with liquor, non-vegetarian food, dance and music!) The full-page article included photographs of officers with glasses of alcoholic drinks in their hands, some of them dancing. This sent shockwaves throughout the district and the officers community. A rattled Sagar cursed the newspaper and vowed to teach the correspondent he suspected of filing the story a lesson.

The article got traction at the state level as well. I did not know whether any explanation from Sagar was called for or provided. I was not asked anything. However, this possibly led to the realization among officers at the state level that it was not a good idea to celebrate the new year in such a manner, and if at all they do so, it should be done with the cost of such an event being met by a contribution made by everyone. No party was held to herald the year 1987. In any case, I was not in town then – Anjali and I got married in late November 1986 and we embarked on an all-India trip thereafter, returning only in the first week of January 1987.

Nasbandi camp's success

As a 'family planning' (a uniquely Indian term!) strategy to control population growth, sterilization had become bad politics after the excesses committed during Emergency under the policies of Sanjay Gandhi, the overzealous son of then prime minister Indira Gandhi. The programme was relegated to the background by the Janata government that took over in 1977 after Emergency was lifted. Indira Gandhi did not push for it when she returned to power in 1980, though it continued to be in force with specific targets for states and districts as one of the key components of the 20-Point Programme she had launched during Emergency.

By the time I reached the district, there was renewed urgency to promote family planning, with sterilization or *nasbandi* as the most visible component of the programme. Persuasion and incentivization had become the usual modes to convince people to go in for *nasbandi*. Besides the government incentive, mobilization of additional incentives from local industrialists, businessmen and charitable organizations had become critical.

The SDO Chittorgarh had targets for *nasbandi*. I was also personally convinced that sterilization was not only in the national interest but also in the interest of every family. My personal experience also had a part to play in this. I was a 15-year-old and studying in Class 10 in Ajmer in 1975 during Emergency, when my mother was pregnant with my youngest sibling. With my father being generally unwell and unwilling to take my mother to the hospital for check-ups, it used to fall upon me to walk her to the dispensary. I would feel deeply embarrassed and was generally angry with my parents for having a sixth child whom they could hardly support. In fact, my embarrassment was so acute that I would take my mother by a longer route to avoid a classmate's home on the shorter route. I saw to it that she went through a *nasbandi* operation when my youngest sibling was born.

With my genuine conviction that family planning was in the interest of every married couple and family, *and* the nation, I mounted a massive outreach programme for a *nasbandi* camp at the Chittorgarh district hospital. Along with the development and revenue machinery of my subdivision, I went to numerous villages, spoke to families, men and, more particularly, women, and explained the economic, health and social advantages of small families. Also, with the help of doctors, I tried to convince them about the easier procedure with the new laparoscopy technology that was virtually risk-free. At the same time, I reached out to the businessmen and industrialists of Chittorgarh who could announce monetary incentives or offer utility items to all those willing to undergo *nasbandi* in the camp. The marble industry was doing well, as were the two cinema halls. The word spread about the good number of additional incentives (saris, utensils, cash, etc.) lined up for a particular camp.

The hard work, mobilization of additional incentives and effective outreach generated a huge response. I had targeted 1,000 sterilization operations on that day. The actual turnout was higher, which even briefly degenerated into a melee. At the end of the day, there were over 1,100 operations with some refusals. This had not happened in Chittorgarh district in many years.

When he learnt of this, Sagar was ecstatic. He had not been aware of my silent efforts to organize the camp to achieve this. He congratulated and lauded me for the achievement. He wrote to the state government as well, highlighting it as a major district success and describing my role. He would cite this camp for many months to other officers and to those higher up in the bureaucracy.

A presidential visit

President Giani Zail Singh visited Chittorgarh in March–April 1986 when the heat had set in. He was to arrive at the Chittorgarh parade grounds by a helicopter. All officers were supposed to be present when he arrived. I, too, was there, but without a *bandgala* (a formal Indian suit) as I did not have one with me at that time. Collector Sagar noticed my attire – I was wearing a shirt, a pair of pants and a cotton jacket – a few minutes before Zail Singh arrived. He asked an assistant collector to take off his bandgala and gave it to me to wear without saying much. I have always hated this protocol, but I complied without demur ring.

Giani Zail Singh was a kind-hearted person. While he would always be immaculately dressed, he was not given to protocol or excessive formality. In fact, he loved regaling the officers around him with anecdotes. I recalled the interaction of our batch when we went to call on him at the Rashtrapati Bhavan during our probation period. He was also known to practise favouritism when he was the home minister before becoming the president in 1982. Any sense of propriety or uniform application of rules was not his forte.

In his effort to show his camaraderie, he would sometimes end up making people laugh. Ranjeev Rakkar, a fellow probationer from Punjab in my batch, was allotted the Gujarat cadre. During the probationers' line-up at the Mughal Gardens, Zail Singh expressed his regret to her that she had to go so far away from Punjab. A few probationers later, when another batchmate from Rajasthan, Rajbala Varma, told him she was going to Bihar, he simply shrugged his shoulders and commented that Bihar was quite close to Rajasthan. We probationers controlled our laughter with considerable effort, but Gianiji kept going. He related the story of his younger days when he was a local-level politician and had landed up at the residence of the district magistrate early in the morning one day to submit a representation. When he saw a young man of about 25–26 years coming out to see him, he asked him to send his father as he could not believe such a young person could be district magistrate!

In Chittorgarh, too, he related many stories – and he was also told plenty of them. The district treasury officer, who doubled as his chief protocol officer for the visit to Chittorgarh Fort, related why the *sharifa* or *sitaphal* (custard apple) was so abundant in Chittorgarh. He explained with much pride that the soil of Chittorgarh was rich in potassium, as was human blood. It was the sacrifice of the brave hearts and warriors of Mewar, he said, that had resulted in the soil of

Chittorgarh soaking up so much blood that it became rich in potassium, which then resulted in it becoming the land of the *sharifa*.

The presidential visit went off well. Collector Sagar did not say anything to me about my attire. But he would later cite the incident as evidence of my indiscipline.

An ex-MLA's gratitude for arresting him

Chittorgarh was a small town. It had only one busy market of some consequence. Traders would encroach upon much of the pavements in the market, some with semi-permanent metal structures, which people found rather inconvenient. The municipality wanted to remove them and came to me. I spoke to the station house officer (SHO) of the Chittorgarh police station. He agreed and supported the removal of the encroachments.

We thought this was a minor matter. Without intimating the collector and the SP, I went along with the municipality executive officer (EO) and staff, backed by the police, to remove the encroachments one afternoon. It created a stir. While the shopkeepers protested, the municipality staff went about swiftly doing their job and removed quite a few encroachments. A former Member of Legislative Assembly (MLA), or perhaps his relatives, also had a shop in the market. He suddenly appeared on the scene and stood between the shopkeepers and the municipality staff. The EO and his staff stopped in their tracks.

I spoke to him and explained that the encroachments were not only unlawful, but they were also creating an obstruction to free movement of people. Seeing him standing there and the temporary halt to the removal, some traders began to rush towards the municipality truck to retrieve their seized goods. The impasse went on for about half an hour. A crowd had assembled by then. Eventually, I told him that I would have to order his arrest if he did not yield. When he refused, I asked the SHO to arrest him. Surprisingly, at this order, he did not resist much and went away with the SHO to the police station. The drive to remove the encroachments resumed.

The word reached Collector Sagar. He asked me and the SHO to come to his residence. I duly set off after asking the municipality staff to continue with their work. A tad upset at not being kept in the loop and a former MLA getting arrested in the process, Sagar was not his usual jovial self. He asked me a little sharply why I had to do what I did. I explained it to him. He listened. After a little while, someone came to report that the encroachment removal had been completed. Sagar did not persist with the matter anymore but asked me to meet the former MLA. I went to see him at the police station. I was expecting hostility from him. Instead, he thanked me for not only removing the encroachments, which he felt were creating a nuisance, but arresting him to break the deadlock. He had possibly calculated that being seen as having stood up to the administration and getting arrested while serving the cause of the traders would reflect positively on him politically.

SDM's jeep burnt!

A minor incident of a suspected killing of an animal by a religious group acquired large communal overtones, and a political party mounted a large agitation. Bhairon Singh Shekhawat, an ex-chief minister and an MLA from the Nimbaheda constituency (adjoining Chittorgarh), was expected to come to town and address the crowd in front of the collectorate building.

A massive crowd began to gather. Around noon, I came out of the collectorate to go for an appointment. At the roundabout just outside the main gate, some people came close to my jeep and 'gheraoed' it. I spoke to them; they moved away after about 10 minutes, and I proceeded for my work.

In the evening, A.L. Jain, a friend and a respected teacher in the local college, called me to enquire about my well-being. To my surprise, he informed me that there was a widespread rumour in the city that my official jeep had been burnt down by the agitators and I barely escaped from their hands.

Amazing! A minor incident of a jeep being stopped for about 10 minutes had been blown out of proportion by rumour-mongers. This incident taught me how much the Indian public relishes rumours. And while there is a widespread belief that there is no smoke without fire, the wild imagination of people can create Frankenstein's monsters from thin air.

Transfer of patwaris irks collector

Chittorgarh tehsil included a large mountainous region, referred to as Magra, with about 10 *patwar* circles located therein. Sparsely populated, with rocky terrain and small patches of agricultural fields in the valleys, they were considered difficult and unattractive postings for patwaris. The ones, those without any administrative godfathers or political connections, usually got posted there. The 25-odd patwaris in the rest of the Chittorgarh tehsil, the fertile zone, had someone or the other to support their cause and ensure they did not get posted to the Magra region.

The authority to transfer officials and staff was delegated to the specific officers under the rules and administrative instructions issued by the Government of Rajasthan. The government, as a matter of routine, placed a ban on transfers of government servants (which included patwaris) for most part of the year in order to control the pressure from MLAs and others for transfers. This ban meant the authorities to whom transfer powers were formally delegated would not be competent to make transfers during the period of ban. The ban, though, was not applicable on the government itself. The transfer ban was lifted for only short periods during a year. There were also usual policy directions that no government servant should be transferred before completing two years in a post.

The SDO was the competent authority to transfer patwaris. After a year or so of my stay in Chittorgarh, I decided to right the wrong done to the Magra patwaris. I planned to bring all those who had spent two to five years in Magra to the plains and post incompetent, corrupt and politically connected patwaris, who had been enjoying the fertile plains for quite some time, to the Magra region. Sometime in July 1986, when the ban on transfers was lifted, I carried out this 'mass transfer' exercise.

This unleashed a major storm. The MLA of Gangrar (the MLA of Chittorgarh, a former royal of a ripe age, was not very active politically) came to my office, expressed his annoyance and demanded the cancellation of the transfer of several patwaris. I refused. The influential Member of Parliament (MP) from Chittorgarh, whose husband was the zila pramukh, also demanded some cancellations. I stood my ground and refused to make any changes. Instead, I asked the Magra patwaris to take charge of their new postings, which they did with some diffidence, being unsure of their fate in future. This left the other patwaris with little option but to also join their new postings.

Someone closely scrutinized the transfer orders I had issued and found that there were a few cases where the patwaris had not completed the minimum period of two years in their present postings. As political influence did not seem to be working, the affected patwaris and their protectors decided to make a formal complaint against me for transfers in violation of the government policy. It was very common to address complaints to everyone who mattered, from the governor and chief minister to the collector.

The aggrieved, including the MLA of Gangrar, complained to Collector Sagar immediately after the transfer orders were issued. Upon his request, I explained the entire matter to him. He did not ask me to change anything, but I could see that he was not quite happy.

T.V. Ramanan, a senior IAS officer who, in next few years, rose to be finance secretary and then chief secretary of Rajasthan, was member of the revenue board at the time and in charge of administrative matters. He decided to look into the matter. Collector Sagar was informed that Ramanan would conduct an on-the-spot enquiry, and I was asked to explain why I had made these transfers, especially those that violated government policy.

I explained in detail, stating the performance record of all the concerned patwaris (there are always mistakes committed and delays made by every field functionary that can be used as justification for transfer) and the transfers made. Four transfers were in violation of the government policy of minimum two-year tenure. The policy used the words 'normally not less than two years'. I justified these four transfers as administratively necessary. Ramanan was a stickler for rules and was a thorough and fair officer. He found all the transfers made in accordance with the rules except for the four transfers that violated the spirit but not the letter of government policy. He was clearly less than pleased with the way I functioned but did not ask for any transfer to be cancelled.

The storm passed, leaving Sagar a little frustrated.

I get on the wrong side of the collector

Collector Sagar was earthy, jovial, witty and pragmatic. He loved being a district collector, which he thought was the only real good posting in the IAS. He would go on to serve five districts as district collector. He would identify the five most important people in the district and ensure that he stayed in their good books. This was his formula for success, and he would openly advocate it. I did not subscribe to this theory.

Two major incidents during my charge of the revenue section of the collectorate convinced me that Sagar was backing people on the wrong side of the law to benefit certain industrial concerns. In one case, a cement company in the Chanderia area of Chittorgarh had unauthorizedly constructed a well in the middle of the riverbed to draw water through pressurized pipes to its factory. In another case, the land parcels of Scheduled Caste (SC) persons were being transferred to another cement factory, on the border of Nimbaheda tehsil, for the construction of a captive power plant. I brought the matter to his knowledge and recorded a note on both files.

Sagar was not happy. I was divested of the charge of revenue section. I had no issue with this. I was perfectly happy to carry on with my core work. Another issue, however, became more problematic.

An ILR used to be the supervisory officer of patwaris. One particular ILR, headquartered at Bassi, was not working efficiently, and his integrity was also questionable. I transferred him to another circle. Though ILRs were a district-level cadre, and their transfers and postings were carried out under the orders of the district collector, I believed I had the right to effect transfers within my jurisdiction. The ILR in question was close to Sagar, who transferred him back to Bassi.

As the episode involved a question of integrity, I decided to place the ILR under suspension, which I was undoubtedly authorized to do, and issued a chargesheet. An enquiry was duly held and he was penalized. While the action sent the right message to the revenue machinery, I probably angered Sagar further in the process.

Sagar complains and targets

R.K. Nair, a very articulate officer with intimate knowledge of the entire cadre, was member of the revenue board. Chittorgarh fell under his supervisory jurisdiction. I had met him in Jodhpur during my probation period, where he was divisional commissioner.

During his inspection visit of Chittorgarh district sometime in April–May 1987, Sagar invited him for drinks and dinner at his residence. I was not invited. The next morning, R.K. Nair visited my residence for breakfast at my invitation. He appeared uncharacteristically grim. Over breakfast, he grilled me on issue after issue: allotment to encroachers against deposits in the panchayat, transferring patwaris without taking the collector into confidence, suspending the ILR because my orders were cancelled by the collector, travelling outside my jurisdiction without collector's permission (I had once gone to a place 50 km beyond my jurisdiction to visit a relative), and so on. It was apparent that such comprehensive questioning could have only come because of Sagar complaining bitterly about me at dinner the previous evening.

I explained everything truthfully and fully to Nair. I thought he would be happy at my having taken risks to do my duty without fear and favour, all entirely in public interest, using innovation to bypass unworkable rules and procedures.

I also informed him about my successful correction of Gangrar settlement records and people-friendly ways of paying Railway land compensation.

I thought he was satisfied with my responses. I was entirely wrong.

About two weeks after Nair returned to the revenue board headquarters in Ajmer, I received a letter from the board calling for my explanation in writing. The letter came to me through Chittorgarh collector's office. While all the issues we had discussed during the breakfast meeting figured in the letter, the matter of making land allotments linked to payments to panchayats was dealt with most prominently and was found to be the one where I was called out for acting beyond established rules and regulations.

I responded, with a copy to the office of the Chittorgarh collector. I flatly denied that I had made any land allotments to any land encroachers, linking it to the payment of the price of land by way of deposit in the panchayat. As for the matter of suspension of the ILR, I attached the chargesheet given to the ILR, along with the enquiry report that I said was self-explanatory.

I did not hear about the matter thereafter. If it had been pursued diligently, the link between the allotment and payment of price to the panchayats could have been established by connecting the dots, though there was no illegality in the entire matter. The allotments were perfectly legitimate and entirely in accordance with the rules. Likewise, there was no illegitimacy in people making voluntary contribution to panchayats.

Evidently, R.K. Nair did not pursue the matter as I did not receive any further communication in this regard. It could be either because he had promised to Sagar to give me a piece of his mind and call for my explanation, or he had been convinced that I was genuinely acting in the public interest.

Either way, I never cared to know. Nor did R.K. Nair ever bring this up with me again. When Nair became chief secretary of Rajasthan, I was in Government of India, in the Department of Economic Affairs (DEA).

3

Dysfunctional Rural Benefits Delivery

The 1980s were the era of a shift – from the trickle-down theory to a direct attack on poverty in the country. The chosen method was to provide investment assistance to the poor to help them set up small businesses to earn an income. The era of direct benefit transfers in the form of cash or in-kind handouts was still far away.

The Integrated Rural Development Programme (IRDP), the biggest poverty alleviation programme in operation in 1987, was launched by the Janata Party government in 1978 and was vigorously continued by the Congress governments of Indira Gandhi and Rajiv Gandhi.

The IRDP continued as the pre-eminent poverty alleviation programme until 1999, when it, along with a few other development programmes, was merged into the Swarnjayanti Gram Swarozgar Yojana (SGSY), which was by and large IRDP in another name. Currently, the National Rural Livelihoods Mission (NRLM), a differently designed programme, serves the purpose of improving income earning of the poor by hand-holding and providing seed capital assistance for individuals organized into self-help groups (SHGs) for taking up micro-entrepreneurial ventures.

The DRDAs were established in each district to help plan and implement IRDP and other development schemes. The central government provided the bulk of the funds, which were routed through bank accounts operated by the DRDAs. These were later merged into the Panchayati Raj institution of zila parishads.

Curious turn of events lands me the DRDA Jaipur job

Before we were married, Anjali, a chartered accountant (CA), had a good job with Indian Petrochemicals Ltd (IPCL), located in Vadodara, Gujarat, a central public sector undertaking (PSU; it was later privatized and sold to Reliance Industries). Realizing that she would not be able to continue in her job, she resigned and joined me in Chittorgarh.

To provide her an opportunity to work professionally in a CA firm and also to satisfy my urge to work in the finance department of the Rajasthan government, I wrote a letter to T.V. Ramanan, who had been appointed to the position of finance secretary of Rajasthan. I requested him to consider me for the post of deputy secretary in the finance department.

Usually, the post of deputy secretary in the finance department was not considered particularly attractive, as it did not come with a government vehicle and other creature comforts. No IAS officer was interested in it. So, when I met T.V. Ramanan with this request, he promised to consider it, though he had a wry smile on his face, probably either remembering the patwari transfer episode on which we had interacted or wondering why anyone would be interested in a deputy secretary post when every IAS officer looked to be in district collector at that stage.

S.D. Srivastava, the collector during my probation in Jodhpur, had been posted in the meantime as special secretary, Department of Personnel (SS, DOP), a powerful position then with a major influence in officers' postings. As I would learn later, my application was forwarded by Ramanan for due consideration to Srivastava. I had not met Srivastava for the posting in the finance department.

Further enquiries revealed that I would only be allotted a small flat in a transit hostel in Gandhinagar. I had a family to support (besides my parents, I had three younger brothers who were studying). Anticipating finance department posting, Anjali and I decided to look for renting a flat in the upcoming colonies of Malviya Nagar or Jawahar Nagar, which were being developed by the Rajasthan Housing Board and the Jaipur Development Authority (JDA). Though this would have taken away a chunk of my salary, we thought that Anjali's potential employment would help bridge the deficit.

When my posting orders came in August 1987, I was surprised to find myself transferred as additional collector (development) and project director (PD) of the DRDA, Jaipur. A field posting in Jaipur, a large district with 18 tehsils in those days, was quite a sought after one. I had never thought that I would get it.

I reckoned this must have been at the behest of S.D. Srivastava. I met him before I joined DRDA Jaipur. He was forthright and told me I did not know what I would have been getting into as deputy secretary in the secretariat. Also, that one should remain in the field and come to the secretariat only when it was unavoidable. I thanked him for this generosity, though it rankled in my mind that I would not be working in the finance department. Srivastava knew better. I was allotted a nice bungalow from the collectorate pool, very close to my DRDA office. I also got vehicular support and other facilities. The work was interesting and entailed considerable responsibility.

I took charge from Ashish Bahuguna, an officer of the 1978 batch and husband of my batchmate Seema. Ironically, Ashish Bahuguna was posted as a deputy secretary in the finance department in the same order. Quirk of fate?

Jai Narain Gaur, collector of Jaipur, was also ex-officio chairman of the DRDA. District Rural Development Agency, Jaipur, when I joined it, operated out of a small single storey rented building close to the collectorate. The PD's chamber was a small 15 ft × 10 ft room. The collector, by stark contrast, had a majestic room in the imposing collectorate building along with many other rooms at his disposal in numerous offices where he was ex-officio head except DRDA Jaipur.

Despite this, every now and then (on an average twice a week), J.N. Gaur would come to the DRDA building and occupy the room of the PD, DRDA, to dispose of collectorate files. He would often come without any prior intimation. The moment he arrived, the PD was expected to break up his meeting or any other engagement he was busy with and shift to the room of the project officer (PO), another small room (10 ft × 10 ft), until Gaur left. I found the whole practice operationally disturbing and personally demeaning when it happened the first time, 10 days after I joined. My staff, with a clear tinge of unhappiness, told me that this had been going on for a while.

After about two more visits, I decided to take up the matter with Gaur. I told him that while he was entitled and welcome to come to the DRDA, it created operational problems for me and the DRDA team. Instead of saying please don't come, I requested him to allot me a room in the collectorate so I could move there to carry on with my work whenever he decided to come to the DRDA. He agreed.

I showed him around the rented premises of the DRDA and the cramped conditions the officers and staff were working in. I made one more request to him to allot a small plot of land lying vacant next to the Jaipur collectorate to construct a new DRDA building. As he appeared interested, I told him that the building could be constructed under the supervision of the engineering staff of the DRDA, at a much cheaper cost than the Public Works Department (PWD) estimates. I had calculated and told him that the cost of building would be paid back in just five years from the rent saved. He had some initial doubts but allotted the land, nevertheless.

Meanwhile, I was allotted a vacant room reserved for additional collectors in the collectorate. It was nice and spacious. In fact, I used it more frequently unconnected with his visits. For reasons best known to him, after about two months, J.N. Gaur stopped coming to the DRDA. He was transferred out in another six months. I, however, continued using my additional room in the collectorate.

We were able to construct the DRDA building in the collectorate complex within a year. I had a tenure of about 20 months, including an overlapping tenure of four months with my posting as chief executive officer (CEO), Zila Parishad Jaipur. I was happy to shift my office and the entire DRDA to the newly constructed building from which I could operate for about three months.

Digging 'wells' in Jaipur

At the time, L.C. Gupta was secretary, Special Schemes Organisation (SSO), the state-level organization cum department responsible for formulating and implementing the rural development schemes of the centre and state. He had also served as the collector of Jaipur for over two years.

Every month, there would be one state-level meeting of all the project directors of the DRDA. As most DRDAs were headed by direct recruit officers of the IAS (at that time, officers of the 1980 to 1983 batches were functioning as PD, DRDA), it was quite exciting to attend the review meetings.

The Government of India had launched a new scheme, named Jeevandhara, in 1987. The guidelines for its implementation reached the DRDA around the time I joined, in August 1987. The scheme envisaged payment of 100 per cent assistance as capital subsidy directly to farmers belonging to the SC, Scheduled Tribe (ST) and bonded labour categories if they constructed an open well in their field. The scheme was meant to incentivize farmers to create irrigation facilities. Constructing wells was a complex process and had become more complicated operationally because the assistance was limited to the extremely resource-poor categories of farmers, although the provision of 100 per cent assistance was a genuine motivator and driver.

About six months later, in the monthly SSO meeting, the implementation of Jeevandhara was reviewed. It so happened that several districts had not created even a single well under the scheme, and about 80 per cent of all the wells dug in the state of Rajasthan were in Jaipur district. Being an unwieldy district with an additional collector (development) usually roped into other, more urgent tasks, Jaipur was generally considered a laggard in implementation of rural development programmes. And here was a newly launched scheme with an extraordinary implementation success in Jaipur district! Wearing a huge smile on his face, L.C. Gupta could not contain his scepticism and remarked that either this number was a typing mistake or it was fake, which evoked laughter in the room.

As I had done my homework, I responded that the number was indeed genuine and could be independently verified. This brought a level of gravitas to the discussion. Gupta directed deputy secretary P.L. Maheshwari to visit Jaipur district in the next week and report on the actual situation about Jeevandhara's implementation.

Maheshwari telephoned two days later in the early afternoon. I invited him to come right away. He arrived the next morning around 10 a.m. I gave him the list of wells sanctioned, in progress and completed under the scheme, and asked him to choose the panchayat samiti he wanted to visit to verify.

Maheshwari went around inspecting the wells the entire day and we returned around 7 p.m. He must have seen about 20 wells spread over 10–12 villages in two panchayat samitis. And he found the progress report to have been completely correct; in fact, in some places, the actual status was better than in the progress reports.

L.C. Gupta was a thorough gentleman. In the next review meeting, he brought up the subject at the beginning and remarked upon the difficulties in Jaipur district and the phenomenal work done in not only the Jeevandhara scheme, which was found to be completely true on ground verification, but also in other development schemes.

Months later, Rakesh Hooja, who took over as the collector of Jaipur from J.N. Gaur, would recommend my name for the state merit award in recognition of the implementation of development programmes in Jaipur district.

Attempts to bring order in development programme delivery

The DRDA implemented about 20 programmes, large and small, to benefit the poor. These programmes basically undertook three types of development interventions: provide an asset or a skill that could be used to establish a tiny business (the IRDP was the largest programme in this class); wage-based rural assets construction programmes (the National Rural Employment Programme [NREP] being the flagship programme in this category); and input/capital subsidization programmes (capital subsidy for land improvement under MASSIVE, a short hand for Massive Food Production Programme, for instance).

The IRDP was mainstreamed after experimental implementation under the predecessor of the DRDA, called Small Farmers Development Agency (SFDA). The IRDP, a universal programme implemented in all the districts of India, provided bank loans and a subsidy by the Government of India to reduce the effective capital cost for the recipient poor. It had a major skill development component called Training of Rural Youth for Self-Employment (TRYSEM), which envisaged government supported training followed by a bank loan cum subsidy for setting up a service business. The core of this programme is currently implemented as the National Rural Livelihood Programme (NRLP).

The NREP funded the creation of community assets with the poor getting wages by working on them. There was a major variant of the NREP called Food for Work, which paid a good part of wages in the form of food grains, priced at a lower rate, raising the effective wages. At the core, it was also a wage-generating programme. Another wage-based programme was the Employment Guarantee Scheme (EGS), under which the identified poor were guaranteed work for about 50 days a year. The EGS, in a way, was the precursor of Mahatma Gandhi National Rural Employment Guarantee Programme (MGNREGA), which is the principal wage programme today.

Under input/capital subsidization programmes, the government would provide a subsidy at a predefined scale depending upon the class and category of the poor. The MASSIVE programme provided subsidy for agriculture inputs. Famine-related works also had certain input subsidization components besides a wage-based programme. The Jeevandhara wells programme was also essentially a capital subsidy programme.

Panchayats prepared a list of the poor manually. All the 20-odd programmes had targets prescribed for the district by state-level agencies, mostly the

SSO. The prevalent practice was to subdivide the district targets under all the programmes among each of the 18 panchayat samitis and allocate funds accordingly. The panchayat samitis would do the same thing and distribute the targets among the panchayats.

I found two major structural problems in delivering these rural development programmes. First, while the basic nature was threefold (productive asset transfer, wage employment and input/capital subsidy) – the programmes were delivered through multiple units with different scales of assistance and guidelines, and second, while all the benefits landed at the doors of poor households, there was no mapping of programmes for delivery to the households in question.

Distributing targets to panchayat samitis was awful and time consuming. As every panchayat samiti was to have targets under each programme, it made the targets of some programmes very thinly spread. It also meant that every panchayat samiti, and by extension most panchayats, remained busy with the implementation of all the programmes. It also made monitoring of programme implementation difficult and tedious. I reckoned all these impacted the quality of programme delivery significantly.

An exercise was initiated to address the problem. All the 20-odd programmes, if necessary, at their sub-programme level, were divided into three broad categories of income-generating, wage-based and capital/input subsidization programmes. This resulted in determination of the total targets for the district separately for these three categories. These were, thereafter, broken down further for SC, ST and other earmarked categories. Finally, we allocated the aggregated district targets to the 18 panchayat samitis and assigned the specific programmes under which targets were allocated to specific panchayat samiti.

The entire exercise resulted in panchayat samitis getting targets under only three–six programmes instead of all 20. We prepared a comprehensive book of development programmes and targets. This did away with the necessity to look at hundreds of circulars. All programme details, allocation of targets and programmes under which targets were allocated became available at one place.

Accurate monitoring and faster implementation of the Jeevandhara wells scheme was partly on account of this streamlined system of target allocation and programme implementation.

I made one more attempt to streamline the programme delivery by writing an accounting and procedural manual for the DRDAs.

The DRDAs were registered as societies under the Societies Registration Act. The administrative expenditure of the DRDA staff was largely borne by the Government of India under what was known as DRDA Scheme. Implementation of the rural development schemes of the Ministry of Rural Development constituted almost their entire work. They were required to prepare annual accounts, including a receipts and payment statement, an income and expenditure statement, and a balance sheet and send the same to the Ministry of Rural Development through SSO.

The Government of India, however, made no administrative and accounting manual for the DRDAs. It would issue comprehensive guidelines for sanctioning of development benefits, the release of payments and furnishing of utilization certificates, and other instructions for each scheme separately. There were no instructions on how to maintain the books of accounts and the procedures to follow while processing the sanctioning of benefits and maintenance of accounts. The governing committee of the DRDA had approved a delegation of powers (that would sanction which benefit/expenditure) dividing them among the governing council; collector and chairman, DRDA; PD, DRDA, cum additional collector (development); and further down to project officers, assistant project officers and so on.

I felt there was a glaring gap. My accounting background also probably made me notice this much more than other IAS officers. I decided to write a comprehensive accounting manual for the DRDA, describing how to authorize and record all sanctions, approvals, authentication and accounting transactions. I sought Anjali's help, who was an accomplished CA, to assist me pro bono in writing the manual.

The manual was taken to the governing board for approval. No one in the governing board, which essentially comprised MLAs, pradhans of panchayat samitis, a representative of SSO and a few other officials, had any interest in or knowledge of an accounting manual. They were willing to give me the benefit of the doubt though some were suspicious of hidden googlies in the proposed manual. The governing board agreed for approval only in principle and further consultation with experts, including government.

I went ahead and implemented the manual in DRDA Jaipur as, in my judgement, this did not violate any guidelines, established procedures, delegated authorities or even administrative instructions. It was supplemental, clarified the responsibility of officials, made processes more transparent and facilitated account-keeping.

Believing the manual would be helpful at the national level, I sent two copies to Indrajeet Khanna, an officer of the Rajasthan cadre who was working as joint secretary in the Ministry of Rural Development. As I got no response in the next two weeks, I decided to seek an appointment with him. When I saw him in Delhi in his office, he directed me to Director Sunila Basant, to whom he had forwarded my letter with the manual. While she appreciated the work that had gone into it (she subsequently sent me a letter to this effect), she felt there was no necessity for the Government of India to issue a manual for the DRDAs. In her view, as far as the ministry was concerned, it worked according to the office manual prescribed by the government, and funds were sanctioned and utilization certificates obtained as prescribed under the instructions of the Ministry of Finance.

IRDP did not make the poor entrepreneurs

The IRDP was the principal instrument of the Government of India's new 'direct delivery' approach. The programme envisaged transforming the poor into entrepreneurs and small businessmen by providing them subsidized loans through the banking system to purchase an income-generating asset.

The most popular 'productive' asset purchased under the IRDP in Jaipur (for that matter all over Rajasthan and across the country) was cattle. As thousands of poor families were being provided loans by banks to buy cattle, a practice of organizing large cattle purchase camps had developed. In these pre-announced camps, typically organized at the panchayat samitis, the cattle sellers would bring their cows and buffalos. All potential beneficiaries of the panchayats would be brought by their sarpanches, panchayat members and village-level workers to the camp. The DRDA and block development office staff and officers would create all the necessary paperwork. The banks would be present to sanction and disburse loans to make payments.

A loan from the bank and subsidy from the government, delivered in this streamlined and efficient manner, was expected to turn the poor into micro-entrepreneurs and lift them over the poverty line.

The logic of cattle purchase as a poverty alleviation measure made some sense to me though it was less logical from the perspective of national GDP and growth. If a cow gets transferred from Family A to Family B, it will continue to produce the same amount of milk, adding no additional value to the district, state or national GDP.

As an instrument of income generation, though, it made sense as villagers were quite familiar with maintaining cattle, milking them and selling the milk. Further, the camp mode of working, which I had used extensively in Chittorgarh, appealed to me. I wanted to see it in operation.

The officers invited me to visit a large camp in Lalsot panchayat samiti. There were thousands of cows and buffaloes at the cattle fair ground. Many banks had organized separate tents to process loan cases. There was a large pandal for district and block development officers. The IRDP PO, P.C. Patni, who was on deputation from agriculture department, told me that at least 1,000 transactions would take place that day.

After some meetings in the tents interacting with the banks and development officials, I decided to venture out on my own to witness the action. The cattle were held in lots. Each cow, when sold against a loan sanctioned under the IRDP was a hypothecated asset. To ensure it was identified with a loan and the loanee, each cow sold was tagged at the corner of the ear. This required a metal tag to be permanently nailed and sealed to the ear as the loan was expected to remain current for three to five years.

To my surprise, many cattle virtually had their entire ear torn out. This made me suspicious. Was the system being gamed?

I enquired about the torn ears. I was told that once the loan was repaid, the tag had to be pulled out and if the same cattle was sold again, another tag was planted. A cow or buffalo had a 'wet' (milk-producing) period of about 10 years at best. It appeared to me that an ear would not be lost unless the same animal had been sold five to six times. This set me thinking. Why was the turnover so high?

I had earlier noted another phenomenon regarding the IRDP loan business. About 10–15 per cent of loanees repaid their loans in just three to six months. Connecting this to the torn ears of the cattle, I speculated in my mind whether the loanees repaid their loans quickly to retain the subsidy, which was the actual financial benefit to them under the programme, and not the cattle!

Discreet enquiries revealed that this was indeed the case in many loans. Further enquiries revealed that cattle owners were told to come to the camp and get their cattle tagged, which they were free to remove after the camp, for a consideration.

After I had spent some time in the camp, the elaborate IRDP loan machine became clearer to me. In most cases, there was no genuine purchase of cattle. Loan papers were made, loans sanctioned, cattle tagged, details noted and loans disbursed – but no actual handover of cattle took place.

The loan plus subsidy amount would come to the beneficiary's account. The cattle owner would be paid off a consideration and carry his fleet back. The beneficiary would get the benefit of the subsidy minus the one-time amount paid to the cattle owner and some corruption costs. I pursued the matter and checked with some beneficiaries. They confirmed that they got about 50–75 per cent of the subsidy.

Having discovered this elaborate, and in a way, fraudulent machinery of the IRDP cattle purchase business, I was in a quandary. Should I raise an alarm and stop the charade?

At the national level, Minister of State for Banking Janardhan Poojary was pushing banks, especially the always compliant public-sector banks (PSBs), at that time to organize massive loan melas to disburse loans and subsidies to the poor to rapidly implement the government programmes. I checked with some bank officials in an indirect way how some cattle get sold multiple times. They seemed to know the reality of the cattle-purchase business.

Upon some more thought, I felt the real advantage of the rural development programmes was to make some financial benefit reach the poor. Most poor people were unlikely to set up businesses to earn income. They would rather earn wages by working on their own or somebody's fields or go to cities for construction and other manual work. If, at the end of this entire process, they were getting some benefit in cash, it was all right. I decided not to make any noise.

However, I learnt a lesson. All government programmes where some benefit is delivered in kind (for example, education delivered by paying the cost of infrastructure and teachers' salary, or wheat or rice delivered through the public distribution system) and those that seek to make the poor entrepreneurs were suboptimal and unlikely to make a real difference. Wages-based programmes or those where the benefit could be delivered in cash were perhaps better targeted.

The IRDP, and its subsequent editions, all convoluted redistribution programmes, survived for many years and were eventually replaced with direct benefit (increasingly cash) delivery programmes, where leakage in delivery was much less or eliminated altogether.

A corruption scandal breaks out

B.K. Meena, an officer of the 1982 batch, succeeded me at DRDA Jaipur in March 1989. One day, about six months after I had left, the Jaipur newspapers ran a front-page story, with *Rajasthan Patrika* publishing the following headline: *'Jaipur DRDA Mein 1 Crore Ka Ghotala!'* (One Crore Scandal in DRDA Jaipur!)

This was a large sum in those days. The Bofors scandal, which had broken out about two years earlier, was pegged at ₹64 crore. A scandal of ₹1 crore in a DRDA, in one of about 500 districts, was a big news. The state anti-corruption agency acted fast. Meena was arrested and put behind bars. Two other officers – an assistant director of industry, D.K. Gupta, on deputation from the industries department, and Ram Kumar Swamy, a junior accountant from the state subordinate junior accountants' cadre – were also arrested.

The scandal remained frontpage news for quite some time. It was reported that the wrongdoing primarily took place in the TRYSEM scheme, under which skill development programmes were delivered through empanelled agencies that trained eligible youths in approved trades. The empanelment, sanctioning the training programme, monitoring the training imparted and sanctioning the funds to the institution and the payment of stipends to the trainees, were managed by Gupta. Swamy verified the work and cleared payments. Meena was overall in charge and the final approving and signing authority in all these cases.

The procedure was clearly elaborated in my DRDA manual. There was a paper trail, and all sanctioning papers had to be signed by the officer in charge of the scheme and the accountant in charge. Procedural excellence, however, cannot eliminate collusion. In this case, a number of fake agencies were reportedly empanelled, fake trainings organized and bills cleared – all following the process laid down in the manual. The sanctioning orders had the signatures of Gupta, Swamy and Meena.

As I was no longer at DRDA Jaipur, I was not concerned. I also did not want to poke my nose into the matter. However, at one stage, the DSP of the anti-corruption wing reached out to me to record my statement.

He first recorded my statement on the applicable process of sanctioning and disbursing funds under TRYSEM. He also questioned my role in two matters. One, he informed me that there was an allegation against me recorded in the statement of B.K. Meena that I had paid a hefty amount to my wife Anjali for writing the manual. Second, he asked me why I had implemented a manual that was not approved by the governing body of the DRDA.

It appeared that he knew the truth about both matters yet wanted my statement on the record. I told him not a single rupee was paid to Anjali for helping me write the manual. I asked why he had to ask me something that could be easily verified from the DRDA records. He then confirmed that they had it in writing from the DRDA that nothing was paid to Anjali in any form, either as a fee, expense reimbursement or anything else. He also told me this was a diversionary tactic employed by Meena, who wanted to implicate me somehow to dilute his own culpability.

As for the implementation of the DRDA manual, I reiterated that I was within my rights and had an obligation to streamline the administrative and accounting procedure. I could have done this by issuing an administrative order. As the manual did not change or violate any other instruction or guideline of the Government of India, the Rajasthan government or the approved process laid down by the governing body, there was no irregularity in implementing it. After I recorded my statement, he told me that it was thanks to the manual that they could pinpoint the role of each of the three officers so clearly in the scandal.

B.K. Meena, Gupta and Swamy remained in jail for a while. They were chargesheeted and convicted by trial courts. However, over the years, the inefficiency of the prosecution and the sheer fatigue of a long-drawn case probably led to their acquittal or the imposition of minor penalties. No one really got punished in the scandal.

4

'Why Do We Need Interviews to Recruit Teachers?'

Under the prime ministership of Rajiv Gandhi, the Government of India started giving importance to panchayati raj institutions from 1985. In December 1988, Rajasthan, led by Chief Minister Shiv Charan Mathur, decided to post direct-recruit IAS officers (in place of officers of the RAS, who usually manned these positions) as CEOs in zila parishads. Panchayats are at the village level, panchayat samitis at block level and zila parishads at the district level.

Along with two other direct-recruit IAS officers, I was posted in a zila parishad. My posting as CEO Zila Parishad Jaipur came in December 1988. No one had been posted at DRDA Jaipur as my replacement till then. I joined my new posting promptly, though the development work in zila parishads was nowhere close to the development work undertaken by the DRDAs. Rakesh Hooja, Jaipur's district collector, asked me to continue as PD, DRDA, and additional collector (development) until an officer was posted to the DRDA. I held the DRDA charge until March 1989 when B.K. Meena took over.

Streamlining teachers transfers and management

Jaipur was a large district with 18 panchayat samitis. Primary school education was entrusted to the panchayat samitis whereas schools from Class 6 were the direct responsibility of the government's education department. The government policy was to take primary schools as close to villagers as possible and equip them with at least two teachers. This required a large number of teachers to be recruited every year. Further, most teachers wanted to be in the panchayat samitis closest to Jaipur, as most came from there or other cities and wanted to live in or closest to the city. Local teachers wanted to be posted in the panchayat samitis they came from.

The recruitment of teachers had been decentralized to the zila parishads. Getting their people recruited in government was the most preferred business of most elected representatives. The MLAs were most interested to see their candidates selected as teachers. Teachers were also useful political workers.

A perfect gentleman, Bhagwan Sahai Sharma from Kotputli was the pramukh of the Jaipur zila parishad. Kamla Beniwal, a very powerful minister in the then ruling Shiv Charan Mathur government, also hailed from Jaipur, from the Bairath area, also (and formally) known as Viratnagar – according to the Mahabharata, this is where the Pandavas are believed to have spent their one year of *agyatvaas* (incognito exile). Kamla had become a minister for the first time in 1954 – I was born in 1960 – and was a very senior minister by experience and standing.

The government's National Informatics Centre (NIC) had set up a district computer centre in Jaipur. Vinod Kumar Agarwal, a very enthusiastic district officer of the NIC, agreed to write a short programme and create two databases. One database was for primary schoolteachers working in different panchayat samitis of Jaipur. It captured relevant and useful information for inter panchayat samiti transfers: date of joining, number of years/months spent in the panchayat samiti posted in, the panchayat samiti where they wanted to be transferred to, the reasons for requesting a transfer, and pending disciplinary matters, if any.

The other database was for applicants who had applied for the job of a teacher – grade III (primary school teachers were designated as grade III teachers) – in the panchayat samitis of Jaipur zila parishad. There was an elaborate schema of marks to be awarded for various degrees, certificates, experience and extracurricular achievements. There were marks for physical handicap, being a woman, and other specified social and economic considerations. Computerization of applications, factoring in all these factors, enabled transparent analysis of the applications and determine the order of merit objectively.

There was no criterion specified by the Panchayati Raj department of the Rajasthan government for inter-panchayat samiti transfers of teachers. General instructions permitted a transfer after two years. There was, however, an additional requirement of a no-objection certificate from both the panchayat samitis – where the teacher was posted and the other where a teacher wanted to go. Though this requirement made the teachers somewhat subject to the whims and fancies of the Pradhans of the concerned panchayat samitis, this was a mandatory criterion. In a way, this provided some leverage to panchayat samitis that traditionally faced teacher shortages owing to lack of interest from teachers to stay there on account of remoteness or relative underdevelopment.

Once the lists were ready and mandatory instructions were complied with, I thought the only rational and least objectionable criterion would be to transfer a teacher to a receiving panchayat samiti who had spent the longest time outside it. For instance, if there were three teachers interested in coming to Panchayat Samiti A, the teacher who had been outside it for the longest period would get priority, and so on. If there were only two vacancies, two teachers in the priority list would get transferred to Panchayat Samiti A.

We first made transfers to the most sought-after panchayat samitis – Sanganer and Amer – which adjoined Jaipur. Thereafter, the next most popular panchayat samitis were taken up. This way, we could order transfers for all teachers who wanted transfers to other panchayat samitis subject to the availability of vacancies.

The transfers received tremendous support from most teachers, except those who had hoped to get to their preferred panchayat samitis, even though they had recently joined, using their connections and other unfair modes.

Recruitment of teachers created upheaval

For new teacher applicants, the state government orders did not prescribe any necessity or process to hold interviews and award marks for them. However, the system prescribed 10 marks out of 100 for the interview; 90 per cent of the marks were for academic qualification, experience, physical handicaps, sports achievements and other objectively defined criteria. There were specific maximum marks for each of these categories and the scale of award of marks was also prescribed. We prepared the list and determined the marks according to the objective criteria laid out.

Interviewing thousands of candidates took enormous time. I was also informed of the charade of interviews held previously. Most candidates were not allowed to sit for even a minute before being turned away, indicating their interview was over. There were no objectively set criteria about what was to be judged in the interview and how the marks could be awarded. This turned the interviews into a farce. However, the stratagem of the interview was very useful for the committee/Pramukh to award high marks to those whom they wanted to favour and low marks to those they did not want selected. As the aggregate marks based on the objective criteria were very tightly distributed, a decent award out of 10 marks were sufficient to select candidates from nearly the bottom of the list and deprive those who were at the top. The interview process made the entire recruitment exercise overwhelmingly subjective.

There was another reason that made me think the interview exercise was wholly unnecessary. The marks awarded for academic performance indicated academic suitability or the lack thereof. The marks for experience objectively rewarded those with experience of teaching. The marks for extracurricular activities catered for the potential of teachers for sports, physical education, social work and other extra-curricular activities in school. Marks for being women, handicapped or SC and ST took care of affirmative action for deprived and marginalized sections of the society. I could not pin down on what else was left to be judged in the interview.

I wrote a long note, after placing the merit list in the file section, for approval of the recruitment of teachers without interviews to Zila Pramukh Sharma. This created a flutter, and he called for a discussion. When he said interviews were the precedent and necessary for judging suitability, I told him frankly there was nothing that could add value in the interview, nor were the interviews required as per the process laid down by the state government. I told him that recruitment could be very well made using the marks awarded to all candidates based on the criteria laid down and firmly stated that I would sign off the recruitment of teachers made only on that basis. I requested him to conduct any test or check he required to ensure the marks were correctly awarded.

He kept the file. And instead of approving or rejecting the list or raising some objections, he rushed to bigger bosses.

Kamala Beniwal summons

Tulsi Ram Varma, an IAS officer 10 years my senior, was director of the panchayati raj department, the government department that interfaced with panchayati raj institutions and exercised considerable authority and powers over the zila parishads.

Kamla Beniwal, though not panchayati raj minister, summoned Varma and me for an urgent meeting. She was in a foul mood and shot rapid fire questions at Varma. How could the process of interviews for recruiting teachers be dispensed with without government orders? Why is the CEO not listening to the pramukh?

It appeared Bhagwan Sahai Sharma had rushed to her to inform that a number of candidates recommended by her or from her constituency would not get recruited as per the list prepared by the CEO unless his ability to manoeuvre was restored through inclusion of interview marks.

Varma, a nice and soft-spoken officer, and too much of a gentleman, could only fumble. He knew there were no orders to award any marks for interviews, but he also knew that almost every zila parishad was doing it. He requested for time to discuss the matter with the district collector and get back to her.

I sought permission to explain. But Beniwal would not grant me that liberty. I tried to explain the position of rules and how transparently we had prepared the merit list. She cut me short and directed Tulsi Ram Varma to get the interview process restored quickly. The meeting disbanded.

Varma took me to his chamber in the secretariat. Despite my detailed explanation, he tried to persuade me to revert to the interview marks. When I stood my ground, he closed the meeting by saying he would discuss the matter with Rakesh Hooja, the district collector.

The next day, Collector Hooja asked me to accompany him to the secretariat. He had got the papers collected the previous evening. In the car, I explained the entire matter to him though he did not seem interested; apparently, he had read the papers quite carefully.

We walked straightaway into the chamber of Chief Minister Shiv Charan Mathur.

Rakesh Hooja did not waste much time in explaining the matter to the CM. It seemed Kamla Beniwal had spoken to both CM and Hooja. Hooja asked CM straight off the bat whether he should cancel the merit list and restore the interviews.

Mathur was a seasoned politician and functioned in the mould of a civil servant. He asked me a few questions. I explained the entire process and how the lists had been prepared objectively. I took the liberty to assert that the interviews would only bring in non-transparency, favouritism and corruption.

I was not expecting Mathur to disregard political considerations completely. In fact, I was ready with a follow-on request should he order restoration of interview process – to transfer me from Jaipur zila parishad. However, he surprised me. Averring that the process adopted appeared perfectly fine to him, he asked Collector Hooja to let the list be approved and appointments issued. He also commented that he had posted young direct recruit officers in zila parishads precisely for the purpose of cleaning up the mess.

I thanked Chief Minister Mathur and mentally saluted him. Rakesh Hooja also smiled and said he would talk to Tulsi Ram Varma and the zila pramukh.

And so, teachers' recruitments were made in the Jaipur zila parishad in 1988–89, without awarding any marks for interviews. Initially, no other zila parishad in Rajasthan followed Jaipur's example. Over the years, the system of recruiting lower-class employees and teachers without any interviews was adopted by many departments. Much later, the Government of India abolished interviews for many positions.

Rakesh Hooja recommends me for merit award

In the same year – 1988–89 – Hooja recommended my name for state merit award for my work at the DRDA, though I was only holding an additional charge there at that time, despite the teachers' recruitment affair.

There were several officers in Rajasthan who judged me fairly and rated me highly despite administrative problems I might have created for them and my very independent style of work.

Rakesh Hooja was the first of such officers.

5

Making the White Elephant Dance

The Rajasthan Cooperative Marketing Federation (Rajfed) procured agricultural crops like wheat, other grains and pulses on the account of the Food Corporation of India (FCI), on its own commercial account or while implementing market intervention schemes of the central or state governments. It was also involved in the distribution of fertilizers and other agricultural inputs.

Sometime in the early 1980s, it was decided to establish a 60,000 tonnes per annum (TPA) plant in the Kota region to process soybean to extract oil and produce de-oiled cake (DOC) as a byproduct. Rajfed was entrusted with this responsibility. It was planned that it would establish a network of oilseeds cooperative societies (OSCSs) in the Kota region and the tribal belt of Udaipur where soybean cultivation was picking up. It was estimated that about 2 lakh tonnes of soybean was produced in that region, adjoining the Malwa region of Madhya Pradesh, where soybean cultivation had taken off earlier. This was a major farmer-friendly move as Rajasthan's soybean farmers were forced to take their produce to Indore in Madhya Pradesh, which effectively reduced their earnings from the crop.

A white elephantine problem

A modern plant to process 60,000 tonnes of soybeans per year was designed and built to process the soybean in Kota, along with 10,000 tons of godown, 5,000 tons of modern silos and other facilities.

The World Bank provided a concessional loan from the International Development Agency (IDA) to the National Cooperative Development Corporation (NCDC), a Government of India undertaking for financing processing facilities in the cooperative sector, under a project called NCDC-III.

A part of the funds from the credit line were used by the NCDC to provide funds to Rajfed. Equity for the soybean project was routed through the state cooperative bank, Apex Bank, which received 40 per cent of the funds as a loan from the NCDC and gave it to Rajfed as equity. The remaining NCDC funds and state government share came to Rajfed as loan from the state government.

The Rajfed Soybeans Processing Plant was the largest processing/manufacturing facility created in Rajasthan in the public sector or the cooperative sector, other than power plants established under the Rajasthan State Electricity Board (RSEB). Over ₹35 crore of capital investment had been made in the project by 1989.

The plant was announced as ready in 1987 but was still formally and technically in 'commissioning stage' in 1989 as it had not met the performance parameters that the project management agency (PMC), the National Heavy Engineering Cooperative Ltd (NHEC), another Government of India enterprise, was to demonstrate before the plant could be taken over by Rajfed.

For about two years, this tussle was on. For more than a year, the plant was operating at less than 20 per cent capacity utilization. It had already run up financial losses of more than ₹10 crore. There was very bad press about it, and unflattering stories were published incessantly.

For most, especially the people of Kota, the plant had become a 'white elephant'.

An amiable and efficient officer of the 1980 batch of the IAS, Atul Kumar Gupta, was first posted as CEO of the Rajfed Soybeans Processing Plant, Kota. He replaced a technocrat, D. Kothari, a senior oil technologist, who was sacked when he could not achieve commercial production in the plant and bad publicity about the plant started creating perceptional problems about the state government. I was to replace a reluctant Atul Gupta.

V.B.L. Mathur, my state mentor during probation and chief secretary of Rajasthan in 1989, called me on the day my posting orders were issued for the Kota Rajfed Soybeans Plant. He was forthright and told me that while the posting as CEO of the project was not an exciting one for an IAS officer, he would like me to try and turn the plant around. For me, a cost accountant by training, the posting appeared interesting as I would get to work as the CEO of a big plant. In any case, there was nothing exciting to do in the Jaipur zila parishad. I assured him I would put my best foot forward.

Atul Gupta was in Jaipur that day. He was also posted out in the same order as the collector in the Pali district of Jodhpur. The next day, we decided to go together for the charge handover. On the way to Kota, a four-hour journey from Jaipur by car, we talked extensively. I wanted to understand everything about the project, and he explained it to me in detail. He filled me in on the plant, its technology, the players in the system, Kothari's experience, the status of construction of the plant and a large colony nearby, and the problems with NCDC and NHEC, among other matters.

It was evident that he had put in a sincere effort to set things right but had not really succeeded in doing so. He was clearly fed up with the way things were going. He was also quite critical of C.K. Mathew, a senior IAS officer who was managing director of Rajfed, and his inability to take decisions. He told me he had requested for a transfer as collector. He also hinted that he was considering going to the US for further studies after the posting as district collector.

Gupta was unambiguous in his assessment of the inadvisability of posting an IAS officer in such a plant when there was an IAS officer working as managing director of Rajfed. He believed that as the Kota facility was largely a technical one, it should be run by a technocrat. Criticizing the state government for not finding a suitable technical replacement for Kothari and posting an IAS officer to waste there, he said, 'You don't post a collector to a tehsil if the tehsildar does not perform.'

I listened to him attentively but held my counsel. White elephantine problem was mine, thereafter.

Horrible state of affairs

Ashok Sharma, a pugnacious but highly competent oil technologist, was in charge of the processing plant. In his assessment, Kothari did not know how to run a plant. I decided to visit the plant and understand what ailed it.

It was indeed in a horrible state.

Two flakers were at the heart of the plant, which crushed and flattened wet soybeans into flakes. These flakes then passed through a moving bed where the solvent hexane was sprayed on them, which dissolved the oil content in the flakes and took it to the bed of the solvent and to the next chamber where the two were separated. One of the two flakers was down and lying on one side of the flaking section. Enquiries revealed that some essential parts had broken down and the requisition for buying replacement had been pending for quite some time. The plant manager was not satisfied with the quality of flaking as well.

The plant had no refinery, although it was sanctioned as part of project, and therefore, the oil produced was sold as unrefined oil. However, a degumming plant had been constructed. Normally, the oil is degummed only when it is refined. If you don't refine the solvent extracted oil, you don't degum the oil. The degumming plant was a standing waste.

Solvent consumption was key to performance parameters. Another critical parameter was how much oil was left in the DOCs. Oil sold at six times the price of the DOC. Any extra oil left in DOCs was an unnecessary financial loss. In Sharma's assessment, the unsatisfactory state of both the critical parameters – hexane consumption and oil left in DOCs – was on account of bad flaking machines chosen by the NHEC, the PMC.

The plant had a larger boiler section with two boilers. One had been down for some time. The plant's large storage capacity (10,000 metric tonnes [MT] of traditional godown storage and 5,000 tonnes of new-age silo storage) was quite fully utilized as farmers' soybeans had to be purchased. As the plant was only operating at less than 20 per cent capacity, large stocks of soybean were lying unutilized for quite some time, with some produce of over two years also stored in the godown. This affected the quality and quantity of extractable oil besides causing financial loss in terms of interest and storage cost.

The DOC produced was brought by a conveyer belt to the DOC godown from the solvent extraction plant and was bagged and then sold. It was high on protein content as almost the entire protein in soybean (soybean has about 40 per cent protein) was left in the DOC. This had become a good item of export as it was very good cattle feed. However, quality parameters existed for it, such as leftover oil, water content and dust. The DOC compliant with quality parameters sold at a premium. But the plant was selling it on an 'as is where is basis', which meant the buyer would assume the risk of extra dust or water present. As it was never easy and cost-effective to make a quality assessment of such a bulky commodity, the DOC from Rajfed Soybeans Plant went at a hefty discount.

There was no care for material balance either. There was no reason why oil plus DOC should not equal the soybean inputted. Sharma told me that t some plants where he had worked, the output weight was higher than the input weight as the water content in DOC was usually higher than in the soybean purchased. However, the Kota plant had an output–input material ratio of about 97, causing big financial loss.

The visit was an eyeopener. I saw evidence of unnecessary investment (the degumming plant), poor quality equipment investment (flakers, solvent section and boilers) and poor management (the storage and DOC godown).

It was a sorry state of affairs, to say the least on the plant side. The situation was no different on the office side.

S.N. Sharma, a competent CA and the finance manager, would push every file for approval to my desk. Aditya Jain, a happy-go-lucky soul and the procurement manager, would somehow manage to get three quotes for small procurements, convene a meeting of the procurement committee and push the file to the finance manager for approval. For a larger procurement such as the flaker parts, a notice inviting tenders would be issued. Generally, there would be no response or some intermediary would respond, building a considerable margin over the cost of the machine or part from the original equipment manufacturer (OEM) or other suppliers. In these circumstances, objections would be raised, and the files would go to and fro, without any resolution. Sharma, the plant manager, would quarrel with the finance manager and other officials as the replacements or parts would not come.

The CEO's office, located on one side of the large land parcel taken for the plant on the Kota–Rawatbhata road (where some of India's nuclear power plants are), presented an even sorrier state of affairs. Files were piling up everywhere. Decisions were not being made by the officers. However, to ensure no one was singled out for causing a delay, there were queries raised on most files, which would either go down to the last clerical level or move to another branch in the office.

Passing the buck – sideways or above – was the most common protection insurance, and the tactic was used by everyone in the system.

First decision: Taking over the plant

Plant performance was contractually the responsibility of the NHEC, the PMC, until the performance parameters were demonstrated and the plant was handed over to the Rajfed management. Uninterested in taking on the responsibility, the Rajfed side would always find some fault, excuse or the something else to avoid taking over.

The contract provided for performance trials to be conducted over a period of seven days with responsibility for the plant, raw materials and other facilities, such as steam from the boiler, hexane supply, etc., on the Rajfed management.

The PMC, along with the plant suppliers, was to run the plant under its supervision and deliver the output in specified capacity (it was a 200 tonnes per day processing plant), specified quality (with respect to quality of oil and DOC) and input consumption (steam, hexane and power).

The last performance trials had been held sometime in 1987.

The NHEC received a per centage of the project cost as its PMC fee. Its managers always said their expenditure on the project was far more than the total fees they received. They wanted to demonstrate the performance parameters and be done with the project. They did not want an outcome where their reputation and future business sank because they failed to demonstrate the parameters. They also had a litany of complaints about the obligations of Rajfed, which was responsible for the performance parameters not having been demonstrated.

Sharma was totally confident that he would be able to run the plant at 100 per cent capacity utilization if the plant were taken over by Rajfed, the damaged flaker replaced, and all required parts for replacement in the boiler and other machines were either readily available in stores or procured quickly as in the private sector – within 24 hours of placing an order.

I also believed real and effective ownership of the plant by Rajfed was critical. No PMC could run the plant for Rajfed forever. While the contract provided for some liquidated damages (LD) to be recovered if plant performance parameters were not satisfied, even if the entire fees paid to the PMC were recovered (an impossible situation), it would only amount to 6 per cent of the cost of the plant. It was also necessary to allow the plant manager to set things right.

We decided to bid the PMC goodbye whether the performance parameters were successfully demonstrated or not. A date for the performance trial was fixed sometime in November 1989, two months after I arrived. The PMC demonstrated most parameters but failed in two of them. We imposed penalties for undemonstrated performance. The plant was taken over, documenting the performance demonstrated and the elements not demonstrated satisfactorily.

It was now a Rajfed processing plant. It was our responsibility.

Second decision: The buck stopped with me

While the plant was taken over to give the managers a shot at demonstrating technical performance, the office had to be converted into a decision-making entity, one that supported the plant in terms of manpower, raw material, parts and other necessary goods and services in real time.

I tried to understand why everyone was always trying to pass the buck when it came to taking a decision. Some questioning helped identify the culprit.

Section 70 of the Rajasthan Cooperatives Act imposed personal liability for every loss incurred on the officer who took that decision. For instance, if a manager procured a part at ₹10,000 and later, on audit, it was found that the part was available in the market at ₹9,000. The audit would determine that the decision caused a loss of ₹1,000, even though due process was followed or even that a ₹9,000 alternative was also a non-serious offer. Section 70 mandated that this loss would be recouped from the officer who signed off on the decision. Take another instance: 100 tonnes of DOC was sold at ₹4 lakh (₹4,000 per tonne) subject to quality parameters ex-plant, and it was found at the port that there was 0.5 per cent more dust than prescribed. This allowed the importer to deduct ₹10,000 from the ₹4 lakh sale price. The loss of ₹10,000 was then determined as the personal responsibility of the sales manager if he was the decision-maker. However, if he could successfully demonstrate on file that this parameter was the purview of the plant manager, the recovery of the ₹10,000 would be shifted to the plant manager.

There were many cases where officers were saddled with notices to recover 'losses' caused by them. They would spend much time trying to explain why there was either no loss or it was not they who had taken the real decision. These harsh provisions of Section 70 had not been able to recover any significant amount to make up for the losses audit determined but succeeded in making all officers non-decisionmakers.

Section 70 was an unjust and unfair law. It was also vague and impractical. Officers in the cooperative registrar business, including the audit organization, did not understand business. They applied the law in such an unimaginative and unfriendly manner that Section 70 ensured that the Rajfed Soybeans Processing Plant became a non-performing asset (NPA), a loss, even before it was commissioned.

That said, the law did exist. Moreover, there were vested interests in the cooperative department and registrar's office for whom Section 70 was a source of power to harass officers and make money. Thus, it was clear to me that officers would remain risk averse if this sword of Damocles hung over their heads.

So, I decided to take a risk. Confident that we would make all decisions motivated by the objective of making the plant functional, I told the officers that the buck stopped at my table and I could be treated as the officer responsible for taking all decisions. If there was any enquiry under Section 70, I would stand responsible. They should take decisions as they saw fit and wherever they had even an iota of doubt that it might lead to trouble later, they could take my approval.

I did something more. An obscure provision in the delegation of power to the CEO from the Rajfed management implicitly permitted the CEO to take a decision on commercial considerations about purchase of parts and sale of material. Using this provision, I issued orders to the effect that for OEM supplies, orders would be placed directly with OEM suppliers and, if necessary, the part would even be airlifted or procured by sending an employee to their factory or warehouse.

These measures inspired tremendous confidence among the officers. Very soon, there was no passing of the buck sideways. Whenever an officer had a doubt, he would come in for a discussion and take oral approval for the course of action he wanted to adopt. If he wanted to be doubly sure, he would record it on the file and get my written confirmation.

The worm began turning. The elephant rose on the feet.

A marvellous turnaround

Taking over the plant from the PMC, entrusting it to the technical team led by Ashok Sharma, expelling the fear of being held personally responsible for hypothetical losses, changing procurement rules to ensure parts and machines were procured rapidly, and boosting the motivation levels of the team made all the difference.

Sharma got the flakers repaired (one was later replaced), fine-tuned the solvent plant and attended to the boiler. Hexane consumption and leftover oil in DOC became the biggest watchwords. His temperament did create some issues on occasion, but I could manage this. He trusted my judgement and abided by it without question. Though he was a poor people-manager, his technical abilities were marvellous, and I ensured these were used to the hilt.

In fact, once, an employee was sent by aircraft from Mumbai to Chennai just to get one part from a supplier located there. Everybody understood the value of 'no downtime'.

Capacity utilization started improving December 1989 onwards. The plant achieved 100 per cent monthly capacity utilization in January, something close to 125 per cent in February and in excess of 130 per cent in March 1990. For the quarter January–March 1990, the plant averaged a monthly capacity utilization of 120 per cent.

It continued its good run in the first and second quarters of 1990–91, averaging more than 100 per cent capacity utilization. By the end of September 1990, the entire raw material stock was exhausted, including stocks purchased from the market. The new soybean crop starts coming in from early October. The plant underwent annual maintenance in September when there were no soybean stocks in the warehouse and silos.

The DOC parameters improved to meet international norms. We switched to selling DOC on a quality-parameter basis. An agreement was struck with Gujarat Oilseeds Growers' Federation (GROFED) to export DOC under the name of Rajfed Kota DOC. This improved price realization. Sharma started adding hot water to the DOC to take the moisture per centage in DOC to the maximum extent permissible. Thereafter, the output–input ratio of the material balance came to being higher than 100 per cent, sometimes as high as 102 per cent; a 3–4 per cent of turnover increase was achieved at a negligible cost of the hot water added to DOC.

The mood was upbeat. I had introduced a uniform for the plant, which everyone started wearing with pride. Public perception also changed totally. The white elephant had begun to dance. Everybody appreciated it.

The World Bank had an elaborate system of project supervision. A team led by the project manager would visit all the projects, have comprehensive discussions at the plant level, corporate level and the state level twice a year. Later, they would brief the concerned administrative ministry and the DEA in the Government of India. The team drew up a comprehensive aide-memoire that recorded project implementation performance and developments relating to all material issues.

Earlier, the aides-memoires for the NCDC-III project, used to flag concerns relating to the disappointing implementation of the Rajfed Soybean Project, termed the project implementation unsatisfactory, which, in World Bank terminology, meant that it was a virtually failed project.

The aide-memoire after the World Bank team's visit in April 1990 sang a very different tune. It recognized vast improvement in project implementation and operational performance. This pleased Mathew as well as M.L. Mehta, who had taken over as the secretary of the agriculture and cooperation department.

Implementing the NCDC-III project was my first introduction to the World Bank. I would later have a much deeper association with it as a director in the DEA and, later, an executive director (ED) on its board.

I solve my boss's problem

In an unusual move, the Rajasthan government gave me the charge of managing director of Rajfed for about a month when C.K. Mathew went for long leave sometime in July–August 1990. I thought this was a great opportunity to learn about the state-level operations of Rajfed and decided to make Jaipur my headquarters for about 10 days at a stretch.

A major issue that came up during this time was the default by the engineering, procurement and construction (EPC) contractor Uma Hitech for the Jalore mustard-oil plant. The contractor had delayed plant construction inordinately and had already been given extensions for many months. He was possibly broke and was not mobilizing workers and machinery to complete the plant. I decided to visit Jalore.

This plant was much simpler than the Kota plant. It had two sections. One section was to extract oil using the traditional *kachchi ghani kolhu* process, a cold-press process that retains the pungency of mustard oil. The second section was a wet-press process through expellers, which squeezed more oil but lost much of the pungent taste in the oil. The plant capacity was smaller at 50 tonnes a day. The installation of the *kolhu*s was half done while the expellers had been installed, and some oil was being extracted on a trial basis. Mustard oilseed had been procured and was lying in the godown.

My enquiries revealed that the contractor was in no position to complete the project. He was demanding an additional advance payment to complete the remaining work, which appeared to be risky as he may have diverted the already given cash towards other purposes.

I, as the officer holding only an additional charge, more particularly of a higher position, was not expected to take any decision in the matter. The usual course of action in such a situation was to leave the matter to be decided by the regular managing director when he returned to work.

However, I decided to take matters into my own hands. I convened a meeting with all the officers concerned in Jaipur and asked for their assessment of the situation. I had made my own assessment during my visit to Jalore. The officers agreed that the contractor would not complete the plant, and acceding to his request for more money, which was not due as per the contract and therefore was a violation of the rules, was not advisable. When I mooted the idea of terminating the contract, they seemed to agree but some of them were not prepared to take the plunge.

Some more discussion followed. While on the merits all of them were convinced that termination of the contract was the only sensible option left, a few hesitated to sign the minutes. I appealed to them to act in the best interests of Rajfed. Some of them could not believe what they were witnessing as Mathew had found this option justifiable but could not act on it for months.

Finally, they all signed on. A day later, we issued a termination letter to the EPC contractor Uma Hitech. The impasse was over and the remaining work in the Jalore plant was completed in the next two to three months using another contractor, at the risk and cost of the terminated contractor (which, after the completion of plant and actual expenditure on excess cost, would be recovered from the terminated contractor).

I get the state merit award and a promotion

C.K. Mathew, managing director of Rajfed, was pleasantly surprised at the turnaround. A project that had given him many sleepless nights had become a source of pride. V.B.L. Mathur also felt vindicated.

In the 1990s, India had decided to take on the challenge of drastically cutting down its edible oil import bill. The strategy involved encouraging the growth of oilseeds and establishment of processing facilities. While the Kota project was funded by the World Bank, India had entered into a deal with the European Economic Community (EEC), which later became the European Union (EU), to use the proceeds of in-kind assistance provided by the EEC to set up oilseed processing facilities. Rajasthan had received assistance to set up five mustard oilseed processing facilities in Bikaner, Sriganganagar, Jalore, Merta and Gangapur.

These plants were at different stages of construction (from near beginning in Gangapur City and Sriganganagar to at a fairly advanced stage in Jalore) when we successfully turned around the soybean project, after throwing out NHEC, and raised capacity utilization from 20 per cent to 120 per cent. All these projects were headed by technical officers, mostly oil technologists. There was one old oilseed processing facility at Fatehnagar in Udaipur district organized under a separate cooperative, which had been taken over by Rajfed recently. Capacity addition at Fatehnagar was also planned.

Mathew asked me to organize a two-day event in Kota to explain the turnaround to these general managers and plant managers. The Kota plant management was very excited to see their performance acknowledged and validated in this manner.

We organized the meetings quite successfully. All other managers came. Our presentation, decision making and risk taking was appreciated. Most officers wanted to follow that path. I was able to persuade C.K. Mathew to improve delegation of powers to all the plants, specifically in terms of procurement of parts and other material. He also agreed to allow the projects to become members of all-India associations of oilseed traders and processing plants to improve industry wide interactions. I attended a few of these meetings, and the pride of my two managers – Sharma and Jain – when they participated in them was palpable.

When he returned to Jaipur, C.K. Mathew recommended my name to the government for the state merit award. The earlier recommendation made by Rakesh Hooja had not resulted in the award for some technical reasons. This time, it materialized. The state merit award, delivered by the governor during the Republic Day or Independence Day function, was quite prestigious.

I received my award from Governor Debi Prasad Chattopadhyay on 26 January 1991. Several officers congratulated me for getting an award for an industrial-sector performance as it was usually collectors who would get such a recognition. A.L. Roongta, a very senior officer who had spent many years in industrial and financial organizations such as the Rajasthan State Industrial Development and Investment Corporation (RIICO), was most effusive in his praise.

Three days later, I was transferred as MD of the newly created Rajasthan Oilseeds Growers Federation, which was later renamed as Tilam Sangh. Atul Gupta had made a proposal to designate the CEO of the Kota soybean project as a joint managing director, which he thought matched the dignity of an IAS officer. Here, I was being entrusted with the responsibility of managing the second-largest manufacturing and processing organization in Rajasthan with projects worth hundreds of crores under execution. In my view, this was an even bigger honour than the merit award.

It was also a much bigger responsibility to build and run a large state-level organization.

6

'Sell Off Before It Is Too Late'

Rajfed, as a business institution, had very little processing experience. From 1985, when the idea of the Kota soybean project had germinated, this marketing organization was saddled with the responsibility of preparing, designing, implementing and running many processing organizations of large capacities.

Rajfed tried to rise to the occasion. It created appropriate positions for managing the processing plants. However, the task of setting up plants and operating them commercially was very different from the DNA of a trading organization.

A decision was taken in 1990 to divide the trading and processing responsibilities of Rajfed in two different verticals and spin off the processing vertical as a separate state-level cooperative federation. The Rajasthan State Oilseeds Growers Federation (Rajasthan Oilfed, later officially renamed Tilam Sangh) came into existence in December 1990. C.K. Mathew took additional charge of Tilam Sangh.

I was appointed its first full-time managing director while I was still working as the CEO of Rajfed Soybeans Project. I took charge of Rajasthan Oilfed/Tilam Sangh on 31 January 1991.

Fast-tracking projects

There were six mustard oilseed projects (including an old one in Fatehnagar) under various stages of construction. There were numerous issues connected with their completion: land allotment, construction of the main plant and associated facilities, water and electricity connections, recruitment of general managers and other plant staff, establishment of oilseed cooperative societies and procurement of mustard through them, and so on.

I had a reasonably good team. R.K. Sharma, a senior oil technologist, joined Tilam Sangh as executive director, Projects. Ashok Sharma was entrusted the responsibility of managing the day-to-day affairs of the Kota project, though I held the charge of CEO for a few more months until Sharma was selected as general manager after a due selection process. There was a very able executive engineer, Civil, P.K. Agarwal, on deputation from the PWD.

I took the matter of execution of the six oilseed projects into my hands, along with R.K. Sharma and P.K. Agarwal. All the plants were basically meant to process mustard, which grew abundantly in Rajasthan, except the Bikaner and Fatehnagar plants, which were for groundnut processing. All were expeller and *kachchi ghani* processing facilities except Bikaner, which had a solvent unit as well.

We would visit each project site every two months. The general managers of the respective plants and all other critical staff were recruited on fast-track mode for all the projects. Tilam Sangh was the largest recruiter in the state at the time, with advertisements appearing for some position or the other almost every week. Sharma and Agarwal would review the projects progress very regularly. The system of writing letters to follow up on construction and permissions related matters with different departments and organizations was complemented by personal calls and visits to expedite decisions.

Faster processes for placing orders for material and machines were put in place. S.S. Singhvi, who replaced P.K. Agarwal later, reminisced to me how unconventional and refreshing the procurement approach was in Tilam Sangh. For instance, to complete the roof of a plant in time, he was allowed to buy steel pipes directly from the market by negotiating with private suppliers for lower price than that of the public-sector supplier, Rajasthan Small Industries Corporation (RAjoint secretaryICO), which had run out of stock.

All these innovations, follow-ups and decisions brought good results. All six facilities were completed and became operational over the next year. The efficient execution emboldened the Government of India and the state government to plan the EEC-II project for another five processing plants.

If a sarkari plant can make money ...

The Kota soybean plant was planned by the state government to provide a reliable sales avenue to farmers in the region to sell their soybean crop, which otherwise had to be sold in faraway Indore and other markets in Madhya

Pradesh. In the meantime, Madhya Pradesh had become a star soybean state with several private industrialists setting up processing plants there. No one had thought of setting up a plant in Rajasthan.

There was trade logic behind this disinclination. In the absence of any major buyer of soybean in Rajasthan, the Madhya Pradesh processors could buy Rajasthan soybean in *mandi*s in and around Kota, or from farmers' villages, at a hefty discount as compared to the 'Indore price', in the name of the cost of transportation to Madhya Pradesh plants and the supposed 'poorer quality' (termed as 'non-FAQ' or 'fair average quality') of soybean produced in Rajasthan. If they could buy soybean at cheaper rates that more than covered the transportation cost, there was no economic rationale for them to set up a new plant in Rajasthan.

The inability of the Kota project to buy soybean from farmers in large quantities until 1989 had also kept the prices in Rajasthan depressed. The dynamics changed massively in 1990. Imposition of customs duty on import of oilseeds and edible oil increased local oil prices. The Kota plant purchased over 40,000 tonnes of soybean in 1990, which raised the effective prices in Kota *mandi*s, substantially reducing the difference between the Indore and Kota *mandi*s. It was no longer feasible for Madhya Pradesh processors to buy soybean from the Kota area at a price that more than covered the difference in the transportation cost.

The technical performance of the Kota plant improved immensely from the last quarter of the financial year 1989–90. Capacity utilization went beyond 100 per cent. The year 1990–91 saw the plant turn in a net profit. The edible oil business was a very low-margin business. It was also a business where private trade evaded taxes to a huge extent, whereas Rajfed and Tilam Sangh units paid full tax. The plant was loaded with unnecessary capital expenditure (like a degumming plant). It also employed more people than necessary. Despite these handicaps, the plant generated not operational, not cash but net profits, after providing for full depreciation.

This major change on the ground made the Madhya Pradesh processors change their plans. One processor set up a 100 tonnes per day unit in 1991 in Baran district, near Kota. Gradually, six new plants came in over a space of two years.

In one of the trade conferences, an industrialist told me in a lighter vein, 'If a *sarkari* plant could make money, we would definitely make far more money,' explaining why he and some others had set up oil processing plants in the Kota area.

'I thought you were testing me'

Tilam Sangh had literally become a wholesale employer in Rajasthan. Seven plants including Kota needed different kinds of workforce: oil technologists, MBAs, finance professionals, human resource (HR) managers, quality managers, marketing managers, administrative managers, and supervisory and operating staff. M.L. Mehta, as chairman of Tilam Sangh, and I as the MD, had one simple objective: We would recruit the best available managers, supervisory staff and operative staff that our pay-scales could get, absolutely on merit. No one would be recruited based on the recommendation of anybody and on any consideration other than merit.

Recruitment of managers was done at the corporate level, while supervisory and operative staff recruitment was delegated to general managers of the plant. A comprehensive HR manual suited for a commercial organization was prepared with the professional inputs of the Management Development Institute (MDI), Gurgaon, with Dr C.P. Shrimali of MDI finishing the job in record time. All recruitments were made in accordance with the transparent process established in the HR manual, including campus recruitments. Appointment orders were handed over on the day of the interview itself, without exception.

Such large-scale recruitment to Tilam Sangh attracted the attention of politicians and bureaucrats. Chaturbhuj (he went by only this name), the Minister of Cooperation under whose charge Tilam Sangh as an organization fell, was also from the Kota region. Many aspirants would urge him to get them an appointment in Tilam Sangh, and he would ask M.L. Mehta and me. We would politely ignore his recommendations. Officers knew Mehta's standards and reputation and had also assessed my no-nonsense approach. No one seriously bothered us.

A very transparent, merit-oriented recruitment system was established in Tilam Sangh. A representative would go from the Tilam Sangh headquarters for the recruitment committee meetings of the plants. All of them also followed best practices and recruitments were made only on merit.

R.K. Sharma once asked why I was so fastidious about merit-based recruitments without *sifarish* (recommendations), whereas it was not a very uncommon thing wherever he had worked and it did not matter much either for some positions. I told him that as the son of a small-time telegraphist, I would have had no chance of being selected in the IAS if the UPSC made recruitments based on recommendations. I owed a duty that everyone recruited under my watch was recruited only on merit.

Some aspirants even approached Chief Minister Bhairon Singh Shekhawat, who had an earthy sense of righteousness and humour. M.L. Mehta was close to him, having worked as his secretary in one of Shekhawat's earlier tenures as the the CM, and was also considered his intellectual alter ego. The CM's information network was fabulous, and he always knew what was going on and where!

Shekhawat would sometimes ask M. L. Mehta, half in jest, whether some people he recommended could be recruited to Tilam Sangh. Mehta would usually tell him how poorly selected managers could cause long-term damage to the interests of the plant. Once or twice, probably to fend him off, he would offer to help if the recommendation were for a lower administrative type of post, where the potential damage would not be significant.

A recruitment for the post of junior manager (administration) was to be made in Jalore. As the post was in the supervisory scale, the general manager, Jalore, was head of the recruitment committee. On the day the interviews were being held, Mehta called me to say that one of the candidates was a distant relation of the chief minister and as the post was not a critical one and he fulfilled all the requisite educational and experience qualifications, he had given his word to the CM that this time he would help.

I was a little uncomfortable but agreed with Mehta's logic. For the first time ever in recruitment matters, I called up V.K. Jain, general manager, Jalore, and advised him to select the candidate in question as long as there was nothing against him on record. I reported to Mehta that I had conveyed my instructions to recruit that person.

In the evening, M.L. Mehta called me again and, with uncharacteristic annoyance, asked me why the person recommended was not selected. As I had no idea what had transpired, I called the general manager, Jalore. He told me there was an outstanding candidate for the post and the committee was unanimous in assessing him as the most meritorious. I asked him why he did not select the candidate I had recommended in the morning. At that stage, he understood that an error of judgement had possibly taken place. He candidly related the entire sequence of events. He mentioned that he had brought up my instructions when the interviews had just concluded. He was not sure why I had asked for such a thing, which had not happened in any selection made by any general manager of any plant. He said he had also checked with the headquarters representative who was there for the meeting, who expressed total ignorance about the matter. The board then concluded that I was testing him, and he would face the music if he made the wrong recruitment.

In a way, he saved me from making the one exception to my rule! I told M.L. Mehta the story, who then relayed it to the CM. Shekhawat was not unduly upset and remarked, '*Mehta sahib, main janta tha ki aap mere ek aadmi ko bhi naukari nahi doge.*' (Mr Mehta, I knew you would not appoint even one of my people.)

Disregarding the union minister's desire cost me a foreign trip

Balram Jakhar, a powerful politician from Punjab, had shifted to the Sikar parliamentary constituency in 1984 in the wake of insurgency in Punjab. He was elected MP from Sikar for the first time in 1984 and again in 1991. He had served two terms from 1980 to 1989 as the speaker of the Lok Sabha. In 1991, he became the agriculture minister of India. The NCDC was under the administrative control of the Ministry of Agriculture.

The mustard projects under implementation in 1991 when I took over as MD, Tilam Sangh, were sanctioned under an EEC edible oil aid programme for financing construction of oilseed processing facilities. Buoyed by the success of the Kota soybean project and speedy completion of mustard oilseed processing facilities, the EEC had proposed a second edible oil aid programme. There was a proposal for constructing four more oilseed processing facilities in Rajasthan under EEC-II.

Balram Jakhar wanted one of these four plants to be constructed in Sikar. The NCDC wrote to us officially through the Rajasthan government to consider including Sikar in the new proposals. I got the proposal examined as part of the larger endeavour to select four potential locations. Unfortunately, Sikar did not make the grade when screened objectively. There was a relatively small mustard growing catchment area; in fact, the Sikar mustard crop was not even sufficient for a small-capacity 50 tonnes per day plant, whereas we were not interested in considering plants with capacity of less than 100 tonnes per day. There was also another operational plant in the adjoining district, Jhunjhunu. It made better economic sense to enlarge the capacity of the Jhunjhunu plant to 100 tonnes per day, which would have catered to the mustard-growing area in Sikar as well.

We furnished a comprehensive report to the state government, suggesting four potential locations (including enhancement of the capacity of the Jhunjhunu plant), which also explained why a greenfield plant at Sikar was completely inadvisable. The state government shared the report with the NCDC.

Around the same time, a visit to Europe and the US to study edible oil processing plants had been planned, led by J.L.N. Shrivastava, managing director of the NCDC, who later became secretary, Agriculture, in the Government of India. My stock had risen quite high in the NCDC. I was proposed as a member of delegation. This was to be my first-ever foreign trip. All the paperwork was done and my passport made.

Siraj Hussain, later food processing and agriculture secretary in the Government of India, was deputy managing director (DMD) of the NCDC. He asked me to come to Delhi for a discussion. Well-meaning and amiable, he laid out the entire issue when we met. In sum, Minister Jakhar had linked approval for the Sikar plant with my place in the foreign delegation. While I was disappointed at the unfairness of the proposal, I reiterated that there was no way a mustard plant was justified in Sikar and that I would not change my earlier report in this regard. He understood my position and respected it. I was replaced in the delegation by Brij Lal Bhadu, who was private secretary to Balram Jakhar. I just smiled away the evaporation of my first foreign visit.

Nonetheless, the Sikar plant never saw the light of the day.

Choice between mindless adherence to reservation policy and running the plant

While completely convinced of the value and advisability of merit-based recruitment in public services, I had genuine respect for the affirmative policy of reservations. Tilam Sangh was also subject to the reservation policy of the government, which was duly enshrined in the HR manual, and posts were reserved accordingly. While making selections against reserved positions, the selection board and I would ensure that the candidate met the minimum expected standards. If you are selecting a quality control supervisor and certain qualifications and experience were prescribed for the post, the candidate must meet that minimum standard. If you are selecting a computer operator, the candidate must know how to operate a computer and run basic programmes.

We were able to fill up most of the posts reserved for SCs and STs. I selected an ST officer and an MBA graduate, K.S. Meena, for an unreserved senior post of joint manager, as he was outstanding, with excellent experience in other state federations. However, we ran into a major problem while filling up the reserved posts of oil technologists, the principal engineering diploma holders in edible oil processing plants. There were no SC or ST applicant for these reserved posts. The case was similar for reserved positions in the accounts and finance wing, which were to be filled by CAs and cost accountants. Almost no one from the reserved categories had applied.

Upon enquiring, I learnt that not a single oil technologist from the reserved category had passed out of the institutions that offered these courses. Likewise, there were very few CAs and cost accountants from the SC and ST communities. We explored the advisability of replacing these qualifications with other substitute qualifications but reached the conclusion that it would not be in the larger interest of the organization.

Therefore, I ordered on file, after recording a note of justification, that the posts of oil technologists, finance managers and joint managers be considered as dereserved and filled with general category candidates. This was done. In one or two interview boards, the representative of the state government, usually a deputy secretary from the cooperatives department, raised a proforma type of objection but did not object to the selection. Tilam Sangh appointed some oil technologists and finance managers from the general category against the posts reserved for SC/ST.

All this was on record. Someone took copies of the appointments made and complained to the SC/ST Committee of the Vidhan Sabha. The complainant brought out only the violation committed, not the justification for the same. This was enough to raise temperatures in the committee. I received a notice to appear before it. As I had not kept the state government formally informed, it washed its hands of the matter and asked me to answer the committee.

I wrote a detailed note with the justification and inevitability of what was done in the interest of the organization. I attached my recorded notes from the files. When I appeared before the committee, I told them the choice was between keeping these positions vacant and letting the organization suffer or filling the posts but technically violating the reservation policy (in my judgement, there was no real violation as no candidate had applied) and serving the best interest of the organization.

Most committee members saw the logic of what was done. While some orally lambasted, no action was taken against me.

MD, Tilam Sangh, does not listen to his minister

Though a mild and soft-spoken person, Chaturbhuj, the Minister of Cooperation in the Bhairon Singh Shekhawat government, was quite unhappy with the way things were happening in Tilam Sangh. He had no formal role in the organization, as the board was headed by Agriculture Secretary M.L. Mehta. He found it difficult to contribute anything worthwhile even to policy issues that went to the state government.

His interests were small: getting some class IV and clerical staff appointed, petty contracts to be awarded to his men, and getting more OSCSs set up in his constituency of Jhalawar. Some of these requests were executed in their normal course, but most were not, which made him unhappy, in fact somewhat bitter, about Tilam Sangh and me.

He wrote a letter to me as MD. This letter had about four complaints. Some were worded in a manner that sounded like I was working in violation of the rules. The letter also had a paragraph that conveyed the message that Tilam Sangh did not care about him and ignored his directions. I found no actionable points in the letter.

Surendra Vyas, an articulate MLA from the Opposition, got hold of the letter somehow and moved a privilege motion in the Vidhan Sabha arguing that by disregarding the wishes of a member of the House (the minister), the MD, Tilam Sangh, had committed a breach of privilege of the house. Clearly, his motive was to embarrass the government.

Anil Kumar, a very senior and effective officer, albeit a little short-tempered, was secretary to the CM (he later served as secretary to Shekhawat when he became vice-president of India). He called me to his office in the Vidhan Sabha and gave me a copy of the privilege motion. I read it and a smile broke out on my lips. Anil Kumar admonished me to not take the matter lightly, as the speaker had allotted time for discussion on the motion that very day and the minister was expected to reply to it late evening.

The motion had created a piquant situation. Lack of respect to the cooperative minister was the alleged reason to have caused a breach of privilege to the assembly. He was definitely miffed over what was going on at Tilam Sangh and cut up by the treatment he was getting. The letter he wrote, in a certain manner, indicated his frustration. In the normal course, he would have replied to the motion. He could not have, however, denied that he wrote the letter. He could not have said everything was hunky-dory when his letter was full of complaints. It was also quite unprecedented for a minister to write such letters.

M.L. Mehta also joined the discussion. The matter was taken to Bhairon Singh Shekhawat. A man I had never seen tense, Shekhawat smiled at the irony of the situation. He asked us to collect all the papers, commendations and data to prove that Tilam Sangh was doing very well. He also decided that Chaturbhuj would not reply to the motion. Another minister, Kailash Meghwal, who was an articulate and forceful speaker, was drafted to reply.

Tilam Sangh's performance was eminently defensible. The record of the Kota turnaround, expeditious implementation of mustard projects, operationalization of Tilam Sangh as a separate entity, profit made for the first time, commendations from the World Bank and Institute of Rural Management, Anand (IRMA), which had done a comparative study of state-level federations, and several other performance parameters spoke for Tilam Sangh.

Kailash Meghwal used the opportunity to provide a stinging and forceful reply, which ran over an hour till about 9 p.m. in the evening. He made the Opposition realize the foolishness of their move, which exposed their ignorance. During the debate and reply, Chaturbhuj was sitting in the house. I was in the official gallery. Once or twice, our eyes met. It was Chaturbhuj who looked embarrassed.

'Let us sell the Kota plant'

India had started opening up its economy in 1991. Indu Bhushan, from my batch (1983) in Rajasthan cadre, was about to resign and move to join the World Bank in Washington, DC. He came over to see me. He jokingly questioned why I was wasting my time running a public-sector enterprise when it was time for the government to get out of business.

I was aware of the folly of government being in business. I had also noted changes taking place, for instance, licensing had been ended for establishing hydrogenated (vegetable ghee) plants in the sector. Yet, agreeing with him in principle and policy, I told Indu Bhushan that my job was to establish and run these plants as efficiently as possible as long as they remained in the public/cooperative sector.

By the second half of the financial year 1991–92, everything was going well for the Kota plant, except some discontent among operational staff. The plant was operating at more than 100 per cent capacity utilization. It was making profits. The OSCS formation work was complete and procurement through OSCSs had made distress sales by soybean farmers a thing of past. The farmers were getting good *mandi* prices for their produce in their villages. The success of the plant had encouraged private industry to begin setting up plants in the area. Almost every objective of setting up the facility seemed to have been achieved.

Operational management, however, had deteriorated. Ashok Sharma, an outstanding technologist, was a poor HR manager. He also had a bad temperament. R.K. Sharma had an inkling of his poor managerial skills. During the selection meeting of GM, Kota (the post was downgraded from CEO to GM about two months after I had taken over as MD, Tilam Sangh), R.K. Sharma hinted at not selecting Ashok Sharma. However, I thought we could handle his poor people-management skills. Ashok Sharma proved to be a disaster as GM. Discontent soon brewed among the staff. So much so that about six months later, when I visited the Kota plant, I was gheraoed, and the union, besides demanding higher bonuses and promotions because of the plant's strong financial performance, asked for Ashok Sharma's removal. It pained me to see such a massive deterioration in the working environment and industrial relations.

Cooperative processing organizations in Rajasthan had a poor record of successful long-term operation. There was a sugar mill in nearby Bundi district at Keshorai Patan, which was established to promote sugarcane growth. The mill was sick and mostly closed in the 1980s and 1990s. There was a processing plant in Gajsinghpur in Ganganagar district, which was set up to extract cotton from cotton balls. It was being run only to keep up the façade of operation. Its annual cash losses were more than the total salary bill, which had made me conclude that it made more financial sense to pay full salaries to the staff without running the mill.

I prepared a note and proposed that Tilam Sangh should sell the Kota plant. My calculations suggested that we would probably get around 80 per cent of the capital investment back. The plant was making a profit, but capital investment was unduly high. Market enquiries suggested that a 200 tonnes per day solvent extraction plant could be set up at ₹10–12 crore instead of ₹35 crore (which Tilam Sangh had invested in the first plant). This was an operational plant and could sell well. There was some land attached to it – I proposed to separate the plant's colony and transfer it to the state for government housing.

M.L. Mehta, who always encouraged out-of-the-box thinking, baulked at the proposal. He had more faith in the ability of Tilam Sangh to grow into a ₹1,000 crore turnover organization. He said it was time to think of taking up the EEC-II project to build more plants in Rajasthan for value addition instead of mustard going out of the state. I argued that the same objective could be achieved by letting the private sector build processing plants. I told him that there was possibly only a short window to sell the plant.

He did not agree. I tried to raise it with him again. I also organized an informal discussion around the proposal at a board meeting. The board, with six farmer representatives of OSCSs, was more obdurate and opposed to the idea.

While the forward march of the public sector did stop with the liberalization introduced in 1991, the proposal of selling off the Kota plant was possibly premature.

End of Tilam Sangh

The writing on the wall was becoming clear. The Kota plant was getting into trouble. Employee unions tended to be short-sighted, and their demands were unreasonable. Ashok Sharma's inability to deal with them (he would always fight with them instead of trying to convince them rationally) made matters worse.

Local politicians wanted local labour supply, DOC bagging, transportation and other contracts to go to their lackeys. Some of them started using high-handed tactics. We tried to find solutions. Contracting for the Kota plant was shifted to the Jaipur headquarters to ensure free competition. Things improved but not sufficiently. Finally, Ashok Sharma had to be fired.

Some other general managers were also not made of the right stuff. The oil business is a very low-margin business. Tilam Sangh had its back to the wall as these small margins were further eroded by tax implications. Tilam Sangh paid the best price for oilseeds. The marketing of oil and DOC was a slippery affair, and managers were cautious and afraid of future inquiries. They would record long notes about price quotes and decisions taken.

Further, there were occasional problems at the port. The train wagons that carried DOC would get 'sick' or the test at the port would reveal different parameters than recorded at the time of despatch from the godowns. Business was indeed a difficult thing for government and cooperative officers to execute.

After my attempts at selling the Kota plant were scuppered in late 1991, I started working on another dramatic way to force the government's hand. Sometime in the first quarter of 1992, I prepared a paper titled 'Tilam Sangh Will Become Sick by 1999'.

The paper tried to crystal-gaze into the performance of Tilam Sangh in the

1990s. I concluded that it would find it difficult to continuously achieve higher capacity utilizations. In fact, I predicted that some of the plants would become dysfunctional for various reasons and the processing function of the body would become weaker by the day. High capital investment would make Tilam Sangh record net losses every year, and at some point two to three years down the line, most of its plants would also go into operational and cash losses like Keshorai Patan and Gajsinghpur. I concluded that Tilam Sangh would become a sick organization by 1999, losing most of its capital.

I discussed the paper with my officers and staff and invited their comments. Most seemed to agree.

I handed over charge of Tilam Sangh in August 1992. It managed to trudge along. The EEC-II project did not take off. Performance deteriorated. By the turn of the century, most of the processing had stopped. Tilam Sangh was transformed into a clone of Rajfed. It started buying wheat and agriculture produce other than oilseeds as well. Its losses kept piling up.

Almost every manager, technologist and administrator recruited during my tenure in Kota and Tilam Sangh left 1993 onwards. They were competent people and saw the downfall coming. They wanted to be part of Tilam Singh's growth story, not its withering away. Quite surprisingly, almost none of the managers, technologists and administrative staff recruited prior to that period left Tilam Sangh. This difference was the biggest testament to the merit-based recruitment system.

In a curious turn of events, I was posted to Rajfed as its administrator in 2009 for a brief period of two months. The former Rajfed employees of Tilam Sangh had formed a separate association in the late 1990s and had succeeded in getting posted back to Rajfed.

In 2020, Rajasthan government approved a plan in principle to merge the sick-to-the-core Tilam Sangh with Rajfed. The broken wheel would have turned full circle when it happens. The proposal was not followed through. Tilam Sangh continues to exist on paper today without a single operational plant. As I write this book, Tilam Sangh Kota plant obtains orders for supplying its branded oil to defence organizations by participating in their tenders but fulfils the same by buying the oil from the market.

7

'You Are Working Well but It Does Not Suit Us'

I joined as collector and district magistrate, Rajsamand, in August 1992, accompanied by Anjali and our two sons, Shrey (a month short of his fourth birthday) and Dhruv (who was still not a year old).

Rajsamand – the district not named after a district headquarter town but rather a lake – was carved out of the Udaipur district the previous year. Rajsamand is in fact a large lake. Two small adjoining towns (Rajnagar and Kankroli) located at the base of the Rajsamand dam together made up the district headquarters of Rajsamand district.

The SDO building was converted into the district collector's office and the PWD resthouse of Rajnagar became the residence. The rest house was situated on top of the dam with an extraordinary view of Rajsamand Lake (which was full to the brim that year). On the lake's side were the famed marble Nau Chauki (nine pavilions with *chhatri*s and pillars) that had exquisite carvings. The walk on top of the dam and along the sides of the Nau Chaukis was an unforgettable experience. On the other side of the dam was more than 2 acres of land, where we were able to raise a good crop of wheat in the winter of 1992. The land also had giant tamarind trees. We distributed the tamarind collected in 1993 to everyone we knew and still had enough for three more years! There were some hazards as well. The lake was a breeding ground for giant water snakes – some of the snakes we encountered were 6–8 ft long. They would often crawl into our residence, and guards would discover them in the garden and around the residence.

The district was largely inhabited along National Highway 8 (NH-8; about a 90 km stretch between Bhim and Nathdwara on the Ajmer–Udaipur section). This stretch was not commercially well-developed and had hilly stretches. Consequently, while it was officially part of NH-8, the road section via Bhilwara and Chittorgarh from Ajmer to Udaipur was more developed and frequented. Much later, this stretch would become the symbol of failed aggressive bidding for build–operate–transfer (BOT) road projects, with a company quoting a negative subsidy of more than ₹700 crore annually in order to get the concession.

The district was relatively small, with only four assembly constituencies: Nathdwara, Rajsamand, Kumbhalgarh and Bhim. Politically, however, it was quite active and prominent. Heera Lal Devpura, former speaker of the Assembly and former chief minister (albeit for a short period), was an MLA from Kumbhalgarh. Mandhata Singh, a minister in the government and brother-in-law of former Prime Minister V.P. Singh, was an MLA from Bhim. C.P. Joshi, later a powerful minister in Rajasthan and a cabinet minister in the union government, was a former MLA of Nathdwara. Girija Vyas, later a minister in the union cabinet, was an MLA from a constituency in Udaipur that included part of Rajsamand district. There were other former ministers and MLAs, such as Lakshman Singh from Bhim. The Shekhawat ministry also had a minister without portfolio, Vijay Singh Jhala (who had earlier served as irrigation minister), who considered the un-bifurcated district of Udaipur his home terrain.

Dharam Singh Sagar, my erstwhile collector at Chittorgarh, was serving as commissioner of the Udaipur division. He had a good company in Namo Narain Meena, Deputy Inspector General (DIG), Udaipur zone. Meena later served as the MP as well as minister of state for environment in the Manmohan Singh government.

Dealing with a minister without a portfolio

Vijay Singh Jhala, a minister without portfolio, not representing any of the assembly constituencies of Rajsamand and not the district in-charge minister for Rajsamand, asked me to convene a meeting of district officials in Rajsamand just a couple of weeks after I had taken charge. I was baffled. Why did he want to chair a meeting of district officials when he apparently had no official business to conduct?

When I asked the district officials, they told me he came from the Nathdwara area and had chaired a few similar meetings earlier. Jhala always had an axe to grind and would pester the officers to do his bidding. Those who did not oblige him would be taken to task and humiliated in the meeting for not doing what he had asked for. I found the whole thing unpalatable and bizarre.

I checked with Rakesh Srivastava, an officer two batches my senior, who was serving as collector in Udaipur. A thorough gentleman who would sometimes be extra accommodating, Srivastava confirmed that Jhala convened such meetings in Udaipur as well and Srivastava had gone along with it as Jhala was a minister in the government. Rakesh Srivastava would later rise to be secretary of the Ministry of Women and Children Development in the Government of India, though he faced some enquiries as joint secretary, Shipping.

I conveyed to V.S. Jhala's secretary that I did not think these meetings were necessary and would not be convening the same. A day later, Jhala called me and demanded why I had not convened the meeting. I told him I would convene the meeting only if he gave me a written agenda prior to it and promised to stick to it. He was furious. He threatened to call the chief secretary to direct me to convene the meeting.

Some more enquiries revealed that he was particularly interested in a water carriage canal in Nathdwara tehsil; its project report had been prepared when he was irrigation minister. It was a very costly project. I worked out the per-acre capital cost of the water this canal would irrigate. It came to about three times the cost of a borewell. I wrote to the state government against the advisability of taking up such a project.

T.V. Ramanan called me. I explained the entire matter to him, including the suspect motives of the minister behind convening the meetings, the humiliation officials faced and the futility of any real performance review without an agenda. I did offer to convene the meeting if an official agenda was proposed. He understood and asked me to write a letter to him.

Jhala did not press for a meeting thereafter. The government was dismissed in December 1992, and he ceased to be a minister.

'I often feel I am not your boss'

Dharam Singh Sagar – who, as I have mentioned earlier, was serving as commissioner of the Udaipur division – had complained bitterly against me in 1987 when I worked under him in Chittorgarh. However, he was a large-hearted individual not given to holding grudges. Very shortly after I joined, he convened a review meeting of collectors of the Udaipur division. I went well prepared. He showed no bias in the meeting and was generally quite appreciative of the grip I had on the issues in the district.

Sagar adopted a policy of no interference in my district. He left matters to me entirely and rarely called. When the Babri Masjid was demolished on 6 December 1992 and there was palpable tension everywhere, he just made a one-minute call to check if everything was all right.

In some meetings, I would bring up the larger context for development programmes being implemented as well as matters like small savings and their fiscal implications. He would find my take interesting. In fact, on one occasion, he remarked that I looked at much larger perspectives than his paygrade, and that I would rise much higher in state and national administration. He wanted me to continue working as I was and not worry about him. '*Subhash, mujhe aksar yeh lagta hai ki main tumhara boss nahin hoon*' (Subhash, I often feel that I am not your boss), he said to me appreciatively.

Unconventional approach to do the right thing

The Rajasthan government conducted a 'Prashashan Aapke Dwar' (administration at your doorstep) camp at panchayat levels to attend to all pending revenue and development matters of people – mutations, allotment of land, allotment of house *patta*s, sanctioning of benefits under development programmes.

During my visits to these camps, I found several matters of schools, hospitals and other public/government offices and entities pending as well relating to land allotments not recorded in their names or requirement of additional lands and the like. The rules prescribed that all cases of more than 2.5 acres were within the powers of the state government.

The normal course adopted in such cases was to make an application, complete all the paperwork and send the proposals to the state government. The approvals never came back.

I realized the futility of doing this exercise again, and in turn, thought of making allotment of the land in anticipation of state government approval and use the camp to transfer the land in the name of the institution concerned and hand over the *patta* or copy of the *jamabandi*, as the case might be to the public institution concerned taking the position that the state government had no reason to refuse these allotments. In the unlikely event of an allotment being rejected, we could always cancel the *patta*/mutation in the land records.

Hundreds of such mutations and allotments were made. As expected, nothing was heard from the state government. I once reminded the revenue secretary about these allotments. He promised to look into the matter. It did not matter to me or the allottees as the land parcels stood allotted and transferred to them.

I had to use similar unconventional approach in another matter involving public land. On one side of the NH-8 opening to the Rajnagar town was a clutch of small hillocks, recorded as forest land.

One day, the divisional forest officer (DFO), Rajasamand, came to my office in a huff. He showed me a copy of a *jamabandi* by which about 3 hectares had been mutated from the Forest Department to government *siwaichak* land. According to him, this was done to allow some local persons to trespass this land for constructing a commercial building. He also apprised me that the local tehsildar had done this in a completely illegal manner as there was no order of any court or higher authority to transfer this land.

I called for the tehsildar. He informed me that on an application that had been pending before him for quite some time, he had determined that the original allotment of the land to the Forest Department was not as per the rules, and he had cancelled the same for that reason.

The action of the tehsildar was clearly indefensible. However, he had passed the order in his quasi-judicial capacity. The rules permitted a revision against tehsildar's order to the revenue board situated in Ajmer, with no authority to collector in the matter. Numerous cases of revision filed in the revenue board were pending for years. It was quite clear to me that there was hardly any probability of obtaining a reversal of the tehsildar's order by filing for a revision in the revenue board.

I reasoned that if I passed an order as collector, while it would also be an irregularity, it would also have to be challenged by someone in the revenue board only.

I issued an order transferring the land parcel and instructed the tehsildar to mutate the land in the name of the Forest Department by the next day. The tehsildar complied. An irregularity neutralized another irregularity.

'Everybody loves a good drought'

The monsoon was poor in 1992. Famine relief in Rajasthan had become a habit and worked like a well-oiled machine. The Indian Famine Code defined famine as an acute water-stressed condition when farmers and labourers were not able to get work and food. Food availability in the country, including Rajasthan, was not an issue in Rajsamand.

The process to declare a famine would begin with the government ordering an urgent *girdawari* (inspection) in late August or early September to assess the state of the crops. The system was built around revenue officials – from the patwari to the collector – visiting the fields and assessing the loss of crops. A loss of more than 50 per cent entitled the *patwar* circle/ILR circle/tehsil to be declared severely affected by drought. The government would sanction famine relief work and increase the number of days under wage employment programmes in drought-affected areas.

Politicians loved drought relief work. It offered them an opportunity to make money on the side in material contracts, movement of fodder and other works, besides ensuring wage earnings to their supporters. District officials too were generally favourably disposed towards getting new works sanctioned under famine relief for genuine reasons and otherwise.

After I received instructions from the government to assess famine conditions, besides ordering the urgent *girdawari*, I asked for two more sets of data to be collected in each tehsil: one, availability of food and inflation in food prices; and two, state of wage employment, including movement in wage rates. Most districts, except Bhim tehsil, were reasonably well endowed with rains and the year 1992 was not too bad either. Rajsamand Lake was quite full.

The early *girdawari* revealed mixed conditions. *Kharaba* (crop damage) was between 50 and 75 per cent only in about 20 per cent of the area. There was no evidence of food prices going up, including in Bhim tehsil. Rajsamand had a flourishing marble mining and cutting industry that attracted labour from across the district and even from outside. The marble industry was doing well and there was no evidence of extra labour inflow or drop in wages rate.

Around the time this exercise was going on, Heera Lal Devpura and Girija Vyas visited my office. During the informal interaction, Devpura referred to the drought and suggested to declare as large a part of the district as possible as severely drought-affected. I brought up the question of impact on wage rate. They still felt that advantage should be taken of a government declaration of a famine, whether there was an actual famine or not, in the interest of development of the district.

I sent my report to the state government enclosing the results of the *girdawari*, the state of food prices and the wage conditions, concluding that there was no famine in the district.

MKSS disrupts power equation

Aruna Roy, who later spearheaded the Right to Information Act (RTI) campaign in India, had set up base in Devdungri in the backward Bhim block of the district. An IAS officer of the 1970 batch she had resigned early from the service and shifted to Tilonia in Ajmer district, where her husband Bunker Roy had set up a Barefoot College, a well-known NGO.

Aruna was joined by Nikhil Dey, son of a retired vice admiral of the Navy, and a few other committed activists. They established the Mazdoor Kisan Shakti Sangathan (MKSS) with their headquarters in Rajsamand in 1992 to take up the cause of poor farmers and workers who worked on wage labour programmes of the government.

The most effective and famous tool they had developed was social audit. This would require government/panchayat officials to bring records of public works taken up under various programmes and announce in a public hearing the name of the work, the cost of the work, materials purchased for the work along with their quantities and prices, and the labour employed on the work, along with their names, the number of days of work and the wages paid to each of them. The key element of the social audit was that the villagers assembled could question any inaccuracies or missing information or suspected made-up information in the records.

Later, the social audit would become part of the official guidelines of many rural development programmes. In 1992, however, this tool was still under development. It had not got official approval and was fiercely resisted by panchayats as it could expose skeletons in their closets.

The MKSS developed two other innovations in Rajsamand. After receiving approval, it set up its first ration shop in Devdungri. Second, it rented a shop in the main bazaar of Bhim to sell products of common consumption at prices much lower than prevailing market prices. By keeping their retail margin next to nothing, they were able to price their products so low.

The traders of Bhim went up in arms. What got their goat most was the loudspeaker the MKSS used to announce their prices. The traders called for a hartal and closed the market.

I had to intervene as it became a law-and-order situation. The traders were told that the MKSS had every right to set up a shop and sell products at whatever price they wanted. The MKSS did not have deep pockets and would never be able to sell below cost, I explained. I agreed with the traders that announcing prices on the loudspeaker was not a good trading practice.

The shop agreed to operate without the loudspeaker with prices of common items written on a board, which was fine. For their part, the traders adopted different tactics. They worked on wholesalers to not supply products to the MKSS shop. The wholesalers raised the prices of products sold to the MKSS and altered the terms of payment – no or little credit. The MKSS had to reduce the gap between their prices and those of other traders. The MKSS shop continued to do business but the edge it had when it started was blunted over time.

Shoot Mandhata's men, if necessary

Another MKSS intervention brought district administration face to face with Minister Mandhata Singh and his men. Politician Mandhata Singh's people had effective possession of a large plot of *siwaichak* land in Devgarh tehsil. The rules required that such *siwaichak* lands be allotted by auction when the monsoon season was over for cattle to graze. In cruel play of misaligned incentive, the patwari of the area ended up working as an employee of the minister instead of the government. Every year, the land would be allotted in the name of some bogus persons acting for Mandhata Singh. Only Mandhata Singh's cattle or those of his henchmen would graze on that large plot, not the people of that area.

The MKSS decided to resist this. They approached me to organize a real bid for the grazing land. I had developed a closer relationship with Aruna and Nikhil. While I did not subscribe to their ideological underpinnings, I saw them as people committed to public interest. In fact, both Aruna and Nikhil would subsist on what a daily mazdoor earned, and they fearlessly championed the mazdoors' cause. I had invited them a couple of times to bring matters of public interest to my notice when they visited Rajsamand. In one of the visits, Aruna told me that as there were only two buses running on the national highway in a day and she had come that day by taking a lift on a truck.

I agreed with them that the villagers should get a fair chance to have the land allotted to them. I asked whether villagers would dare to bid for fear of the minister's henchmen. They said they would ensure it. I also asked whether Mandhata Singh's men would simply outbid them to break their resolve. They conceded that this was a real possibility as the villagers could not bid beyond a point.

So, instead of an auction, I decided to fix the price after considering the maximum price at which the land was allotted in the previous three years and asked the SDM of Bhim, Hari Singh Rathore, to ensure allotment by way of lottery. Rathore, a young RAS officer, ensured the allotment was made at the determined price to a number of people, at about an acre to a person, by lottery. More than 75 per cent of the land got allotted to the MKSS applicants.

Rathore was present on the site when possession of the land was to be given by the patwari to the allottees for the season. Around 11 a.m., he called me on the wireless, agitated. Some of Mandhata Singh's henchmen had come to the land on horseback, he told me, and a couple of them were armed. They were threatening to shoot if anyone dared to graze cattle there.

I told Rathore to shoot anyone who tried to take the law in their hands. He was a brave officer and felt emboldened when he got clear orders. He announced unambiguously to the miscreants that he would order the police to open fire if anyone obstructed the process of handing over possession of land. A few hours later, he reported that the resistance dissipated after the miscreants sensed the administration's resolve. Possibly, Mandhata Singh also advised them to back off.

For the first time in many years, the coveted *siwaichak* land was used by villagers to graze their cattle instead of serving as the private grazing ground of a powerful former zamindar and minister.

Unjustness of land allotment to the poor, again

The allotment of surplus land to the poor has been discussed in an earlier chapter. The issue cropped up again in Rajsamand, but this time I had to deal with it in my capacity as appellate authority over allotments made in the district.

The collector's court had several cases challenging allotments made to landless farmers. Typically, a powerful person who had either encroached upon land allotted to a poor landless farmer or coveted that land would hire a lawyer and file an appeal. There were two respondents in such cases: the state of Rajasthan represented by the tehsildar concerned, and the allottee. In almost all cases before me, I found that the allottee concerned could not hire an advocate and, in some cases, had even stopped attending hearings as well. For their part, the tehsildars were not in a good position to counter legal arguments of advocates, nor were they highly motivated to defend allotments.

I decided to take matters into my own hands. I argued that as the land allotments had been made by the state and I was a representative of the state, I could, in a manner of speaking, represent the state. The advocate would, therefore, must convince me that the land allotment was irregular. I also decided that the advocate would get one day for a case to explain the matter in the tehsildar's presence who would have all the records.

This changed the rules of engagement. Now, it was the advocate who had to prove his case with neither the tehsildar nor the allottee defending it. There were about 40-odd cases. I disposed of them all in three months. The allotments had to be cancelled only in a few cases.

In a few months after my assuming charge, there was not a single case pending in the collector's court. Collectors were required to send a monthly report of land records and court matters to the revenue board. When I sent a nil court case pendency report, the revenue board asked me for an explanation for what was a bizarre situation for them. I reaffirmed, with data, that there was indeed no court case pending in Rajsamand collector's court.

A public warning from ex-chief minister

In December 1992, the Bhairon Singh Shekhawat government was dismissed in the wake of the demolition of the Babri Masjid, though without any apparent justification. Governor Chenna Reddy assumed the administration of the state. Shekhawat immediately went into campaign mode for the next round of elections, which were expected to take place in second half of 1993.

The Nathdwara Temple, with Shrinathji as its presiding deity, is a revered place of worship for followers of the 'Pushtimarg' tradition of Bhagwat Vaishnavism. The temple had been taken over legally by the government, and a Nathdwara Temple Board, headed by the Tilkayat (head priest), was formed to run its affairs. At that time, Nathdwara was the second-richest temple in India, after Tirupati. An RAS officer was posted as the CEO of the board to manage day-to-day non-religious affairs.

The entry into Nathdwara town was from NH-8. The road coming from the Udaipur side had a steep downward gradient. The bus stand was at the mouth of the entry. This caused considerable chaos, with the bus stand teeming with private buses bearing devotees. Inside the temple town, roads were narrow. Some spacious cottage complexes had been constructed near the temple for VIPs and wealthy devotees, who would go there by car to rest before darshan. These cars crowded the bus stand and temple road further.

There was a large piece of open land available in front of Nathdwara Police Station on NH-8, about 100 m from the existing bus stand. After consultation with the CEO of the temple board and revenue and police officials of Nathdwara, I decided that a new bus stand should be constructed on the vacant land. For the transition period, the undulating land could be levelled up and the buses parked there. Further, we decided that no vehicle would be allowed inside the town; they would have to be parked at the place vacated by the buses. In addition, a parking charge was imposed on vehicles that chose to park in the assigned place.

I thought this will help everyone besides easing the traffic. Nathdwara, though, was a volatile town. Yet, the firmness of the administration ensured that a temporary bus stand was made, the buses shifted and an entry barrier installed to stop cars from entering the town. We were determined to do it despite some discontent and objections from local Nathdwara residents.

Elsewhere, in a place called Gomti Chauraha, about 15 km on the other side of the NH-8 from Rajnagar, a small temple was coming in the way of road widening. A few days before the bus stand was shifted in Nathdwara, the administration shifted the temple in Gomti Chauraha 15 ft inside, without much opposition. However, there was some simmering discontent in the surcharged atmosphere in the wake of the Babri Masjid demolition.

At this point, Bhairon Singh Shekhawat visited Nathdwara for the first time after being ousted from chief ministership. He had always wanted to keep Nathdwara in good humour and visited every three/four months. I had received and briefed him as the CM twice during my stay of four months before his government was dismissed.

Shekhawat convened a public meeting at the site of the old bus stand. Obviously pandering to the public mood in Nathdwara, he demanded that the status quo must be restored and issued a warning that he would deal with me appropriately once he formed the government again. In his address, he was critical of the shifting of the temple at Gomti Chauraha as well. He also wrote a detailed letter to me, which seemed to be a rehash of the representations of local politicians, asking me to undo the damage done to the 'spirit of Nathdwara', whatever that meant.

Prime Minister drops in to make amends

In Nathdwara Temple, the deity, Shrinathji, was worshipped and exhibited for darshans at different times of the day, in different moods and appropriate attire according to the season, weather and time of day. For instance, in winter, for the first darshan – Mangala – in the morning, the Lord would get up late and wear heavy clothing. In total, there were eight darshans a day. This meant the temple would be opened eight times a day from early morning to the evening. The period between two darshans was used to change the idol's attire and ornaments. It was a small but beautiful idol and the darshan, with different *shringar* (adornments), was spectacular.

Unfortunately, the deity could only be viewed through a small door, which opened into a small hall, which then opened into the larger temple premises. There was an uncontrollable rush of devotees when the small hall was opened for these short darshans. Everyone tried to get to the door of the inner sanctum to have as close a darshan of Shrinathji as possible. For the administration, it was a nightmare scenario.

There was always a big rush of VIPs for darshan. They were stationed in an adjoining gallery and brought through a side door a little while before the door opened. This way, they were able to have a close darshan for a short time, usually a minute or so. The most favoured were allowed to sit at the base of the inner door for a longer period while the darshans were open. After darshan, the VIPs were moved out through a separate dedicated gate.

Haryana Governor Dhanik Lal Mandal was given additional charge of Rajasthan for about a month in May–June 1993. He wanted darshan at Nathdwara. The trip started with a disaster. His first stop was at Eiklingji, the presiding deity of Mewar kings, just before the border of Rajsamand district. Mandal was wearing torn socks, and a photographer clicked them when he removed his shoes to enter the temple, embarrassing the governor. When he came out of the temple, I was waiting to receive him. As it was hot in June, I did not wear a *bandgala* and was in a plain shirt. He asked who I was. Sagar, who was with him, informed him that I was the collector of Rajsamand. He looked a little askance at me but did not say anything. The party moved on to Nathdwara, where a bigger disaster awaited.

As per protocol, we took Governor Mandal to the reserved waiting area adjoining the temple. It was time for the Rajbhog darshan, which opened around 11.30 a.m. We were there at 11.30 a.m. but the darshan had not opened. We waited for about 15 minutes. It still didn't open. I checked with the CEO of Nathdwara and other officials. They said the darshan was delayed sometimes. We waited another 15 minutes. It was inordinately late and the temple doors to usher in the governor had still not opened.

I became concerned. An official whispered in my ear that the temple staff seemed to be up to some mischief. Nathdwara had a troubled history in permitting Dalits in for darshan. I did not know earlier that Governor Mandal was Dalit. Sagar must have known. I kept quiet. Another five minutes later, the governor said something abusive and left in a huff without the darshan. As he had no other business in the district, he drove off to Udaipur. Along with him, Commissioner Sagar and DIG Meena also departed. I returned to my residence in Rajnagar.

Around 3 p.m. in the afternoon, I received a call from the soft-spoken and pleasant N.R. Bhasin, a veterinarian who had got promoted to the IAS in Rajasthan and later rose to become president of the Indian Dairy Association. At the time, he was secretary to the governor. He asked me regarding an allegation that I had breached protocol by receiving the governor in a half-sleeved shirt. I admitted it was a fact as I found wearing a *bandgala* a pain in the hot summer. I also told him the entire story. It was apparent that Sagar had filed a report, which, among other things, had included a description of my indiscretion. I did not hear anything about the matter.

I had not fully heard the abuse Mandal probably uttered when he left the temple, nor did I know if anyone else had heard it. However, some hot-headed Nathdwara residents, possibly from among the large army of priests (there were more than 200 *panda*s (priests) who participated in the puja at the temple), decided to avenge the so-called 'insult' to Shrinathji.

Letters were written to Prime Minister P.V. Narasimha Rao about the impatience Governor Mandal displayed and the insult he hurled at Shrinathji. These letters went to many authorities. The collector, Rajsamand, also received a few copies. Knowing the volatility of Nathdwara as well as the undue delay in opening the doors that day, we decided to not to act on these letters.

About three weeks later, much to my surprise, Prime Minister Narasimha Rao visited Rajsamand. His helicopters landed at the helipad at a tyre factory in Kankroli. I received him. He asked no questions. He drove straight to Nathdwara, had a darshan of Shrinathji, returned directly to the helipad and left for Delhi via Udaipur airport. He had no other business in Rajsamand or Udaipur.

Sagar believed and told us that he came to Nathdwara to apologize for the 'misdeeds' of Dhanik Lal Mandal.

'Your continuance does not suit us'

Every IAS officer loves a district posting and one's first district posting is truly special. Rajsamand was my first district posting – though it turned out to be the only one. I put my heart and soul into not only the developmental transformation of Rajsamand but also its cultural one.

Rajsamand has several places associated with Rana Pratap, the legendary Rajput king whose battles with Akbar are the stuff of Indian pride. The district included Kumbhalgarh, where Pratap was born, and it was the site of the poignant sacrifice made by Panna Dhai, his nursemaid, who sacrificed her own child to save the king's son. Haldi Ghati, where Pratap fearlessly fought the Mughals and Chetak, his legendary horse, breathed its last, is a few miles away from Nathdwara. I initiated programmes to renovate the sites in a way that celebrated their history. I formed a society headed by the district collector to develop land on top of a hill for a Chetak memorial that overlooked the valley where the horse died. I encouraged Pratap enthusiasts like Mohan Shrimali, a teacher in the education department, who later constructed a very nice museum in the valley that has become a popular tourist destination.

After the exhaustion of marble in Makrana, the beautiful dolomite found in Rajsamand became quite popular and a large marble industry developed in Rajsamand. Many traders from Rajsamand had moved to Mumbai (then Bombay) and set up marble trading shops and other businesses. They remained emotionally attached to their roots in Rajsamand. The Rajasthan government had started a programme called 'Apna Gaon Apna Kaam' (Our Village, Our Work). The scheme was simple. If any donor contributed 30 per cent of the cost of a project, the government would contribute the remaining 70 per cent and allow the donor to name the building as they desired. The immigrant traders of Rajsamand invited me to come to Mumbai, organized a large function to honour me and committed about ₹7 lakh for various public works. Rajsamand became the district with the largest utilization of funds under the Apna Gaon Apna Kaam scheme.

Rajsamand was known for its Molela terracotta art and the Nathdwara school of art, which specialized in the *picchwai* style of painting. I allocated a large piece of land to establish a Molela clay art complex. Girija Vyas sent a message that she was expecting to be invited as chief guest for the function. It was the period of President's Rule in Rajasthan. She was not invited. In fact, no politician was invited to any of the public programmes I organized during my tenure in Rajsamand.

Quite unexpectedly, I received my transfer orders in early August, less than a year of my joining. To her credit, Girija Vyas was a polite and frank person. She called to say: 'Subhashji, you have been doing excellent work. To tell you honestly, we had asked for your transfer as your continuance does not suit us.'

I thanked her for her candour, and Anjali and I soon packed for my next posting station.

8

Challenges of Transfers and Short Tenures

From Rajsamand, I was transferred to Spinfed as its managing director. Like Tilam Sangh, Spinfed was an apex federation of three old spinning mills at Gulabpura and Gangapur City in Bhilwara district and Hanumangarh in Hanumangarh district, and a modern cotton complex which was then under construction at Ganganagar. My background in turning around the Kota soybean project and Tilam Sangh might have had something to do with this posting.

Gangapur City was located only about 50 km from Rajsamand. We packed up our household stuff, kept all of it in one room of the collectors' residence, and planned to take our belongings to Jaipur after we could rent a house there, using liberal lease facility available from corporations and federations like Spinfed.

After taking charge of Spinfed in Gangapur City, we had stopped at Circuit House, Ajmer, for lunch en route Jaipur. I received an intimation there that my transfer orders to Spinfed had been cancelled and I was now posted as Inspector General, Registration and Stamps (IG [R&S]) in Ajmer! My batchmate Ashok Singhvi was interested in going to Spinfed. He pulled some strings to get what he wanted. Singhvi would get into major trouble later as Mines Secretary, including spending few years in jail for alleged corruption.

We were literally waylaid. Anyway, we went on to Jaipur. I handed over charge of Spinfed next day to Ashok and assumed the charge of IG (R&S) in Ajmer the following day.

We become homeless

A bigger tragedy awaited me and my family. It turned out that there was a stay order on allotment of government houses in Ajmer. No house could thus be allotted to me in Ajmer as a consequence.

I reached out to Chief Secretary Ramanan to allot me a government house in Jaipur and shift my headquarters to Jaipur. He refused. At my salary, I could not afford to rent a house in Jaipur for the family and in Ajmer for me. We were left homeless.

In the circumstances, I had to take a painful decision, for which Anjali has not forgiven me till now. She and the children went to Baroda, where my in-laws lived, while I divided my time in three places: 10 days in Jaipur Circuit House (which was the maximum limit an officer was allowed to stay in a circuit house), 10 days in Ajmer Circuit House and 10 days touring all over Rajasthan.

Drastic situations also force one to look for long-term solutions.

I had purchased a 240 square yard plot of land in 1991 in Nemi Nagar, Jaipur, in a cooperative society promoted by a private group, at a cost of ₹42,000. Land in the city was quite cheap in those days.

We decided it was time to construct our permanent home in Jaipur. I acted quite fast. The foundation was laid on 15 August 1993, less than a week after we left Rajsamand. The basic structure was completed in about five months. We moved into the house, which was still not fully complete, on 9 January 1994. The roof over the staircase, which led to the first floor, was not constructed, nor were glass-panes installed in all windows. That night, it rained; it was the coldest month – January. We had a horrible time. We took solace in the fact that our family was reunited, and we had a permanent roof for the family.

The total cost of construction for that semi-finished house was less than ₹2 lakh. We completed the house over the next four years, including replacing some of the temporary arrangements, at a final cost of ₹6 lakh. Our investment in the house inflation-proofed us from land price to a great extent. We eventually sold it in 2007 at ₹65 lakh, which met a substantial part of our purchase of a flat in Delhi the same year at the cost of ₹90 lakh.

That said, we have never forgotten the irony of our situation in 1993. After living in a palatial house in Rajsamand, in just one week, we became homeless.

'We don't have the luxury of three months'

The post of IG (R&S) was quite ill-defined. While on the registration side, IG (R&S) had formal authority and responsibility of superintendence and regulation making under the Registration Act, 1908, the position had no formal role on the stamp side as the authority of collector of stamps and chief controlling revenue authority under the Indian Stamps Act was not conferred on IG (R&S). The administrative system, however, expected IG (R&S) to achieve the stamp revenue targets and supervise the stamp system for the entire state.

The department also had a poor reputation in terms of integrity and public service orientation with many terming the department as a 'coal mine', where people make money but get their reputations tarnished. The department was also quite outdated in terms of modernization of office systems, record retrieval and most other matters.

My posting as IG (R&S), despite not being a core finance job or in the secretariat, was my entry into the finance department of the state government.

The principal expectation from the IG (R&S) was to ensure that the revenue target was met; this was a little over ₹100 crore for the financial year 1994–95. Achievement of the target depended upon fuller collection of stamp duties besides the general state of the property market in the state. Undervaluation of sale documents was rampant and was the principal avenue of revenue leakage. This widespread practice had eaten into the vitals of the department officers and there was a general perception that the department was corrupt. I was reminded of the Phalodi tehsil episode of ₹25 per registry for the tehsildar.

The department was old-fashioned, hugely procedure-oriented and bureaucratic. I figured out quickly that the only way revenue targets could be achieved and corruption leakage reduced was to ensure that the valuations of land in the documents presented for registration were close to market prices and the process of registration was fast, which would leave little room for corruption. I, therefore, adopted two immediate goals: one, the registration of documents must happen on the same day they were presented; and two, finding systemic solutions to eliminate undervaluation.

I collected data on the number of days it took for the documents to get registered and the reasons why it could not be done the same day. This data, along with discussions with officers and my visits to field offices, pinpointed some common issues: Documentation was kept pending to verify the land in question and its market price, necessitating field inspections of the concerned properties. These inspections would be undertaken according to the whims and fancies of the concerned officer, and the cost was borne by the landowner; the absence of appropriate benchmark property value; the non-availability of stamp papers of exact denominations; the absence of a sub registrar, since they were involved with other duties such as elections, law and order, relief work etc. There were numerous classes for buildings depending upon the state of construction (which had to be determined). Arbitrary modes of determining stamp duty also added to the chaos.

The provision of superintendence authority granted to the IG in the Registration Act came handy for me. After studying the processes carefully and discussing the matter thoroughly with field officers, I issued many orders and circulars in my first month of posting to set things right.

This started showing results by improving the proportion of registration made on the same day, with the onus of explaining non-registration of documents being placed on the sub registrar concerned. When the matter came to his attention, Finance Secretary Indrajeet Khanna called me. He would go on to become chief secretary and serve in the DEA in the Government of India as an additional secretary.

Indrajeet Khanna was a conventional civil servant who set great store by precedent. He concluded that the spree of circulars I was issuing was, in some way, usurping the powers of the state government. He also felt that the matters at hand required cooler consideration. He told me not to issue any orders or circulars for at least the first three months of my tenure. On that occasion, I recalled what the legendary IAS officer Nagarajan Vittal, credited with crafting the telecom policy which ushered in mass mobile telephony and software services revolution in the country, had told me in a vertical training session – that the times of IAS officers working as if they were playing a cricket test match was gone and, in the then current model of one-day cricket (T20 had not emerged on the scene), officers were supposed to start playing shots from the first ball they faced. So, I protested and told Khanna that as postings in the state were averaging six months to a year, I did not have the luxury of sitting on my haunches for three to four months.

I continued doing what I was doing, and the matter did not escalate. Coincidentally, Indrajeet Khanna proceeded on central deputation to Delhi very soon thereafter. After a few months, I compiled all the changes I made in a booklet manual and circulated it to the collectors and officers in the registration department. This improved same-day registration remarkably: 1994–95 was the first year stamp revenues crossed ₹100 crore despite a weak property market.

When a bribe is refused ...

A cement plant in Udaipur district was possibly proving to be a drag on the finances of the largest sugar company in India at the time that owned it. It sold the plant and presented the document for registration with the sub registrar in Fatehnagar. The sub registrar impounded the document, as per applicable procedure, on account of underpayment of stamp duty and sent it to the collector (stamps), Udaipur, who calculated the duty payable to be more than ₹5 crore.

The managing director of the company, called on me in my modest office in Ajmer. He was visibly tense. I heard him out patiently. After he had related his litany of woes, I explained to him that the company had sold a plant. The sale of any asset, whether a profit-making or loss-making one, attracted duty at the normal rate of 8 per cent. This was not a transaction of sales of company shares, which attracted much smaller duty. He realized a mistake had been committed but expected me to order the registration treating it as a sale of shares, not an asset.

When I conveyed my assessment of the case to him, including the powers the department had to seize assets pending payment of full stamp duty, he panicked. He then offered a down payment and said he would take care of me and my family throughout our lives if the document was registered as transfer of shares at a nominal duty.

At that stage, I requested him to leave my office.

Two days later, I received a call from N.C. Goel, an IAS officer of the 1982 batch, who was deputy secretary in the finance department with administrative responsibility for IG (R&S). President's Rule was still in place in the state. Goel informed me that Governor Bali Ram Bhagat, who had in the meantime replaced Chenna Ready, had received a complaint alleging that I had misbehaved with the MD, including making him wait for over an hour. He wanted a factual report within 24 hours.

I prepared a report and submitted it to the state government. The case came to be described loosely as an offer of a bribe of ₹35 lakh. A lot of time was spent processing the file. I also briefed Dr Adarsh Kishore, who had taken over as finance secretary after Indrajeet Khanna moved to the centre.

While a lot of to and fro took place, the department's decision stood. There was no relief to the company from the governor or government. Its MD's false allegations against me of mistreatment also did not find any sympathy.

A naysaying system

Reforming the stamp and registration system required amendments in rules and the law. These could be done only by the government. The general mindset of the government was to preserve status quo. Any proposals for change would be examined from the standpoint of identifying how to reject the proposal.

The examination would typically begin at the level of section officer, who would usually put together the existing law and rules on the subject and write that the proposal was contrary to them. A more constructive section officer would simply reproduce the proposed change and submit it. It was never the case that the section officer would recommend acceptance of the proposal.

The proposal would move through the deputy secretary, special secretary, finance secretary and minister to the chief minister and cabinet. At every stage of this hierarchy, every officer had the authority to reject the proposal. If rejected by the deputy secretary, the file would come back and the disapproval of the government would be conveyed. However, at no stage of the hierarchy was the proposal accepted, as the delegation of powers did not confer authority on anyone except the minister and the cabinet to change the rules and law. For a change in the law, the Assembly would also have to pass the amendment law.

It required endless sessions at different layers of authority to explain the proposal. I learnt a very important lesson: The secretariat was essentially designed to say no, rather than say yes. This mindset needed to be changed if the secretariat were to be more productive.

However, during budget time 1994, the system became quite efficient. I carried several proposals for amendments in stamp laws and rules. While the system put these proposals on file, I discussed them with Dr Adarsh Kishore. He agreed with several. Some proposals required reference to the existing rules, calculations of financial implications and discussions with other officials. All that was agreed upon was placed on file and got approved at every level in a jiffy. The other lesson learnt was to use budget time and the device of the financial bill more strategically and liberally to carry out required changes.

The bribe that wasn't

Jaipur had two independent sub registrar offices. One looked after Jaipur city and the other the rest of Jaipur tehsil. As Jaipur was rapidly expanding outside municipal limits, both the sub registrars' offices were among the largest revenue generators in the state. Correspondingly, the potential for corruption was also quite high. Jaipur tehsil had another problem as well. A lot of land that earlier belonged to the princely state of Jaipur was claimed as government *siwaichak* land by the government. There were court cases pending on most of these lands and their status was disputed. The state government had also followed a faulty policy of not allowing private housing societies or builders to build houses in the state. Only cooperative housing societies were allowed to undertake house-building besides state agencies of the Rajasthan Housing Board. The government, in its wisdom, had also put a ban on the formation of new housing cooperative societies, which made existing ones hugely profitable and prized assets. These cooperative societies were 'cooperative' only in name and were controlled by powerful politically backed toughies or businessmen.

Jaipur also has the JDA. However, it was not in the housing space. It came out with some housing schemes in which it only allotted land plots. Given the paucity of undisputed government or JDA land in Jaipur, such schemes would come up only once in a decade or so and that too for a small number of plots. The JDA also tried to acquire private land. Prithviraj Nagar was one of the largest housing schemes planned on the land to be acquired. This, unfortunately, also got mired in court cases and rampant encroachments by existing cooperative housing societies.

The housing situation was, to say the least, terrible. There were rampant rivalries among powerful local politicians and the land sharks they backed.

Satish Sharma was one of the two sub registrars in Jaipur. Only the most connected and politically acceptable tehsildars could be sub-registrars of Jaipur city. He must have been well connected. He was also an ace astrologer. I have never believed in astrology. The kind of astrology Sharma peddled, however, opened many doors of senior politicians and bureaucrats for him. He was appointed during the Bhairon Singh Shekhawat regime but continued after the government was dismissed.

Powerful rival interests were not happy with him as he was not serving their needs. One toughie in the state, Suresh Punia, decided to fix him. He organized a trap by the anti-corruption agency of the state, most likely with the tacit consent of the ruling establishment. Sharma's house was raided by a team from the Anti-Corruption Bureau (ACB). The trap, however, failed. They could not catch Sharma red-handed. Still, the ACB team arrested him because of some documents that, in their judgement, constituted circumstantial evidence that he had demanded bribes. They prepared the papers and sent them to the state government recommending his suspension.

Sunil Arora, secretary to the chief minister, asked me to prepare the case for Sharma's suspension. I studied the papers. There was no smoking gun. There was evidence of Sharma refusing to register some documents the Punia group had presented. Though Sharma did raise objections, there was no clear case to determine that these objections were raised to elicit bribes. In fact, some of these objections were genuine, considering the backdrop of the anarchic land situation in Jaipur.

I concluded that there was no clear case for charging Sharma with any misdemeanour or conduct unbecoming of an officer. I wrote out a detailed report to the state government. I recommended that as there was no case for chargesheeting Sharma, there was no need to suspend him. I further noted that disciplinary rules provide for automatic suspension if a government servant remains in police or judicial custody for more than 48 hours. My recommendation was that if the ACB believed it had a case, it could have kept him in custody for over 48 hours, which would had led to his automatic suspension.

The state government, with my report filed in, did not find the evidence strong enough. Sharma was released before 48 hours. He was not suspended. He remained sub registrar for some more time before he was transferred out.

A scurrilous complaint

One day when I was at the site where our house was being constructed, a letter was delivered by post. It was from the ACB. A four-line letter asked for my comments on an enclosed complaint alleging that I was collecting bribes during my tenure as IG (R&S). It further alleged that my house was being constructed from the proceeds of this ill-gotten money.

The complaint was made by a certain Sita Ram Garg, which happened to be the name of my father. The complaint was not only scurrilous but mischievous. I was forced to start the construction of the house in most trying circumstances when my family was rendered homeless. When it began, we did not have enough cash. For the first few weeks, construction material was taken from a Vaishinagar trader, and the bills had piled up by the time this letter arrived.

HDFC bank had taken a bold decision to start lending for house construction on land plots of cooperative societies even though there was no legal *patta* from the JDA, if the scheme had been approved by it. I had applied for a plot in the Chitrakoot scheme of the JDA. However, I did not get the allotment in the lottery. So, I had purchased the Nemi Nagar plot – this was also in the class of a scheme approved by the JDA but without a JDA *patta*. I applied for an HDFC loan, which was sanctioned. This helped me clear the pending bills for construction material.

The complaint sent by the ACB was more amusing than anything else. It was a wild allegation without any evidence. The complainant was probably trying to have fun at my expense by using my father's full name.

I wrote back to the ACB, also in just four lines. I told them the complaint was scurrilous and mischievous, and my father's name had been misused as the complainant. It had provided no other details of the complainant or complaint. My last line asked the ACB whether it really wanted to waste its time on the matter.

I did not hear anything about it thereafter.

9

Personnel Battles in Agriculture Development

I was transferred to the Department of Agriculture as the director at the behest of M.L. Mehta, the chief secretary, soon after the Bhairo Singh government returned in early 1994. The agriculture department was massive and technically challenging. It employed thousands of officers and agriculture workers. Through its extensive outreach, it touched the lives of all farmers in the state. Rajasthan, being predominantly agricultural, with agriculture GDP more than one-third of the state's GDP, ensured the department was a significant developmental institution for the state government.

In the decade preceding my arrival, the central and state governments' focus on agriculture since the Green Revolution had translated into new World Bank-assisted agriculture development programme resources. This had transformed the technical and manpower base of the department, its modernization and infrastructure. An imposing modern building, Krishi Bhawan, had been constructed next to the secretariat building, which was also maintained in a very professional and sleek manner.

The department was predominantly manned by technical officers recruited as part of the Rajasthan Agriculture Service. This was the only department where, other than the director, there was no IAS or RAS officer in any capacity or post. The technical officers did all the administrative work as well.

Gyan Singh Chaudhury, who had once been president of the student union of Rajasthan University, Jaipur, was the agriculture minister. Narendra Singh Sisodia, a very senior IAS officer of the 1968 batch, was 'agriculture production secretary (APS)', as the agriculture secretary in the state was formally referred to. After about three months of my joining the department, C.S. Rajan, who had earlier served for long as director, Agriculture, took over as APS.

Crop biology, agronomy, technology and agriculture development projects, though technical, were quite fascinating. I wanted to understand what went on in the entire process of farming, from producing seeds to harvesting. There were many state and national institutions dedicated to the subject, including an agriculture university in Udaipur and another newly set up one in Bikaner.

A stand-off over transfers

Less than a fortnight after I joined, I received an unsigned list on a plain paper containing about 100 names for transfer from and to a particular place, without any reference whatsoever. My personal staff told me that the list was for issuing 'transfer orders' and was received from the office of the agriculture minister.

I found the process and contents of list preposterous and demeaning. The departmental officers handling HR personnel matters told me this was the usual practice. I was told that such 'transfer lists' received earlier used to be taken on file and orders issued routinely. If the department or the director had a serious issue with any particular transfer, the director would speak to the minister, who would generally agree to delete that name from the list.

First, I decided to get the business of receiving unsigned list formal. My doubts about the authenticity of the unsigned list were duly communicated by an officer of the establishment section to the minister's office. After some time, the same list came back with the signature of Antar Singh Nehra, an RAS officer (later promoted to IAS) serving as executive assistant to the minister, which made the list orders 'in writing'.

I asked the officers to examine the proposals on merit. The scrutiny revealed that more than 85 per cent of the transfers ordered were not desirable from one point or the other. I, therefore, decided not to issue orders on the list, which was conveyed to the minister's office.

This made the student leader-turned-agriculture minister quite furious. He found it difficult to believe that such a thing could happen. The transfers expected to be made were within the delegated powers of the director, agriculture; the state government, however, had overriding authority. Considering my stand, the minister was advised by his staff to get the orders issued as a government order.

Ministers determine the level and authority for the disposal of different matters for the agriculture department in the secretariat. Gyan Singh

Chaudhury had issued these rules of delegation in such a manner that every matter was practically and finally disposed of at his level. Sisodia was absolutely disgusted but abided by the delegation. He sent the file with the proposal to issue a government order for the transfers to the minister for consideration and approval. The minister approved it. I received 'government orders' for all the 100-odd transfers that I had first received as an unsigned list.

As a director, I had to normally carry out the government orders. This time, I decided to fight back. I wrote a semi-official letter to Sisodia to reconsider the government order, enclosing a tabular factual report with my letter, indicating why the transfers were not in the public or the state's interest. This created a flutter as it was entirely unprecedented.

Sisodia called me and advised me, acting as a senior colleague, not to question the minister's orders in this manner and make the transfers. He offered to write back saying that the government had considered my views and still decided that the transfers be carried out. I politely refused to accept this advice. I found it difficult to stomach ordering the transfer of hundreds of employees with questionable integrity and poor track records to largely serve political interests. When I persisted in refusing to do such a blatantly wrong thing, Sisodia cautioned me, referring to the minister: 'Such people can go to any extent, including physically harming you.' I told him that I was prepared to run the risk. At that stage, he said he had no option but to resubmit the file for the minister's orders. He said he knew what the minister would do. As a measure of some comfort for me, he decided to route the file through Chief Secretary M.L. Mehta.

This caused some consternation in the minister's office as Mehta could not be taken for granted by the minister. At that stage, the minister asked me to see him. I explained the reasons of my discomfort with the cases I had questioned. What followed was quite unexpected! Perhaps it was because of his apprehension that M.L. Mehta might agree entirely with me, or sit on the file, or even tell Chief Minister Shekhawat about what was going on in the agriculture department! The minister went deep into each case and seemed to understand why I was opposing the transfers. Finally, he asked me how many transfers I would agree to make. Based on analysis which we had done earlier, I said around 15, maybe half-a-dozen more. He, with a sense of resignation, asked me to make 25 transfers out of the list, which I broadly agreed to do.

We prepared a list of 25 that we had no real problems with and gave it to Sisodia, who recalled the file from the chief secretary's office and placed the list for the minister's approval. We issued the transfer orders for the 25. A good spinoff of the entire standoff was that no such list was received again during my tenure. A very powerful message went across the department as well that no one would be able to manage a transfer through political connections.

I was tested on the transfer matters once more while I was at the agriculture department. Sunil Arora, secretary to the chief minister, asked for the transfer of a corrupt lab assistant. (Arora later worked as secretary to Chief Minister Vasundhara Raje Scindia and rose to be the information and broadcasting secretary in the Government of India and the chief election commissioner.) I went to Arora and explained the reasons why the transfer was not desirable. When he insisted I do it, I held firm and related the story of the transfers ordered by the minister. He knew about the episode but still wanted it done using the reflected authority of Chief Minister's Office. The transfer did not happen but kicked off the beginning of an uncomfortable relationship with him.

'Will treat your mass casual leave as a break in service'

The department functioned in several silos under the control of the senior-most agriculture service officers of the rank of additional and joint directors. Every silo was responsible for some scheme of the Government of India or some thematic area. The central government, around this time, was shifting to a cropping systems-based approach, rather than a particular crop-based programmatic approach. The officers in different silos would propose guidelines for implementation of that scheme in the state and allocate targets. After approval of the director, the scheme would be circulated to field formations along with the targets. As there were numerous schemes, numerous such circulars would be issued every year.

I found this suboptimal and decided to integrate all the schematic guidelines as part of a major document called the annual programme of agriculture development. The targets under different schemes were also aggregated and allocated on a rational basis. This had the effect of breaking the silos and bringing integration in the functioning of the department. It also brought a lot of transparency and synergy between different programmes. The officers, however, resented it. They thought that I was interfering in technical subject matter and their fiefdoms, of which they were the masters.

On the personnel side, there was a very well-organized drill in the department to get annual promotions done through departmental promotion committees

(DPCs). This exercise received top priority of the departmental officers as their personal interests were involved. I somehow thought departmental work was a bigger priority. I decided to go slow on the DPCs and gave overriding priority to bring out the annual agriculture development programme as it had been delayed that year for various reasons – elections, late passage of the main budget and others. The departmental officers thought I was deliberately and unjustifiably delaying their promotions.

There must have been some other pinpricks as well. In the last week of September 1994, I called a meeting of all the officers, including from the field, for final discussions on the plan and to approve guidelines and allocation of targets. Around 10.30 a.m., half an hour before the commencement of the meeting, I received a notice that the officers had decided to proceed on mass casual leave and they would boycott the meeting.

I was somewhat shocked but decided to act tough. I ordered on the same paper that notices be issued to all individual officers who did not turn up in the meeting that their casual leaves were refused, and in case they failed to attend the meeting, they would be treated as wilfully absent from duty. I used an infrequently used but very powerful provision in service law, which allowed wilful absence to be treated as *dies non* or 'the day does not exist' and recorded as such in the service records of the officers concerned. This had the effect of forfeiture of all service prior to the *dies non*, which would also impact their pension and other retirement benefits.

I went to the meeting hall at 11 a.m. There were only a few officers of the lower cadres at the headquarters. We started discussing the plan. Meanwhile, cracks started appearing among the agitating senior functionaries. Some of them were horrified at the prospect of losing all service. They were also not very sure about their ability to understand administrative law. A couple of officers walked in at 11.30. By noon, there was a total collapse of the agitation. Everyone showed up. We discussed and approved the annual agriculture development plans and targets.

I had a tenure of about a year in the agriculture department. I did not face any administrative resistance during the rest of my stay.

Rajasthan Canal transformed the desert

Agriculture is essentially a field subject. With many agroclimatic zones, large canal network-based agriculture in the west, and massive groundwater-based agriculture in most parts of the state, my posting offered a delightful opportunity to tour the state and see agriculture at close quarters.

I decided to make a trip from the northwest point in Sriganganagar district along the Rajasthan Canal (now Indira Gandhi Canal) to the state's southernmost point in Barmer district. The main canal runs for over 600 km in Rajasthan.

In the irrigated areas of the Ganganagar and Hanumangarh districts, the cotton–wheat routine was the main cropping system. The area had the highest water allowance. Despite this, in the tail areas, there was paucity of water. In the areas close to the canal network, however, there was excessive application of water, which waterlogged long stretches. Farmers in the tail areas demanded *diggi*s (water tanks to store canal water to be applied with sprinklers and drips to get more crop per drop), whereas farmers in the waterlogged areas asked for pumps to drain out excess water. My visit to Gharsana Mandi revealed the intense relationship between farmers and *adatia*s (the traders in the *mandi*s), which made them akin to Siamese twins.

Further down the Rajasthan Canal, groundnut cultivation in Bikaner district, especially in the Loonkaransar area, had transformed the desert geography, topography and economic life of the people. Groundnut cultivation had spread to the Jaisalmer area as well. In the newly developing areas of Nachna tehsil in Jaisalmer, groundnut was picked by labour with labour payment decided on a per kg basis. Labour was scarce in the canal area and labour charges thus made up a major part of the overall cost of growing groundnut.

The government charged nothing for the water supplied by the large network that included the main canal, minor canals, distributaries and field channels. Most of Rajasthan drew water by digging wells hundreds of metres into the earth and paid for electricity or diesel charges for pumping water besides paying the capital cost of equipment. In canal areas, however, field channels were also constructed at government cost. The inequity of the two situations was stark. I proposed a scheme for the construction of *diggi*s by the government, with 40 per cent of the cost contributed by farmers, which became quite popular. Much later, solar pumps began to be used to pump and distribute water from the *diggi*s.

Agriculture extension was not all official

Agriculture department, in essence, was for providing technology extension services to farmers. For most, the extension work in the department was the most important. Agricultural universities were supposed to conduct research and develop new seed varieties, machinery and equipment and better ways to apply inputs. All these would lead to the formulation of the packages of practices to transfer the research and development in actual fields. The agriculture department was the bridge that extended the outputs of research to farmers.

Agriculture workers delivered these services., Rajasthan had created one position of agriculture worker in each panchayat, resulting in a cadre of over 10,000 workers. These workers delivered extension services through a variety of programmes: mini-kits (certified seeds and recommended fertilizers delivered in small doses free of cost to farmers to encourage their use); demonstrations (showcasing better results from better seeds and practices compared to traditional cultivation); and visits to farmers who had successfully adopted the good seeds and practices.

In contrast to the popular perception of farmers being traditionalist, I found them very receptive to new ideas, technologies and practices. Exhortation, however, did not work. Highly knowledgeable scientists and well-educated agriculture officers just could not get through to farmers unless they could demonstrate actual utility. What cut through the ice for farmers most effectively was a demonstration of the recommended change implemented by another farmer and its value demonstrated by improved production and price realization when compared to their own.

Workforce issues afflicted delivery of these valuable services. Agriculture workers wanted to live in cities, not villages. They also wanted to live in bigger cities. Those who had no one to speak for them ended up in remote areas, tribal areas and areas that did not grow the major crops of wheat, mustard and groundnut. In one visit to the Rann of Kutch area of Jalore district (before the river Luni meanders into the Rann), I met an agriculture worker who had been there for more than eight years. When I asked him why he was there for so long, with a resigned look, he said he had no connections. I recalled the gross inequity of the transfers ordered by the minister facing me. Though I transferred him to a more habitable place, I realized there would have been many more like him languishing in other corners of the state.

While the government's extension services did make some difference in many areas of Rajasthan, my visit to Jalore revealed that non-official channels were in fact working very effectively as well. This area, adjacent to the Unjha area of Gujarat, was growing non-traditional crops like *jeera* (cumin), *methi* (fenugreek) and *dhania* (coriander). Cumin is quite a delicate crop. There was not one certified seed developed by the state research system for cumin. No package of practices was recommended by the department for cumin. When I went to see a few cumin fields, at one place I found two people sitting on a charpoy. The farmer later introduced them as visitors from Unjha who were teaching him how to grow cumin. Enquiries revealed that cumin cultivation in the districts of Jalore and Sirohi in Rajasthan has been taught by farmers from Gujarat for many years. These visiting farmers also helped establish marketing linkages with the Unjha *mandi,* the biggest market for cumin.

Promotional services for some other crops, like castor seeds, were being provided at places by workers of the companies that produced these seeds. Some farmers, in different parts of Rajasthan, would produce better crops of traditional (*desi*) varieties and sell their crops as seeds.

The department needed to mobilize all agents instead of working only through its agriculture workers, and for all crops instead of only three to four major ones.

I tried to introduce a line of business for the Rajasthan State Seeds Corporation (RSSC), which I headed as chairperson in the truthfully labelled seeds (TFL) seeds category despite opposition from scientists and purists. For the scientists, the seeds produced in their research chain – basic seeds, foundation seeds and certified seeds – were the only genuine seeds. The effort of marketing the farmers seeds – TFL seeds – did not amount to much, though.

Charging a nominal amount for soil tests

Testing soil for nutrients (nitrogen, phosphorus and potash) and micronutrients (iron, zinc) helps determine what kind and amount of supplementary nutrition in the form of fertilizers and manure needs to be provided for growing a healthy crop. Facilities for testing micronutrients were just beginning to get established (these machines were quite costly as well) in the state soil-testing laboratories. Testing for the three major nutrients – nitrogen, phosphate and potash – was relatively cheaper and substantial testing capacities had been built.

The soil-testing system operated purely as a government service at the time in Rajasthan. Agriculture workers of the department would collect samples (they would weigh several kilos and were typically carried in large sacks) and deposit them with the laboratories. The laboratories would dissolve the soil to ascertain the extent of nutrients. Finally, a report would be written in the form of a 'soil card' and the findings conveyed to the farmers. The farmers were expected to apply the requisite fertilizers to the recommended extent.

The communication of test results and the assessment of the quantity of deficient nutrients was the real test of the entire exercise. However, there were serious issues at every stage in the chain. Agriculture workers could not collect soil samples on any scientific basis. This ended up in samples being collected from similar soil conditions and soil from different conditions missing in the samples. Usually, the samples would not reach the laboratories on time. Weighty soil samples would end up occupying a lot of space in the laboratories. I saw numerous samples piled up at the Jodhpur soil-testing lab.

Farmers were unable to fathom the test results, too. They were not confident of the right quantity and type of fertilizers that needed to be applied. As fertilizers came cheap, with most of the cost covered by the government in subsidy, farmers generally went by the belief that it was better to apply more than less.

Finally, farmers had no stake in the testing enterprise. While the cost of testing one soil sample was only about ₹10 in those days, the farmers paid nothing. They did not care for the results either. On the other hand, the laboratories were starved of the chemicals required for testing as the government only gave them a fixed budget every year. The sacks of soil samples lying in Jodhpur were also because the budget had been exhausted.

I proposed to charge ₹2 per sample from farmers. For farmers, though, even such a nominal payment mattered. I proposed to keep this income in a fund in the public account to supplement the budgets of laboratories. The officers showed me the rules. Charging any fee was a non-tax income of the government and could only be done with government approval. I decided to initiate the charging of a fee and sent the proposal for approval. The agriculture department sent the proposal to the revenue division of the finance department. They raised quite a few issues. Nevertheless, in the meantime, the new system of charging ₹2 per sample got established and the farmers started having a stake in the value of the testing.

The matter could not be decided by the government during my short tenure in the directorate of agriculture.

A major business process re-engineering of RSSC

Along with the charge of director, agriculture department, came the responsibility of managing director of RSSC. The corporation was in the business of raising and buying seeds and selling them to farmers. While the agriculture department was a real technical department, RSSC was no different from any other commercial organization. Tilam Sangh also did some business in seeds as part of its service to oilseed cooperative societies.

C.S. Rajan, an IAS officer of the 1978 batch, was rated among the best performing officers of the cadre. He had served as director, Agriculture, for about six years until a year before I took over. Rajasthan State Seeds Corporation's accounts had fallen into more than seven years' arrears, which Rajan worked very hard to set right. By the time he left in 1993, the arrears had almost been cleared. The corporation, though, was still a loss-making organization in 1994.

In the seeds business, the certified seed was the type of seed RSSC was primarily supposed to produce or procure and sell to farmers. It was produced from foundation seed, which, in turn, was produced from basic seed. Basic seeds and foundation seeds were mostly produced by scientists in the farms of agriculture universities.

The corporation procured certified seeds in three different ways. First, the state government, through an agency called Rajasthan State Seeds Certifying Agency (RSSCA), registered good farmers to raise production of certified seeds from the foundation seeds provided by the agriculture department/RSSCA. The government provided an incentive over the market price on such production. RSSC procured seeds from such registered farmers. Second, RSSC had farms of its own in which it produced certified seeds hiring labour for cultivation. Third, it bought seeds from the National Seeds Corporation (NSC) and other state agencies like the Andhra Pradesh Seeds Corporation, which produced the bulk of bajra seeds for Rajasthan, taking advantage of good climatic conditions in winter preceding bajra cultivation season. Rajasthan State Seeds Corporation had not ventured into hybrid seeds. It met the bulk of the certified seeds requirement of the state.

The team of officers in RSSC was quite competent and knew the seeds business well. However, it was largely clueless about the losses the corporation suffered year after year. It had not made a profit in at least 10 years. Using my accounting background and knowledge of business, I, after undertaking a comprehensive analysis of the accounts and the business model, found four principal reasons for the losses RSSC made every year. First, the government had a small equity in the corporation, but had given large loans to it, making its debt-to-equity ratio close to 10:1. It did not pay the interest, which made the government debt continue to pile up. Second, RSSC lost money heavily on seed production on its farms. Third, it was selling the certified wheat seeds at a price lower than the price of even the normal wheat crop in the market, by passing on all the liberal subsidy it received from the government on seed production. Fourth, every year, about 5–10 per cent of all the seeds remained unsold. Since such seeds were not usable for human or animal consumption as they had been treated with chemicals, they had to be virtually thrown away. Rajasthan State Seeds Corporation did not get subsidy from the government for such unsold seeds as well, making it suffer a double whammy.

I decided to deal with two issues first, which were entirely in my jurisdiction.

The corporation sold about 8,000 tonnes of certified seeds of wheat every winter. Wheat had one of the highest subsidies on production of certified seed. It sold at about ₹4 a kg at the time. The price of certified seed amounted to about ₹3 a kg after adjusting for the incentive. There was excellent demand for RSSC-certified wheat seed and all of it was sold without any effort. There was never any wheat seed left unsold.

I checked with the officers about the impact on demand if the price were raised by ₹1 per kg. They recoiled at first as the price was derived from the formula fixed by the state government after factoring in the subsidy. When pressed, they confirmed that there would be no adverse impact on demand. In fact, an officer informed me that the NSC was selling the seed at higher prices as well. The matter was taken on file. I approved the decision to raise the price of certified wheat seed by ₹1 per kg; 8,000 tonnes of certified wheat seed brought an additional income of ₹80 lakh to RSSC.

Certified seed left unsold caused a loss of about ₹75 lakh to ₹1 crore every year! Well in time, we adopted a policy that no seed would be left unsold at the end of the financial year, i.e., on 31 March 1995. All officers were instructed to demand the seed required in their area, keeping in mind that there was to be no leftover seed at the end of the year. Further, if some seed remained unsold around the time sowing season was getting over, they were asked to intimate headquarters and take permission to sell the unsold seeds at a lower price. Leaving no seed unsold became such a high management priority that the RSSC officers became much more alert about the quantity of seed they had and made a better effort to sell the entire quantity. More than 99 per cent of the seed available was sold at the normal full price that year. Small leftover quantities of seed were disposed of at discounted prices. Some farmers bought seed for sowing it a little later, while others bought it to keep for the next season. The corporation had zero stock of seed pending from the financial year 1994–95 on 31 March 1995.

These measures virtually wiped out the annual losses from RSSC's profit-and-loss account.

Trouble in contracting out seed farms

The solution I found most suitable for cutting down losses from the seed farms was contracting out seed production on RSSC's farms to private farmers. On my visits to Ganganagar and other areas as director, Agriculture, I had seen the widespread practice of contracting agricultural land out for crop production. In those days, land was contracted out for about ₹ 4,000 per hectare with no share in costs and production. Rajasthan State Seeds Corporation had the added advantage that the seeds produced in its farm, being certified seeds, would earn farmers a higher price in the form of incentive income as well. Contracting would also solve the problem of keeping RSSC staff and hiring labour (there were court cases to regularize the services of some of this labour). The expected increase in productivity would bring an additional quantity of certified seeds to RSSC as well.

To me, it appeared to be a no-brainer. We decided to contract out all the farms of RSCC. Advertisements were issued, bids examined, and over a period of three months, all the farms were contracted out on two basic terms. One, the farmers would hand over all the seeds to RSSC at a price determined in accordance with the state government formula with an incentive paid to them. Second, they would quote a per acre rate to get the lease/concession to raise the seed crop with all costs borne by them.

Rajbir Singh, additional general manager, RSSC, made some quick calculations. The corporation would get a neat profit of ₹2 crore per annum from contracting out the farms besides getting about 25 per cent extra seed production, he found. Farms were handed over to the selected farmers after entering into contractual agreements with them.

After joining as agriculture secretary, C.S. Rajan, who was also chairman of RSSC, called me one day. After confirming that I had decided to contract out the RSSC farms, Rajan questioned the decision. He informed me that the farms were state government land that had been leased out to RSSC. As per the rules applicable on land leasing, the lessee had no right to sublease it, he said.

I had known the legal implications of contracting out leased farms. It was indeed a violation of the rules. However, in my judgement, it was only a technical violation. It did not really matter whether RSSC raised certified seeds by employing its own labour or giving the land on contract. I told Rajan that the pith and substance of the transaction was basically a labour contract, not subleasing. I further said I had taken the decision without referring to the state government precisely to avoid such technical objections being raised by some officer in the secretariat. I also informed him of the kind of profits RSSC would get and argued that such a good proposition should not be sacrificed on a mere technicality.

Rajan was not very happy but he did not pursue the matter further. The arrangement I instituted remained in force for many years after I left.

Got the loan converted as well

Dr Adarsh Kishore, finance secretary, had formed a good opinion of me when I was IG (R&S). Quite a few of my innovative proposals for raising stamp duty and registration fee revenues were incorporated in the budget for 1994–95. He also involved me in the preparation of the budget speech for that year.

I went to him with a proposal for partial conversion of the large government loan to RSSC into equity, as this would save it the interest cost. Dr Kishore would not, even in accounting terms, ever agree to forgo interest on the state government loan by converting it into equity. His first reaction was expectedly unfavourable. I told him the facts. The corporation was not paying interest on these state government loans. The interest burden was making RSSC report losses. The debt-to-equity ratio had become completely out of line for any prudential financial re-engineering of any company. Thereafter, I told him about my efforts to make the organization a profit-making one.

Finally, I offered him a deal. I requested that only one-fourth of the state government loan be converted into equity, which would bring the debt-to-equity ratio to about 3:1. I also suggested that the remaining loan will be paid off by RSSC in five equal annual instalments and the interest payment resumed the same year.

Dr Kishore saw the rationale of my proposal. He must have certainly been persuaded by the prospect of the state government loan being paid back and resumption of the interest income. He agreed. RSSC had its debt converted into equity, which contributed its might to turn the loss-making corporation into a profit-making one.

True to our promise, RSSC paid back the first instalment of the remaining loan and due interest that year. 1994–95 was the first year it made a profit after many years. The officers of RSSC were visibly proud of their achievement.

I get my first less-than-outstanding ACR

Rajan had difficulty with my unorthodox solutions.

Contracting out the RSSC farms was the first major point of Rajan's annoyance with me. He might have genuinely felt that it was not right to act against the explicit rule of the lessee not being competent to sublease. It might have also been some envy at my having pulled off a turnaround that he could not do during his six-year tenure. He was certainly annoyed at my style of functioning, as I was taking major decisions without even bothering to inform him (he was not only chairman of RSSC but also the APS.

I held a dim view of procedural niceties. I believed that as the MD of RSSC or director, Agriculture, I was the executive head of the organization. I was not only entitled to take decisions but had to do so at my level to ensure I was fully responsible for them. Such decision-making also saved lot of valuable time. I told him this when he questioned me about the legality of giving RSSC farms on contract. That said, Rajan was an extremely competent and reasonable person and a balanced officer. I worked with him several times later as well. The rough edges were possibly still to smoothen.

There were also a few other instances during that nine-month tenure together. Once, he phoned me during a holiday and complained bitterly about my lack of respect for him and his office. He was severely critical of my way of working and handling officers in the department. Though he said that I was innovative and made decisions that would serve the interest of the department, he pointed out that the manner of making those decisions was not in line with established procedures. I replied that what mattered to me were results, not government procedures. I reiterated that I would risk personal well-being in the interest of serving public interest, the way I saw it best.

Annual confidential reports (ACRs) were not disclosed to the officer concerned in those days. Only adverse remarks were conveyed. In terms of rating, officers were rated as 'outstanding', 'very good', 'good', 'satisfactory' and 'unsatisfactory'. Only unsatisfactory ratings were communicated.

I had never bothered to know about my ACRs until then. Much later, around 2010, when the government decided to provide copies of old ACRs, I also got copies of my ACRs since 1985. The ACR of 1994–95 was the only year I was rated less than outstanding. Rajan had rated me as 'good' that year. M.L. Mehta had upgraded it to 'very good' but not 'outstanding'.

Rajasthan agriculture receives a national award

There had been an undercurrent of hostility towards me during my short tenure in the directorate of agriculture. The post of director, Agriculture, was in the cadre of the Rajasthan Agriculture Service, which meant the post was normally filled by promoting an eligible additional-director-level officer to the position of director. In the eventuality of there being no eligible officer, the post could be filled with an IAS officer.

For many years, the post had been managed by IAS officers, and departmental officers retired as additional director. If an officer became eligible to become director, Agriculture, he or she was posted to another equivalent post in the agriculture sector as director, Horticulture, or director, Soil Conservation (later director, Watershed Management).

It was the turn of Dr Sushil Kumar Sharma, a competent and respected officer of the department, when I was serving. The system decided to give him the honour and opportunity to be director, Agriculture.

I had no problem with it. I happily agreed. Dr Sharma's posting has been the only posting of a technical officer as director (later upgraded to commissioner), Agriculture, in living memory.

I drew a lot of satisfaction from my posting though.

Besides improvements in production and productivity of Rajasthan's agriculture, the transformation of RSSC into a completely modern and up-to-date company in terms of accounts and holding AGMs received national attention. Rajasthan got the National Agriculture Award for 1994–95. The factor that made the largest contribution was the stellar performance in the growth of certified seeds distribution and its management.

The awards were finalized during the financial year 1995–96 for the performance of 1994–95. I had left the department by that time. Normal courtesy would have been to invite the head of the department – director, Agriculture – responsible for the performance of the year assessed. I was not invited. The award, when presented by the president of India, was received by a batchmate who had taken over as director by that time.

It was fine with me. I worked as a public servant. Receiving recognition and awards was not that important to me, doing the task well was.

10

Getting Waylaid by the Wheels of Corruption

In June 1995, I was shifted as managing director of Rajasthan Roadways. I was transferred within the next six weeks, consigned to the post of director, State Insurance and Provident Fund (SIPF), a position considered by most as a punishment post. In local administrative lingo, I was put in deep freeze (*barf mein laga diya*).

Why this swift turnaround in fortunes?

A corrupt organization

Rajasthan Roadways was a massive organization, considering the size of the states' public-sector organizations. The corporation owned more than 4,000 buses and bought about 700–1,000 buses every year (barring some exceptions), a purchase worth about ₹100 crore in those days.

It operated about 30 depots and employed over 25,000 people with a person-to-bus ratio of about six employees per bus. It had three large workshops to maintain and repair its fleet. The depots and workshops were divided between two manufacturers, Tata Motors and Ashok Leyland, who competed but had an assured supply of orders for buses in the long-accepted ratio of 60:40. Rajasthan Roadways ran diesel pumps from its own premises to supply fuel to its fleet. The bus business had a large follow-on procurement as well, manufacturing bus bodies for the chassis supplied by Tata Motors and Ashok Leyland, procurement of tyres and other materials.

Bus operations were notoriously corrupt. The conductors responsible for issuing bus tickets (there were no online pre-bookings then) were known to carry many passengers without issuing tickets. The conductors channelled the money to other staff of the Roadways. The conductors' postings were controlled by the depot managers, whose posting and transfers were controlled by the minister. The Roadways was a big corruption machine. At the time, the chairman of the Roadways was also a person of dubious reputation.

There were three key dramatis personae involved in making purchase decisions, transfers and postings of depot managers and conductors, and, in general, running the Roadways.

Transport Minister Rohitasva Kumar, a flippant and loud-mouthed man, had the worst reputation in terms of integrity. However, he was the leader of 12 independents who were crucial for the survival of the 89-member Bharatiya Janata Party (BJP) government at the time, led by Bhairon Singh Shekhawat, in the legislative assembly of 200.

Mahendra Singh, chairman of Rajasthan Roadways, was a senior IAS officer who fancied himself as the leader of SC and ST officers and as a future political leader – he later contested the state assembly election and lost. G.S. Sandhu, an IAS officer of the 1979 batch, was the outgoing managing director.

This was the first time I was being posted to serve in an organization that was widely viewed as notoriously corrupt.

'Minister wants to interview you'

Before I was to assume my charge in the Roadways, M.L. Mehta asked me to see him. He told me three things frankly.

First, both the minister and chairman were corrupt and were fighting each other over share of the spoils. The MD was either not in a position to act or might have also joined the gravy train. The government was hugely concerned about the reputation and state of indecision in the Roadways.

Second, I was expected to restore some sort of order and protect the interest of the government, as it was the government that ended up providing the funds for the procurement of buses and to cover the losses of the organization. He also warned that there was a real possibility of me falling between two stools, meaning thereby that both the minister and the chairman may target me, and therefore, advised me to be tactful and careful.

Third, the transport minister was reluctant to accept me in the Roadways and had asked for the cancellation of my posting. However, Mehta had told the minister that I was knowledgeable in financial matters and would help in restoration of the financial health of the Roadways. He added that the minister wanted to do his due diligence, and I would have to meet him before I joined.

I realized the gravity of the situation and agreed to see Rohitashva Kumar. Our meeting happened in his study at his residence.

He appeared amiable and forthright. He was candid enough to state that he had heard some not-so-good things about my dealings with ministers in the past and was concerned about my streak of independence.

The reason he wanted to meet me was to assess whether I was a 'practical' person. To test my pragmatism, he posed a question: 'If I ask you to transfer a corrupt depot manager from place A to place B, would you have an objection or carry out the order?'

Thinking on my feet and assuming that I could possibly deal with the case differently when I was in the seat, I told him it did not matter if a corrupt officer worked at place A or place B, as he would probably be as corrupt in both places. He seemed visibly relieved.

Some more small talk followed. He signalled I might join the Roadways.

I reported the interaction to M.L. Mehta and assumed charge as MD of Rajasthan Roadways.

60:40 split between Tata and Leyland: Root of corruption

The matter of purchasing 1,000 new buses had acquired urgency in view of the government's decision to modernize the ageing fleet. The normal life of a roadways bus was considered six years and about one-fifth of the fleet needed to be replaced every year. There was documented data that older buses were significantly inefficient in diesel consumption and the cost of their maintenance was much higher.

Within a day or two of joining, I had to convene a meeting about the purchase. Bids had been invited but had not been opened, and instead of giving the requisite funds from the state budget, the government had agreed to provide a state guarantee for the Roadways to borrow from the banks on its strength.

Tata had a clean reputation and had quoted a lower price per bus. Ashok Leyland's reputation was poor and its price was higher as well. The officials had prepared a note, probably on the lines of what had been done on previous occasions, justifying the higher price of Ashok Leyland on account of its lower lifecycle cost, which looked suspicious.

Rajasthan Roadways's fleet comprised Tata Motors and Ashok Leyland buses in a 60:40 ratio. I asked them why we were locked into this 60:40 approach and why we could not abandon this practice. It was obvious to me that they had addressed this question earlier as well and offered two primary reasons. First, the structure and operations of depots and workshops would be upset if the buses were not purchased in this ratio. Second, the monopoly of one supplier might lead them to charge higher prices and supply spare parts at a higher-than-normal cost too.

The 60:40 ratio might have originated as a historical accident, but over the years it had acquired a deep structural base. The depots that retained the buses on an overnight basis and were responsible for minor repairs were either Tata or Leyland depots. For major repairs and what they called 'overhauling' work, there were two state-level workshops for Tata buses and one for Ashok Leyland buses.

I asked them about the technical feasibility of one set of depots and workshops taking a higher number of buses and augmenting repairing facilities and workshops. They did not have cost estimates but confirmed that land and space would not be a constraint. I asked them if the cost of augmenting the workshop/depots could be considered a part of the bid. They seemed to agree that it could be done.

As for the fear of one operator becoming a monopoly and the consequential adverse impact on future prices and workshop supplies, I found this to be baseless. In fact, if word was convincingly spread that the entire order could go to the supplier with the lower bid, the chances of them bidding lower competitive prices would be substantially enhanced.

There were side negotiations going on between the chairman's and minister's confidants about the kind of money that would be paid to them per bus. I did not witness these deliberations in person but got an inkling when a Tata senior manager came to see me and complained about the 'excessiveness' of the demand.

After understanding the matter in its entirety, a couple of days later, I submitted the file to the chairman and minister, making an unequivocal recommendation that the bids received should be rejected and fresh bids be called after making it clear that the 60:40 rule had been scrapped and the Roadways would be free to place the order in any configuration.

This set the cat among the pigeons.

Minister's transfer test got tested

June–July is when transfers of depot managers were done. Some applications were pending and there were some references from the minister's and chairman's offices as well. I prepared the proposals keeping the best interests of the Roadways in mind and after giving due consideration to references from the minister and chairman.

Whether some officers went to the minister to stall the proposed transfers or for some other reasons, the government decided to call for the file related to the proposed list of transfers. The roadways and transport department in the secretariat operated on a single file system and the proposals originating in the Roadways were sent on the same file to the transport department. I recorded my note on the file and sent it to the transport secretary without bothering the chairman about the matter.

Rajiv Mehrishi, with whom I would spend considerable time later in different postings and capacities, was transport secretary. He would go on to become principal finance secretary and chief secretary of Rajasthan, economic affairs secretary and finance secretary in the Government of India, and the comptroller and auditor general (CAG). This was the first time I was interacting professionally with him.

Mehrishi called me to his home on a public holiday considering the urgency of the matter. He asked me about three-four cases quite specifically. I gave him my honest opinion about the concerned officers. He agreed with my assessment. In a note he typed at home, he endorsed the transfer list I had prepared and sent the file to the minister.

The minister must have surely felt that he was taken for a ride in the interview he conducted.

'Get this man out first'

The state government had approved a foreign training for me in the Philippines at a workshop organized by the Ford Foundation on a farmer-to-farmer extension while I was still in the agriculture department. All permissions, including from the state and centre, had come, some of which after I had joined the Roadways. The Ford Foundation was keen for me to join the workshop as India had considerable experience on the subject: farmer-to-farmer exchange. I decided to proceed for the training after sending a formal note of information to the chairman, which he received after I had left.

On the second day of my week-long workshop in Manila, I received my transfer orders out of the Roadways.

It was quite obvious that things moved very quickly after I left Jaipur. Nonetheless, I completed my stay at the workshop.

I was told by officers upon my return to Jaipur that the chairman was furious at the proposal of doing away with the 60:40 split, that too made on file without any prior consultation with him. He was also upset at being bypassed in the transfer file, which was directly sent to the transport secretary without taking him into confidence. They also told me that the minister was highly upset at the transfer proposal and the potential personal loss of 'income' in the bus purchase deal. I had it from them that both the gentlemen indeed met, buried their differences for the time being and decided that the first thing to do was to get me immediately transferred from the Roadways. Both chairman and transport minister met the chief minister separately.

The chairman complained bitterly to the chief minister about my way of working, bypassing and ignoring him, and my impractical approach in dismantling a well-settled decade-old buses purchase system. He also complained about transfer proposals file sent to government without routing it through him.

The transport minister repeated much the same story and insisted that I be transferred out that very day to such a place outside Jaipur that I would remember it all my life. He reportedly threatened to withdraw his support to the government if I was not transferred that very day.

Surviving on a slim majority, the government was on thin ice. M.L. Mehta told me that it was with great difficulty that he could convince chief minister Shekhawat to instead 'dump' me into the SIPF department, which was, as he told the CM, the worst department in the state.

It was a single-order transfer. It was issued in such a hurry that no one else was posted in my place.

I assumed my responsibility at the SIPF department the day I returned from the Philippines. I had no regret or worries.

Strangely, the government asked me to hold additional charge of the Roadways till my replacement was appointed, which I did for 12 days.

I finally bid goodbye to the Roadways when Umesh Kumar, my batchmate, was posted. My conscience was fully satisfied, and I was convinced I did the right thing. It did not matter that the posting in Rajasthan Roadways, including additional charge, lasted for only 40-odd days.

11

In the Den of Union Leaders

Creating work in the 'dumped' department

Some progressive princely states of India, including Jaipur, in the pre-Independence period, had started providing life insurance cover to their employees. To do this, the Jaipur princely state had set up an insurance organization. After Independence, this transformed into the state insurance department (SID). When the life insurance business was nationalized in 1956 and amalgamated into Life Insurance Corporation (LIC), and general insurance business was nationalized and consolidated in four public-sector general insurance companies, the SID was allowed to continue with life insurance for state employees and fire insurance business for state government properties.

Provident fund (PF) accounts of state government employees, other than class IV, are generally kept by the offices of the Accountant General (part of the CAG). Rajasthan, in a progressive and assertive move, took over the maintenance of PF accounts of all state government employees and of All India Services (AIS) officers in the late 1970s. This work was entrusted to the state insurance department, which then became the SIPF department.

In the early 1990s, the state government decided to offer general insurance services for state government, and public-sector and associated organizations. For this, the general insurance licence of the department, which had become virtually defunct, was revived. The state government directed all these entities to mandatorily take fire and general insurance only from the SIPF department.

The SIPF department set up a general insurance division in addition to two major divisions of state insurance and PF. The state government also decided to offer a group accident insurance policy to all its employees by paying a lumpsum premium to the SIPF department.

In terms of work profile, Rajasthan's SIPF department was unique in the country and had a wide array of insurance and PF products to offer. Its clients were, however, largely the state government employees.

The SIPF department was a classic *babu* organization. Its job was to collect the details of entries of deductions of state insurance, PF and other contributions of state government employees, post these in manual ledgers (called broadsheets), and process the cases of loans and final payments to state government employees from their accounts. The SIPF employees thus had control over six lakh state government employees and would take bribes from them to process their loans.

Two of the field offices – Jaipur City and Jaipur Rural – functioned from the directorate building. Many government employees came to these offices to get loans and resolve other personal cases. There was rampant absence of employees from their offices resulting into visiting staff complaining bitterly about the rounds they had to make to get their work done. There were complaints of corruption as well. The miserable state of record maintenance did not help the matters as well.

The director literally had no work to do. Almost nothing came to the director. Processes were all routine and ended up with the heads of offices. The work was manual and there was no computerization worth the name. I had always kept long office work schedules as there was always much work to do. However, I realized on the very first day that my physical presence in the directorate was necessary, if only to keep order and ensuring that the employees remained in their offices.

I decided to do two things.

First, I thought the abundant availability of free time was a great opportunity to read up to understand state finances and accounts. One thing led to another. I studied the chart of accounts, state government finances and the state cash management system. This was to prove very helpful to me later.

Second, I decided to revamp of the processes of the department, complete individual ledgers and accounts (pending for more than 17 years) and bring some discipline to the department.

Nerve centre of employee unionism

The SIPF department was deeply involved with state government employees as they had to approach it to take loans from their state insurance and PF accounts.

Their final retirement benefits were also in control of the employees of this department. The leadership of state employees' union was heavily concentrated in the department.

The 1990s were times of strident employee unionism. The SIPF employees headed rival Maha Sanghas (state-wide federations). The Jaipur headquarters particularly had numerous leaders who wielded considerable influence not only on employees but also on politicians. They were generally beyond the pale of any discipline and would not hesitate to take on even directors. Departmental officers were completely under their thrall. In fact, the union employees had locked one of my predecessors in his room. The other one had to sneek out through a backdoor to avoid being hackled. The state of indiscipline and threats of personal harm were so serious that many directors avoided coming to the directorate regularly.

I decided to deal with the employees' absenteeism, including by the union leaders head-on.

Attendance registers were maintained in every office as per the rules. Any employee who reported late by half an hour three times would have half a day's leave deducted. Also, if the employee was not in the office within an hour or so of office opening time, he/she was required to be marked absent for the day.

The union leaders cared two hoots for these rules. On the pretext that he was on a tour of the state for union work, the president of the Maha Sangh, Lakshman Singh Rajawat, would mark himself present once in four to five days when he deigned to come to office. Other union leaders would also behave in more or less the same way. Even if they were present, they would not mark attendance. Some union leaders expected the registers to be brought to them by peons to record their signatures rather than signing them in the officers' chambers where the registers were kept.

I found the practice not only highly objectionable but also the primary reason for indiscipline in the directorate. I asked officers to put a cross against absentees' names if they did not report by 10.30 a.m., as was the rule. The officers were too afraid to do so.

Thinking that an invisible system would be more powerful, I asked the administration to get one deputy or assistant director to stand at the gate of the directorate and record the time at which the habitually non-compliant employees, including union leaders, came in, went out in between, came back, if they did, and finally left the office for the day.

These officers, including women (there was a good proportion of women officers in the SIPF service) did the needful unobtrusively and produced the list to me at the end of the day. I would issue orders every day for the concerned heads of offices to deduct leave or mark whole day's absence, as the case might be. The officers had to do it as they had written orders.

This practice started making an impact. Employees started reporting on time and the incidence of coming late substantially reduced. After a few days, the officers and employees witnessed a spectacle – the Maha Sangh's president Rajawat (who was obese) getting through the gate, literally running out of breath, to be in on time. The problem of coming late and getting out for long hours almost disappeared.

A systemic overhaul – Switch over to a new A-to-Z system

A careful and comprehensive study of the processing of employees' application for loans and withdrawals from their PF and state insurance accounts (permitted by rules) with the officers of the department (the SIPF department was managed by the officers of the SIPF service recruited along with RAS officers who were generally quite competent and sincere) revealed that the system in vogue required a loan/withdrawal application to move through seven to eight clerks before it was finally approved by the officer.

This system was tailormade for delays, buck-passing and corruption. An application, in the obtaining practices, would get processed on an average in four to five days. Some would get delayed much longer. The absence of any person in the chain would put a stop to the process. The system was ideal for rent-seeking, as anybody in the chain could sit over an application or raise an objection and send it back. The sordid state of records provided readymade excuses to return the application to the office of the employee concerned to provide certificates of deductions that might be spread over tens of years. Even peons, who were responsible for fetching the employee record (called the 'bag' in the system) from the record room, would sometimes report the bag missing. If a bribe was paid or the clerk/peon otherwise pleased, the missing bag would be found and the case processed.

The key to repair this state of affairs was to allocate only a limited number of state government employees to one SIPF employee, allow their bags to remain in the custody of such an employee and task that person to complete all the work relating to an application. I was aware that this proposed system was not in line with the classical preference of accountants to adopt the principle of internal check/auto-checking, which required the work of an employee checked by another in the chain, but, in our case, the only way to avoid buck-passing and pinpoint the sole responsibility for approving the application was to adopt the system I had in mind.

The changed system was institutionalized and came to be popularly described as the A-to-Z system. The new system envisaged an application going only to a single clerk who was to process it in a time-bound manner (a couple of hours, not days) and, after getting it vetted from his supervisor, release the pay order the same day. No second day under any circumstance was the rule.

This brought very quick results but created massive consternation among the employee leaders.

The introduction of this system jolted the employee union, as rent-seeking came under existential threat. The unions launched a big agitation. Dharnas began at the entrance of the directorate. When I would enter the directorate, the leaders would get more activated, and the slogan shouting would get shriller.

Union leaders and delegations went to the chief minister and finance secretary, questioning the legality of the A-to-Z system. They taunted the government as well by alleging that the director had usurped and was exercising powers that belonged to the state government.

The finance secretary, Dr Adarsh Kishore, called me to ask why I was changing the well-established system, that too without taking prior permission of the state government. I explained the system and asserted that it was purely an operational matter; no specific guidelines or order from the state government existed on the subject and the director should have the full liberty to undertake such operational changes. I offered to refer the matter to the state government for review on the condition that the implementation of the new system, which had already become fully functional, would not be suspended. Dr Kishore decided to get the new system reviewed at the government level.

Shyam Agarwal, who was special secretary (revenue) in the finance department to whom the directorate of SIPF primarily reported, meticulously scrutinized the changed system, including in meetings convened with the union leaders. He concluded that there was no violation of state government policy and rules and conveyed this to Dr Adarsh Kishore.

After a lot of hemming and hawing, the government finally 'approved' the A-to-Z system, which remained in practice for many years thereafter until computerization of the department, which also I had a chance to usher in as principal secretary of finance department later, replaced it.

Backlog cleared

There were two primary pain points in the matter of arrears of record. One, updating the deductions made from salary bills of lakhs of employees for insurance, PF and other schemes that had not been posted in the scheme ledgers (called broadsheets) for years. There were large gaps in the broadsheets, which in those days were prepared manually. The broadsheets gave aggregate picture and were the base for making entries in individual accounts. Second, as a consequence, the entries in individual accounts, calculation of interest due and making individual accounts up to date was hopelessly out of date.

I initiated a switchover to a computerized system that would pick up the entries directly from treasury bills and help make automated interest calculations. This system would take some time to be implemented. In fact, the contract for the system was finally completed when I returned to the state. The herculean task of completing years of backlog of broadsheets was fast-tracked. Broadsheets for state employees were allocated to the same SIPF employees, assigned the accounts per the A-to-Z system. They were to do it with the help of treasuries and concerned heads of department wherever needed.

Some strong-arm tactics were also used. If employees were not able to complete their backlog in the time assigned, they were served with a chargesheet for a minor penalty under Section 17 of disciplinary rules. I must have issued about 100 chargesheets on this score alone. As Section 17 chargesheets had no rigid rules about holding enquiries and taking elaborate evidence, and there was a reasonable degree of discretion in terms of imposing penalties, the employees who appeared to make a sincere effort were spared while those who showed lack of application were penalized. As these penalties affected their promotions, even though they were called minor penalties (stopping an increment, recorded warning), their impact on employee productivity was substantial which resulted in real good progress.

The officers of the department also rose to the occasion. After many years of finger-pointing they had faced, they were finding purpose and recognition in doing something that brought them credit. Their collective determination saw the entire process through in a record time of 15 months. The entire backlog was cleared. The department started sanctioning loans and withdrawals the same day and retirement dues routinely on the last day of the service of the employee.

The SIPF department was a backwater that no one really gave any attention to. However, the clearance of the backlog and prompt payment of employees' dues brought a lot of positive feedback. We were able to serve the neglected sections of the government servants well through these improvements.

Entrenched unions kept agitating

The employee unions, however, expanded their agitation. They picked up other issues as well. They demanded a meeting with me in the open and not in the confines of the director's room. I agreed and invited their leaders to come to the rostrum – a staircase in the front hall served as a makeshift rostrum.

We had a discussion. I explained the A-to-Z system and other reforms being undertaken to clear the backlog of records. I also spoke about implementation of the government's orders to deliver all dues to employees by the last day of their service life. I spoke of the efforts many of the assembled employees as well and the difference they were making to the well-being of their fellow employees.

The employee leaders did not really have anything substantial to say. One complained that I had tightened the department too much, which was causing undue distress. Another complained that employees were not able to complete their work (A-to-Z and clearance of arrears) during the day and had to take work home. I countered that a little tightening was necessary and that any rope served its purpose best when it was tight. We had created the backlog together in the past and we would have to clean it up, I asserted.

The employee leaders, for obvious reasons, were not satisfied and warned that they would expand their agitation all over the state. The Maha Sangh leaders went to the chief minister again and probably warned of losing the support of employees in the next election 'if corrective step' were not taken. The CM directed them to meet Dr Adarsh Kishore, who agreed to intervene, but did not like getting messages from the chief minister though the union leaders.

Dr Kishore called me a couple of times. I updated him on the situation and how the core function of the department was improving by the day and the backlog was getting cleared. Over some weeks, Dr Kishore got weary of the intrusion into his space by employee leaders who would descend on him at all times with their litany of grievances.

One day, he told me he did not want the union employees to come to the secretariat and disturb him. I politely reminded him that it was I who faced their agitation the most. I was sitting among them in the directorate without any protection whereas only a few employee leaders could enter the secretariat, that too only when permitted. I requested him not to grant any time to the employee leaders if he did not want to be disturbed as I could not guarantee that they would not come to the secretariat.

'It takes one hole for a dam to burst'

The SIPF department had less than 1,500 people spread over 30-odd field offices. About 300–350 officers and employees were at the Jaipur headquarters, with the rest posted in offices in various districts of the state. A good chunk of the staff originated from Jaipur (as originally the department was located in Jaipur while the field offices came into existence much later) and preferred to be posted there.

As was the case in most other departments, this resulted in 'connected' employees remaining in Jaipur – there were four offices in Jaipur: the headquarters, Jaipur City, Jaipur Rural and a newly established office for the general insurance wing. The SIPF department being the citadel of employee unions, many employees posted in the Jaipur offices had a connection with union work or were office-bearers of unions.

I received several representations from employees posted outside to be transferred to Jaipur. Some had families in the city; some had been away for years. It was a fair expectation on their part. Those who were in Jaipur also had their own reasons for staying put, though their case was weaker after having served for a long time in the city. Union employees had a long-standing understanding that their office bearers would not be transferred out. The biggest problem was that the ratio of those wanting to come to Jaipur and those who could be sent out was quite adverse.

It did not appear feasible to do what I did in Chittorgarh to get the patwaris perched on the mountain moved to the plains by exchanging positions. We had to design something new and more acceptable. I came up with a scheme to transfer headquarters employees out of Jaipur for a fixed period of one year and assure to bring them back at the end of it. To make the whole thing credible, the transfer orders to post an employee out of Jaipur mentioned the commitment of re-transfer after a year. This arrangement was more acceptable as a one-year period was much less troublesome for employees as their families could continue to remain in Jaipur. Despite some annoyance, most employees accepted the deal. Those who were coming in were also assured that they could stay for two to five years as another batch of employees would be sent outside after a year without disturbing them. They would go out only when their turn came, and then too for a one-year period. About 30 employees were thus transferred.

As the employees posted out were chosen according to an objective formula (longest stay being the most prominent element), the transfer list included people connected to politicians and other influential persons. Sanwar Lal Jat, a prominent and assertive minister in the government (he later rose to be a union minister), called me to ask for the cancellation of a transfer of an employee. I explained the entire scheme and regretted my inability to disturb it. Clearly unhappy, he then forcefully complained, 'Why can't you make one exception?' I told him that it takes only one hole for a dam to burst. If I made one exception, I would lose all my moral authority, and no one would abide by the scheme that was based on an objective formula and implemented without favour or malice to anyone. Sanwar Mal Jat was not pleased, but he did not get his way.

'Stubborn' in public interest

Dr Adarsh Kishore would have liked some compromise in handling the A-to-Z system and other issues connected with the employee unions, which might have been more politically correct. He possibly had larger considerations in mind. The scheme was implemented without any concession to the unions. Also, in his judgement, one or two exceptions in the matter of transfers would have possibly been a small price to pay for the larger good. These incidents made him form an opinion that I was inflexible.

Manju Mathur, one of two senior-most additional directors of the department, was quite ambitious. The rules of the SIPF service provided that the director would be from the SIPF service; only in the event of no officer being eligible would an IAS officer be posted as director. Manju Mathur, wife of a senior government advocate who became a high court judge after some time, was preparing herself for the role. She had maintained a good relationship with senior officers, including Dr Adarsh Kishore, as well as union leaders. I found her a little superficial. After some time, I transferred her from the position of additional director (insurance), which was in the headquarters, to additional director (general insurance), which was based in another building. Though the post was equivalent, she was piqued to move away from the headquarters and interpreted it as a deliberate attempt to cut her down to size. Though she joined her new appointment, she reached out to Dr Kishore, complaining about being badly treated. When I found her work less than outstanding and pressed her to do a better job at general insurance, she complained again. Dr Kishore was convinced that I did not handle the issue well.

Another officer in the department, Ragini Saxena, who was senior accounts officer, had an excessively rule-bound approach in financial matters and tended to raise objection to most proposals, including of reforms. There was nothing wrong with raising objections as such. I would respond to all her points on file and then, with reason, overrule her whenever I found her objections either not in accordance with the rules or not in the interest of the department. Under the executive instructions of the government, the accounts head had the authority to refer to the state government any matter they felt was being decided in a manner not in accordance with the rules. She referred a few matters to Dr Adarsh Kishore exercising her authority. When he sought my comments on these, I would respond, usually countering points raised by her providing full fact-base and the position of rules.

Many such issues accumulated on Dr Adarsh Kishore's table. Then, he wrote me a semi-official letter to me asking me to reconsider some of my decisions, calling me 'stubborn'. I promptly and politely responded, accepting it as a compliment and reiterated my resolve that it was necessary, in my judgement, to be stubborn in the larger public interest and that I would continue to do so.

Dr Adarsh Kishore had a larger-than-life image in Rajasthan. Having been a powerful secretary to Chief Minister Shiv Charan Mathur and having become finance secretary at a young age, he was considered a central figure in the Rajasthan cadre. Dr Kishore did not pursue the matter thereafter. He also had a large heart. He gave me an outstanding ACR.

I got opportunity to work with him later in my career as well, as director in the DEA when he was additional secretary in the fund-bank (the division in the DEA that handled matters related to International Monetary Fund [the fund] and World Bank [the bank]), and as a joint secretary in the Department of Expenditure when he was posted first an officer on special duty (OSD) and later became secretary, Expenditure. I believe he always respected my judgement and had full faith in my fairness and firmness.

'It is easier to get concessions from officers who get angry'

Employee leaders of the directorate would seek time to discuss their 'grievances' at the drop of a hat. I would invariably give them time. I had no shortage of it. The first few meetings were reasonably cordial. I would discuss each of their grievances comprehensively and get the officers concerned to suggest ways to sort them out.

Many grievances had their roots in the hopeless state of records and the divided responsibility between the treasuries that made the deductions and payments. I would engage with the employee leaders, whom I would refer to, tongue in cheek, as the doyens and seniors of the system, to diagnose the root causes of their grievances and ways to set the house in order.

I have a smiling face and an inquisitive mind. I found that the employee leaders were good at agitation and mobilization but not particularly good at doing a root-cause analysis and finding long-term sustainable solutions. These discussions would often expose their lack of understanding of the rules and processes. Slowly, the impression formed among the employees' leadership that they ended up exposing themselves and 'losing the deal' in these meetings. They reduced their requests for meetings and unfortunately decided to use their agitational approach.

Their agitational approach also did not yield much results either. They reached out to Uday Singh Rathore, one of the tallest employee leaders of Rajasthan, who had interacted with me in the agriculture department as well and later became a member of the Rajasthan Legislative Assembly. He visited me once, leading a delegation of leaders of SIPF employees. After the meeting, he stayed back.

He told me that he had dealt with several IAS officers, including those at the highest levels in the state. It was his life's lesson, he told me, that he, as a union leader, could get better concessions from officers who got angry in meetings and lost their tempers. His parting shot was that the employees would not get much from me as I would never lose my cool and always had a smiling face.

His words of wisdom only strengthened my belief in the approach that until then I was probably adopting only subconsciously.

Farewell with a garland of shoes

After serving in the SIPF department for about 20 months and completing its streamlining and backlog, I was transferred to the education department in the secretariat as special secretary in April 1997.

The employees' unions were never at ease during my tenure in the department. They felt marginalized and irrelevant and resorted to agitational tactics quite a few times. Most of these agitations did not risk my personal safety. I had the confidence that they would never gather the courage to cause any physical harm to me. However, on a couple of occasions, they came close to doing so. In one agitation, when I reached the office, about 50 of them had gathered at the entrance gate. As I started walking towards my room, some of them tried to push me from behind. However, when I stood firm and looked back, they withdrew. On another occasion, they gheraoed me in my office for about three hours, not allowing me to get out. I had to call the police on that occasion. After three hours of hard negotiations, the gherao was lifted. On another occasion, they tried to disrupt the Independence Day flag-hoisting function in the directorate. I had to lodge an FIR, including a charge for disrespecting the national flag.

They had concluded that they would not be able to get their way as long as I was there. My transfer brought them major relief and probably joy. In their high, some of the leaders planned to give me a send-off by garlanding me with footwear as a farewell. The departmental officers got highly concerned by this. They tried to dissuade them but failed. I was not aware of these plans. When the officers failed to convince the union leaders to abandon their plans, they came to me and requested me to leave that day from a side gate.

I refused to do so. After handing over my charge to the additional director, Administration, I walked out of my room to get to the car. The employees saw me confidently walking out with a smile on my face. They knew I would not buckle under any kind of pressure. As I looked at their faces with confidence, the crowd started melting away. No one dared to come near me. I sat inside the car. As the driver switched on the engine, some men pushed the car from behind. This was all that they could muster the courage to do.

12

Conducting Board Exams Without Teachers

The education department employed a few lakhs of teachers, constituting 40 per cent of total state government employees, and was allocated about 30 per cent of the state budget, almost 95 per cent of which was spent on teachers' salaries. There was a single education department until the early 1990s. Later, a higher and technical education department was established with a separate minister and a secretary, while the education secretary handled primary, elementary, secondary and Sanskrit education. There used to be one position of special secretary, Education, under the unified education department, focused on aided educational institutions (schools and colleges). After the division, too, the special secretary served both departments.

I joined as special secretary, Education, in April 1997. It was my first secretariat posting. From 1985 to 1997, I had always been the chief executive of an office, department or organization. In the secretariat, an officer's decision-making authority is formally limited to what is assigned to him in the rules of business approved by the minister in charge. There is, of course, considerable enhancement or diminution of authority depending on the priorities of the minister and secretary, and how much they want to use an officer for the department's work.

With two departments, there were two ministers. Education Minister Gulab Chand Kataria was a former schoolteacher. A well-meaning man, Kataria was hugely interested in bringing order to the messy world of school education. Kataria later held many other important ministerial positions and served as the governor of Assam and Punjab. Higher and Technical Education Minister Lalit Kishore Chaturvedi was far more vocal. With his strong roots in the Rashtriya

Swayamsevak Sangh (RSS) system, he was one of the most influential ministers in the Bhairon Singh Shekhawat government. Kataria considered Lalit Kishore as his *bada bhai* – elder brother.

Priyadarshi Thakur was secretary, Education, and Anil Vaish was secretary, Higher and Technical Education. Both the secretaries decided to route most of the files of their departments, not limited to aided institutions, through me, partly out of tradition and partly because I could help them with the objective and thorough examination of issues.

Rajasthan State Textbook Board printed textbooks for schools. A few years back, the government had decided to provide all textbooks free of cost to all students in Classes 1–8. The textbook board had its hands full. Priyadarshi Thakur, in line with the general practice, decided to hand over the responsibility of executive chairman of the board to me. The post of director, Sanskrit Education, was also lying vacant for some time, which I was also entrusted with.

The directorate of school education was the largest field organization of the government with about 2 lakh teachers and other employees on its roll. Bonu Shekhar, an idealistic IAS officer, headed the department. The director, though, lived a miserable existence with no respite as thousands of teachers chased him for transfers everywhere he went. Transfer of teachers was the biggest issue in the department it seemed; imparting education was almost a by-product.

A minister refuses to make transfers

While there was a well-laid-out transfer policy in the education department, a large chunk of teachers, coming from Jaipur, Ajmer, Alwar and Bharatpur districts, brought immense pressure on the education minister and chief minister to post them to Jaipur.

All ministers and other influential people would write scores of letters to the education minister recommending, and often demanding, transfers in deviation from the transfer policy. The chief minister's office also recommended many transfers.

The pressure to accommodate as many of these transfers as possible would reach a crescendo around July–August. It was the case in 1997 as well. Gulab Chand Kataria was, however, made of sterner stuff. He had stated very categorically in June itself that no government order would be issued from the secretariat ordering such transfers. It was quite unusual for a politician to make such a statement. I developed huge respect for him. Priyadarshi Thakur had a softer heart but also felt hugely relieved at such a principled stand taken by the minister.

No government order was issued for transferring in the months of June, July and August 1997. The big bad world of the education department found this unbelievable. While most teachers and their well-wishers accepted that 1997 would be an unprecedented year, the most powerful still did not relent.

Finally, the chief minister's office cast the first stone – some transfers would have to be done, Priyadarshi Thakur was told. The state assembly elections were due in 1998. When told by Thakur that the CM wanted some transfers to be made, Kataria refused to cave in for some days but finally agreed to make only a few exceptions.

I came to know when Priyadarshi Thakur told me, in case I also had to make any pressing recommendation for transfer. Thakur compiled a list of the 100 most pressing cases. Kataria did not include anyone from his side. I made two recommendations which I thought were quite deserving, though I was quite unhappy to see the big principle and policy being violated.

The sole government order with 100 teachers' transfers was issued in September 1997. It was still extraordinary in the annals of Rajasthan. Gulab Chand Kataria was truly an exceptional minister.

Para teachers to substitute absent teachers

Abhimanyu Singh, a highly regarded officer of the Rajasthan cadre who had spent years in the education department in the state and at the centre, was joint secretary in the Ministry of Human Resource Development, Government of India. He was also in charge of a Rajasthan-centric programme called Shiksha Karmi. He organized a foreign trip to learn and exchange best elementary education practices, which took Kataria and me to Zimbabwe and Chile.

The Shiksha Karmi programme was designed for primary school students in remote, tribal and desert areas of Rajasthan, where no qualified teachers posted there stayed. To impart education to children in such schools, the programme selected a local secondary-educated boy or girl, trained them so they were good enough to teach, and appointed them with a decent enough honorarium, though a fraction of regular teacher's salary. These 'para-teachers' were called Shiksha Karmis and were assessed to be doing a reasonably decent job.

When a presentation was made to administrators and teachers in Zimbabwe, not a very advanced country in terms of education attainment, on the Shiksha

Karmi scheme, the audience of teachers and administrators looked bewildered. Soon enough, one educational administrator asked, 'What, the qualified teachers you appoint do not stay in school and teach? And instead of disciplining such errant teachers, you appoint para-teachers to run classes?'

The question, in the class of the aphorism 'the king is naked', exposed the hollowness of the entire edifice of government-funded education. Teachers who are appointed and paid to teach do not teach, and the government runs alternative development programmes to substitute them with para-teachers who are neither fully qualified nor fully paid!

Government schools are the costliest schools

Government schools and colleges charged a nominal fee from students. I paid ₹14 fee per quarter when I attended Government College, Ajmer. Twenty years on, the college fees were the same.

The government might not charge from students, but a school cannot be run without paying salaries to teachers and other staff, constructing and maintaining buildings and other infrastructural facilities, and incurring numerous other expenditures. The government in fact ends up footing this entire bill.

In addition to government schools, there were private schools, which charged full fees from students to cover all their expenditure. Then there were charitable schools that charged some fees but met most of their costs from government aid. These were termed private-aided schools.

While the government provided 'free' education in government schools, parents flocked to English-medium private schools even in rural areas. Our informal surveys in rural areas revealed that parents paid as much as ₹100 per month per child for private schools that had no facilities worth the name and employed teachers at a fraction of the salaries the government paid its schoolteachers. Yet, the demand for these 'English' schools was so high. An estimate suggested that about 30 per cent of students in rural areas were getting educated in these unrecognized private schools at that time (per centage has risen much higher by now). It was also reported that many students simultaneously enrolled in government schools to get free textbooks and midday meals.

I thought we should revise the fee structure. Kataria was open to the idea. Priyadarshi Thakur, however, had a different view. He felt the difference was too large to bridge even if the fees were raised two to five times. In his judgement, which also appeared to make sense, such an increase would not contribute much to reduce the burden of the government but would invite a major backlash from the public. In his inimitable style (he is an urdu poet as well), he said, '*Na Khuda hi mila na visal-e-sanam. Na idhar ke hue na udher ke hue ham*.' (I did not get God, nor did I get the beloved. I was left neither here nor there.) The effort was abandoned.

There was and still is a widespread belief that government schools provided free education whereas private schools fleeced parents. There was obviously an evident difference between the fees parents paid at private schools like SMS School (the most elite school in Jaipur at the time) and the negligible fees they paid at government schools. However, there was only a little understanding of what it cost the government to teach a student in a government school.

To gain clarity, I collected data relating to the overall cost of elementary education in Rajasthan in different districts and the number of students that passed out of Class 8 in both government and private schools. I also collected data on the fees payable by a student from Class 1 to 8 in private schools, including in the costliest schools of Jaipur and other major district headquarters of Rajasthan. With the help of this data, the cost of educating a student in all eight classes of elementary school was computed for private schools. The state budget for elementary students was divided by the number of students passing Class 8 to calculate the cost per student of passing eight classes in government schools. The conclusions were startling.

To build awareness, show a mirror to government teachers and start a debate, I published the findings in a signed article in the education department's official magazine, *Shivira*, and sought feedback and comments.

The per-student cost of education in government schools, until Class 8, came to be ₹1 lakh on an average. In district headquarters like Jaipur and Jodhpur, the cost worked out to be roughly twice that amount as the number of students passing Class 8 from government schools in these places was much lower, whereas the strength of teachers was disproportionately higher. The cost of education at SMS School in Jaipur, by comparison, was only around ₹75,000 per student (the fees of all eight classes added). There was no district in Rajasthan where the cost of educating a student in government school till Class 8 was lower than ₹75,000.

My conclusion was that government school education anywhere in Rajasthan was costlier than the most elite school in Jaipur. As the writeup was based on factual numbers, there was not much argument raised by anyone. The NGOs also did not dispute this as they were aware that the cost in the government system goes up further for schools that received substantial grant support under government programmes.

Education in government schools was not, and still is not, a free lunch. The cost of government education is higher and paid by taxpayers collectively instead of individual parents.

'Have your children studied in Hindi-medium schools?'

Government schools in Rajasthan introduced English-language education only from Class 6, i.e., at the elementary school stage. As English was not taught as a language in the first five years of school education, there was no question of any textbooks being available in English.

Private schools were mushrooming, including in rural areas, which taught English from Class 1. Parents preferred schools teaching English and using English as the medium of instruction. While urban areas had many private English-medium schools, government schools there did not teach English as a language. As a result, government schools in urban areas did not have any students except from poor families. The government had a list of schools located in the heart of major cities like Jaipur and Jodhpur, which only had a few students. In a couple of schools, there were more teachers than students. The introduction of English-language education and English-medium education was an idea whose time had come.

Education Minister Kataria wanted the introduction of English education in government schools. I carried out the necessary groundwork. We put together a team of teachers to write English-language books for each of the five classes and prepare some subject books in English. This preparatory work proceeded without any fanfare, efficiently and in a time-bound manner.

The introduction of English education in government schools, however, was a decision that had to be made at the cabinet level. We prepared the cabinet note. Priyadarshi Thakur, a polyglot, enthusiastically pursued the proposal. Kataria wholeheartedly supported it and Chief Minister Shekhawat approved the note for discussion in the cabinet.

The proposal disturbed the conventional mindset and comfort level of many cabinet members, most of whom were backward looking. Ironically, the fiercest opposition came from Lalit Kishore Chaturvedi, the most educated member in the cabinet. He had ideological objections. He launched a fusillade. How could India teach her young students in English and make them acquire the *ghulam manovriti* (captive mindset) seeded by Macaulay? He was quite vociferous and taunted Gulab Chand Kataria a few times.

We were sitting on back benches in the cabinet room and beginning to lose hope about the proposal going through. Kataria tried to offer a defence and resistance, but Lalit Kishore Chaturvedi shot him down. Some other ministers also sided with Chaturvedi. Almost no one spoke in the proposal's favour.

When he had heard it all, Shekhawat asked Chaturvedi, in his inimitable light-hearted style, about the type of school his children went to. Did they study in Hindi-medium schools? This made Chaturvedi squirm in his chair. Shekhawat was rightly targeting the moral duplicity of people like Chaturvedi. He did not respond.

The proposal to introduce English education was approved by the cabinet. Our motivated teachers and experts at Rajasthan State Textbook Board burnt the midnight oil and prepared all the requisite textbooks on time. Government schools started teaching English from 1998. The textbook board also began providing primary school subject textbooks in English for use in private schools and some government English-medium schools.

The government actually delivered books to each student

There were about 200 panchayat samitis and 9,200 panchayats in Rajasthan with about 10 lakh students in elementary schools. When the government decided to provide free textbooks to all students, the textbook board began delivering the sets of books at the panchayat samitis in a designated warehouse or at the secondary/senior secondary school. The books were supposed to be carried to respective schools by schoolteachers, which caused a lot of hassle, and in most cases, resulted in the distribution of books to students many weeks and months late.

When the proposals for calling tenders to hire trucks to take the books to the panchayat samiti headquarters came to me for approval, I asked G.K. Tiwari, secretary of the board, why the books could not be delivered directly by the textbook board trucks to all the 9,200 schools, which would only require the books to do a single trip to the final destination. Tiwari came up with a detailed note on file to the effect that it would be impractical and cost would go up at least by 50 per cent.

The commitment of the government was to deliver free textbooks to students, which meant reimbursement of full cost of delivering the textbooks right to their destination, the school.

I wrote out a comprehensive note rebutting every argument Tiwari advanced and ordered that the textbooks be delivered by the board right to the schools, with the board recovering full transportation cost from government. Tiwari carried out the order quite efficiently. From that year, 1997, textbooks started getting delivered to students in their schools.

With the full support of Kataria, we carried out a major revamping of the education department's administrative structure as well.

To give right impetus to elementary education and to allow the director, Eduation, to focus on quality education in secondary schools, a new Department of Elementary School Education was created. Again, to eliminate the artificial distinction between boys' and girls' schools being managed by two separate management structure, the two vertical structures were combined to create a single administration structure.

These two reforms transformed the managerial structure of education department for ever.

Lok Jumbish or DPEP?

Anil Bordia, an IAS officer of the Rajasthan cadre who had been secretary, Education, in the Government of India, was considered the czar of education throughout India, particularly in Rajasthan. He had experimented with and fathered many educational initiatives. Anil Bordia came from Udaipur and treated Rajasthan as his laboratory. He is responsible for starting the Shiksha Karmi programme as well.

In 1992, after his retirement, he initiated a mega programme called Lok Jumbish in Rajasthan with the help of the Government of India, the Rajasthan government and the Swedish International Development Cooperation Agency (SIDA). The programme – *lok* meaning people in Hindi and *jumbish* meaning movement in Urdu – supervised by a state-level NGO, Lok Jumbish Parishad, which Bordia headed, had created an alternative education delivery structure in many blocks of Rajasthan. This brought in many education innovations: village mapping by motivators; participation of parents in running schools; and formation of school construction committees and management structures at cluster (a group of 20–25 villages), block and district levels. Compared to government schools, Lok Jumbish had large resources. True to its spirit, it also created a lot of awareness, improved identification of education-deprived segments and delivered education to marginalized people. There was, however, an undercurrent of resentment, if not hostility, among mainstream schoolteachers and government managerial cadres about the resources the Lok Jumbish programme got from the government and international funding agencies.

About a year before I joined the education department, the Government of India had launched a mega elementary school education programme called the District Primary Education Programme (DPEP), which was partly funded by the World Bank. The DPEP adopted an almost similar approach as Lok Jumbish except that it was more integrated with the education systems of the states and offered resources for educational improvement on par with Lok Jumbish. The Government of India had begun promoting the DPEP and was planning to close Lok Jumbish or merge it with the DPEP.

The central government wrote to the Rajasthan government as well to adopt the DPEP in the state. However, Anil Bordia was opposed to it tooth and nail. He loved his own creation, Lok Jumbish, too much. Abhimanyu Singh, who represented the Government of India in the Lok Jumbish Parishad, also felt that Rajasthan should stick to Lok Jumbish.

The matter landed on my desk. I attended a meeting of Lok Jumbish Parishad besides reading up on the programme and how it was doing. I also studied its financial implications for Rajasthan. P.R. Dasgupta, who was the education secretary in the Government of India at that time, called a meeting of the DPEP. I attended on behalf of the state. I thoroughly studied the DPEP document and its implications for Rajasthan as well.

After analysing the educational and financial implications of the two competing programmes, I proposed a split of districts: 13 for the DPEP and 12 for Lok Jumbish. The DPEP was proposed for the districts where Lok Jumbish either had no block or had been started in only one or two blocks. I also recommended that over the years, Lok Jumbish be folded into the DPEP.

Anil Bordia was mightily displeased, though Kataria and Thakur were convinced of the merit of my proposal. Several rounds of meetings took place, including in the finance department and at higher levels. My proposal was finally approved and the DPEP made its entry in the state in 1998. Gradually, Lok Jumbish kept ceding ground, and sometime around 2003–04, it was terminated.

Teachers went on a strike

Teachers of grade III taught primary classes up to Class 5 in those days. They also taught elementary school classes, although a complement of subject teachers – teachers of grade II – did bulk of teaching at the elementary education stage, i.e., between Classes 6 and 8. Teachers of grade III, including in panchayati raj schools, constituted about 65 per cent of the total strength of teachers. They typically received/moved over to three pay scales during their service life. Their entry scale was lower than that of equivalent teachers in the central government setup, but under the scheme of timebound scale promotion in Rajasthan (popularly known as the 9-18-27 scheme), they got a much higher pay upon the completion of nine years' service than what central government teachers got upon in-situ promotions after nine years, under the central scheme.

Grade III teachers had a grievance about their initial pay scale. They wanted their entry scale to be made on par with the central government grade III-equivalent teachers. While the demand was long-standing, it became more strident near election time, which were due in 1998. The teachers' associations, themselves quite powerful on account of their numbers, were joined by the employees' Maha Sangh as well. The chief minister's office became the biggest pressure point closer to the elections as, going by precedent, CMs were seen as softer targets during such times.

We examined the demand. As suspected, the details of the central government setup pay structure were conveniently hidden by employees' unions. The education department was also more tuned to examine the demands teachers' demand with reference to employees of the state government in other cadres. They had not obtained details about the full structure of the central government teachers' pay scale and had made no comparative lifetime analysis.

I obtained the entire structure of pay scales for primary school teachers in the central government. My examination revealed the advantage state government teachers had at the next stage of in-situ upgradation under the 9-18-27 scheme.

After doing the calculations, we furnished our assessment of the union's demand and the likely financial impact, and sent our recommended response to the CM's office. Our offer was simple: Either take the central package in full or maintain status quo. Taking the central package would have benefitted about 75 per cent of the grade III teachers straightaway, but it would have also meant reducing the existing pay packages of about 25 per cent of the teachers who had moved up under the 9-18-27 scheme. It was a choice they could neither easily accept nor reject.

In the face of plain facts, CM's office could not accept teachers' demand. The teachers decided to show their might and went on strike.

Conducting board exams without teachers

The teachers had another ace up their sleeve. The examinations for secondary and senior secondary classes, already delayed during the year, were to be conducted in August–September.

Some rounds of negotiations took place. In exasperation at their inability to counter our arguments to move the needle, the teachers decided to boycott examination duties. Teachers conduct invigilation in thousands of schools where secondary examinations are held, besides managing work relating to receiving examination papers in sealed covers, storing them securely, opening the earmarked packets for the day, distributing papers and answer sheets, collecting these and securely sending them to the board and other designated places for evaluation. The task is mammoth and specialized, and requires experienced handling.

The call for the boycott of board examinations created uncertainties in the mind of Priyadarshi Thakur. However, Kataria was not willing to cave in. I made some quick calculations. The non-teaching staff was not on strike. Likewise, the school principals were also not on strike. I proposed, after some calculation, that we hold the examinations without teachers. The plan envisaged the use of police stations to keep papers securely and the ministerial and class IV staff of the state government to conduct invigilation and other duties. Tehsildars, block development officers, and other tehsil- and district-level officers would manage the entire affair.

After some rounds of discussions, the proposal was approved by Thakur and Kataria. I was made in-charge of conducting the operation. We mobilized the district administration. Quite unusually for the education department, we used wireless communication, along the lines of law-and-order management, to pass on instructions to districts and education authorities. A couple of times every day, the long messages that I drafted were transmitted through the wireless network.

The teachers initially laughed at our decision. They were cocksure that the department would never be able to hold examinations without them. We suspected there might be some sabotage from them. To tackle this, we conducted a kind of stocktaking exercise in towns and villages and spoke to parents. In the process we discovered a surprisingly low level of support and respect for teachers. The teaching community had lost much of the respect of people on account of absenteeism, lack of professionalism and falling learning standards of their wards. Additionally, many years of extraordinary enhancements of their pay scales vis-à-vis other government servants had made teachers the most pampered lot in villages and small towns. We heard stories of teachers having turned into moneylenders. We also heard of teachers deputing someone else to teach classes at a fraction of their fat pay, while they employed themselves elsewhere, earning double income. Parents clearly wanted the examinations to be held. There was an unequivocal message of assurance from the villagers that they supported the government's resolve to hold the examinations and that they would not allow, under any circumstance, the teachers to disrupt them.

While teachers watched from the sidelines, villagers stood guard at the gates of schools and ensured there was no glitch. The first two examinations were held without any disruption. This bolstered the confidence of the government and directorate team that the next 15 days would also pass without any serious interruption. The education department's resolve to stick to its stand in negotiations was further strengthened.

Some miscreants among the teachers did try to sabotage the examination process, which, after five days, seemed to have settled into a well-oiled routine. On one occasion, somebody succeeded in getting hold of a question paper three days before the exam and leaked it in the newspapers. The teachers' union felt that the government would surrender and accept their demand. We had other ideas.

The board approved three sets of examination papers for one subject paper. We quickly got hold of the alternative paper, got it printed and delivered to all the schools before the scheduled day of the exam. On the day of the leak, we issued a denial that the paper had been leaked. When the paper in the examination turned out to be different from the paper the teachers had leaked, their credibility suffered further dent. This was on the eighth or ninth day of the examinations.

After this leaking incident, teachers started losing confidence in their leaders. Many of them started reporting to back to work. We did not use their services in the examinations, though they were allowed to mark their attendance. The union also seemed to be weakening. They attempted another paper leak; this time, they succeeded in doing it the day before the examination. We accepted there was a leak and rescheduled that examination.

Despite some hiccups, the education department pulled off a near-impossible feat of conducting secondary and senior secondary examinations without the participation of teachers.

Shekhawat chuckles at Arora's expense

Sunil Arora, secretary to the chief minister, believed it was in Shekhawat's political interest to keep the teachers on his side even at the cost of the state's financial soundness or at the risk of acting unfairly.

Right from the beginning of the teachers' agitation, Arora was in favour of accepting their demand as it would have earned the gratitude and loyalty (actually, meaning votes) of over 2 lakh teachers. When the charter of demand was initially received, he had seized upon the contention that the starting pay of grade III teachers in Rajasthan was lower than the pay of equivalent teachers in the central government setup. For him, this was adequate reason to accept the demand. The finance department, normally quite stingy in accepting pay revisions, had also accepted the fact of the pay scale of grade III teachers being lower in Rajasthan, though in its submission it had disagreed with the acceptance of the demand, citing the state's weak financial position.

As mentioned above, we carried out a thorough examination and proposed that the demands of teachers be accepted as a package on the principle of pay parity with the central government at all stages of service life, bringing out better pay scales of grade III teachers of Rajasthan after nine years of service. Arora still advised Shekhawat to only accept the initial pay scale demand without revising downward the pay scale given to teachers at 9-18-27 year revision.

Shekhawat waited and watched to see if the department succeeded in conducting the examinations without the teachers. Possibly, he knew that the teachers had lost much of their respect and clout at the ground level and parents wanted the examinations to be held.

On the tenth day of the agitation, signals started coming from the agitating teachers that they wanted to resume negotiations. They reached out to Sunil Arora again to broker an honourable settlement. We played hardball. After two more days of negotiations, the teachers finally conceded. They agreed to not press for the revision of pay scale of grade III teachers and to study the central teachers' pay pattern more thoroughly; they also agreed to the appointment of a committee that would study their demands.

When this 'honourable settlement' was signed, Shekhawat called Kataria, Thakur and me to his office. Sunil Arora was, of course, present. Shekhawat, addressing us with a smile, said that Sunil Arora had been telling him all along to accept the teachers' demand, but Subhash Garg kept bringing all sorts of analyses to take the sting out of their demands. Sunil Arora usually succeeded in having his way but this time he was bested, he said.

I had no point to prove. I was happy that the correct thing had been done. Sunil Arora probably noted in his mind one more 'favour' to be returned to me appropriately at some other time.

Attending to private schools' just demand as well

The Rajasthan Non-Government Educational Institutions Act, 1989, which became a law in 1992, regulated the recognition, aid and other affairs of private aided and unaided educational institutions.

As special secretary, Education, I was primarily concerned with the administration of this Act. Two major tasks were: administration of the aid budget of the state for aided educational institutions, and policy aspects relating to both aided and unaided educational institutions. The Act covered all kinds of educational institutions and, therefore, the special secretary was common to both school education and higher and technical education departments. Over the years, a tradition had developed that the special secretary, Education, operated virtually like a secretary in such matters, though the files to ministers (for matters that required approval of the minister or cabinet) went through the two respective secretaries.

Two primary conditions for any educational institution to become eligible for aid were: first, it had to be affiliated to a university or a board of secondary education, or recognized by the directorate of education or any competent authority; and second, it had to be established by a society or a trust and managed by a committee as per the composition mandated in the law. Aid from the government was not a matter of right.

The 1989 Act imposed many obligations on aided educational institutions. It also placed some restrictions on unaided ones. Further, there was a bias in the minds of education administrators, which was reflected in their tendency to extend the obligations of aided institutions implicitly to unaided educational institutions as well.

All schools were required to be recognized to be considered eligible for holding state-wide examinations for Class 8. All unaided schools that wanted to move over to the Central Board of Secondary Education (CBSE) required a no-objection letter from the directorate of education. Disciplinary action against any teacher or other employee, even of an unaided school, needed to be approved by the director, Education, or his authorized officer.

The government was not able to make the fine distinction between aided and unaided private schools. There were some flaws in the drafting of the 1989 Act that indicated an implicit bias against private educational institutions.

Gulab Chand Kataria recognized this unfairness and unnecessary interference in the affairs of private unaided institutions. He was completely convinced of the genuineness of the fee structure of most private schools, though there were some black sheep. He would also argue that while the law did not succeed in catching these black sheep, who could easily receive many payments under the table, it made the life of genuine societies and trusts really difficult.

I set about correcting the biases. The task of reviewing every single circular issued by the government was taken up. Wherever there was any obligation that was found to be beyond the literal reach of the 1989 Act, it was removed by withdrawing or modifying it. As a matter of standard operating procedure, circulars applicable to aided institutions were not automatically made applicable to unaided institutions. Circulars for private unaided educational institutions were issued as part of a separate series. The idea was to liberate private unaided educational institutions as much as possible.

For aided schools, we could not carry out the necessary and desirable changes.

Government aid came with many strings attached; some strong enough to make genuine aided institutions hung themselves with those strings. The broad construct for determining aid was to compute the total admissible expenditure based on the norm, as prescribed in the rules of the 1989 Act, and reduce the fees, incomes and donations – and pay 90 per cent of the resultant gap as aid from the government, subject to an overall ceiling based on the number of students. However, when calculating the normative requirements, the method excluded funds required for payment of gratuity, leave encashment and arrears of pay (though institutions were obliged by law pay these). Thus, there was always a structural gap for the aided schools between the funds required and funds available, including government aid.

The aided schools tried to cope with this using different strategies. Some brought in more donations from good Samaritans (but this did not work as it was counted as resources available and deducted from the aid requirement). Many did not pay teachers and other staff what was formally required to be paid to them (this would allow them to carry an unfunded gap in the accounts). Many did not pay their teachers and other staff gratuity, leave encashment and arrears as the government did not provide aid against these items of expenditure. All these cases ended up in the Rajasthan Non-Government Educational Tribunal (set up under the Act) and in courts. Invariably, the judgment went against the institution and the government, and was in favour of the teachers and staff who had been affected. The government would always take the view that the institutions pay from their own resources, which were just not there. Often, contempt proceedings would be started against the education secretary as well. When there was no escape, the government would pay in those specific cases. The system worked on the principle of judgement *in personam*, not *in rem* (against the person, not applicable to all such cases automatically), which provided relief to the government but worked against the public interest.

The situation simply could not be improved as it stood. The only way was to amend the law and make these items eligible for aid as well, or disengage aided institutions from these liabilities, as in the case of private educational institutions. Kataria and Thakur recognized the problem. I drafted the amending law, but the government did not muster the courage to take it to its logical end.

The wound kept festering. After a few years, the government decided to bite the bullet but in a different way, which ended up costing it much more. Almost 90 per cent of aided institutions in the state were taken over by the government with full liability for salaries, allowances and retirement benefits for teachers and staff. The remaining 10 per cent institutions converted into purely private institutions.

Impractical laws and regulations have a way of coming to bite you in the end.

'We are also educated'

College education in western Rajasthan, especially in the districts of Jhunjhunu, Sikar and Churu, was mostly confined to private colleges set up by charitable institutions. The district of Jhunjhunu had the distinction of producing the largest number of industrialists in India. These industrialists, corporate houses and other charities had set up many colleges where the fee was nominal, and did not receive any aid from the state government either. It so happened that Jhunjhunu, at that time, did not have any government college or government-aided college.

While the cause of college education was admirably served by these charitable educational institutions, there were some constraints emerging in their finances. As teachers' salaries kept rising, the gap in funding required for running the colleges increased, forcing some of the otherwise rich backers of these institutions to feel the heat of maintaining them.

Hari Shankar Bhabhra, who had served as speaker of the State Assembly for two terms, was deputy chief minister and finance minister in 1998. He had got elected from Ratangarh constituency in Churu district. On being approached by some of these charitable institutions, he decided to accommodate them. Anil Vaish had just been replaced by another senior but not quite well-grounded IAS officer, Harish Nayyer.

On a day when I had gone for a tour, matters moved very swiftly on a file. The file was moved by the higher education department directly to Harish Nayyer (as I was away), proposing the takeover of a private charitable college in Jhunjhunu district to make it a government college. The file was duly approved by Higher Education Minister Lalit Kishore Chaturvedi. It went to the finance department. As the file had the blessings of the finance minister, the department agreed. On its way back from the finance department, it landed on my table. In a day, the proposal to take over a private college by government was approved on file!

The 1989 Act had provisions for the government taking over the management of any recognized educational institution, but that power was to be exercised only if the its managing committee did not perform its duties or failed to manage the institution properly, making a takeover necessary in the public interest. There was no such case made out in the file. It was based on the application by the trust, pleading its inability to meet the financial burden.

The government had also given an assurance in the Assembly that it would not take over any private education institution. If there was financial difficulty, the right course was for the institution to apply for financial aid and the government to support it by providing aid. Instead, Bhabhra had decided to make the government take over the institution in such a swift move.

I felt it was my duty to bring all the relevant facts and the legal position to the notice of the higher education secretary and the finance department. I wrote out a note on the file that had been already approved, proposing that the government reconsider its decision. Harish Nayyer simply signed the file and sent it to the finance department. When it landed in the finance department and was placed before Bhabhra, he was furious. He called Harish Nayyer, who pleaded complete innocence, having joined only a couple of days before.

Bhabhra assembled an inquisition. Both the education ministers, Lalit Kishore Chaturvedi and Gulab Chand Kataria, were in his room. Harish Nayyer was called but not Priyadarshi Thakur. I was called in. Both Bhabhra and Chaturvedi pounced on me. Chaturvedi asked how I could dare to write that note after the deputy chief minister and finance minister had approved the matter. Bhabhra tried to show off his knowledge of rules and procedures and caustically commented, 'We are also educated.' Kataria tried to intervene and said I was a very fine officer. He was summarily dismissed.

After they had vented their anger, I spoke. Without expressing any regret for my action, I stated that it was my duty to put the matter for reconsideration, especially when the relevant facts, factors and legal position had not been brought up on the file. I said that the government could make a speaking order reiterating the decision, which I was duty-bound to carry out even when I believed it was wrong, as I had exercised my right and duty by putting the matter for reconsideration. (A 'speaking order' clearly states the reasons for a decision, ensuring transparency and accountability.) Harish Nayyer sheepishly tried to plead for me. I requested him not to do so.

The meeting was dismissed. Bhabhra asked for my transfer the same day. I was dumped in the University of Rajasthan as a registrar. Priyadarshi Thakur was devastated. Kataria, too, felt very sorry. I took the transfer in my stride as usual and reported for duty as registrar the next day.

13

A University Student's Tragic Suicide

I am a product of Rajasthan University, having graduated in commerce in 1980 from Government College in Ajmer. I had also pursued a three-year graduate programme for an LLB degree spread over some years, finally culminating in 1985.

I was made its registrar.

Unruly university handed over to administrators

The university's affairs had seen massive deterioration in the 1990s, forcing the government to appoint as its vice-chancellor (VC) a retired IAS officer, V.I. Rajagopal, who had earlier served as home secretary overseeing maintenance of the law and order in the state.

The post of registrar was usually held by a university official. Whenever the situation there worsened, the government sometimes posted an IAS officer. The last such officer was Abhimanyu Singh, sometime in the mid-1970s. I was posted more to punish me for my impertinence than to improve the affairs of the university. However, I was determined to do my best to set the house in order.

At that time, the university did not have any college affiliated to it. It was a completely on-campus university. Even colleges located in Jaipur city were affiliated to another university. This campus-only system meant the university's teachers and staff were non-transferrable. The fee structure was the same as government colleges. The university had a very small research programme. There was a big gap in its finances, for which it was dependent on the state government. The management and faculty believed it was their birthright to get the difference in financial receipts and requirements from the state government with no questions asked.

The governance structure was complicated. There was a senate with representatives drawn from MLAs, teachers and other academicians. There was a complete disconnect between the senate's powers and its accountability. Senate meetings tended to be hugely acrimonious. There was also a syndicate to decide academic matters. Neither the senate nor the syndicate had any responsibility to manage the university's expenditures and administrative order.

Timebound promotions had become a matter of right. Teaching hours were limited. Professors were supposed to teach for only 16 hours a week. The university had employed hundreds of teachers without following a due process. There were widespread allegations of favouritism in these appointments, neglect of reservations and other issues.

Professors spent more time in campus politics, agitations and verbal fights than teaching classes. Consequently, students stopped attending classes. Some classrooms had not been opened for months. Student leaders wanted elections, and degrees, without attending classes or learning.

The situation was truly disturbing. There were tensions every day and instances of manhandling and gheraoing of the VC and registrar were not infrequent. Things were so bad that a large contingent of policemen was kept stationed in a nearby building and one of the bigger houses of the university had been converted into an office for the additional SP.

Rajagopal was a very sincere, conscientious and able administrator. However, he was a rank outsider and alone in the badlands of Rajasthan University. He had felt strengthened with my arrival and started tightening the administration somewhat.

A teacher wrote a letter asking for the locks of the classrooms in the Commerce College to be opened so that he could at least go and sit in class, hoping that the students would start coming in. The doors of most classrooms in the Commerce College had not been opened since the academic session began. The teacher was considered a maverick by his colleagues. After consultation with Rajagopal, we opened the doors of the classrooms, and some students started trickling in.

Acting Governor Navrang Lal Tibrewal inspected the university campus. He went around buildings, offices and record rooms. He found filth and dust everywhere. At one place, he lost his cool and told the staff, 'Even a dog cleans the place before it sits anywhere. And here you work with this filth.' This got reported in the newspapers the next day to the utter shame of the university administration.

The university got its water supply from two large overhead tanks. On inspection, I saw these two tanks lacked covers. This was symptomatic of a general lack of sanitation and cleanliness. I organized a self-service campaign to clean up the university campus. We launched it on a weekend. Along with some enthusiastic teachers, staff and students, I undertook the cleaning of the two tanks. There were dead birds inside. After a thorough cleaning, the tanks were given new covers. The general standard of cleanliness and sanitation started looking up.

There was a big mismatch in the finances of the university. Steps were taken to find long-standing solutions to cover the major deficit in the pension fund by selling a part of the building that housed a branch of Rajasthan Bank to the bank. Some improvement did take place, although it was not enough to make a material difference.

Teachers on strike and teaching simultaneously

The university did not require teaching staff to record their attendance anywhere. It was assumed they took all their classes and attended to university matters, unless somebody applied for a leave. The salary payment system processed salary bills without any confirmation of attendance. There were cases where academic staff had gone away for months without any intimation to the university, yet their salaries were paid without fail.

The most bizarre spectacle was when teachers declared a strike, sat on dharnas and participated in agitations or marches, issued press releases with their photographs for being on full strike yet their salaries were drawn with the certificate that they had attended their classes!

A few days after I joined, the teachers had a showdown with the VC. The police had to be called in, which enraged the teachers further. They decided to call a general strike and began a dharna. Photographs of their leaders on strike were published prominently in the newspapers.

When the salary bills came for my approval on 1 September (I joined in August), I asked about the attendance certificates. I was told there was no tradition of recording attendance. When I saw the bills of teachers who were prominently taking part in the strike with the certificates duly recorded that they had given all their classes without any default, I pointed out the grave inconsistency. The officials agreed the certificates were incorrect but pleaded helplessness since they had no record of non-attendance.

I realized that stopping salary bills at that stage would result in further deterioration of the situation. It would also alienate many teachers who regularly attended university and were not participating in the strike. It was also not possible to single out all those teachers who were on strike with the documentation I had.

I, therefore, decided to allow the salary bills to be passed, but with a rider. I asked for a certificate to be taken from all teachers based on self-certification that he/she did not participate in any strike in the month of August and were always available for teaching classes. I further recorded that necessary adjustment in salaries be made in the next month for those teachers who either did not respond or responded by admitting that they were on strike. A letter was written to each teacher on the rolls of the university to state their position within 15 days.

This created a furore. Some teachers responded by writing that they had not participated in the strike. Most huddled with the striking leaders. Madhukar Shyam Chaturvedi, president of the teachers' association, spat fire and directed everyone not to respond. Someone told him that no response meant that the concerned teacher was on strike. After a few days, he came to see me. I told him that teachers could not have their cake and eat it too. If they believed in their cause, they should courageously offer to forgo their salaries for the same and own up that they were on strike.

The teachers decided to pile on more pressure. Tensions escalated.

A student immolates himself

A meeting of the senate was scheduled in the month of October. By this time, the elections to the Assembly had been ordered and the Shekhawat government was acting as a caretaker government, constrained by the restrictions of the model code of conduct. University examinations were running far behind schedule. The students were on edge as a result and were in agitation mode.

Besides other items on the senate meeting agenda was one that sought its approval for the recovery of salaries and allowances paid to teachers who had not confirmed in writing that they were not on strike in the months of August and September. The teachers did not want this item to be approved. They had made all kinds of efforts to get the senate meeting postponed, including going to the High Court to obtain a stay.

The senate met as scheduled. Teachers' representatives, including Madhukar Shyam Chaturvedi, tried to disturb the meeting on some pretexts. Rajagopalan stood firm. After the loss of about two hours, the meeting commenced its business by taking the agenda. At that stage, teachers' representatives walked out of the meeting.

After about an hour or so, there was a loud thumping on the door of the meeting hall. The ACP, a female IPS officer, had come running to inform us that a student had poured kerosene over himself and set himself on fire. The police had initially seen it as a stunt with some teachers casually egging him on. It had gone horribly wrong, and the fire had engulfed the student. Attempts to douse the fire had not succeeded and the student had been rushed to the hospital. All this happened in a space of 10 minutes.

The meeting had to be adjourned. The VC did not rush to the hospital. Instead, he went to his chamber in the university administrative building and wrote his resignation letter. After asking the letter to be delivered to the university chancellor, the governor, the devastated Rajagopalan walked out and went home. I visited the student in hospital. He had more than 80 per cent burns. He was rushed to Delhi by air ambulance for treatment but did not survive.

The teachers succeeded in keeping the agenda item concerning their salary deduction off the table by literally abetting the immolation of an innocent student.

Everything begins going downhill with the new VC

Tibrewal, who had developed a liking for me and had invited Anjali and me for a meal at Raj Bhawan a couple of times, called an urgent meeting on the day of the immolation itself. Besides his secretary, Chief Minister Shekhawat and I were present. He wanted names for a new VC to be suggested immediately, as the university could not be left headless in such a volatile situation. Appointing another IAS officer was ruled out.

I proposed two names: Professor Kanta Ahuja and Professor Ramesh Arora. The CM seemed to agree that these were good options. The meeting was deferred to reconvene the next day. Prof. Arora came to see me. He was an excellent motivational speaker and connected well with his audience. However, I had watched his administrative performance in some meetings, where he did not seem to fare very well. I knew Prof. Ahuja personally and she commanded an excellent reputation as a leading economist of the state. She had handled administrative responsibilities as well, having worked as principal of Maharani College.

Before the meeting reconvened the next day, Governor Tibrewal called me alone to discuss the matter. He said he trusted my judgement and wanted me to suggest categorically which of the two would be a better choice. I suggested Prof. Kanta Ahuja and gave my reasons for doing so. He seemed to agree. He met the chief minister again. By evening, Prof. Ahuja was appointed VC.

When I met Prof. Kanta Ahuja after her selection but before the public announcement, I briefed her about the difficult administrative situation in the university, including the matter of deduction from the salary of teachers for the days they were on strike. She thanked me profusely for supporting her candidature and entirely agreed that disciplinary issues had to be handled with a tough hand.

Over the next two days, after Prof. Ahuja assumed office, the teachers bombarded her with several representations for their demands, one of which was my repatriation to the state government. There was a flurry of activity with hordes of teachers, other staff and students wanting to see her immediately with their demands. In the first couple of meetings, I sat with her and tried to present the factual position when some teachers and other staff tried to present a distorted or incorrect picture to her. Surprisingly, after two or three meetings, she asked me not to bother as the people she was meeting with were 'her own people'.

Soon, the teachers prevailed upon her to press the state government on matters such as pending grants, covering the gap in the pension fund, passing the ordinance for regularizing teachers, completing the process, ignoring the state government's orders, granting promotions to everyone who had completed nine years of service, and many such issues. They also persuaded her to drop the matter of recovering the salary paid for the period when they were on strike.

She asked me to draft letters to the state government on all the above issues and initiate action to make promotions. She also asked me to close the matter of recovering salaries for the strike period. She would not even agree to deduct leave for this period. I realized that everything in terms of bringing some discipline was lost. I refused to comply with her orders though.

Ahuja stops my salary

I decided to see the chief secretary and secretary to the chief minister. Besides briefing the about the actual state of affairs in the university and the disappointing decisions being taken by VC Ahuja, I suggested that the situation had become so ugly that my remaining in the university was unlikely to serve any purpose. I requested that the state government might consider recalling my services.

The chief secretary was sympathetic but said the matter could be addressed only after the elections, which were only a few days away. Sunil Arora, secretary to the CM, seemed to particularly enjoy my plight. At one stage, when the matter of self-immolation of the student was discussed, he said, referring to the risk of violence I faced, that it did not matter if one or two officers got sacrificed in the cause of duty.

Officers had a leave travel concession (LTC) facility once in four years to travel to any part of the country with their family with the fare paid by the government. The year 1998 was the last extended year for which LTC could have been availed for the block of years 1993–97. I decided to avail my LTC. Kanta Ahuja approved the proposal and sent it to the state government with a recommendation, possibly a way of getting me out of the picture. The LTC was approved by the government, our tickets purchased and everything organized for travel in the last week of December.

Within weeks of her taking over, however, my relationship with Prof. Ahuja had deteriorated as she kept granting concessions to teachers and taking steps that, in my opinion, were not in the university's and students' real interest. I tried to reason with her, but she seemed to have concluded that the only way she would survive as VC was to keep the teachers happy and on her side.

So much probably happened that she decided to teach me a lesson instead. Two days before I was to proceed on leave, I received a note from her cancelling my LTC as my services were needed 'to handle administrative matters', including preparing for the student union elections that were many weeks away. She had no power to do so. The LTC was granted by the state government, and the university had no authority to cancel it. She was also aware that if I did not avail the LTC in the last week of December 1998, it would lapse. I was convinced that she had done this under pressure from the teachers' association.

I decided not to comply with her order and wrote a detailed note explaining that LTC had been approved, tickets purchased, stay arrangements made and that 1998 was the last year for me to avail LTC, as well as the fact that the last week of December was mostly a holiday week and there were no urgent administrative requirements till 3 January, when I was scheduled to return. After sending the note to her, I proceeded on leave.

Kanta Ahuja refused to accede to my request. She ordered non-payment of salary to me for the month of December 1998 and no reimbursement for my LTC admissible expenditure.

Ashok Gehlot took charge as chief minister of Rajasthan for the first time on the back of a large majority (153 out of 200). C.K. Mathew took over as his principal secretary. Immediately after my return from leave, I explained the entire matter to him, including the kind of compromises Kanta Ahuja was making.

I was immediately transferred as special secretary for the energy and mines departments. I was also assigned the duty of being the CEO of Rajasthan Energy Development Agency (REDA). I relinquished charge at the university immediately. I did not care to meet Kanta Ahuja and left to join my new positions, two of which were in the secretariat and one at REDA.

As the university had refused to pay my salary for December and the balance of LTC payment (total cost of travel minus advance taken), I moved a case for recovering my dues from the grants paid by the state government every quarter to the university. This was as unusual a proposal as Prof. Ahuja's orders for stopping my salary. It has not been done in living memory in the education department, Department of Personnel and finance department.

C.S. Rajan, who became my boss again upon being appointed energy secretary, supported my proposal. After much back and forth over two months, the government decided to approve my proposal. It deducted an amount exactly equal to my dues from its grant to the university and allowed me to draw the amount. I received my dues.

The leaders of the teachers' association ensured that Kanta Ahuja did not make any deduction from their salaries for the period of their participation in the strike.

Kanta Ahuja could not handle the affairs of the university well despite her attempt to buy peace with the teachers by pandering to their unjust demands. She did not last long. Within a year, she was replaced by Prof. K.L. Kamal.

14

Rajasthan Begins Its Journey on the Renewable Energy Path

The 1990s was a decade of major change in power generation and distribution and marked a shift towards renewable energy. The Ministry of New and Renewable Energy (MNRE) has its roots in the Department of Non-conventional Energy Sources set up in 1992. Along with national organizations, renewable energy development agencies were set up in the states. Rajasthan also set up Rajasthan Energy Development Agency (more commonly known as REDA). The day-to-day affairs of REDA were in the charge of the CEO.

The agency's job was to administer the renewable energy development programmes of the Government of India and the state government in Rajasthan. Its largest programme was installing solar home lighting systems that had a heavy subsidy from the centre and the state. There was also a small solar streetlighting promotion programme.

Rajasthan Energy Development Agency was also the policy and programme adviser for the state on renewable energy. It was responsible for other important renewable energy initiatives in the state. Two such initiatives were especially important in January 1999 when I joined REDA.

First, with the support of the Global Environmental Facility (GEF) and the Government of India, Rajasthan had initiated work on a large (50 MW) solar energy generation plant, which was to be located at Mathania in Jodhpur district. The loan portion for this project was to come from the German KfW Development Bank.

Second, there was an agreement for supply and installation of a 2 MW wind power generation plant in Jaisalmer with Bharat Heavy Electricals Ltd (BHEL). For the implementation of this project, the government had established Rajasthan State Power Corporation Ltd (RSPCL). The CEO of REDA was the managing director of RSPCL as well.

As mentioned previously, I was posted as special secretary in the energy department. C.S. Rajan, secretary of the energy department, was also the chairman of REDA. Many states, including Rajasthan, had signed numerous memorandums of understanding (MoUs) with whoever offered to establish a generation plant during the Shekhawat regime (1993–98). Most had not made any progress. A major task assigned to C.S. Rajan was to review all the MoUs through a committee of ministers, headed by the finance minister. A World Bank team was working with the state from 1994 with the objective of persuading the state to unbundle the vertically integrated RSEB into separate generation, transmission and (a few) distribution companies. Rajasthan had engaged PricewaterhouseCoopers (PwC) to assist the state to prepare the project for the World Bank financing.

My job as special secretary, Energy, was to support Secretary Rajan and handle these important initiatives and other administrative issues connected with the power sector in the state.

My third charge was of special secretary, Mines. There was not much activity in the mines department for both a secretary and a special secretary to be busy. The role of secretary, Mines, allowed me to focus mostly on energy issues.

People willing to pay for solar lights

The solar home lighting programme envisaged supply and installation of a solar module to generate either 11 or 18 W of electricity in the daytime, supply of a battery to store it as chemical energy, which would supply two small lights in two rooms for about four to six hours. The entire system cost about ₹7,200. Rajasthan Energy Development Agency also entered into a maintenance agreement with the supplier agency to maintain the systems for five years. The beneficiaries were supposed to pay only a token amount of ₹30. The Government of India provided the bulk of the subsidy (₹5,400 per system), with the state government footing the rest of the bill.

As the beneficiaries got the systems virtually free of cost, the solar home lighting programme became a kind of welfare programme. Moreover, the notion that tribals and other disadvantaged people deserved to be assisted first had ensured that almost half the 'targets' were in tribal areas. The Government of India allocated a target of roughly 10,000 solar home lighting systems for

Rajasthan. As the beneficiaries paid next to nothing, there was no problem in achieving the target as suppliers were quite happy to dump the systems at the houses of the selected beneficiaries. With solar insolation being weak in tribal areas and the stake of beneficiaries quite insignificant, the lighting systems were reportedly to be grossly under-used or not used. The state was achieving its targets, but the use of solar lighting was not spreading.

During my tours of the state, many people, especially in the rich rural belt of Ganganagar, Hanumangarh, Jodhpur and Jaisalmer, expressed interest in acquiring solar home lighting systems. The well-to-do farmers of these sparsely populated areas that were not connected with grid electricity were quite willing to pay the cost of the system as well.

I proposed upending the implementation of the scheme. I questioned why we should take solar lighting systems to only the poor and difficult areas like the tribal belt first. As our object was to promote solar lighting, it would make much better sense to take it to areas where there was demand for it. I also proposed that the state government withdraw its subsidy from the lighting system and allow REDA to undertake additional installation of solar lights with the money allocated by the state government. In essence, I proposed to sell the solar home lighting systems at their market cost minus the Government of India subsidy and raise the distribution/sales target by 50 per cent in the first year.

After some initial hesitation, Rajan supported the proposal. The reformed scheme was a big hit. We could not only complete 100 per cent of the Government of India target and the additional 50 per cent target the state allowed with its subsidy budget, but, on my persuasion, the Government of India also allocated the unutilized targets of many other states to us in Rajasthan.

People pay for refrigerators and many other durables to improve their quality of life. Lighting brings one of the biggest improvements in living conditions. We also got relatively lower prices for the home lighting systems as volumes went up. People were more than willing to pay for about 30 per cent of the cost of the system (total cost minus Government of India subsidy) for a service they valued.

Mathania project fails to take off

A 50 MW solar power project was envisaged in the early 1990s and was awarded to an American consortium. The project did not make any progress and the contract was cancelled. The project had global recognition, as the GEF had agreed to provide it a grant of $50 million in addition to a project preparation grant of $4 million – at that time, this was the largest sanctioned grant in the world! For Rajasthan as well as India, the Mathania solar power project was a matter of pride. KfW had agreed to provide a soft loan for the project.

When I arrived in January 1999, the project was in disarray, though there was near consensus on a few key issues. Acknowledging that the solar photovoltaic (PV) technology at the time was not quite suitable for large-scale power plants, solar thermal technology was considered more promising. It uses the power of heating from solar insolation. It was also agreed that the plant had to be operational 24 hours as power supply was needed 24/7. Taking all this into account, a broad design had emerged to change the project configuration from a 'solar only' project to an integrated solar combined cycle (ISCC) project that used both solar energy as well as a thermal source such as naphtha to generate power continuously in a combined cycle mode.

All power projects in the country required techno-economic clearance (TEC) from the Central Electricity Authority (CEA), though the licence requirement for setting up power plants had been dispensed with in the early 1990s. Later, TEC was also exempted for power projects awarded on an open competitive bid.

I worked with the KfW team and the project developers on feasibility reports for a 140 MW ISCC project. After approval of the state government, we took it to Ministry of Non-Conventional Energy Sources (MNES), later renamed MNRE, and CEA. After considerable discussion in the CEA meeting, in principle, TEC was granted to the Mathania project.

That was the most advanced stage the project could reach. It is now more than 25 years since then. No bids could be called before I demitted office in May 2000. The papers kept making the rounds between the Rajasthan government, Government of India and CEA in India and KfW and GEF overseas. There were several reservations about the project design. The solar thermal component of 35 MW had problems. Naphtha availability and cost were a problem. Even other plants based on naphtha had started experiencing major problems.

The bids for the Mathania project could not be called until 2015. Thereafter, the project was virtually shelved. In fact, with the rapid development of PV technology and cost of solar power plants based on this technology dropping, it is now more cost-effective to set up solar power plants compared to coal power plants for most locations in India. Today, gigawatt-scale solar power plants are being established in India and many parts of the world.

The Mathania solar power plant represented a wrong technology choice at a time when there was so much uncertainty and too great a cost disadvantage in establishing solar power plants. It is good that it failed to take off.

Rajasthan unbundles electricity board

Political preference for locating high-cost coal-based power plants in Rajasthan, expanding the electricity grid network to every nook and corner irrespective of cost, electricity connections to lakhs of farmers at very low cost without charging the infrastructure cost, and providing electricity to farmers, residents and other preferred groups at zero or very low rates had made the power sector finances go for a toss in the state of Rajasthan as well, as was the case in most other states.

Rajasthan State Electricity Board (RSEB), the integrated power utility in the state, owned all the thermal power generation plants, and the state transmission and distribution network. It supplied electricity to about 40 lakh households and businesses, and was assured a 3 per cent rate of return under the Electricity (Supply) Act. The difference between the statutory rate of return and the actual loss incurred by RSEB was supposed to be paid by the state government as a grant. Instead, the state government used to cover this deficit by providing equity to RSEB instead of grants. This kept the revenue deficits of the state in control, but fiscal deficits expanded. For RSEB, this meant loss of cash every year, forcing it to raise borrowings from banks, issue bonds and use other means as equity was primarily meant for spending on new projects. Rajasthan State Electricity Board's finances, as a consequence, were in terrible shape.

The World Bank, supported by the Government of India, offered to provide concessional loans to states if they adopted a power-sector reforms package. This package aimed to make power-sector utilities financially viable and structurally more independent of the state government. It was built around three key elements. First, unbundling RSEB into a separate generation company that owns and runs the generation plants (with an assured rate of return), a separate transmission company (again financially viable by recovering its cost plus a return through transmission charges), and three distribution companies in Rajasthan organized on a regional basis. Second, establishing an independent state electricity regulatory commission to determine tariffs that would ensure financial sustainability of the electricity companies. Third, instead of covering the deficit as before, the state government would provide upfront budgetary support in case it wanted some consumer segments to receive electricity at tariffs lower than the regular rate determined on the basis of cost of supply.

The reforms were well-conceptualized and structured except that the entire package depended upon well-intentioned implementation by state governments and the disciplining and reorientation of power-sector engineers.

The whole package was, however, not very easily understandable to most politicians, though Chandra Bhan, a well-meaning and educated energy minister, was hugely supportive. Chief Minister Ashok Gehlot was not so sure. Its long-term implications and political fallout were not very apparent to him. He hesitated. Dr Adarsh Kishore also seemed to go along with him initially. However, the team in the power sector – C.S. Rajan (secretary, Energy), M.D. Kaurani (chairman, RSEB), Umesh Kumar (he had joined as member, Finance, in the board) and I – worked incessantly to explain every aspect to everyone who mattered.

Finally, the government agreed to bite the bullet. A law was passed by the Assembly vesting all the RSEB assets in the state government and revesting the assets in three generation, transmission and distribution companies at new fair values. These new power-sector companies could start on a completely clean slate without any losses on their books. Rajasthan became one of the early states in India to unbundle the electricity sector and move to a new structure of business.

After the electricity sector was unbundled, the work on completing the documents package for the World Bank loan got fast-tracked. This loan had been in the preparation phase since 1996. It supported investment in building power-sector assets.

The package actually moved to the Government of India after I had gone to Delhi on deputation. I was assigned the responsibility of the fund-bank division in the DEA. Loans from the World Bank are formally taken by the Government of India. The director handling the concerned sector in DEA headed the team that went to Washington, DC, to negotiate the loan and sign the initial papers.

I had the pleasure of leading the negotiation team, which included C.S. Rajan, Umesh Kumar and an officer from the Ministry of Power. It was a satisfying end to a long process of initiating reforms in a complicated sector.

First steps to make Rajasthan a wind power giant

Wind power generation had taken off in the country in the 1990s, though India had achieved wind power generation capacity of only a couple of thousand megawatts by 1998.

During a visit to Kanyakumari in Tamil Nadu, I was mesmerized to see hundreds of wind power generation mills dotting the skyline. Another visit to Madhya Pradesh showed me that wind power generation was at the take-off stage there as well. Gujarat and Maharashtra were also mentioned as seriously advanced states in wind power generation.

Rajasthan, on the other hand, had made a very cautious beginning. Only a 2 MW wind power-generation project had been sanctioned by the Government of India for the state a few years earlier in 1995. It took more than three years for the project to be awarded.

The Government of India had promoted a renewable financing company, the Indian Renewable Energy Development Agency (IREDA), which provided loans for renewable energy projects. The IREDA was supposed to finance the loan portion of the demonstration wind power plants approved by the Government of India. Rajasthan had approached the IREDA for financing but was rebuffed.

Rajasthan was a seriously power-deficit state. It was investing in establishing hundreds of megawatts of power-generation capacity based on coal, fetched from thousands of kilometres away. Yet, the state government was not very enthusiastic about wind power projects.

Why was Rajasthan not on the wind map when most parts of the country were embracing wind power with gusto?

Enquiries revealed that the MNES, Government of India, had carried out a survey of wind power potential of all the states and divided them in three zones: good, medium and low. Rajasthan was classified as a low wind power-potential zone. The technology available at that time would at best operate at 16 per cent power-generation potential in Rajasthan at that time.

This was seen as a serious handicap. As a result, the state had not developed and approved a wind power-generation policy, there was no master financing agreement with the IREDA, and the matter of renewable power purchase by RSEB was pending.

My visit to Indore, Madhya Pradesh, and the developing wind power generation technologies convinced me that the so-called low wind-power potential zones could generate a lot of wind power, especially in view of the fact that Rajasthan and Gujarat had large lands and unrestricted wind flow to make it happen at much lesser capital cost.

I decided to fast-track the 2 MW power plant in Jaisalmer.

CM inaugurates the first wind power project

As mentioned above, REDA had awarded the contract for a 2 MW wind power-generation plant to BHEL a few months before I joined. The project envisaged installing eight wind power generators of 250 KW each in Jaisalmer, which would supply the grid. The project cost only about ₹10 crore. The Government of India had agreed to a grant of about ₹4 crore. The rest was to be raised as debt, which could be provided by the Rajasthan government or raised from the IREDA. The BHEL engineers were quite keen to complete the project and demonstrate its successful operation. However, progress on ground was slow.

Three matters needed to be sorted out immediately. First, the Rajasthan government had to approve a wind power-generation policy that provided for, among others, land allotment for private-sector wind power plants, purchase of power by RSEB at the rate fixed by the MNRE, and the fiscal support offered by the government. Second, a power purchase agreement had to be signed with RSEB. Third, loan financing for the project had to be tied up.

I quickly drafted the wind power-generation policy of Rajasthan based on the guidelines of the MNES and the policy of Madhya Pradesh. Rajan organized discussions among the stakeholders, most importantly with RSEB. M.D. Kaurani, chairman, RSEB, supported the policy. By March 1999, Rajasthan's first wind power-generation policy, approved by the government, was put in public domain.

The Government of India had mandated promotional electricity tariffs to make renewable power schemes commercially viable taking into consideration capital subsidy. A tariff was fixed for the year 1995 and was to escalate every year by 5 per cent. For 1999, it came to ₹2.75 per unit. Though the power to be generated by wind projects was a drop in the ocean of the power produced and purchased by RSEB, correspondence with the board on this took a long time. A special-purpose vehicle, RSPCL, was formed to take up REDA's commercial projects, such as the wind power project. No power purchase agreement (PPA) had been concluded between RSEB and REDA/RSPCL.

I walked over to see M.D. Kaurani, who had sound business sense. He saw the rationale for an administratively fixed price and virtually miniscule financial implications for RSEB. He agreed and cleared the draft. After the PPA was approved, it was quickly signed between RSEB and RSPCL.

I reached out to the IREDA to finance the loan to structure the project as a commercially viable one (with the Government of India's capital grant support) and free up the state's fiscal resources. A few rounds of discussions followed. Finally, the IREDA agreed to fund the loan portion with a state government guarantee. I was able to convince the state government to provide a guarantee in place of full loan funding. The IREDA financing materialized.

With all policy and other associated clearances and agreements tied up, work on the Jaisalmer project was expedited. By August 1999, BHEL completed the project. Although contractual issues such as imposition of liquidated damage for delayed completion arose, we resolved them taking a pragmatic view of the performance of both parties.

In early October, Chief Minister Ashok Gehlot, accompanied by Energy Minister Chandra Bhan, inaugurated Rajasthan's first wind power-generation plant. Both were enormously happy. I travelled with the CM on the way back to Jaipur, my first trip in the state aircraft. We discussed the renewable power-generation potential of Rajasthan as well as power-sector reforms.

With that first wind-power plant of 2 MW, a small but firm step was taken to bring Rajasthan on the wind power-generation map of India. I organized one more demonstration power plant in the Deogarh area of Banswara district by getting three generators of 750 KW each, the biggest available at the time.

The 2 MW wind power plant generated profits for RSPCL. In due course, RSPCL would establish over 25 MW of wind power-generation capacity on its own. The success of the plant demonstrated that the vast land mass of Jaisalmer offered good potential for the private sector to invest in wind power. In May 2024, Rajasthan had over 5,000 MW of wind power-generation capacity. Jaisalmer district alone boasts a wind power-generation capacity of more than 3,500 MW.

Gold jewellery in a sweets box

One day, Tulsi Tanti of Suzlon, who had significant interest in putting up wind-power generators and establishing wind farms in the country, dropped in at my office. He wanted to know about the third wind power plant REDA was planning in Phalodi in Jodhpur district.

The Phalodi wind-power generating station was only at the planning stage, as there was no promised subsidy support from the MNES for it. I provided Tanti this basic information as I would do to anyone who might be a potential bidder or supplier in REDA's future projects.

When Tulsi Tanti was leaving, he placed a box on my table, which I assumed to be a package of sweets. I expressed my view that any gifts were not acceptable, but he politely insisted. Wishing to avoid a disagreement over what seemed like a small matter, I placed the box on a side table.

Later that evening, when my wife Anjali opened it, we were surprised to find that it did not contain sweets but pieces of gold jewellery. I was taken aback and felt bad by the unexpected contents.

The next day, I asked my personal assistant to connect me to Mr. Tanti. When we spoke, I conveyed my sense of anguish. He responded by saying it was not intended as a bribe, but rather, was a Diwali gift – something he mentioned he had extended as a matter of routine to others as well. I informed him that I could not accept it and asked that he arrange for someone to collect the box. Although he agreed, no one came over the next few days.

I contacted him again and told him that if the item was not collected within two days, I would place it in the donation box at the Birla Temple in Jaipur. This time, appropriate arrangements were made and the item was collected.

Solar power-generation policy follows

In 1999, it was estimated to cost ₹200 crore to establish solar power-generation capacity of 1 MW. In comparison, it cost about ₹3 crore to install 1 MW of thermal power-generation capacity. Even wind power generation cost about ₹4–5 crore per MW, although its capacity utilization was low, at 16–18 per cent. For effective 80 per cent capacity equivalent generation, wind power would cost ₹16–20 crore per MW. Solar power was in a different league altogether.

Solar power-generation technology was at an experimental stage at the time. Many prototypes were being tried. There was immense promise. The cost was also expected to come down as the volumes improved. In 1999, solar power generation on a commercial scale was a big leap of faith. In contrast to its potential in wind power generation, Rajasthan unquestionably had the best solar insolation in the country.

The MNES was promoting the formulation of a solar power-generation policy. While we saw no immediate or near-term prospects of it happening in

Rajasthan, in order to sell the potential of the solar state of India and capitalize on any future opportunities, we decided to go ahead and formulate a solar power-generation policy for the state.

There was not much discussion over the policy I proposed, and a few months after the wind power-generation policy of the state, Rajasthan had its first solar power-generation policy as well. This policy provided for liberal allotment of barren land to establish solar power plants. Later in 2014, when I was principal secretary, Finance, Rajasthan, we conceptualized the notion of solar power generation as agriculture. In agriculture, plants perform photosynthesis using sunlight. The solar power plants harvest sunlight directly into electricity. This did away with the hassle of converting land into non-agricultural land for setting up solar power plants.

Today, Rajasthan is India's leading solar power producer. At the end of December 2024, the state has solar power-generation capacity of over 17,000 MW.

A batchmate does me an unintentional favour

Our IAS batch had become a large one. Ten of us were originally allotted to the Rajasthan cadre. Three more joined by transfer from other state cadres. One of the three, Seema Bahuguna, came to Rajasthan from Jammu and Kashmir, along with her husband Ashish Bahuguna (1978 batch) from the West Bengal cadre. Usually, the entire batch got a higher scale or promotions together. However, in view of our large batch, we got our senior scales (from the entry scale of the IAS to the next scale, which made us eligible to be posted as additional collectors, collectors, deputy secretaries and the like) in 1987 in three instalments. Being the topper of the batch in Rajasthan, I got the senior scale in the first instalment, along with four other batchmates, whereas Seema Bahuguna got it in the last batch (officers who came on transfer from other cadres were given seniority after the last officer originally allotted to the cadre). She was certainly not amused by this staggered promotion policy and her being placed so low in the seniority list.

In 2000, again, after the batch had completed 16 years of service, the government decided to give super time scale (officers used to become eligible for secretary-level postings in the state and joint secretary-level posts) to only three of us. Orders were issued to post the three of us, including me, in the super time scale as members of the Board of Revenue in Ajmer.

Seema Bahuguna decided to make noise this time. She met Finance Secretary Adarsh Kishore, Chief Secretary Indrajeet Khanna as well as the CM, and asked for all the officers of the 1983 batch to be promoted to super time scale together. Her efforts led to the government changing the promotion policy. The government decided to adopt a new policy for the promotion of the 1983 batch to super time scale. Worried about the lack of enthusiasm in the officers to go to Delhi for central deputation, which Chief Secretary Indrajeet Khanna considered highly desirable, the government decided that promotion would be given only to those officers who went to the Centre on deputation. Of course, as per the standard practice, all the officers senior to such an officer in the batch would also be given the scale.

The position in the revenue board was literally a waste of time, as this anachronistic organization existed without any real 'revenue' function with it. None of us three were enthusiastic to serve in the Board of Revenue, except for availing the benefit of super time scale.

My orders, along with the orders for the two other officers, were cancelled. Thanks to Seema, I was saved from going to the Board of Revenue. A few months later, this decision paved my way to go to the centre, which was possibly the biggest turning point of my life in the IAS.

Lok Ayukta pursues a non-issue against me

One local supplier was quite keen to get contracts for at least some of the districts for supply, installation and maintenance of solar home-lighting projects. We had decided to move to an open competitive tender system to award the districts under the programme. The party filed its bid but lost out on both price and quality. It tried to match the price of the best offer we had but that was not allowed as it would have meant putting the party that had offered the best price and quality in the open bid to an unfair disadvantage. This bid and subsequent offers were rejected.

The party filed a complaint alleging favouritism and disregard of the local party preference rules. The allegations were all false and wholly evident as such on the face of the record itself. As was the wont in the state, copies of the complaint were sent to everyone that mattered, including the state government, Government of India and the Lok Ayukta of Rajasthan. Everyone wanted a factual report, which was duly submitted. The Government of India and the state government decided not to take any action and closed the matter. The Lok Ayukta, however, decided to take cognizance of the matter and investigate.

I received a notice from the Lok Ayukta to appear in person and explain the matter after I had moved to the Government of India on deputation. I sent a curt reply, essentially saying everything concerning the tender was available on the file, and I saw no reason to appear personally to appear before him and testify. After a few months, a similar notice came again. I again referred to my earlier response and regretted my inability to appear before the Lok Ayukta. After a year or so, the notice came for the third time. This time, I was a little more abrupt in my response. I stated that I had no defence other than what was available on file and the Lok Ayukta could decide whatever it had to without any statement from me.

The Lok Ayukta, Justice Milap Chand Jain, was probably offended at my insistence on neither appearing before him nor reaching out to him. About three years after I went to Delhi, in 2003, he passed an order. The order found nothing wrong with the award of the tender and rejection of the complainant's tender, which was also explicitly stated in the order. However, the Lok Ayukta found me guilty of 'a conduct unbecoming of a senior officer' in persistently refusing to appear before him despite several opportunities given. The order conveniently ignored the fact that I had waived all rights of defence and thus there was no need for me to appear if I did not want to defend myself.

The Lok Ayukta law of Rajasthan did not confer any powers of punishment on the Lok Ayukta. That authority remained with the state government. The state government examined the order and the matter. I received an advisory warning signed by Chief Secretary Anil Vaish to conduct myself more gracefully before the honourable Lok Ayukta. As this advisory meant nothing, I simply ignored it.

'Do you have any objection to going to the Government of India?'

Chief Secretary Indrajeet Khanna called me on phone one afternoon. Referring to the decision of the Rajasthan government to encourage officers to go on deputation to the centre to make up for the shortfall in utilization of the state's deputation reserve, he pointedly asked me whether I had any objection to going to the Government of India.

The established process for going on deputation to the Government of India at the level of deputy secretary/director required the officer concerned to be eligible (nine years of service with minimum three years of field experience) and his/her specific willingness to go on deputation, conveyed in writing. Officers were also required to choose whether, besides being willing to be considered for deputation with the Government of India, they were also willing to be considered for other posts under the control of Government of India.

The thought of going to the centre had crossed my mind a couple of times. However, I had agreed with Anjali's opinion that it was preferable to go after I became eligible for a joint secretary's position. As the Government of India was empanelling officers for joint secretary after about 20 years of service, we were interested to go only after three more years.

I told the chief secretary I was not doing anything hugely important in REDA, though there were a couple of initiatives, like establishing Rajasthan as a wind power-generating state and taking the Mathania project to the bidding stage, which might require my continuance in the position. I added that I had no objection to going to the Government of India if the government considered it appropriate in the circumstances.

A similar call went to other batchmates as well. Two officers said they were willing but most others either sought time to respond or enumerated reasons why they were not in a position to go. I told Anjali about this in the evening. She felt I should have taken time for a day or so to discuss with her and respond the next day that I would prefer to go only at the joint secretary stage. Anyway, the die was cast.

There was no follow up from the chief secretary's office or from the Department of Personnel of the Rajasthan government. As my stated preference expressed at the beginning of the year was not to go on deputation that year, I thought the call meant nothing. We went about our business as usual.

However, he treated my response as consent and sent my name for deputation to the Government of India, which I would discover a few weeks later.

When I left REDA and RSPCL in May 2000, my 15-year-long stay in the state also came to an end.

Part B

Budget and Finance in Rajasthan

15

In and Out of Helming Finance in Rajasthan

I landed back in my cadre, Rajasthan, in 2006 after serving in Delhi for nearly six years. Those six years established my credentials in economic and financial management. Anil Vaish, with whom I had peripherally worked in the education department in the mid-1990s, had been chief secretary. Rajiv Mehrishi, who was transport secretary during my short stint at Rajasthan Roadways, had taken over as principal secretary, Finance, after the untimely demise of S.P. Gupta.

Vasundhara Raje had won an incredible majority in 2003 elections for the BJP, for the first time in Rajasthan. She was comfortably settled in the chief minister's chair. She had decided to be her own finance minister, probably for the first time in the history of Rajasthan. Govind Mohan, an IAS officer of Sikkim cadre, who had worked with Vasundhara Raje as her private secretary in the Department of Personnel & Training (DoPT), had joined as her secretary but had left in June 2005 under unclear circumstances. Sunil Arora was her principal secretary when I joined. Rajasthan had three finance secretaries assisting the principal secretary, Finance. They dealt with budget, expenditure and revenue.

Rajiv Mehrishi had sounded me to come to Rajasthan to work in the finance department after he took over in April 2005, when I was still working at the expenditure department of the Ministry of Finance. It did not work out as I wanted to stay in Delhi until March 2006 to see through my son Shrey's Class 12 examinations. Upon my return to Rajasthan in April 2006, I was posted as secretary, Finance, and was given the responsibility of the budget division.

The 2006–07 budget had been presented and approved in March 2006. My task was to implement it. During the year, the position of expenditure secretary was also vacant for some time. I doubled up to discharge both duties.

The 2007–08 budget, presented on 8 March 2007, was the first budget with which I got fully involved. As a convention, the secretary, Budget, was the principal custodian of the budget in Rajasthan. It was dictated and typed out in his or her anteroom. I also worked with Rajiv Mehrishi to get the 2008–09 budget prepared and steered through the system in March 2008.

'Please relieve me of my responsibilities'

Within a few days of joining, I had to make an unusual request to Rajiv Mehrishi to be relieved of my responsibilities.

Rajiv Mehrishi had an excellent command over English and wrote impactfully even in mundane government files. Combined with his impatience against mediocrity and way of dealing with official matters, many of his file notings used to become a kind of diatribe. He would write his notes questioning, sometimes ridiculing, and passing his orders, which sometimes seemed to be a result of sudden rush of anger. The secretaries working under him in the three departments would receive the files back with trepidation, as passing down some such files was humiliating. While Rajiv Mehrishi's observations were always sharp, that rush of blood sometimes made him overreact and pass orders that were not most appropriate on the merit of the case in question.

His ire was mostly reserved for one finance secretary who was excessively conservative and had a poor command over the language and, therefore, was not in a position to communicate well, and other officers that were negligent and lethargic in their work.

One day, when a set of my files came back from Mehrishi, I found a file with a note written in his signature, acerbic style. That was the first such file out of the hundreds of files that I had submitted to him until then, though I had spent only a few days on the job. I looked at the file again. He had missed the crucial facts based on which I had submitted my proposal. His pontificating note, based on an incorrect appreciation of the proposal and facts, shocked me.

I decided to protest. That evening, when I was returning home after clearing all the files on my desk, as was my usual practice, I wrote him a message on phone from my car. I said that I found the note on the file simply unacceptable, more so as it was based on an incorrect reading of the file and facts. At the end of the message, I requested that I be relieved from the finance department the next morning.

Rajiv called back within 15 minutes, apologized, and requested me to stay on. As he was one of the brightest officers of the cadre with a sharp mind to understand complex issues quickly, I relented. I served with him for my entire tenure in the finance department as secretary (close to two years). He never wrote a nasty note again. We enjoyed a relationship of mutual respect for next the 14 years and more until he demitted his last charge as the CAG in 2020.

Empty treasury

Rajasthan was not an industrially advanced state, thanks to over 60 per cent of the state being a desert and growing crops in tough conditions being dominant economic activity in the rest. Lack of industrial opportunities resulted in Rajasthani businessmen migrating to all parts of the country for better prospects. With agriculture contributing to over 40 per cent of the state's GDP, tax revenues were relatively low as well. On the other hand, expenditure responsibilities were much more on account of the state's vast geographical area, making the cost of infrastructure and utilities supply very high. As the government was the largest employer, the state spent a good portion of its revenues on salaries and pensions. The large deficits, funded by debts taken liberally until the year 2000, not only raised state's outstanding debt stock but also led to interest payments rising disproportionately.

The gross fiscal deficit (GFD) (gross fiscal deficit and fiscal deficit are used inter changeably) of the states in general had started rising ominously after the Pay Commission award in 1998. While GFD in aggregate was only 2.8 per cent of GDP during 1990–95, it rose to 3.5 per cent during 1995–2000. Gross fiscal deficit was 4.7 per cent in 1999–2000 and gradually reduced to 4.1 per cent in 2002–03.

Rajasthan had the fourth-highest ratio of GFD to GSDP (state GDP) of 6.3 per cent in the country during 2000–03, after Bihar, Orissa (now Odisha) and West Bengal. Rajasthan's GFD deteriorated to become the worst in the country during the three-year period of 2002–03 to 2004–05, at 6.6 per cent. Bihar, West Bengal, Uttar Pradesh and Punjab followed Rajasthan. It was one of the five most fiscally stressed states in the first part of the first decade of the twenty-first century.

Though debts and fiscal deficits are staid and boring subjects, the worrying state of debt and fiscal deficits in Rajasthan had been a political hot potato since the late 1990s. There were frequent discussions in the Assembly on the subject. The government had brought out a White Paper in 1998, which tried to justify the inevitability of debt for Rajasthan. The Ashok Gehlot government (1998–2003) usually pleaded fiscal helplessness: '*Tijori khali hai.*' (The vault is empty.)

Vasundhara Raje questioned the Gehlot government's financial management record during her election campaign and promised to bring in efficient financial management when voted to power. *Kushal Vittiya Prabandhan* (efficient financial management) had become the buzzword of her government after she took over as CM.

The fiscally stressed position of the states usually showed up in the number of days the state availed ways and means advance (WMA) and overdraft (OD) from Reserve Bank of India (RBI) in a year. Rajasthan remained in WMA for as many as 303 days and in OD for as many as 94 days in 2003–04, the year Vasundhara Raje took over the reins in December 2003. Stress was writ all over state's finance.

An unconventional-though-efficient system

Rajiv Mehrishi worked out an excellent arrangement with Vasundhara Raje for efficient disposal of the business of the finance department.

The CMO in Rajasthan normally operated through a bevy of officers headed by the principal secretary to the CM. The departments were divided among these officers who, after studying every file that came for disposal at the level of the chief minister, initiated a new note (which remained the property of the CMO), proposing specific actions/decisions. The CM disposed of the departmental file after considering the suggested course of action in the note, either in accordance with it or as it pleased him/her, by recording an approval or another order on the departmental file.

Rajiv Mehrishi got Vasundhara Raje to agree to the arrangement that all files and matters that required a judgement call or had serious financial implications would be taken personally by him to her instead of being routed through the CMO. The files would be disposed of by the CM and appropriate orders recorded on the departmental file during the discussion. Rajiv brought the files back with him. The arrangement ensured that Sunil Arora did not get a chance to even look at the file, leave alone influence the CM's decision. He did not like the arrangement but had to put up with it.

I accompanied Rajiv on several of these exclusive sessions with the CM, as many proposals and files emanated from my side. The same arrangement continued even during budget discussions, with Sunil not joining in most of the time.

From overdrafts to active cash management

I have described major decisions taken at the central government level to turn around state finances from 2002–03 to 2005–06 including debt swap, debt write-off, prepayment of costly debts, and the like in Part II. These measures had started making an impact on state finances. There was also a massive turnaround in international financial flows to emerging markets, including India. Foreign direct investment (FDI) and foreign portfolio investment (FPI) in India, including in external commercial borrowings (ECBs) and debt, zoomed 2002–03 onwards. India added about $100 billion to its paltry foreign exchange reserves of less than $50 billion in three years. There was liquidity all around. Interest rates crashed. The Government of India and RBI had to bring in a market stabilization scheme (MSS) in 2004 to suck out excess liquidity (the government paid interest on these deposits without using the proceeds). Inflation came crashing down as well.

All this had a positive impact on the states' finances and cash position. In 2004–05, Rajasthan did not have to get into OD for even a single day and could manage with being in WMA for only 85 days. Ways and means advance disappeared in 2005–06. In those days, the state governments' cash balance with RBI could be invested in four types of short-term papers. There was automatic deployment of states' cash balance over a nominal amount in 14-day treasury bills (TBs). These carried a low interest rate linked to the reverse repo rate of the RBI. There were also three investment-type TBs: 91 days, 182 days and 364 days. These carried market-linked rates of interest.

By the time I joined the finance department in April 2006, the stress on cash management was largely gone. But there was still widespread fear that spectre of overdrafts could return. The RBI used to provide the position of states' cash and investment in TBs every day. Rajasthan's cash balance was almost entirely invested in automatic 14-day TBs as these could be converted to cash anytime, whereas dated TBs (91, 182 and 364 days) could be converted to cash only at the end of maturity. There was no market for selling these TBs, in case that was required for raising urgent cash. The position of cash balances was kept hidden from the CM, who was also the finance minister, lest she get any 'wrong idea' and loosen the purse strings.

I initiated active cash management in the state. We started making broad calculations of likely cash demand and putting securely excess cash in dated TBs. There was a differential of 2–3 per cent in terms of interest. Some unanticipated payments in March 2007 created a difficult situation. We were in danger of slipping into WMA/OD if we did not sell our dated TBs. As there was no market, I called up Dr Rakesh Mohan, who was deputy governor of RBI at the time, to allow us to sell our dated TBs. As this was the first time RBI was faced with such a request, Rakesh Mohan had to call up ICICI Bank to buy the TBs. We could successfully sell them and avoid the dreaded WMA/OD position.

I decided to use the extra cash to earn better returns and worked with RBI to allow Rajasthan to buy back its securities. As high coupon securities had swelled up, we had to pay a premium, which was made up by the higher rate of interest the state government received on its own bonds. We created a state investment account to hold these bought-back securities. The state had issued securitization bonds in 2003–04 to clear the power-sector dues following the one-time settlement scheme. We exercised our call options on these bonds and persuaded some holders to sell the bonds to us.

Rajasthan became a kind of pioneer in active cash management in the country.

Vasundhara Raje scuppers my foreign training

Almost all officers of my batch in Rajasthan had done a foreign training course. Under a programme known as the Colombo Plan, every year, the DoPT would sponsor officers for long-term training of about 10 months, which resulted in a degree as well.

After obtaining permission, including from Vasundhara Raje, before the 2007–08 budget was presented in March 2007, I had applied for a course. the DoPT nominated me for a public policy programme at the University of Minnesota in the US, which was considered quite prestigious. After a long process of application, scrutiny and exchange of communications, I was selected and got approval from the DoPT by the end of May.

As my children had decided to continue with their educational pursuits in Delhi, I sold my house in Jaipur in May 2007 – it was to be handed over in June. My family had been living in a Type 4 sublet house in the capital's

R.K. Puram Sector 12 since June 2006. We used the proceeds of the sale of the Jaipur house and a loan from HDFC to buy a DDA flat in Delhi to get rid of this arrangement and establish our small home in Delhi.

There were two other officers from India joining the Minnesota course, which was expected to begin in August 2007. In early July, we got together and located a flat to rent near the university campus. Just as we were about to conclude the rent agreement, Vasundhara Raje decided to withdraw her consent for my leave for the training. She simply said I could not be spared. I was left stranded and disappointed. However, I respected her decision, though it caused considerable personal dislocation. I never got the opportunity of foreign training again.

'Youngest' principal secretary, Finance

In the middle of March 2008, after the 2008–09 budget was presented and passed, Rajiv Mehrishi decided to go to Delhi, which he had been intending to do for quite some time. However, Vasundhara Raje would always refuse his requests to allow him to go. One day, he decided to proceed on leave and went to Delhi. He did not return to work in Jaipur. I was neither party to nor aware of what was going on between the CM and Rajiv. However, I was senior-most among the secretaries in the finance department, though I had not been promoted to the grade of principal secretary. I was asked to step in to coordinate the work.

After two or three weeks, Vasundhara Raje reconciled herself to the fact that Rajiv Mehrishi would remain in Delhi. He opted to be posted as principal resident commissioner, Rajasthan, in the capital. The promotion of our batch to principal secretary grade had been pending since January 2008, yet Chief Secretary D.C. Samant seemed to be in no hurry. We got our promotion orders only in early April 2008. All subsequent batches in Rajasthan have been promoted on the first day of the calendar year, beginning with the promotion of the 1984 batch on 1 January 2009.

Rajasthan had 65 officers senior to me in the grades of additional chief secretaries and principal secretaries on the day my batch was promoted. The position of finance secretary in the state (held by the senior-most officers in the cadre in their respective grades, whether additional chief secretary, principal secretary or secretary earlier) was considered extremely high in responsibility, next only to that of chief secretary.

Rajiv Mehrishi alerted me that I was being considered for the position of principal secretary, Finance. It was April 2008, and elections were only seven to eight months away. Delivering Bhamashah, announced in Budget 2008–09 with considerable fanfare, was not an easy task. Sunil Arora was persistently pursuing a populist agenda at the CM's office. I was apprehensive about accepting the responsibility in such turbulent times.

I told Rajiv that I needed to speak to the chief minister before the honour was conferred upon me.

Vasundhara Raje called me for a discussion. I told her the circumstances were difficult, but I was willing to accept the responsibility and was also confident of implementing the budget. However, I told her that I had a few conditions. She was quite surprised at my audacity of speaking of conditions to accept one of the most powerful and coveted position in government. Yet she asked me to tell her.

I told her that the administrative arrangement of file disposal must continue as it was during Rajiv Mehrishi's time, i.e., I should have the same liberty of not routing the files through the CMO or Sunil Arora. I told her further that she would be flooded with populist proposals in coming months from not only Arora but from several others. I said it was her right to take the final decision, but she must hear me out on every such proposal. Lastly, which was quite ambitious for me to ask, if any proposal was received in the finance department with her approval as either minister of the department she headed or as chief minister, but without the finance department having been consulted, I must have the liberty to bring it to her for discussion/reconsideration before the final approval was granted thereon.

She was at her charming best and agreed to all my conditions liberally smiling all through. I was appointed principal secretary, Finance, an officer of the batch promoted to the grade only a few days earlier – in a way a youngest and 'junior most' finance secretary of the state.

Transferred out on Day 1 of the Ashok Gehlot government

Vasundhara Raje lost the 2008 elections, although she managed to win as many as 78 seats of 200. Ashok Gehlot took the oath of office on the evening of 13 December 2008. He came to the secretariat the next day and held a meeting of the secretaries. I was still the principal finance secretary and was present. A copy of the Congress manifesto was handed over in the presence of all senior officers to Chief Secretary D.C. Samant. It was announced that the manifesto had been accepted as the government policy and would be implemented as such.

In the evening, the appointment and transfer orders of only a few key officers were announced. T. Srinivasan was appointed additional chief secretary to the CM. I was transferred to the Bureau of Investment Promotion (BIP) as commissioner. C.K. Mathew was appointed in my place as principal secretary, Finance. I gladly handed over charge to Mathew the next morning and assumed my responsibilities at the BIP.

The Gehlot government decided to appoint a three-men committee under the leadership of former chief secretary Indrajeet Khanna to examine the irregularities and corruption of officers under the Vasundhara Raje government.

I was never called for questioning by the committee, though they took over many files of the finance department, including files relating to the Bhamashah scheme. One of the members spoke to me informally. I told him two things: First, in the eight months that I helmed the finance department, there was not a single decision that could be termed even populist despite it being a pre-election period, and corruption in any case was simply out of question; second, every decision I was party to had been recorded in the files, as were the reasons for taking those decisions. The committee was free to draw its conclusions from files and my notes.

I never heard from the committee or it questioning any of my decisions.

Lost a year's performance report

The BIP was an untypical government organization. Unlike the regulatory or implementational role, which most government departments or organizations play, the BIP was meant to roll out a red carpet to investors. It was to showcase Rajasthan and promote industrialization of and investments in the state.

D.C. Samant, chief secretary under Vasundhara Raje, was retained in his position by the Gehlot government, possibly because he had only a few months of service left. After that, Kushal Singh replaced him.

One of the major initiatives of the Vasundhara Raje government had been to organize the first Resurgent Rajasthan Summit in December 2007. Organized by the BIP under the leadership of Umesh Kumar, it was considered a highly successful event resulting in investment interest of thousands of crores of rupees from state, national and international investors captured in hundreds of the MoUs signed.

Samant would diligently and meticulously monitor implementations of the MoUs as chief secretary and head of the State Steering Committee. The committee would meet every fortnight during Vasundhara Raje's time, keeping the BIP always busy as it was the secretariat for the committee. Samant would personally brief Vasundhara Raje after each such meeting.

As soon as I took over as the BIP commissioner, I initiated preparations for the next meeting of the steering committee, which took place in early January in a business-like manner with Samant taking considerable interest. Later, when he went to brief the new chief minister, I believe he received a lukewarm response. Soon, Samant, taking the cue, lost interest in even convening steering committee meetings. Kushal Singh had no interest in it either. Rajasthan stopped resurging.

The annual performance appraisal reports (APARs) for the year 2008–09, which covered a large part of the period under Vasundhara Raje, were due. Many officers, including I, submitted our reports in March 2009 for Samant to complete the APARs on time. Though Vasundhara Raje was chief minister for most of 2008–09, the rules did not permit an outgoing chief minister to be the accepting authority of performance reports, making Ashok Gehlot the accepting authority for my performance report. For whatever reasons, Samant decided not to write my annual performance report for the year 2008–09. It remained a gap in my APAR record.

Booted out for getting an airport cleared

Delhi suffers from fog every winter. It tends to disappear near the Behror–Kotputli area close to the Haryana–Rajasthan border. The idea was conceived to build an aerotropolis around a greenfield airport in this area to serve as an alternative airport for Delhi and to divert Delhi-bound aircraft on foggy days. As the distance was only about 90–100 km by road (aerially somewhat less) from the capital, the airport could serve Delhi well. It would also be close to Jaipur, around 150 km. We thought of building a new rail line from Delhi to Jaipur to connect this airport with the two cities and to develop the newly conceived nodal city in the Delhi–Mumbai Industrial Corridor (DMIC) plan in this area.

A consortium of private parties, in partnership with Frankfurt Airport, signed an MoU for this aerotropolis project during Resurgent Rajasthan. A major hitch in the plan was that it fell within 100 km of the Delhi airport. The contract with GMR for the Delhi airport concession required a no-objection certificate. In addition, the Airport Authority of India (AAI) and the Ministry of Civil Aviation, in principle, were not favourably inclined towards an additional airport within 100 km of an existing airport.

I worked on this project immediately after joining in the BIP and completed most of the work required for its clearance. In the project sanctioning committee meeting in Delhi held in June 2009, I was able to convince the committee, headed by the civil aviation secretary, that it was in the national interest to have an alternative airport to decongest the Delhi airport (the airport close to Jewar in Uttar Pradesh was not even in its concept stage at that time). This could also help national and international flights to operate more smoothly from near the capital, as our proposed location fell outside the foggy zone, which used to disturb many flights during winters.

The committee agreed to grant us in-principle approval.

Soon after I left the meeting and was on my way back to Jaipur, I received a call from a Jaipur-based journalist. He was aware of the meeting and wanted to know what had happened. I told him it was approved in principle. The news was immediately flashed on local TV and made it to the front page of local newspapers the next morning.

I was transferred the next day afternoon from the BIP for the ostensible reason that instead of informing the chief minister and senior authorities, I chose to speak to the press 'to claim credit'.

Rajasthan did not get final clearance for the project, for reasons I am not aware of. Instead, the Jewar airport near Noida received the clearance in 2020.

Back to Delhi via Rajfed

Ironically, I was transferred to Rajfed, the organization that had set up the Rajfed Kota soybean project in the 1980s, as its administrator.

I had applied for central deputation in April 2009 as soon as my mandatory cooling period of three years was over. The Rajasthan government gave its 'no objection' to this sometime in May 2009.

It was expected that I would get my central posting in a couple of months. Despite this, I was transferred from the not-so-significant position of the BIP commissioner to a still more insignificant post in Rajfed. I joined my new posting the next day. It did not have any work for the administrator. I whiled away my time in Rajfed.

My central deputation orders for a joint secretary in the Department of Agriculture came in mid-August. With that I bade farewell to Rajasthan again, hoping that I might possibly be able to spend the remaining 11 years of my service in the Government of India.

16

State-Level Finance and Budgets

During the two years I worked in the finance department of Rajasthan as secretry, Budget, from April 2006 to April 2008, I got the opportunity to learn and master budget-making at the state level. No budget was presented during the eight-month period (April 2008 to December 2008). I worked as principal secretary, Finance, though this period proved highly eventful as I steered implementation of Budget 2008–09.

Getting the budget speech ready

Vasundhara Raje accorded budget-making her biggest priority. She was also an ideal finance minister from the perspective of expenditure management. She prepared very hard for her budget speech. It was a long drill. I witnessed this all and managed through it for Budget 2007–08 during February–March 2007.

The budget team – Rajiv Mehrishi, director, Budget, and I – would meet her in the evening around 6 p.m. with our budget draft. Over the next four to five hours, she would read the speech aloud. In this process, issues connected with flow in delivery would be identified and addressed. Further, every proposal or formulation she did not fully comprehend or wanted to understand better would be discussed threadbare. All the facts and references relating to the matter would be brought to her knowledge. Each paragraph of the budget speech would get okayed only after a complete buy-in from her. She would do about six to seven rounds of such readings before the speech was finalized.

Rajasthan had a bad system of finalizing and printing the budget speech. It would not be final before 11 p.m. or midnight of the day before the budget presentation in the assembly; only then would it be handed over to the risograph people waiting in the secretariat for printing.

Once this was done, Rajiv Mehrishi and I would thereafter sit down to prepare the budget highlights in both Hindi and English versions. In the meantime, when the budget speech was printed, I would go to the CM's home to hand her the final budget speech at about 4 a.m. in the morning. On both the budgets I worked on in 2007 and 2008, it was only at about 7 a.m. on budget day that I could go home to freshen up before going to the House to meet the CM and watch the finance minister deliver her speech.

A rare revenue surplus budget

Rajasthan witnessed an unprecedented budget on 8 March 2007. It was the first revenue surplus budget of the state after 1991–92 with a revenue surplus of ₹214 crore. What's more, the revised estimates for 2006–07 also had got converted into a revenue surplus. Many states presented a revenue surplus budget for the year 2007–08. It was, however, a special feat for Rajasthan, which was India's most fiscally stressed state only a year before.

Neither Rajiv nor I were very keen to present a revenue surplus budget as this was likely to lull the political executive into believing the fiscal crisis was over, allowing them to ramp up expenditures, especially as the elections were only a year and a half away.

Therefore, we put a good part of the surplus into buckets where it could be used in future for more worthwhile activities, which was an unprecedented fiscal prudence ever shown. We also discharged certain obligations of electricity utilities, including retiring a part of the equity given earlier to cover the power-sector deficit, another first which made the electricity utilities quite happy. They had never hoped to get cash in lieu of equity earlier.

Vishwakarma Scheme inspires three central schemes

The 2007–08 budget contained several innovative schemes and practices. The Rajasthan Social Sector Viability Gap Funding Scheme was initiated, with an outlay of ₹100 crore, for social-sector projects like schools, water supply and health centres. The government proposed to give only capital assistance under the scheme. The separate feeder scheme to segregate the agricultural and non-agricultural load to assure 24-hour electricity supply for the non-agricultural load (primarily residential use) in rural areas was scaled up substantially. Clear incentivization for people to take ownership of the scheme was built in, based on loss reduction in the feeders. The government made complete provision for all the new and innovative schemes under a lumpsum head to ensure that funding would be available for rolling out the budget schemes from Day 1. This was followed by all financial allocation made available in the month of April.

Pride of place among the schemes went to the Vishwakarma Contributory Pension Scheme for unorganized-sector workers like rickshaw pullers, street vendors, cobblers and so on. The government promised to pay up to ₹1,000 a year, equivalent to the amount contributed by every worker who opened a pension account under the scheme. This was the first co-contribution pension scheme in the country for unorganized-sector workers. I had proposed it, though it fell in the domain of the labour department. As the labour department did not have any background about the scheme, I helped implement it quickly. I brought in an outfit headed by Gautam Bhardwaj, one of the authors of the original Dave Committee OASIS report, to create a computerized system to enrol such workers. It was a tough task, but we were able to enrol more than 50,000 workers in the first year.

The Government of India adopted the Vishwakarma idea to launch the Swavalamban Pension Scheme in Budget 2010–11. I was contacted to provide the details and was happy to see it become a national scheme. Swavalamban had the same features – a contribution up to ₹1,000 per annum, equivalent to the contribution of each citizen in the unorganized sectors, who joined the New Pension Scheme (NPS).

Swavalamban was replaced by Atal Pension Yojana (APY) in 2015. Atal Pension Yojna changed the architecture of the scheme with introduction of the minimum guaranteed pension of ₹1,000 per month or more at the age of 60 depending on the contribution made by the unorganized-sector workers.

Finally, the Government of India came up with one more contribution-based pension scheme, Pradhan Mantri Shram Yogi Mandhan Yojana (PM SYM), in the interim budget of 2019–20, when I was secretary, Economic Affairs. There is not much difference between the architecture of APY and PM SYM except that the latter is being implemented by LIC instead of Pension Fund Regulation and Development Authority (PFRDA). The monthly pension amount depends upon the monthly contribution made, though the ambition of PM SYM is to help workers receive a monthly pension of ₹3,000. Unfortunately, PM SYM has not really succeeded, with hardly any new addition taking place in the years 2022–25.

A rainy-day fund

The global push of liquidity and demand during 2003–07 led to investments, production and profits booming in India. This translated into higher value-added tax (VAT) revenues for states and larger transfers of central taxes to them. On the other hand, milder inflation and interest rates meant lower increases in dearness allowances and interest payments. This, besides efficient and nimble fiscal management, had brought Rajasthan to a revenue surplus.

Good times do not last forever, though. Assimilating the advice of saner fiscal experts that such surpluses should be kept aside in some sort of a rainy-day fund, the state created a Rajasthan Development and Poverty Alleviation Fund from the outgoing financial year 2006–07. A formula was adopted to compute extraordinary growth in revenues to determine the amount to be transferred in the rainy fund. ₹100 crore was transferred from the budget of financial year 2006–07 and the budget provided for another transfer of ₹200 crore in 2007–08.

Vasundhara Raje spoke of the demand of the times to avoid 'short-term populism' and display 'statesmanship' in the management of finances for comprehensive and accelerated development of the state, better governance and fiscal responsibility while creating the fund.

The fund was entirely my idea, and I was glad that both Rajiv Mehrishi and Vasundhara Raje adopted it and translated it into reality. The chief minister was able to establish her credentials for visionary financial management in the long discussion that took place in the Assembly, using the examples of the Vishwakarma Scheme and the rainy-day fund, besides other feathers in her cap, such as pushing up capital expenditure and transforming the energy sector.

Populism bested by Bhamashah

Budget 2008–09 presented in March 2008 provided us the best opportunity to think of something truly transformational.

Elections for the Legislative Assembly were due in November 2008. The model code of conduct would get applied some 45 days earlier. Effectively six months only were available to deliver programmes in the financial year 2008–09.

In Rajasthan, there was a long-established but bad tradition of casting aside all pretentions of fiscal prudence in the election year budget, despite the fact that the state's finances had been under severe stress for at least two decades. By contrast, the Vasundhara Raje government had the record of having delivered two revenue surplus budgets and was in a position to deliver another one, which could have been viewed by many as a great opportunity to unleash unprecedented populism.

In the past two Assembly elections in Rajasthan, the incumbent had lost: the BJP in 1998 and the Congress in 2003. Ground reports and the general opinion about the performance of the government were not great – it was expected that Vasundhara Raje would lose the elections.

Against this backdrop, the populist lobby led by Sunil Arora wanted to take control of Budget 2008–09. He marshalled all his persuasive skills, deployed various actors who worked behind the scenes on Vasundhara Raje and emerged with a slew of populist proposals. He had a long list, of which three proposals particularly had very large fiscal implications.

First, make power free for farmers or at least bring it down to 50 paise per unit (Rajasthan charged 90 paise per unit; the national consensus was a minimum 50 paise; some states like Punjab and Andhra Pradesh provided power free of cost). Second, provide 5 kg of fortified wheat flour free of cost to every poor family, or at best, charge ₹2 per kg for it – the National Food Security Mission had promised wheat at ₹2 per kg to most ration-card holders. Third, announce a loan waiver for all farmers other than those fully covered by the Central Farm Loan Waiver Scheme in the central budget. We calculated financial implications. The bill for these three schemes alone would have been over ₹2,000 crore per annum.

Rajiv Mehrishi and I were not in favour of any populist schemes. We took our alternative proposals before Vasundhara Raje. We brought to her notice with the fact that such populist measures and giveaways had not won any elections for any party in the previous 20 years in Rajasthan. We presented a better alternative. We proposed she continue with her reforms and launch a mega scheme to overhaul public welfare schemes to establish direct contact with the households and transform the administrative system in the process. Our argument was that there were vast leakages in the current set of schemes; these were also too thinly funded and very poorly targeted. The welfare message was lost in the implementation of programmes. Instead, if she reached out to a very large number of households and made a direct appeal to the women promising transfer of a good amount, such a scheme would make far bigger impact.

The chief minister was in two minds. Her cabinet colleagues were clearly on the side of the proposals Sunil Arora had put forth. However, she sensed the advantages of breaking with the past and not falling in the trap of wasteful populism. That said, she was clearly unsure whether anything spectacularly game-changing could be done in the last half year of the government that had not been done in the previous four-and-a-half years.

We proposed what was named the 'Bhamashah' programme later. The core idea was simple: Reach out to at least 60 lakh families of Rajasthan (of an estimated 125 lakh), give them a smart card to access schematic benefits like ration and health services, and bundle up many welfare schemes in a direct cash payment of ₹1,500 per annum to be delivered to the female head of the household. The scheme required a gargantuan IT setup, registration of 60 lakh families, issue of smart cards and delivery of at least ₹1,500 in their accounts.

Several rounds of discussions took place. Sunil tried to appeal to the CM's electoral insecurity to champion his well-understood and politically acceptable cocktail of programmes. We stuck to our ground and marshalled several go-getters, including the now disgraced Hari Sankaran of Infrastructure Leasing & Financial Services (IL&FS), to convince her that the programme we proposed was deliverable as well as administratively and politically savvy.

Vasundhara Raje finally decided to reject Sunil Arora's proposals and go with ours. The 2008–09 budget announced the Bhamashah programme along with quite a few other pathbreaking initiatives, such as a public–private partnership (PPP) programme in the education sector (Gyanodaya), which promised capital subsidy and educational vouchers to families that opted to study in private schools. Trained teachers were given the option to establish their own small school, 'Adhyapak ka Apna Vidyalaya', funded by educational vouchers.

When the 2008–09 budget was presented in the Assembly on 25 February 2008, legislators from both the ruling party and the Opposition could not believe that an election year budget did not have a single populist announcement.

First state to implement Sixth Pay Commission report

The Sixth Central Pay Commission (VI CPC) released its report in February 2008. As soon as the report was available in the public domain, we started preparing to adopt it in Rajasthan. I took over as principal secretary, Finance, in April 2008.

Pay Commission reports not only alter the basic pay and readjust the start date of dearness allowances, but they also affect pay parities among different groups or sections of government servants, many types of allowances and associated benefits like pensions, leave encashment, and so on. The rates of recoveries applicable for the use of different facilities, like house rent, also need to be reworked considering the new structure and scale of pay and allowances.

An examination of the VI CPC report in the context of Rajasthan revealed that its adoption, as it was, would lead to some major distortions. The VI CPC had merged some scales in the middle that would have meant that scales of two or three levels in the hierarchy – like junior accountant and accountant – would become entitled to the same pay. The pay scales of schoolteachers had been raised in such a manner that, at one stage, the pay of a primary schoolteacher equalled the pay of a block development officer.

While we decided to adopt the VI CPC report broadly, the recommendations that would distort the administrative structure of the state, we believed, should be accepted only with the insertion of additional grade pay to safeguard the existing structure. Scales and allowances that Rajasthan had not made equal to the central government, like house rent allowance or LTC, were also decided not to be extended to state employees. Discussions with Chief Minister Vasundhara Raje suggested that she was on board, again despite the elections being round the corner.

The Government of India announced implementation of the VI CPC's recommendations on 29 August 2008. Usually, Rajasthan and most states appointed a state committee to consider the report and central government decision to make its recommendations to the state government for consideration. This process normally took many months after the announcement of implementation by the central government.

We decided not to appoint any such committee in 2008. A team of officers worked during May–June 2008 under my leadership to adapt the recommendations for the state. We had our draft orders ready on 29 August. We took the proposals on file and submitted for the chief minister's approval though the chief secretary the next day. Despite some reservations of Chief Secretary Samant, the proposals got formally processed about 10 days thereafter.

On 12 September, Rajasthan became the first state in India to announce implementation of the VI CPC's recommendations. It was also not an interim award but a complete and comprehensive one. The Rajasthan Civil Services (Revised Pay) Rules 2008, a compendium of adoption of the new rules and amendment in all the necessary rules, running to about 140 pages, was issued under my signature on 12 September 2008.We anticipated some backlash from employee unions against our adaptation of the VI CPC's recommendations and abolition of some allowances that were not recommended by the CPC. In effect, the net gains that the employees were anticipating were smaller than what the central government employees got. There was another matter to contend with. Vasundhara Raje had given a written assurance in 2003 to employee unions, before the elections, that several of their long-pending demands would be granted. This included promoting employees in the ninth, eighteenth and twenty-seventh years of their service in place of granting them monetary benefit of the next scale only. She had also agreed to grant LTC facility to state government employees. It was very difficult for her to go back on these assurances after she took over as chief minister. However, her good sense of expenditure management enabled her to resist all these pressures, and she did not yield to any of these demands during her five years at the helm.

The employee associations decided to protest. They sought intervention of Sunil Arora. A senior politician of the BJP also spoke sympathetically for the employees.

Vasundhara Raje, however, stood firm. Even while going to elections, she was able to resist the temptation of giving any quarter to the employees. The implementation of the VI CPC's recommendations in Rajasthan was the harshest of any state. After coming to power, the Ashok Gehlot government reversed some of the decisions taken in September 2008 and gave benefits to the employees.

17

Bhamashah Got Stalled Just Before Elections

There were no Jan-Dhan (zero-balance electronic) bank accounts for the poor in 2008; many public-sector banks were implementing the banking inclusion programme by opening manual zero-balance accounts in their branches. Almost all these manual accounts remained inoperative. Banking was almost fully branch-based, and RBI was in the initial stage of permitting banking correspondents to carry out limited banking transactions – deposit and withdrawal of cash – as an increasing number of banks embraced core banking solutions that converted their deposit accounts into electronic deposit accounts.

At this point, Nandan Nilekani had only written about the concept of a unique identity number, which was later named Aadhaar. The Government of India had not started any programme to build a unique ID system for the country. However, it had started a programme called Rashtriya Swasthya Bima Yojana (RSBY), which registered poor households for a publicly funded medical treatment plan. Rashtriya Swasthya Bima Yojana had initiated the use of smart cards to store identification details of the family, including fingerprints, for correct identification in empanelled hospitals.

Mobile telephony had permeated across India, though the total number of mobile phones had not crossed 40 crores in 2008. Penetration of mobiles in rural areas was much lower, only about 10 per cent. Mobile-phone banking was nowhere on the horizon. There was no UPI, IMPS or any other form of electronic payment and transfer.

In short, there was no JAM (Jan-Dhan, Aadhaar and Mobile) trinity in India in 2008. In fact, the building blocks of the JAM system did not exist. It was at this time that Rajasthan had audaciously embarked on the Bhamashah programme.

Three key players we were dependent on

ICICI Bank had promoted FINO, now a payments bank, to take advantage of the emerging correspondent banking. FINO was establishing itself in Rajasthan and had highly ambitious plans. Its scaling up of correspondent banking envisaged enrolling poor households in the state as an extended arm of ICICI Bank and delivering banking services of deposits and withdrawals close to their doorsteps by building a network of retail stores and self-employed persons as banking correspondents. Our discussions with ICICI Bank and FINO representatives were reassuring, though we never told them of the Bhamashah programme, or the scale envisaged.

Hari Sankaran, the flamboyant CEO of IL&FS (who, along with Ravi Parthasarathy, believed nothing was impossible) had partnered with Vijay Mahajan's grassroot organization Basix and they were independently offering us the facility to register every Rajasthan household to deliver government benefits.

The Government of India had offered to launch RSBY in eight districts in Rajasthan in financial year 2008–09 and register every eligible poor household with the issue of a smart card. We thought that by offering to take RSBY to every district, we would be able to leverage the smart card to securely deliver ₹1,500 cash transfer and other government benefits.

No project feasibility exercise had been undertaken. In fact, the idea emerged quite late, sometime in January–February 2008, basically to stop the populist schemes that Sunil Arora was trying to implant in Vasundhara Raje's mind. Rajiv Mehrishi and I could develop only a perfunctory understanding about the infrastructure for the Bhamashah programme at the time of its announcement. It was a leap of faith.

Vasundhara makes the ambitious budget announcement

Chief Minister and Finance Minister Vasundhara Raje built up the momentum for the Bhamashah Vittiya Sashaktikaran Yojana (the Bhamashah financial empowerment scheme) in her budget speech by first talking about scaling up medical insurance under RSBY. She claimed credit for the Government of India announcing RSBY for families below the poverty line (BPL) in eight districts of Rajasthan: Jalore, Jhalawar, Tonk, Bikaner, Rajsamand, Baran, Karauli and Sawai Madhopur. Then, stating that for her every district and every citizen of Rajasthan was equal, she announced that the state government would implement the same scheme in the remaining 20 districts from the same year (2008–09) at its own cost.

The leverage of the RSBY smart card was built into this announcement. She continued to announce that every BPL family would be provided with a smart card and expressed her desire for them to open a bank account linked with the smart card. She said '*Main chahti hoon ki sabhi* BPL *pariwar saath hi iss* smart card *se chalta apna* bank *khata bhi khulwa lein*.' (I would like everyone in the BPL family to also open a bank account, which is operated with this smart card.)

Taking advantage of the sentiment building in favour of direct cash transfer as a more effective mode of transferring assistance to people and to secure the loyalty of her women support base, she declared that every family that received a smart card for the health scheme and opened a bank account in the name of the woman in the family would get a transfer of ₹1,500 in her account from the government as incentive. Vasundhara Raje was happy to allocate ₹500 crore for BPL families under the Bhamashah and health schemes.

The list of BPL families did not cover all the vulnerable and marginal sections of the state. The idea was also to reach as many households as possible as subsidized electricity and food schemes reached bigger beneficiary groups. Therefore, she continued with her enunciation of the Bhamashah scheme in her budget speech. Styling herself as the benefactor of Rajasthan, she declared that the benefit of ₹1,500 incentive would not be limited to BPL families. She expanded the coverage to other vulnerable groups, specifically mentioning SC and ST families, and small and marginal farmers. Estimating this additional group of people at about 25 lakh, she estimated an additional expenditure of ₹400 crore for this purpose.

She expressed her confidence that the entire scheme would be rolled out by 30 June 2008. She did not forget to add that this was possibly the biggest and most ambitious scheme in the world.

The challenge to deliver Bhamashah thus began on 25 February. We had four months to deliver an incredibly complex scheme at the most ambitious scale based on technology and a financial system that was at best only at the experimental stage.

Anil Swarup plays spoilsport

Anil Swarup, an IAS officer of the 1981 batch serving as joint secretary in the Ministry of Labour, was the architect of the RSBY scheme. While RSBY was a health insurance scheme, by targeting the labour force and defining it as all households below the poverty line, Anil Swarup succeeded in convincing the Government of India that the RSBY scheme should be implemented by the Ministry of Labour, not the Ministry of Health (eventually, in 2015, the scheme was transferred to the Ministry of Health before being merged with the Ayushman Bharat Scheme in 2018).

The smart card was a high-grade technological innovation of the RSBY scheme. The scheme also envisaged the creation of a central database of RSBY beneficiaries and electronic deduplication based on identity data captured as part of the registration processes on laptops, which were to be carried to all villages by enrolling agents. The process was tedious, time-consuming and, consequently, slow-moving. Anil Swarup, however, remained convinced that slow and steady would ultimately win the race.

Rashtriya Swasthya Bima Yojana could only be rolled out with the active cooperation of the states because it needed the on-ground machinery of the state government. The authentication of persons registered was completely dependent upon these functionaries. Rashtriya Swasthya Bima Yojana's benefits were expected to be delivered by state government hospitals and private hospitals located in the state. The state-government also paid a part of the RSBY premium.

With the additional challenge of implementing RSBY in all districts of Rajasthan and seeking to press all the field machinery of the state into the service of RSBY, Rajiv Mehrishi and I went to see Labour Secretary Sudha Pillai in March 2008. As expected, Sudha Pillai redirected us to Anil Swarup. We explained our offer and wanted him to build a facility of identification for banking purposes to deliver the ₹1,500 incentive and for the development scheme benefit. We also wanted to use the back of the RSBY smart card to print family details.

Anil Swarup, a professional narcissist, saw our offer as diluting his exclusive hold over the pioneering RSBY scheme. He came out with several technical reasons why this was not possible. He also told us that the RSBY card was an exclusive Government of India card and it was not possible to share it with any state government. He also expressed his fear that security features would get compromised if data from any other scheme was placed on the card.

His technical arguments probably had some merit. However, we were confident that these issues could be solved. But he was not willing to make the effort. His virtual refusal to converge the two platforms on a single RSBY smart card disappointed us but did not dampen our enthusiasm to find a solution.

We quickly develop the basic architecture of the scheme

Hari Sankaran came up with a grand offer in the inimitable IL&FS overconfident style. He wanted the Rajasthan government to pay ₹150 per smart card and provide the services for grassroot registration. Infrastructure Leasing & Financial Services would create the entire system and register 40 lakh households in one year. We refused to walk into this trap as it would have made Rajasthan completely dependent on IL&FS, which would have owned all the databases and been the only pipeline for all operations. If IL&FS failed or defaulted, the government would have nowhere to turn. Moreover, paying ₹150 for a smart card without discovering the price in an open bid would have been an invitation to allegations of gross financial irregularity.

We discussed with IL&FS the design aspects of the card and whether all that we wanted to deliver through the card was possible. Further, we wanted to explore bank linkages, the registration process of beneficiaries and how the database would be centrally managed. We also thought of looking at other players in the market. One company, Bartronics, had built a good franchise in the smart-card business. We invited them to meet us. Besides discussing the basic architecture of the technological system to deliver the benefits of Bhamashah, we encouraged them to test their offerings in field conditions working with FINO, other banking correspondents and banks to evaluate whether the cash incentive could be easily withdrawn from using the smart card and electronic bank account.

These discussions, held at a breakneck speed, as we hardly had any time, led to the development of the basic architectural features of the central database management and family smart card system for Bhamashah. However, not fully knowing whether there were other technological options to achieve our desired goals, we decided to specify our ask in the form of outputs in the tender documents keeping technology options open.

We decided to call for expressions of interest (EOI) to deliver a 50 lakh smart card-based and bank/banking correspondent-linked digital benefit transfer system for two key schemes – RSBY benefits to all poor families and ₹1,500 to all poor, SC, ST, small and marginal farmer families of Rajasthan – with further flexibility to deliver cash as well as non-cash benefits which the government decided from time to time.

I present Bhamashah to officers and ministers

Very early in April 2008, Vasundhara Raje organized a meeting to which all ministers, secretaries and heads of departments were invited. I explained the ambition of the government in the design of the Bhamashah scheme and how we proposed to roll it out in six months all over the state.

Further work made us conclude that we should be able to enrol about 40 lakh families under the Bhamashah scheme. I informed the audience that all the 40 lakh BPL, SC, ST, and small and marginal farmer families of Rajasthan would be registered through a hybrid system. Every eligible family would be registered, with a woman as head of family, along with all family members. For digital registration, the workers of the registering agency would fan out in rural areas, along the lines of RSBY registration, capture the requisite details and upload them on the central database server. For places with physical registration, the data collected would be transcribed into digital form at panchayat samiti camp offices and uploaded. This operation was Aadhaar in the making. The bank account of the beneficiary would also be opened along with the registration.

Health insurance to all BPL families and cash incentive of ₹1,500 to 40 lakh BPL, SC, ST, and small and marginal farmers were the two key deliverables in the scheme. Ration cards would be merged into the smart cards and ration would be delivered with online and offline identification of the person using the smart card. The system of benefit transfer we envisaged was bigger than the direct benefit transfer (DBT) scheme later implemented by the Government of India.

The Bhamashah digital architecture and smart-card system was being designed and linked to the bank account such that the cardholder would be able to make banking transactions at the branch and with the banking correspondents as well as conduct online purchase transactions such as booking railway and bus tickets. This was Jan-Dhan, mobile banking and more.

Finally, Bhamashah would become a vehicle for major administrative reform. The government would make a layered database at the core, schematic and general levels, and government services would increasingly be linked to the digital database being created under Bhamashah. Driving licences would, in due course, be issued using Bhamashah databases. Grant of pensions and other benefits would be subject to verification through the Bhamashah portal, and the like.

It was indeed the most ambitious of schemes. And while some officers were quite enthusiastic and confident that they could pull it off in the short window of time available, many sceptics were conveying through their body language that Vasundhara Raje was being led up the garden path.

Rajasthan selects IL&FS as principal vendor

Maintaining a frantic speed to deliver, we floated the request for proposal (RFP) in the second week of April 2008, asking companies to submit their technical proposals and financial bids in two separate covers. Eight companies responded. We asked for all the companies to make their presentations before a large committee of officers, which I chaired. Even though something altogether new was happening and the scope of work and expected deadlines were audacious, we went through the technical presentations very carefully and in detail. In a month from the date of issue of the RFP, the technical evaluation was completed and four of the best companies in the country were technically approved. Besides IL&FS and Bartronics, these included Financial Technologies India Ltd, which had provided software for the National Stock Exchange of India (NSE) and FINO. Infrastructure Leasing & Financial Services was adjudged the best firm on technical considerations.

On 16 May, the financial bids, which were called for the seven divisions of the state separately, were opened. Bartronics emerged as the lowest bidder in all the seven divisions. We did not want to place all our eggs in one basket. Negotiations were held with the technically best and financially lowest firms. After completing the entire process, the letters of intent were issued on 23 May. It was a strenuous process with so much unknown about the product, technology and expected delivery. Yet, we pulled it off. The fieldwork commenced before 31 May 2008.

I had taken over as principal secretary, Finance, in the first fortnight of April and directed the entire effort at breakneck speed. Rajiv Mehrishi extended enormous support from Delhi. He joined in many meetings and discussions in Jaipur and agreed to become a member in many committees I chaired.

This incredible feat of selecting within two months agencies that could commit to deliver the expected 40 lakh registrations before 30 September was not music to the ears of many. Sunil Arora was not amused. Yaduvendra Mathur (the planning secretary, where the execution of Bhamashah was formally placed) was not happy. Even Chief Secretary Samant felt he was being taken for granted.

Suddenly, over three continuous days, a front-page 'scoop' appeared in *Rashtradoot*. Though it was not a frontline newspaper in Rajasthan, it still had a considerable following. The newspaper termed Bhamashah a scam by questioning the tendering process and the divisions awarded to IL&FS, which was not the financially lowest party. The paper quoted extensively from unnamed sources and minutes of the tender evaluation. Obviously, some insider was providing grist to the mill. Samant immediately asked for a full report on the allegations. I responded to all the allegations and innuendos on file while continuing with the delivery of the programme at the same speed.

The contract we had negotiated and structured with IL&FS and Bartronics protected Rajasthan's interests fully. We did not pay them any advance. In fact, we took ₹10 crore from them as performance guarantee. Both the companies were to make all the investment in the digital system, hire the enumerators and complete the registration. The government agreed to pay only for the completed registrations, which were then deduplicated, checked, authenticated – and only upon the successful upload of the data on the bank's portal. The final rate per Bhamashah card we received was very low, around ₹75 per card – nearly half the price IL&FS had quoted initially.

Nothing came out of the sensational claims made in *Rashtradoot*.

We rope in Punjab National Bank

FINO, the ICICI affiliate, was shaping up quite well in the banking correspondent business. We were banking on FINO to deliver banking services. FINO bid for the entire Bhamashah system, registration and smart-card issuance tender. It was one of the four technically short-listed. However, they lost out due to a very high bid. They could have still joined to provide the banking transactional services. However, they asked for a rate of ₹10 per transaction, which was what they were getting in other states such as Andhra Pradesh. We thought we should get a more competitive rate, as we would be making bulk transfers to a massive number of accounts. Further, there was unnecessary uncertainty with respect to payment of transaction fees by the account holders themselves for withdrawals and personal deposits. We wanted to pay for only those transactions where one party was the government. FINO soon got disinterested with our terms.

We opened a channel of communication with Punjab National Bank (PNB). K.C. Chakraborty, the loud-mouthed but efficient and risk-taking chairman and managing director (CMD) of the bank, got sold on the massive scale of financial inclusion Bhamashah promised. He wanted an audience with Vasundhara Raje, which we happily arranged. Punjab National Bank agreed to charge only for those transactions where one party was the government, at a rate of ₹5 per transaction. S.P. Singh, general manager of PNB, took over the task of putting the system together in Rajasthan. The bank worked with outstanding speed and conviction.

In the first week of August, connection was established between PNB's core banking system and the Bhamashah points of service (PoSs). With this, the entire system of digital bank accounts, unique identity-based registration system and operations through the smart card system came into existence.

Vasundhara Raje makes Bhamashah her USP

The completion of the Bhamashah platform's design and award of the letter of intent to IL&FS and Bartronics before the end of May removed any nagging doubts Chief Minister Vasundhara Raje might have had. Roping in PNB as the financial vehicle convinced her that the Rajiv–Subhash team would deliver the smart card and ₹1,500 in millions of accounts before the election took place in November 2008.

She used the women-centric nature of the programme to reach out to over 3 crore women of Rajasthan. She drafted a communication to every woman in the state in the form of a direct letter. She extolled the centrality of women in the development of Rajasthan. And she conveyed how the Bhamashah programme empowered them by registering every family with the woman as the head of family, issuing a smart card in her name, opening a digital bank account in her name and transferring ₹1,500 in the account, which only she could withdraw.

Very efficient mobilization of household registration and data collection agencies, mostly NGOs, by IL&FS, including Vijay Mahajan's Basix, achieved an almost miraculous feat. By September, the agencies had collected data from more than 43 lakh households. The district administration extended extraordinary support.

Punjab National Bank opened about 15 lakh accounts within six weeks of the system going live in the middle of August. The government started issuing sanctions for transferring ₹1,500 per family for families whose data had been captured in the central database and been checked for deduplication and whose digital bank account had been opened. By means of about 10 sanctions between the middle of September and the first week of October, the Rajasthan government transferred over ₹200 crore to PNB for deposit in the Bhamashah accounts.

We had tasked PNB to engage one banking correspondent for every 2,000 people. This roughly corresponded to one correspondent to three panchayats. Punjab National Bank started organizing its banking correspondents from the second fortnight of September.

Vasundhara Raje delivered the first set of smart cards to a group of women in a village in the second fortnight of September – they received their cards and a welcome letter from the bank with their account details. These women could withdraw the money by using the PoS machine that the banking correspondent carried. While it was a full rollout only in a few panchayats, Vasundhara Raje was convinced that the Bhamashah scheme had been delivered within the promised six-month period. Her ministers were also convinced. The CM, ministers and the party began using Bhamashah as a symbol of women's empowerment and a major instrument for poverty removal.

Ashok Gehlot moves heaven and earth

The Opposition, the Congress, under the leadership of Ashok Gehlot, was initially convinced that Bhamashah would remain a pipedream or turn out to be an administrative disaster. The unexpectedly quick rollout of the programme and its actual field implementation by September alarmed Ashok Gehlot. He decided to stop the juggernaut.

A writ petition was filed in the Rajasthan High Court in September 2008, alleging that the government was distributing ₹1,500 in cash to all households of Rajasthan, and it was a corrupt practice, especially in view of the Assembly elections that were around the corner. The matter was listed with a judge friendly to Gehlot's cause. The Election Commission had not announced the poll schedule, which was considered the earliest point of reference for stopping the announcement of 'new programmes'. However, the judge stayed the transfer of ₹1,500 to the accounts of the women beneficiaries. The order came the day after Vasundhara Raje had delivered the first set of smart cards and benefits.

We moved the division bench quickly. The division bench maintained the essence of the order of the judge, though it agreed that Bhamashah was an ongoing programme, not a new one. We had to move the Supreme Court, which agreed to hear the matter. The whole process, from the judgment of the single bench to the appeal in the Supreme Court against the order of the division bench, took place in a span of three weeks.

A day before the Supreme Court hearing, on 14 October, the Election Commission announced the election schedule. The Supreme Court also impleaded the Election Commission as a party. In the next hearing, the Election Commission also questioned the desirability of transferring cash in the Bhamashah accounts of women. The apex court refused to interfere with the order of the division bench in view of the announcement of elections.

The sum and substance of the court orders were that the incentive amount of ₹1,500 could not be transferred to the accounts of the beneficiaries. All other activities under the scheme – registration and issuance of smart cards – could continue. However, the declaration of the election schedule sowed the seeds of doubt in the minds of State Election Commissioner Vinod Zutshi, Chief Secretary Samant and some collectors. One or two of them referred the matter to the chief secretary and state election commissioner asking for clarification about continuing registration camps. The state election commissioner opined that even the registration camps should be discontinued. Despite our vehement arguments backed by provisions of the model code of conduct, Samant, a conservative and play-it-safe bureaucrat, sided with the view that the registration camps must be discontinued.

With all these interventions, judicial and administrative, the Bhamashah rollout came to a sudden stop.

Bhamashah in deep freeze

Ashok Gehlot put the Bhamashah programme in deep freeze as soon as he joined as Chief Minister.

Infrastructure Leasing & Financial Services had taken Aruna Sundararajan, an IAS officer of the 1982 batch of Kerala cadre, on deputation. She had excellent credentials as IT secretary in Kerala. Aruna was put in charge of the Bhamashah project.

We had crafted the agreement between the Rajasthan government and IL&FS over many sessions. The agreement with Bartronics was similarly modelled. In addition to outcome-based payment for actual services delivered, the agreement also provided for events of default and the compensation to be paid for taking over project assets in both events of default – by the government or IL&FS.

Aruna Sundararajan, Hari Sankaran and the IL&FS team made several efforts to convince the Gehlot government about the unique nature of the Bhamashah platform and how it was a trendsetter in the country. The government refused to budge. It appointed a committee of officers, which took about a year to give its report.

In the meantime, default occurred in terms of the agreement. However, IL&FS could not muster the courage to serve a default notice on the government. The project remained shelved during the entire five-year term of the Gehlot government.

During this period, the Government of India initiated the Aadhaar programme and, later, around 2013, DBT for LPG (cooking gas). The Gehlot government decided to go with the Government of India programme but moved in a characteristically slow manner.

The IL&FS board wrote off about ₹90 crore of investment in Bhamashah. It had made tons of money at the cost of most state governments in India. In this project, it lost money!

The threads of the Bhamashah programme would be picked up again in 2013 when Rajiv Mehrishi joined the next Vasundhara Raje government as chief secretary and I again as principal secretary, Finance. It would be combined with the Aadhaar and Jan-Dhan initiatives of the Government of India and successfully completed. Bhamashah, the legendary philanthropist who gave away all his wealth to Maharana Pratap, then stood immortalized in Rajasthan in the form of Bhamashah cards and numerous Bhamashah schematic variants the platform spun off.

Ashok Gehlot returned as chief minister in 2018. This time, he could not dismantle the scheme as it had been fully rolled out and become an inalienable part of Rajasthan's system of governance. He flirted with the idea of replacing the Bhamashah cards with so called 'Jan-Aadhaar' cards. After some time, he did change the name. Its basic structure and functionality, however, remain the same despite the change of name.

18

Two Budgets in Six Months

As soon as the Vasundhara Raje-led government assumed power in Rajasthan again in December 2013, I received a call from the new CM. She pulled my leg by commenting that I had not cared to even congratulate her for her victory in elections. She then told me to come back immediately to Rajasthan and work as principal secretary, Finance.

On the day she assumed responsibility, the Government of Rajasthan posted Rajiv Mehrishi as chief secretary and me as principal secretary, finance. The CM wrote to the prime minister, asking for the two of us to be relieved immediately. The Government of India did some formalities. Asked for my willingness, I conveyed no objection. In 48 hours, we received our relieving orders. I landed in Jaipur on 23 December 2013 for my second shot at the post of principal secretary, finance.

Reforms and investment instead of populism

A quick review of the state of finances revealed the serious impact of the contrasting approaches of Vasundhara Raje and Ashok Gehlot. Ashok Gehlot had adopted a populist approach unlike Vasundhara Raje's solid investment-oriented approach.

From 2008 to 2013, the Rajasthan government had not undertaken much capital expenditure. It had also suspended governance reforms envisaged under the Bhamashah programme. There were no good initiatives even under Aadhaar-linked direct benefit initiatives.

Instead, the government had raised social-security pensions and lowered eligibility age to 55 years. Further, a lackadaisical enrolment approach for the pension scheme (it was not linked to Aadhaar; there was a massive number of ineligible enrolments) raised the annual pension outgo four times, from about ₹600 crore to about ₹2,500 crore.

The government had not touched electricity tariffs for five years, resulting in a jump in the outstanding liabilities of the power sector from ₹15,000 crore in 2007–08 to ₹75,000 crore in 2013–14, with over ₹35,000 crore being purely short-term debt.

To appease government servants before elections, a stationery allowance of ₹750 per month, a completely impermissible allowance, was introduced for every employee, on the excuse that the government was not able to provide them paper, pens and pencils for office work!

Vasundhara Raje recharges field machinery

I was keen to build a long-term investment and governance reforms agenda for Rajasthan. Vasundhara Raje wholeheartedly supported this. The arrival of Rajiv Mehrishi as chief secretary strengthened her resolve further. The appointment of a relatively junior officer, Tanmay Kumar, as secretary to the chief minister assured that there would not be any roadblocks from the CMO.

Vasundhara Raje embarked on a strong field-connect programme, which envisaged the entire government (all cabinet ministers and senior officers) going to a region, staying there for at least three days, discussing issues with local representatives and organizing discussions with industrialists, investors and consultants about initiatives needed to solve the development issues. Cabinet meetings were also organized during these camps and on the spot decisions were taken. The finance secretary is present in all cabinet meetings in Rajasthan. The finance secretary also has, conventionally, the right to speak on any agenda before the Cabinet.

The Rajasthan government decided to first present its interim budget for 2014–15, which was done on 20 February within two months of the Vasundhara Raje government taking over. The modified regular budget was presented on 14 July.

Three ambitious programmes in interim budget

Normally, new programmes are not announced in the interim budget as it is generally intended to present the revised numbers for the current year and seek authorization for four to five months of expenditure before the regular budget is presented. This norm, however, is more appropriate for outgoing governments before elections, not incoming governments. Incoming governments must articulate at least major initiatives to guide the state machinery to productively work in the period between budgets. We also thought that we would be able to work out implementational details as the model code of conduct for the upcoming Lok Sabha elections remained in force.

Vasundhara Raje's first mega initiative was to announce a 25 GW solar electricity generation programme. This programme, intended to leverage the enormous natural advantage of Rajasthan, was beyond the imagination of most, as India had a total capacity of only about 2.3 MW of solar power generation in 2013. Later, this fitted in very well with the ambitious 175 GW renewable energy generation programme announced by Prime Minister Narendra Modi in 2015, which had 100 GW contribution from solar energy.

The second ambitious programme in the interim budget related to road construction and improvement. Vasundhara Raje announced that Rajasthan would build new east–west corridors of over 1,000 km to complete the grid of world-class roads in the state. She also announced that the state would undertake road improvement to raise 20,000 km of state highways and major district roads to the standard of mega highways. In line with her emphasis on building utilities infrastructure, she announced a programme to provide potable drinking water to an additional 20,000 villages (about one-sixth of total villages and over 80 per cent of underserved and problematic villages).

The third ambitious announcement related to picking up the threads of the stalled Bhamashah programme. She categorically stated that Bhamashah would be the vehicle to deliver 'all individual beneficiary schemes for the poor and incapacitated families' of Rajasthan.

With these announcements, she set the most ambitious goals for the state for her five years of government. Most people and officers in Rajasthan thought these were impractical. However, Rajiv Mehrishi and I were completely confident that the government would be able to deliver them and place Rajasthan at the frontline of Indian states in terms of growth, development and benefits to the poor and vulnerable.

Bhamashah is rolled out, finally

As soon as the team was assembled in the last week of December 2013, the Bhamashah programme was back on the table. Noting developments at the national level, most specifically the commencement of the Aadhaar programme, we decided to make the Bhamashah platform a universal programme for all residents of Rajasthan. We retained the basic architecture of the Bhamashah system, which envisaged it as a household registration system with a woman as head of the family. Every member of the family would be individually registered as part of the Aadhaar system and then the family would be digitally joined together by linking all individual members with their Aadhaar identity into the Bhamashah family. We also decided to leave the choice of bank account to the family concerned, with the condition that the bank should be the core banking facility so that the accounts become completely portable. This meant cooperative banks were out of the system. That was fine with us.

We also decided to build a first-class, state-level data centre and facility management system. The IL&FS team came back, asking they be paid for the losses suffered during the past five years. We told them not to entertain such thoughts. In the changed circumstances, we also informed them that they would not have exclusive right to register families. The Aadhaar ID system would be called upon to collect these details for the Bhamashah portal. Infrastructure Leasing & Financial Services was given the choice to become one of the registrars for the Aadhaar system and place onboard any data they had collected earlier by organizing the Aadhaar-cum-Bhamashah camps. This synergetic linking of Aadhaar and Bhamashah made a big difference, and Rajasthan became a leader in bringing the state's residents on the Aadhaar platform as well. We bid out the contract for a state-level data centre and the Bhamashah facility programme. Infrastructure Leasing & Financial Services won in the open bid. The total value of this contract was not even one-sixth the value of the work assigned to them in 2008.

The system had three-layered data for each Bhamashah family. First was basic identity data. This was the same as Aadhaar data, though hosted separately on the Bhamashah platform. The second layer had other important data like bank account details, ration card identification, basic educational and employment status, members of family, and the like. The third layer was individual, scheme-oriented and scalable. It captured the details required to avail benefits under the scheme such as education and institution details for those availing scholarships. The details of the first and second layers were collected at village-level camps organized and onboarded on the Bhamashah platform. The details of the third layer could be provided by the concerned individual by accessing the Bhamashah portal through thousands of common service centres (CSCs).

We mobilized the entire state machinery. Within three months, we had every part of the system working. All the banks came on board. In fact, there was competition among them. Later, when the Government of India announced the Jan-Dhan scheme to open an electronic bank account for every family, Rajasthan had already brought more than 50 per cent of families under banking coverage. In fact, families in the state had a full banking account in contrast to the basic Jan-Dhan account that offered limited facilities.

In the regular budget presented in July 2014, Vasundhara Raje announced a full suite of facilities and benefits to be delivered through the Bhamashah platform. Terming it as a harbinger of the biggest 'delivery' reforms, she made it clear that every cash and non-cash benefit under government programmes would be delivered through the programme. She also promised to resume payment of cash assistance to the woman-headed families, raising the amount to ₹2,000 per family. She announced insurance-based health coverage for every family covered by the food-security programme under the Bhamashah platform.

Energy sector reforms

Agriculture connections bleed electricity utilities in two ways: large under-recoveries of cost on account of free or highly subsidized supplies; and huge capital investment in laying infrastructure to reach electricity supplies to dispersed farmlands. While the first is well-known and widely prevalent, the second put enormous financial burden on electricity utilities in states like Rajasthan, where the farms, in particular in western Rajasthan, are located at great distances from the grid.

The Rajasthan government decided to deal with both.

There were over 3 lakh applications for agriculture electricity connections pending when the Vasundhara Raje government assumed power. The electricity utilities released about 30,000–40,000 connections every year. It was decided that this large backlog would be cleared in a market-based manner.

The chief minister announced two market-based decisions.

One, contrary to the demand of water conservationists, the government announced delivery of on-demand electricity connections in 'dark-zone areas' (where the water table was depleting on account of negative recharge) from 2015–16 at full cost of infrastructure, and further subject to full electricity tariff being charged. The idea was simple. If farmers found it worth their while to invest in taking an electricity connection at full market infrastructure and power tariff rate (which would not be the case for most farmers), the government would provide the connection on demand as it caused no capital or revenue loss to the utility.

Second, a few years earlier, the pragmatic and non-conventional electricity board chairman, P.N. Bhandari, had started a faster track route to save on electricity subsidy burden by giving out-of-turn connections to farmers willing to take connections for horticulture purposes (called 'nursery') at higher tariffs. The populist Ashok Gehlot government had discontinued the nursery scheme before the elections to give more 'normal' connections. Vasundhara Raje not only revived the nursery scheme but used it as a fast-track arrangements in non-dark zone areas, recovering not only higher (though not full) tariff as well as the capital cost of connections, again on demand.

These two decisions were expected to make the pending list of electricity connections evaporate, enable the electricity utility to recover full capital cost and bring down the electricity subsidy burden substantially.

No other state government in India had dared undertake such deep market reforms in the agriculture sector.

Restructuring road transport

The institutional and policy structures of India's road transport sector got frozen in the 1950s and 1960s. There were three pillars of this structure. One, the states nationalized all the important routes, irrespective of them being on national highways, state highways or on major district roads. Second, the bus transport business was nationalized as well and placed under a state-level or regional state-owned road transport corporation, in which the central government also had an equity stake. Third, small private operators (mostly owners of one to two buses) plied on non-nationalized, mostly 'other' district and village roads and clandestinely operated on nationalized routes in the name of using the connecting roads. These buses were not allowed anywhere near the bus stands operated by the state transport undertakings.

Rajasthan also meticulously followed this policy and institutional arrangement. Over 16,000 km of highways in the state were nationalized, on which Rajasthan State Road Transport Corporation (RSRTC) was the official monopoly operator. Illegal bus operations though were rampant and RSRTC had accumulated about ₹2,000 crore of losses and continued to lose money every year. There were about 80 bus stands largely operated by RSRTC (some were with local urban bodies) that, in general, provided horrible amenities and services to passengers.

The 2014–15 Rajasthan budget proposed fundamental reforms for all three problems. Vasundhara Raje made an unambiguous announcement to 'denationalize the entire nationalized routes'. She proposed the establishment of Rajasthan State Bus-Port Corporation (RSBSC) to develop the state's 80 bus stands as modern bus-ports for operation of buses of RSRTC and private operators. She divested RSRTC from the ownership of RSBSC and launched a business-like reforms programme for RSRTC to shape up or ship out, with budgetary assistance linked to progress of the reform timetable.

Indian states had seen the withering away of state road transport undertakings (for example, in Madhya Pradesh and Chhattisgarh) as they could not maintain their services on account of mounting losses and inability to acquire buses. Some, like Punjab, had also started bus-stand modernization programmes. However, no state had attempted a bold and comprehensive road transport-sector reform programme of complete denationalization, creating a PPP to develop and manage bus-port facilities, and subjecting the state transport undertaking on a reform-linked programme to either restore its health or let it fade away, with organized private-sector bus operators taking over.

Accompanying taxation reforms included establishment of computerized border check-posts and electronic weighbridges in PPP mode by abolishing physical check-posts on all 16 interstate border points, levying a green tax based on the engine capacity of vehicles and simplifying the transport tax structure on commercial vehicles.

Listing and privatizing PSUs

Rajasthan had some good, commercially managed public-sector undertakings (PSUs) like RIICO and the Rajasthan State Mines and Minerals (RSMM) company. Power-sector companies at the national level, such as NTPC and Powergrid, had demonstrated the commercial viability of the power-generation and transmission businesses. NTPC and Powergrid had been listed on stock exchanges to help raise much-needed equity capital to fund projects. Gujarat had also listed many state-level companies on stock exchanges. Rajasthan, however, had not listed even one. The state had produced many industrialists and entrepreneurs whose listed companies dominated the stock exchanges in the twentieth century. The non-entrepreneurial character of the government and its public enterprises was evident by their being totally averse to listing. This mindset and ingrained behaviour required a major jolt.

Vasundhara Raje sought to seize the bull by the horns in her 2014–15 budget. She announced the restructuring of the power-generation company Rajasthan Rajya Vidyut Utpadan Nigam (RVUN) and the transmission company Rajasthan Rajya Vidyut Prasaran Nigam (RVPN) to make them commercial entities by allowing them to earn regulatory return on their equity employed. She also announced 10 per cent divestment in both companies.

Expressing her surprise at the fact that Gujarat had 15 listed state enterprises whereas Rajasthan had none, she announced a mega divestment programme of 10–25 per cent equity in three profitable and commercially run enterprises: RSSM, RIICO and Rajasthan State Road Development Corporation (RSRDC).

Rajasthan's political and administrative leadership had imbibed feudal (*bado hukum*) values from its erstwhile princely states instead of the entrepreneurial spirit of the industrialists and businessmen it had produced aplenty. Vasundhara Raje's 2014–15 budget was an attempt to turn feudal Rajasthan into entrepreneurial Rajasthan.

A liberal dose of tax reforms and transparency

Announcing that she was guided by the principles of tax efficiency, effectiveness, stability and equity, Vasundhara Raje announced a slew of measures that showed her resolve to deal with difficult sectors for taxation, making the tax system transparent and eliminating the physical interface between taxpayers and tax administrators as much as possible.

Taking on holy cows, she imposed 5 per cent VAT on handicrafts and certain textiles that cost above a set price, and on whole spices. Micro, small and medium enterprises (MSMEs) that had been given unlimited exemption from taxation were brought into the tax net by reducing the central sales tax (CST) rate to 1 per cent and limiting the exemption to 10 years.

Fast-tracking digitalization of tax management, Vasundhara Raje declared that all assessments would be made online from 1 April 2015. She further announced that the VAT tax administration would be improved such that every tax-related service would be available electronically and online by 31 March 2016 using appropriate measures like digitization of the demand collection registers and payment of all tax and related payments.

To establish Jaipur as a parking station for aircrafts, VAT on aviation turbine fuel (ATF) was brought down from 20 per cent to 5 per cent. Amongst other new tax measures, an agriculture and infrastructure cess was imposed to collect revenue for improving agriculture infrastructure, and a new Entry Tax law was announced to take care of constitutional issues arising from the earlier 1999 Act.

Major reforms were undertaken under the stamps and registration taxation provision. Stamp duty for documents registered in the name of women was reduced to 3 per cent. Tax rates for documents executed by government departments (including old, unstamped and inadequately stamped) in favour of private parties were subjected to a one-time low payment. Resale of apartments was subjected to a very small stamp duty – ranging between 1 and 3 per cent, depending upon the time within which the flat was resold. Rent deeds were subjected to a very low rate of taxation.

The taxation package of the 2014–15 budget recognized the emerging digital economy and tried to mould the taxation system to this economy.

Governance reforms

Rajiv Mehrishi and Labour and Employment Secretary Rajat Mishra (previously secretary to Chief Minister Ashok Gehlot) had begun working on a slew of reforms in industrial and labour laws immediately after the Vasundhara Raje government assumed office.

The Industrial Disputes Act was amended to raise the limit of employed workers from 100 to 300 for enterprises to require permission from the government to close. Compensation payable upon retrenchment and such closures was raised by 50 per cent. Reforms were also undertaken in the Factories Act, Contract Labour (Employment and Regulation) Act, Apprentice Act and Boilers Act. The budget alluded to these reforms, which had come to be known nationally as the 'Rajasthan model of labour reforms'. The chief minister announced the revival of the Rajasthan Mission on Livelihood, which had become an excellent fulcrum for interface between employers and labour (it had been shut down by the Ashok Gehlot government). A labour market information system (LMIS) was proposed to create an online database of all willing youths looking for skill training and employment.

Significant institutional reforms were announced in the education sector: an English-medium higher secondary model school in each of the 248 panchayat samitis; establishment of a senior secondary school in each of the 9,177 panchayats of the state; consolidation of primary and upper primary schools to eliminate the problem of schools with no students or fewer students but with a higher number of teachers; and many more.

The government also announced the scaling up of digital delivery of its services by bringing 100 departments (from the existing 35) within the fold of CSC services. Digitalization was to be further supported by establishing an IT service centre in every panchayat and bringing all the public information with the government departments and organizations under one Rajasthan GIS (geographic information service) platform.

New institutions and ventures were established to capture newer opportunities. A Rajasthan State Petroleum Corporation was announced to be established in a joint venture with GAIL to undertake city gas distribution. Mining was permitted in tribal areas with adequate safeguards. A customized package was proposed for the defence sector to take advantage of the liberalized defence procurement policy announced by the Government of India.

Large government residential colonies like Gandhinagar in Jaipur and older government offices and properties like the Indira Gandhi Nahar Pariyojana building were proposed to be rebuilt by a joint venture with the National Building Construction Corporation (NBCC), which had successfully redeveloped a major residential complex in New Delhi.

State budgets do not receive due attention at the national level. However, they should be vehicles to undertake fiscal and policy reforms. Rajasthan's 2014–2015 budget introduced pathbreaking policy reforms across a very wide range of the real sector. This budget had the potential to transform the governance, economy and welfare of the people of the state.

Playing a major part in conceptualizing, designing and formulating this budget left me with the satisfaction of having done my duty.

19

'I Don't Want to See Him in the Cabinet Today'

My second innings as Rajasthan's principal secretary, Finance, had a very different setting as compared to my first stint in 2008. When I assumed charge in April 2008, the state was to go for elections in six months. This time, in 2014, I took over after the elections. The budget for 2008–09 had been presented in February 2008 while Rajiv Mehrishi was still principal secretary, Finance. This time, I was in charge of both the interim and regular budgets. The principal task in 2008 was to implement the newly conceived Bhamashah scheme and resist pressure for political giveaways in the run-up to elections. The principal task in 2014 was to lay the foundations of reforms and rapid economic progress in the state.

The arrival of Rajiv Mehrishi as chief secretary made the task doable. We held similar views on governance, economic reforms and financial management. Rajiv was a little more of a fiscal fundamentalist than me. He also did not mind using some amount of subterfuge to achieve the right goals. The financial position of the state in 2003, when Vasundhara Raje assumed power for the first time, was terrible. In 2013, it was not that bad. While some costly populist programmes were announced by the outgoing Gehlot government, it had actually failed to spend full budget allocations during its five-year tenure. There was no overdraft (overdrawing from a state's account with RBI at a higher rate of interest, which had to be cleared in 10 days to avoid the state's payments from being suspended) or WMAs (at lower interest rates within the limit approved by RBI). However, Rajiv Mehrishi was keen to show that the fiscal position was worse than it actually was, for two reasons: to paint the previous government in as bad a light as possible and to ensure

Vasundhara Raje did not splurge. I accommodated him to the extent that I did not have to utter or present a lie.

I had served as principal secretary, Finance, in 2008 for about nine months. My 2014 tenure was also for about nine months. The second innings had three time slices: one, the period of January–March until the Lok Sabha elections were announced when the Congress was in power at the Centre; second, April–May, when the model code of conduct was in force; and third, June–September, when the BJP-led National Democratic Alliance (NDA) had formed the government at the centre under the leadership of Narendra Modi. These three periods were quite different from one other.

Rajasthan set a hectic pace to figure out its development and reforms programme at the beginning of calendar year 2014. Experts were called in to advise on education, labour and employment, infrastructure, power, and so on. Vasundhara Raje reviewed the status of programme implementation in every department over about 50-odd meetings. I was part of all these meetings. It was a great opportunity to learn and test ideas.

The Fourteenth Finance Commission (FC-XIV) was at work. It was awaiting Rajasthan's memorandum, and its state visit was overdue.

There was some functional change in the relationship with the CMO and secretary. While the practice of all important files being taken directly by the principal secretary, Finance, to the chief minister continued, Vasundhara Raje started calling Tanmay Kumar, her secretary, to some of these discussions. Unlike past practice, Chief Secretary Rajiv Mehrishi got involved in budget-making. Tanmay was also invited to most of the pre-budget discussions. I did not mind this. They functioned more as sounding boards, which improved the quality of preparation. Most reforms described in the previous chapter were my ideas and I was happy to see most of these ideas incorporated in the budget speech, with the CM taking full ownership of them.

Larger share in central taxes had a Rajasthan connection

One of the first major tasks to complete was preparation of the state memorandum for the FC-XIV. Vinod Pandya, a sincere and knowledgeable officer of the Rajasthan Accounts Service, who was promoted to the IAS, had prepared the basic draft. I was expected to bring in a bigger policy perspective, considering my previous work in the state finance division in the Ministry of Finance and my general standing in this area.

I thoroughly revised the draft memorandum. Rajiv took great interest in the process, and we were able to prepare a memorandum that was rich in federal fiscal issues. Taking a national perspective, among other major recommendations, Rajasthan's memorandum argued for the closure of multiple channels of resource transfers like central assistance to state plans, additional central assistance, centrally sponsored schemes, and so on, and replace them with one single untied mode of transfer (transfers which have no conditions attached to them, like the share in central taxes) – a hike in the share of central taxes from 32 per cent to 50 per cent. We argued for this national realignment of resource transfers when the Commission, headed by Dr Y.V. Reddy, visited Rajasthan in March.

While the erudite FC-XIV would have its own reasons and rationale, it finally recommended raising the states' share in central taxes to 42 per cent – one of the largest jumps ever, which was possibly unanticipated by the central government. In its recommendations, it also said that the centre may discontinue other schematic transfers including centrally sponsored schemes (CSSs) to keep its overall resource transfers to 48 per cent of gross tax revenues, as was the case during the FC-XIII period.

As luck would have it, Rajiv Mehrishi became finance secretary in the Government of India when the recommendations of the FC-XIV came up for acceptance. He ensured that the government accepted the recommendation of 42 per cent share of states in central taxes.

Excessive generosity to Barmer refinery clawed back

Discovery of crude oil in the exploration areas originally given to ONGC in Rajasthan by Cairn Energy in 2003 raised political ambitions to build a petroleum refinery in Barmer district. There was no real economic case for the refinery. The crude produced in the state was heavy, which normal refineries could not process. It sold at a discount. The projections of resource availability suggested that the resources would not be sufficient for even a 9-million-tonne refinery. India had already built refining capacity that was more than its crude processing requirement. India had emerged as a major exporter of refined petroleum products. Barmer district was located deep in the desert where consumption demand was small. Compared to a shore-located 40-million-tonne refinery like at Jamnagar, any 9-million-tonne refinery in Barmer district was bound to be born sick and loss-making.

Yet, the Gehlot government made the construction of the Barmer refinery its biggest political bet during 2008–13. The obliging SBI Capital Markets (SBI Caps) produced a techno-economic feasibility report for a 9-million-tonne refinery and petrochemical complex at Barmer based on a mix of Rajasthan crude and imported Middle East crude. To make the refinery financially viable, the project report envisaged payment of over ₹54,000 crore by the Rajasthan government in interest-free loans over a period of 15 years, while the refinery cost was projected at about ₹60,000 crore. The Gehlot government agreed to pay this massive subsidy as interest-free loans in addition to taking 26 per cent equity and granting VAT concessions amounting to thousands of crores. Racing against time, the public-sector HPCL (Hindustan Petroleum Corporation Limited) was pushed to set it up. The foundation stone was laid in September 2013, just before the declaration of the model code of conduct, when the project had not even achieved its financial closure.

Examination of the file related to concessions granted to the Barmer refinery in the finance revenue department revealed the government's superficial understanding of the financial and technical aspects of the project. There was no examination of the financial viability projections made by the consultant SBI Caps. No one tried to understand why ₹54,000 crore of interest-free loans were needed. The technical risks relating to heavy crude requiring excessive investments, impact on profitability, the cost implications of bringing Middle East crude to Barmer, transportation costs of taking final products to consumption centres, and other related issues were not considered. It was truly pathetic.

We examined the matter thoroughly. It was clear that excessive padding had been done to make Rajasthan cough up ₹54,000 crore in interest-free loans for its trophy refinery. Our calculations suggested that there was no justification for more than ₹15,000 crore of interest-free loans and most tax concessions on crude oil and final products to generate a 14 per cent return on equity. Anticipating the fading supply of crude oil in Rajasthan and to offer a better mix, we found an option that envisaged the use of about 60 per cent of light Middle East crude oil to be most suitable.

I sought the approval of the chief minister to renegotiate the project with HPCL; she agreed.

When confronted with this analysis, HPCL officials found it difficult to disagree. Our demand that the interest-free loans would have to be taken out of the package agreed earlier was difficult for them to accept. Hindustan

Petroleum Corporation Limited was not really interested in putting up the refinery in the first place. It was doing it because the government asked it to, and it wanted to keep its financial returns safe by fleecing the ill-equipped Rajasthan government. To show that we really meant business, we offered to raise the equity stake of the Rajasthan government to 49 per cent if it provided HPCL comfort.

The chief minister, highlighting the gross bankruptcy of the commitment of the Gehlot government to pay ₹54,000 crore in interest-free loans, announced her government's resolve to renegotiate the project in the budget. I attempted to persuade her to abandon the project, but she found this too politically hot to handle.

The project remained in negotiating limbo after Rajiv Mehrishi and I left for central postings in September–October 2014. In 2018, HPCL finally agreed to the package we had proposed in July 2014. The interest-free loans were reduced from ₹54,000 crore to ₹15,000 crore. In tune with the political/election cycle, the project was reinaugurated by Prime Minister Narendra Modi in 2018, again before the elections.

The refinery project achieved financial closure in 2019, and some critical contracts were awarded. There was a race to 'commission' the refinery during 2018–23, when Ashok Gehlot headed the state government. It could not be done. As I complete this book in July 2025, the refinery is making some production but is expected to be commissioned only in December 2025. I had handled a white elephant, the Kota soybean project, in 1989. The Barmer refinery project proved to be a herd of white elephants.

The game in excise

In my first innings as principal secretary in 2008, I was not really involved in excise policy and its implementation – the budget had been passed, excise policy announced and shops allotted by the time I took over in April. In 2014, however, one of my first tasks was to get the excise policy for 2014–15 approved and operationalized.

On the pattern of Karnataka and a few other states, Rajasthan had done away with the system of contracting out 'areas' for sale (the *theka* system) of both country-made (*desi*) and India-made foreign liquor (IMFL or *angrezi*) in 2005, and created the Rajasthan State Beverages Corporation Ltd (RSBCL) to channel liquor sales through designated shops. Manufacturers were required to notify their prices for the brands they wanted to sell in the state, give an undertaking that the price offered was not more than the lowest price offered elsewhere, and stock their liquor in Beverages Corporation godowns from where designated shopkeepers picked it up. The sales price was formally approved by the excise commissioner.

Rajasthan had experimented with reviving its 'royal' desi liquor brands under the heritage liquor class during Vasundhara Raje's earlier tenure; the state undertaking Rajasthan State Ganganagar Sugar Mills (RSGSM) in Sri Ganganagar produced this heritage liquor. As there was not much traction, production was stopped in 2008. Principal secretary, Finance, was chairman of the Beverages Corporation, and the excise commissioner was the managing director. Day-to-day work was managed by an RAS officer appointed as ED.

Excise Commissioner Dinesh Kumar, carrying on from the previous Gehlot regime, did much of the hard work in preparing policy proposals before he was replaced. O.P. Yadav, a promoted IAS officer who was a bit controversial and overly loyal to the chief minister but quite hardworking and efficient, took over.

The excise policy was formulated and announced in February. Vasundhara Raje wanted to liberalize the pricing policy by eliminating the condition of subjecting the price to minimum price elsewhere. I had welcomed the idea as this condition had resulted in some corrupt practices in the department. Vasundhara Raje also wanted to appoint a consultant, an expert in heritage liquor, who could reboot the production and sale of royal heritage liquor. I had agreed to this proposal as well.

Liquor shops were allotted by lottery in 2014. While the *theka* system had been abolished, there were still some groups with deep pockets and long arms that were interested in cornering as many shops as possible. As there was a restriction on allotting more than two shops to one retailer, these groups filed numerous applications for each shop in the names of their family members, relatives, friends and agents. This generated revenues of more than ₹100 crore in application fees alone. The designation of shops (somewhat reduced from the previous number) and allotment of retail contracts was completed in time and the system was ready for sale of liquor from 1 April 2014. Following a process of competitive applications, a person was appointed as consultant for promoting heritage liquor as well.

Manufacturers filed their price lists for the liquor brands they wanted to sell. Formal approval by the excise commissioner was expected to be virtually automatic as there was no requirement of verifying that the price they offered was the lowest in the country. Thus, I was quite surprised when the excise commissioner did not approve the price lists even after 10 days. All sale was taking place on a provisional price basis.

When I checked with Excise Commissioner Yadav, he told me that as per instructions received (obviously from the CMO), the files had been sent to the consultant and was awaiting approval. The consultant was not supposed to handle this work. There was clearly some game afoot. It became apparent that the policy of free pricing was not intended to give freedom to the manufacturers but most probably to fix a higher cut (share) in the approved price (paid as a bribe) of the liquor that would be sold during the year.

In 2005, it was rumoured in the state that the sudden stroke that S.P. Gupta – the then principal secretary of finance – suffered had something to do with pressure for overlooking corrupt practice in the implementation of excise policy. I was determined not to allow corrupt practices to gain ground during my stewardship of the department.

I brought the matter of pending approvals to the notice of Rajiv Mehrishi. We discussed it with Vasundhara Raje. She insisted that the consultant might be undertaking only a routine check. To me, it appeared that she was trying to brush the matter under the carpet. I did a further background check on the consultant selected. It turned out that he had been in the liquor business but had a shady past. Nor did he have any real experience in the heritage liquor business. I moved a proposal to terminate his services. I also took the entire matter of price approval on file to the CM besides sharing a piece of my mind with the excise commissioner in the board meeting of the Beverages Corporation.

Things moved quickly. The chief minister first tried to keep me out of the excise issues by specifically telling me not to bother myself with the implementation of the excise policy. I refused to oblige. There was no way the consultant could have continued after I placed details of his shady past on file; he was fired. The price lists were approved soon. In the meantime, Praveen Gupta, an energetic but compliant officer, who was in Vasundhara Raje's staff in her previous tenure, had joined as revenue secretary. I was soon divested of the charge of chairman of the Beverages Corporation, which was given to secretary, Revenue.

Vasundhara Raje had mastered the art of an official split personality, which was in evidence in her first tenure as well. On one side was her extraordinarily efficient, transparent and sagacious management of expenditure and development programmes. During the three years from 2006 to 2008, when

I basically dealt with budgets, expenditures and development programmes, there was not a single decision she took that appeared to be motivated by any consideration other than public interest. However, she operated differently in revenue-earning departments like excise, land allotment, JDA, and the like.

The excise episode created a lack of trust, but I did not consider it enough to make it a breaking point. As described in the previous chapter in the context of the state's most reformist budget, almost everything on expenditure, tax reforms and policy reforms was moving well. She also agreed with my proposal to close the controversial Sports City project that Lalit Modi was trying to foist on the Rajasthan government.

The Binani Cement affair kept us on our toes

Rajasthan has rich deposits of limestone, which are attractive to the cement industry. It did not require much government incentive to attract investment in cement plants. Further, most of the cement produced in the state went outside and enjoyed relatively liberal interstate sales tax rates in the 1990s. The cement industry, however, kept pushing the state to give it some incentives. The investment promotion policy of Rajasthan, therefore, had alternated between no sales tax incentives (negative list) to limited incentives.

The investment promotion policy for other industrial investments was progressively made more liberal. In the 1990s, it was expanded to categorize investments in large industries as 'prestigious' and 'very prestigious', promising increasingly higher incentives. By amendments in the investment promotion policy in 1996, 'prestigious' industries were exempted 75 per cent of annual tax due for up to 25 per cent of total investment made.

The cement industry, which was in the negative list prior to this, was made eligible for limited incentives by specifically providing an incentive structure in an annex of the policy, which restricted sales tax incentives for cement plants to only 10 per cent of the annual tax due.

There were, in all, seven categories of general industries for incentive purposes. The scheme specifically excluded the cement industry for incentives in clauses relating to six of the seven categories. Inadvertently or otherwise, for the large general industry category (all industries other than cement), the specific exclusionary clause was missing.

Binani Cement established a plant in Sirohi district of Rajasthan and claimed 75 per cent tax exemption, arguing it was a large general industry. The tax authorities allowed only the 10 per cent tax exemption available for the cement industry. The difference meant a tax liability of about ₹200 crore by the time I assumed charge as principal secretary, Finance, in December 2013.

Rajiv Mehrishi had fought this case tooth and nail from 2005 to 2008 when Binani Cement, promoted by Braj Binani, managed to get orders from tax tribunals and Rajasthan High Court to the effect that the unit was entitled to 75 per cent tax exemption. The case finally reached the Supreme Court. In February 2014, the Supreme Court upheld the contention of the Rajasthan government and ordered that Binani Cement was entitled to only 10 per cent exemption, reversing the High Court order.

We acted fast. The orders, formally passed by the commercial tax officer in Sirohi, were carefully drafted, with Rajiv Mehrishi taking an active interest. A demand of over ₹154 crore was slapped on Binani Cement and all its 26 bank accounts were seized. Braj Binani used every tactic to pressurize the government. He shut down production in the cement factory and persuaded workers to agitate, threatening them with loss of jobs. We stayed firm. He went to court. One particular judge in the High Court had always favoured Binani. He tried to bring pressure on the government, at one stage, threatening to summon me to court and, at another hearing, pontificating that the government did not know how to argue its case, even appointing a lawyer to represent the government! We stood firm despite all these tactics and threats. At one stage, Binani interfered with the attachment orders by getting an order that only a fraction of the due amount would be recovered. Essentially, he wanted us to accept a 10-year-long, interest-free arrears payment plan.

Despite trying every trick in the book, Braj Binani did not succeed. Vasundhara Raje also backed us. We threatened to take over the plant. After some time, the plant was restarted. We were able to recover more than 25 per cent of the due amount within four months. I don't have details of the recoveries made after I left in September 2014. Binani Cement went into bankruptcy later and was acquired by Ultratech Cement in 2018.

'Can you come over to Delhi today?'

At about 11 a.m. on 9 September 2014, Dr P.K. Mishra, additional principal secretary to Prime Minister Narendra Modi, called me and asked whether I could come to Delhi.

I was taken completely by surprise. When I asked him the reason, he was not specific, only saying he was speaking to five officers regarding a financial-sector assignment. I was due to travel to Singapore the next day as part of a delegation led by C.S. Rajan, then additional chief secretary, Infrastructure, to discuss some investment proposals. I asked Dr Mishra whether I could see him the next day as I was scheduled to travel from Delhi anyway. He told me it was urgent and that I must come that very day.

Vasundhara Raje was in her fort palace in Dholpur and was not taking calls. I spoke to Rajiv Mehrishi. He allowed me to travel to Delhi to see Dr P.K. Mishra. He, too, could not guess the reason for this sudden call.

I took the 3 p.m. flight, reached Delhi by 4.30 p.m. and was at the PMO by 6 p.m. Dr Mishra met me around 6.30 p.m. and we chatted for about half an hour.

Dr Mishra knew me, though we had never worked together. He was part of the Gujarat delegation to negotiate the Gujarat earthquake project in 2001, which I had led as director, DEA. Thereafter, at a training course in Mussoorie, where he had spoken as a power-sector regulator, we had discussed some issues related to the power sector.

Other names on his list of potential candidates, provided by the DoPT to Dr Mishra, included my batchmates K.P. Krishnan and D.B. Gupta, and two other officers, as he told me.

In the discussion, he mentioned that one of the positions for which he was speaking to these few officers was that of India's ED in the World Bank. The moment he mentioned this (he was guarded and was exploring the possibility in case I was chosen by the prime minister), I told him plainly that while I would be interested in the job, there was no likelihood of me being available. Under no circumstance would Vasundhara Raje agree to my moving outside Rajasthan. He asked whether the chief secretary could persuade her. I said it was absolutely unlikely.

Dr Mishra then sounded me out about the suitability of other officers in the list. I gave my opinion about the officers I knew. I told him K.P. Krishnan was the most suitable person on the list. When he asked me to suggest someone outside the list, I suggested the names of Rajiv Kumar, then chief secretary, Uttar Pradesh (earlier joint secretary in the cabinet secretariat) and J.S. Deepak, in the Department of Telecom.

The meeting ended with these enquiries. Nothing more was said or indicated. Convinced that I had sufficiently conveyed my unavailability, I returned to Jaipur the same night as I had to dispose of some urgent files before I left for

Singapore the next day. Both Rajiv Mehrishi and I agreed that the matter was over. D.B. Gupta went to meet Dr Mishra the next day, again with the approval of Chief Secretary Mehrishi. He was told that the Government of India was putting together a panel of four to five officers for financial-sector positions that could be used when necessary. No specific position was mentioned to him.

On 10 September, I left for Delhi by the afternoon flight along with C.S. Rajan and Veenu Gupta. We took the late evening flight to Singapore and reached on the morning of 11 September.

Around 11.30 a.m., when we were on our way to a scheduled meeting, my phone rang. It was Dr Mishra. Congratulating me, he informed me that the prime minister had approved my appointment as India's ED in the World Bank and that orders were being issued that day. I was flabbergasted. C.S. Rajan and Veenu Gupta, sitting in the same car, congratulated me.

Later, I gathered that the last date for making nominations for the Indian constituency, which included Bangladesh, Sri Lanka and Bhutan, for the election of EDs for the next two-year cycle beginning 1 November 2014 was 11 September. The Modi government, which had taken over at the end of May and had no list of favourites, decided to continue with the policy formulated during Chidambaram's time to post officers of senior joint secretary or additional secretary levels to the ED's post at the World Bank and the Asian Development Bank (ADB). As the deadline was approaching and the government had not made up its mind, there was a tearing hurry to complete the entire process of interviewing shortlisted candidates over a 48-hour period from 9 to 11 September.

Vasundhara Raje felt 'cheated'

The establishment officer, DoPT, issued the orders on the evening of 11 September. Our delegation in Singapore went about its business on 11 and 12 September and reached Delhi on the afternoon of 13 September.

Unbeknown to me, all hell had broken loose in Rajasthan.

Vasundhara Raje returned to Jaipur on 11 September and was informed of the Government of India order. She was infuriated and felt cheated. She summoned Rajiv Mehrishi and declared, 'Subhash is not going anywhere.' On her insistence, Rajiv Mehrishi spoke to Dr P.K. Mishra. Dr Mishra told him that these were the orders of the prime minister and that he could not do anything about it.

Vasundhara Raje decided to take the matter in her own hands. She asked Rajiv Mehrishi to draft a letter to the prime minister intimating him of her decision not to relieve me for the central deputation. Rajiv advised her against it but drafted the letter for her signature when she insisted. Some confabulations took place on the political grid as well. She was told that the prime minister was unlikely to accommodate her request, even if it was made in writing. The relationship between the two was also not very cordial.

She decided not to send the letter.

'I don't want to see him in the cabinet meeting today'

A cabinet meeting was scheduled for 3 p.m. on 13 September. Among other things, the cabinet was to consider the new Rajasthan Investment Promotion Policy (RIPS), 2014. Formally within the domain of the industries department, RIPS was essentially a finance department affair, as it used tax incentives as the principal mode of promoting industrial investment. I was instrumental in formulating quite an unconventional policy and was expected to present it to the cabinet. Incidentally, Industries Secretary Veenu Gupta had also travelled as part of the Singapore delegation.

As we could not have landed in Jaipur before 4.30 p.m., we had requested that the meeting be scheduled for 5 p.m. We learnt in Delhi around 2.30 p.m. that the meeting had been rescheduled for 5 p.m. As I was about to leave for the secretariat at about 4.45 p.m., I received intimation that the meeting had been further rescheduled for 7 p.m. Happy to get some time, I went through the agenda papers for the meeting.

On my way to the secretariat, I sent a message to Gajanand Sharma, special secretary to the chief minister, who handled her appointments, requesting a meeting with her any day in the coming week for a courtesy visit by me and Anjali my wife.

As was the practice, I went into the cabinet room with my papers and took my seat at 7 p.m. All the ministers were present, and the chief minister was expected anytime. Half an hour went by; there was no sign of Vasundhara Raje. I went outside to say hello to Rajiv Mehrishi and Tanmay Kumar. They conveyed nothing. We exchanged greetings and I went back to the Cabinet room and sat down.

At about 7.45 p.m., Rajiv Mehrishi came in and asked me to step out. He asked me to collect all my papers and sit in Tanmay's room. I sensed something was amiss. I asked him what the matter was. He told me to stay put in Tanmay's room till the Cabinet meeting was over. I asked about the RIPS item. He said Veenu Gupta would take care of it.

At about 8 p.m., when I was still in Tanmay's room, I received orders placing my services at the disposal of the Government of India. I was also relieved of my charge with immediate effect to proceed on deputation to the centre. Prem Singh Mehra was appointed the new principal secretary, Finance.

Vasundhara Raje came around 8.15 p.m., after my orders were out. She had told Rajiv Mehrishi she did not want to see me in the cabinet meeting.

I could only smile at the turn of events. I sat in Tanmay's room for the duration of the cabinet meeting, which was about 45 minutes, and left the room after she had departed, thinking how quickly times could change.

Arvind Mayaram would not initiate a note to create OSD position

I was expected to assume the position of ED in the World Bank only on 1 November 2014. There were more than one-and-a-half months to go. Almost always, in the past, officers had gone to the International Monetary Fund (IMF) and World Bank while they were serving in the Government of India.

There was much procedural work to be completed after the appointment. The World Bank had to complete its election process. Thereafter, it had to complete the formal process of appointment. The US government had to issue appropriate diplomatic visas and confer an ambassadorial rank.

I was not required to be in the Government of India while these formalities and processes were being completed. Vasundhara Raje's decision left me hanging. I was not to continue in the Rajasthan government, but there was no post for me to join in the Government of India, from which my salary for the intervening period could be paid.

Complying with the order, I cleared my table and pending work on 14 September and was relieved with effect from that afternoon. I decided to use the 'joining time' of 10 days (provided to officers being transferred as they shift to the new place of posting) to wind up my household in Jaipur and shift it to Delhi.

During a visit to Delhi during this period, I met and requested Arvind Mayaram, who was secretary, DEA, to propose creation of a new temporary post. My request did not find a sympathetic ear. There was some coldness in our relationship and Mayaram refused to move the proposal and asked me to request the PMO to direct the Cabinet secretariat to do it directly.

There was only one precedent of creating a position of OSD for drawing a salary before the officer joined as ED in World Bank/IMF. Former cabinet secretary Surendra Singh had been posted as ED, World Bank, in the late 1980s. The post of OSD was created for him for the time after his tenure as cabinet secretary until he joined the World Bank.

Dr P.K. Mishra issued the necessary instructions directly. The cabinet secretariat completed the process to create a post of OSD by temporarily upgrading a vacant post in the DEA.

I joined the DEA as OSD on 24 September. The period of a little more than a month came in handy to examine the major India-related issues in the World Bank and also understand more about the work that awaited me in Washington, DC.

Vasundhara Raje's tiff with PM Modi

One theory offered by people, especially Vasundhara Raje's detractors, for her anger and unexpected behaviour at my sudden World Bank appointment, was that Prime Minister Modi wanted to deprive her of the two pillars on which her administration rested: Rajiv Mehrishi and I. I was taken away first; Mehrishi, a month later, as he was appointed finance and secretary, DEA, with a promise that he might be the next cabinet secretary.

Another theory suggested that people unhappy with my style and approach to work played on her insecurities by telling her that I had been angling for the World Bank position behind her back. She was told that I knew about my selection all along and went to Singapore to have a joyride at the cost of the state.

I don't know anything about the first theory. I don't think it was true either.

As for the second, D.B. Gupta confirmed her frayed mindset. She was upset with him, too, for having gone to Delhi to meet Dr Mishra without first telling her. When they had a person-to-person discussion a couple of weeks later, she told him that I was aware of my ED posting. She further told him that I should not have gone to meet Dr Mishra, and she would have refused permission if I had asked for it. Her grouse was also that I should not have accepted the assignment.

While it is untrue that I knew anything about the posting or had angled for it, I do think there was good reason for her to suspect such motives or be upset with the way the episode played out. I had helped her deliver one of the most reformist and ambitious budgets only two months earlier. She could have spoken to me directly.

To implement these major reforms, she needed me in Rajasthan, more so because almost the entire establishment was against these reforms. My sense is that she felt most upset at prime minister Modi taking away my services without consulting her or even mentioning it to her. Her difficult relationship with the prime minister perhaps made her find the whole thing quite unfair and meant possibly to cut her down to size.

I made one more request to see her before I departed Jaipur lock, stock and barrel on 24 September. Her secretary did not revert. I decided that was the end of the matter.

I never reached out to her thereafter. We have neither met nor spoken to each other since September 2014.

Part C

At the World Bank and the Centre

20

'You Must Be a Dummy Candidate'

My first posting with the Government of India in 2000 as director in the DEA happened in the unlikeliest of circumstances. This posting transformed the future of my life in the IAS and provided me an unprecedented opportunity to work and excel at managing economic affairs nationally and internationally.

This also had its challenging moments. Chandra Babu Naidu, holding the levers of power in New Delhi, was riding roughshod over other states and taking away an unprecedentedly large proportion of multilateral resources to Andhra Pradesh. My analysis and resistance led to stopping him somewhat in his tracks, and had him baying for my blood.

The DEA posting also ended in very unusual circumstances. First, I was deprived of my promotion to a joint secretary position for many months. Quite a few officers joined in the positions vacant in the DEA, but I was not promoted. Finally, I was shifted to Department of Expenditure, which I had no objection to, instead of being promoted in the DEA itself.

The DEA posting was the longest of my service life – three years and four months. This chapter recounts the drama associated with my posting in DEA, the Andhra interlude and my exit. In Chapter 21, I recount my stint in the World Bank and IMF ([fund-bank] division of DEA). Chapter 22 includes an account of other important developments during my stay in the DEA.

Not a dummy candidate

Sometime in March 2000, I received a call from Bhaskar Khulbe, my batchmate and then director in the DoPT, Government of India (later, secretary, PMO, and advisor to the prime minister in the PMO). He said I had been 'retained' and asked me to come to Delhi to complete some missing information in my executive sheet.

At the first go, I did not quite comprehend what he was saying. He explained that after the state government sent my name for consideration for posting at director's level, my service record had been examined, and I had been shortlisted for a posting in the Government of India. I told him I would come soon.

As I had not given any formal consent to go on deputation to the centre, I went to the secretariat and checked with the secretary, DoPT. I was told that after his telephonic talk with me a few days ago, Chief Secretary Indrajeet Khanna had recorded that I had consented to be sent to the Government of India. My name was duly forwarded by the DoPT for appropriate consideration.

I went to Delhi a few days later and met Bhaskar Khulbe. There were some missing entries relating to my professional qualifications of cost accounting and company secretaryship, which I provided. My ACR record was complete. I came to know for the first time there that six out of my last seven ACRs, which were considered by the Central Staffing Board (CSB) for assigning officers to vacant posts, were outstanding.

Bhaskar felt I was likely to be considered for vacancies in the next meeting of the CSB due in a week. Things were moving fast.

The DEA was considered a highly prestigious department in the Government of India in those days. Deputy secretaries/directors in the DEA dealt with externally aided projects, headed negotiations with multilateral and bilateral agencies, and travelled abroad frequently. Considering all this, many influential people (ministers, senior secretaries) pulled strings to have their wards and relatives in the civil services posted to the DEA. Finance ministers had their own preferences. The doors of the DEA generally opened only for the powerful, influential and well-connected.

The system of the CSB, in 2000, operated with the DoPT proposing three names for each post. The DoPT minister personally cleared the names, especially for posts that were considered in great demand, like the DEA and Department of Commerce. These names were considered by the CSB, chaired by the cabinet secretary – the secretary of the department with the vacancy and the secretary, DoPT – were also present. The CSB placed the three names in an order of merit.

The file with the CSB recommendations went to the Appointments Committee of the Cabinet (ACC), which then comprised the DoPT minister, home minister and prime minister, and then came to the minister concerned for concurrence (in the case of the DEA, it was the finance minister). After the approval of ACC and the concerned minister, the DoPT issued orders asking the state government concerned to send the officer on deputation to the Government of India.

Priyadarshi Thakur, my education secretary only two years earlier in Rajasthan, had moved to Delhi as managing director of National Agricultural Cooperative Marketing Federation of India (NAFED). When my name was retained by the Government of India, I met him as well. He offered me the post of deputy managing director (DMD) in NAFED. I thought it would be great to work with him. And a posting in NAFED also meant that the transition to Delhi, with its notorious shortage of living accommodation and vehicular support, would be a little easier. I collected some papers about NAFED, including the terms and conditions of the appointment and the role of the DMD, and returned to Jaipur.

A couple of days later, Bhaskar Khulbe informed me that my name had been included in a panel for the post of director in the DEA. He did not say anything more. I immediately called Priyadarshi Thakur. Without batting an eyelid, he said, 'You must be a dummy candidate.' What he meant was that the DoPT had fine-tuned a strategy of placing one strong candidate (whom they wanted selected by the CSB) and two weaker/uninfluential 'dummy' candidates for posts in departments like the DEA, which facilitated the selection of the preferred candidate. The remaining two candidates were not serious contenders.

The name of my batchmate and friend Devendra Bhushan Gupta was sent, I came to know, as part of another panel for the DEA two weeks earlier. D.B. Gupta did have some influence. Still, he was not selected. S.P. Gupta, an outstanding officer of the Rajasthan cadre on deputation to the Government of India as joint secretary, Mines, felt that while I had merit on my side (as a professional cost accountant and company secretary besides being a batch topper), people who were being picked up for the DEA those days were either Kayasthas or from Bihar, as reflected in the composition of officers in the DEA at that time.

I did not entertain any serious hopes of being selected for the DEA and focused mentally on the DMD position in NAFED.

No. 1 in the DEA panel

In early April, the evening of the CSB meeting, I called Bhaskar Khulbe. He was not very forthright (he was possibly under instructions not to divulge too much about the CSB meeting) but dropped hints to indicate that I was at the top of the DEA post panel.

After a few days, the file came back to the DoPT. Khulbe then officially confirmed my selection by the ACC and that the file would go to the finance minister soon.

How did it happen?

Vasundhara Raje, then minister of state in the DoPT, was an MP from Rajasthan. She probably wanted to do a good turn to Rajasthan cadre officers. When I met her and Govind Mohan, her private secretary, for the first time after my file had come back from ACC with approval, I learnt that the DEA was one of the key places where she was determined to see a Rajasthan officer posted. She had insisted on including D.B. Gupta's name when the last vacancy had arisen in the DEA. She was not happy when Gupta was not selected.

Just about the time my name entered the retention list, another vacancy arose in the DEA. This time, the vacancy was caused by the departure of a Rajasthan cadre officer, Diwesh Saran, who was proceeding to the ADB on a staff appointment. Vasundhara Raje, believing that replacement of an outgoing Rajasthan cadre officer by another was most justified, included my name in the panel.

E.A.S. Sarma, a real gem of an officer who rose in the service by dint of sheer merit and hard work, was secretary, economic affairs, at the time. When I first met him upon joining the DEA in late May, he recalled my professional degrees and performance in my examinations. Impressed as he was with my qualification, he also decided to advance my candidature, spoke in my favour at the CSB meeting and was quite instrumental in placing me at first place in the panel.

At this stage, sometime in the month of April, which was the admission time in schools in Delhi, I enrolled my children, Shrey and Dhruv, in the newly established Sanskriti School, which gave precedence to officers coming to Delhi on 'tenure' (a fixed period of posting on deputation – officers got a tenure of four years as deputy secretaries and five years as directors), without waiting for formal appointment orders.

However, the file got stuck at the Ministry of Finance. During this period, a visit to Germany and Spain materialized in connection with the Mathania solar power plant. The DEA is the administrative ministry for the KfW bank as well. In a visit to the DEA in connection with this project and visit, I met

Naveen Kumar, joint secretary, Administration. He told me the file was under examination. There appeared to be some reservations at the minister's level.

Along with Anjali, I travelled to Germany and Spain in the middle of May – it was her first foreign visit. The day we landed back in Delhi, around 20 May, the DEA cleared the file after keeping it pending for a little over a month.

I joined the DEA on 27 May 2000.

Chandrababu Naidu bays for my blood

As part of the portfolio review, I discovered in a review meeting in September 2000 that the state of undivided Andhra Pradesh, at that time led by Chandrababu Naidu, had cornered more than 40 per cent of the total portfolio of projects approved by the World Bank in 1999–2000. The Government of India and the World Bank, it seemed, existed primarily for Andhra Pradesh. Chandrababu Naidu carried enormous heft in Delhi during those days as the Atal Bihari Vajpayee government was crucially dependent on his support for survival.

This was clearly unfair and lopsided. World Bank assistance, specifically cheaper credits from the International Development Agency (IDA), was meant for low-income and poorer states. Using the efficiency of his administration and his political clout, Chandrababu Naidu was able to manoeuvre the system in Delhi, including the DEA, to divert a disproportionate part of the Government of India budget and external assistance to Andhra Pradesh.

I prepared a detailed analysis highlighting the lopsided nature of the external assistance portfolio being negotiated with the World Bank and how this practice for the past few years had already made the overall portfolio Andhra Pradesh heavy. I proposed to limit the allocation of the annual World Bank country assistance system (CAS) for Andhra Pradesh to no more than 15 per cent a year.

This created a flutter. However, the unethical nature of the disproportionate allocation to Andhra Pradesh could not have been justified in any objective manner. Moreover, once it came on the record, it was also not very easy to be pushed aside. Secretary Ajit Kumar sent the matter to the PMO. It was explained to them as well.

The PMO directed that a balance should be restored. With this direction, I put some of the Andhra Pradesh projects on the slower lane. Chief Minister Chandrababu Naidu did not like it. In the year 2001–02, the share of Andhra Pradesh got markedly reduced, though it was still higher if you take the ratio of the state's population to the national population into account.

Sometime in November 2001, the Andhra Pradesh Structural Adjustment Loan (SAL) for $250 million came to be negotiated with the World Bank. As there was dislocation in the US after the events of 11 September, it was decided that this loan would be negotiated in New Delhi. The package also included one of the largest ever grant from the Department for International Development (DFID) to India of $100 million.

At the DEA, we had structured SAL on the standard terms of transfers to states, applicable at the time. Both the DFID grant and the World Bank loan were to go to Andhra Pradesh on the standard 70:30 loan–grant ratio. The Andhra Pradesh government thought otherwise. It entered into an understanding with the DFID, without the DEA's concurrence, that its grant would go to the state as a 100 per cent grant. Its understanding with the World Bank was that its loan would go to the state in the standard 70 per cent loan and 30 per cent grant basis.

While it was made clear to the Andhra Pradesh government before the negotiations started that the World Bank loan and the DFID grant would be on standard DEA terms, I had suspected that it would play some mischief in the negotiations. I had prepared the negotiation brief highlighting this point and had explained the matter to Dr Adarsh Kishore, who also felt that the funds should flow only on standard terms.

In the negotiations, the World Bank team usually prepared a draft of minutes in advance, which was then discussed and negotiated. When I saw the draft minutes, I spotted the mischief. It contained a paragraph that said that the financing package had been prepared on the basis that the DFID grant would go to Andhra Pradesh as grant while the World Bank loan would go on the standard 70:30 basis.

As the meeting was held in Delhi, the Andhra Pradesh delegation had at least 15 members, including its chief secretary, finance secretary and energy secretary. I told the Bank and the Andhra Pradesh team that the fund-flow arrangement was not in line with the DEA's policy and, therefore, was not acceptable. The head of the state delegation stated that this matter had been discussed by the chief minister with the highest authorities in the Government of India and that they had agreed. I told them categorically that I did not have any instructions in this regard, and even if there were instructions, I would not have agreed until the official policy was changed in writing. Therefore, there was no question of my agreeing to the changed fund-flow pattern proposed in the draft minutes.

After some argumentation, the Andhra Pradesh delegation realized I was not going to relent. At one point, I did offer an alternative if the standard terms were to be modified. In that case, the modification would only be in the form of taking the entire World Bank loan as a loan or the entire DFID grant as a grant. That alternative, however, would have reduced the total grant component of the package by about $5 million, as 30 per cent of a $250 million loan or $75 million was higher than 70 per cent of $100 million grant or $70 million. Obviously, this was not acceptable to the Andhra Pradesh delegation. Someone in the state delegation then told me they had to speak to the chief minister. The meeting broke for lunch. I briefed Dr Adarsh Kishore during this time on the clear stand I had taken. He seemed to approve of my stand.

During the lunch time, the Andhra Pradesh delegation reached out to Chandrababu Naidu, who was somewhere in Ireland at the time. When we resumed negotiations, the head of the delegation informed me that they were able to catch hold of the CM at a traffic intersection and that the CM finally relented to agree to the standard terms.

The draft minutes were modified to incorporate the standard terms (both loan and grant as 70 per cent loan and 30 per cent grant) and initialled by everyone.

Around the time these negotiations were taking place, C.M. Vasudev took over as secretary, Economic Affairs (he later went as India's ED to the World Bank after about seven months in the DEA). Two days after the negotiations were completed and the documents initialled, he asked me to come to his chamber with the Andhra Pradesh SAL file. He was visibly agitated. When he asked why I had insisted on not giving the state the grant as grant and the loan on standard terms, I told him the DEA policy and the fact that the same principle and practice had been applied to every case without exception.

He asked me to submit the file again to him. I recorded the note and sent the file to him. After two to three days, the file came back with orders, approved by the finance minister, that an exception be made in the case and that the DFID grant be given to Andhra Pradesh as a 100 per cent grant.

Evidently, on his return to India, Chandrababu Naidu had moved heaven and earth and forced the government at the highest level to agree to his completely unjustified demand. As the orders were absolutely specific and there was nothing new that could be submitted to reconsider the matter, I passed on the file to the section for necessary action. After a few days, an amendment in the negotiated agreement was agreed to between the Government of India and the World Bank. What Chandrababu Naidu wanted was incorporated as the fund-flow arrangement.

I had met Chandrababu Naidu for the first time in December 2000 when World Bank President James Wolfensohn visited India. I was attached to Wolfensohn as the representative of the DEA/secretary, Economic Affairs, during his visit to India, which included Andhra Pradesh besides Gujarat, Karnataka, Uttar Pradesh and Rajasthan. I also visited Andhra Pradesh for a preparatory visit.

During this visit, I could see the transformation the state was undergoing under the reformist leadership of Chandrababu Naidu. The glittering IT parks coming up in Jubilee Hills, cleaning of Hyderabad roads at night, efficient and fast-paced preparation and execution of reform projects and rapidly expanding use of IT in government work were impressive. My batchmate Randeep Sudan, as secretary in-charge of IT, was driving the e-governance reform agenda.

Chandrababu Naidu appeared to be the ideal reformist chief minister India needed in all the states. I encountered the flipside later.

The utter disregard for fair distribution of central government resources to all the states and the manic zeal and insistence to grab all resources for Andhra Pradesh were disturbing. The way he managed to get the DFID grant transferred as a 100 per cent grant with utter disregard for all principles also convinced me that he valued only his interest, not the larger national interest.

As I was in charge of the state in the DEA (directors/DSs were assigned states to deal with state-specific issues and references), I got to see many other issues such as Andhra Pradesh questioning its poverty headcount that influenced allocation of resources under some CSSs, issues connected with the recommendations of the previous Finance Commission, and so on. Everywhere, there were attempts to relax or ignore objective criteria in a bid to nudge resources to the state. I always carried out a brutally objective examination of the issue and submitted my recommendations without any fear or favour.

Andhra Pradesh secretaries possibly identified me as an irritant in the way of their boss. V.S. Sampath, finance secretary in Andhra Pradesh (he later became chief election commissioner of India), who was also involved in SAL and other externally aided projects spoke to me a couple of times. I would always explain the entire matter to him with facts, reason and logic. I found that he understood my viewpoint but had a job to do.

V. Srinivas, PS to Jaswant Singh, later told me that Sampath sought his help to 'find ways to fix Subhash'. When he did not seem to be succeeding (I was only doing my duty in the most objective manner in the larger public interest), Chandrababu Naidu's patience ran out. C.S. Rajan told me later that Naidu asked for my transfer out of the DEA.

Empanelled, but no posting for months

In January 2003, the 1983 batch got empanelled as joint secretaries. I also made the grade. The topper of the batch, Praveen Kumar, had left the service to join the World Bank some years earlier, and I had moved to the second rank in the batch. As Keshni Anand, the topper of the heap at that point of time, was not posted in the capital, I happened to be the first among the empanelled officers of the 1983 batch in Delhi in 2003. Quite naturally, I expected to be posted as joint secretary as soon as the posting of 1983 batch started. Normally, an officer serving as director in a ministry/department was posted as joint secretary in the same ministry/department.

There was no immediate vacancy at the DEA at that point of time. However, soon after the arrival of Jaswant Singh as finance minister, from March to May 2003, as many as three vacancies arose in the department (six in all in the Ministry of Finance). Joint secretaries (Siddharth Behura, Naveen Kumar and G.S. Dutt) were either placed on a compulsory wait or transferred to other ministries. I had no direct knowledge of the reasons why so many joint secretaries had to be booted out of the department in such a wholesale manner, but speculation was high (also reported in the newspapers) that Jaswant Singh was not convinced of the professional competence of most of these officers; he felt they were there because of considerations other than merit.

These vacancies were filled by bringing in other officers while I was waiting in the department. Dr Adarsh Kishore was also somewhat rattled after the arrival of Jaswant Singh. Though he was handling the administration division as well, he never told me why I was not being considered for a joint secretary post. Dr Kishore was posted out of DEA at the end of June 2003, and took charge as secretary, statistics and programme implementation. No IAS officer having Dr Kishore's profile would have been sent to Statistics and Programme Implementation unless a message that he/she was not favoured by the government anymore was intended to be delivered. That possibly explained his discomfiture for some time.

Quite a few of my batchmates got postings as joint secretaries in their respective ministries/departments or even in newer ministries/departments. Some officers also came from the states to serve as joint secretary in the Government of India.

For me, the wait was getting longer.

As a matter of principle, I have always felt that it was for the Government to post me where it considered appropriate. I would never seek a posting or meet anyone for a posting.

Chitra Chopra from the Rajasthan cadre was serving as establishment officer in the DoPT. I had met her, along with Tapesh Pawar and D.B. Gupta, once in late 2002 to enquire about the progress of the batch's empanelment. She did not receive us well. There was no question, both on principle as well as personally, to see Chitra Chopra for a posting.

At one stage, Dr Adarsh Kishore, informed me that my name had gone for a posting to the Department of Ocean Development as joint secretary. However, someone else got appointed.

One day, the PS to Health Minister Sushma Swaraj, Anshu Prakash (who later retired as telecom secretary), called me on phone to come and see the minister. When I asked him the reason for the summons, he informed that my name had come for consideration as a joint secretary in AYUSH (Ayurveda, Yoga, Naturopathy, Unani, Siddha, and Homoeopathy) Department. He said it would be advisable if I came to see her for the same, which will help in consideration of my name favourably.

I told him I had no problem with joining AYUSH if the government appointed me there as joint secretary; however, I would not come to see her for this purpose. I was not selected. My batchmate Tara Dutt, a scholar of Sanskrit and Ayurveda, got the posting. Sushma Swaraj picked the right person.

Dr Adarsh Kishore would often tell me during our time together at the DEA that I was the best person to go to the World Bank/IMF as advisor to the ED. While three DS/directors went to Washington in these organizations from 2001 to 2003, I was not one of them.

Sometime in June 2003, Dr Adarsh Kishore told me that my name had been recommended for consideration for deputation as minister, Economics, in Japan. The proposal seemed quite unexpected to me, though the position was usually filled by sending an officer from the DEA. Anup Kumar Thakur of the 1979 batch was the other officer in the panel. He was selected. I was not disappointed as I was not really expecting this to materialize.

Finally got a posting in the Department of Expenditure

The extraordinary delay in my appointment as a joint secretary did cause me some concern. By July, about seven months had passed since the empanelment. I decided to approach the finance minister directly.

I wrote a note to Jaswant Singh, mentioning some facts that indicated that I was a professional in the finance and accounting field. I also mentioned some of the work I had done in my three years at the DEA. I even offered that he, or anyone he appointed, could test me about my claims and suitability for a posting in finance ministry. I wanted to be considered on merit for appointment as joint secretary in the Ministry of Finance.

I did get an opportunity to meet Jaswant Singh. It was a short meeting. He was quite courteous and promised to set the matter right.

After Dr Adarsh Kishore's departure in early July, B.P. Misra took over as the AS, Fund-Bank. He soon developed a liking for me and once asked me why my posting as joint secretary was not taking place. I told him I did not know but informed him about the note I had written to the finance minister.

B.P. Misra investigated the matter and came to the conclusion that S. Narayan, who had taken over as secretary, DEA, in July 2002, was dead against me. He also discovered that the PMO believed that I was angling for a foreign posting. I told Misra that I had never applied for the Japan posting, nor did I speak to anyone to propose my name. I also confirmed Narayan's bias against me.

Around August, another vacancy arose in the DEA. The services of Joint Secretary Sanjeev Mishra, who had just been promoted as an additional secretary, were requisitioned by Home Minister L.K. Advani, who wanted him as his OSD. Things moved rapidly after B.P. Misra was asked by Jaswant Singh to find an appropriate officer for the post.

Two joint secretaries in the revenue department were interested to move as joint secretary, Fund-Bank. After the arrival of B.P. Misra, the Fund-Bank division had been assigned to Sanjeev Mishra as joint secretary. A joint secretary in the DoPT was keen to move over to the DEA. And Ranjeet Banerjee, joint secretary, Plan Finance I (PF-I), in the Department of Expenditure, was also keen to shift to the DEA.

B.P. Misra asked me whether I would like to be considered for the post of joint secretary, PF-I, in the Department of Expenditure. I said I would be quite happy to work on the state finance side, which, I was told, was the real financing function. Although he felt sorry about not seeing me in the DEA as joint secretary, Fund-Bank, which he thought I was best suited for, I assured him it was fine.

In September, my orders were issued as joint secretary, PF-I/State Finances Division. Thus, my association with the DEA came to an end and I could experience the expenditure side of the Ministry of Finance.

21

Resetting India's Relationship with the World Bank and IMF

The DEA was primarily responsible for interfacing with multilateral and bilateral aid agencies. India's ambition in those days was to get about \$3 billion in loans and grants every year from the World Bank, but it was getting less than \$2 billion a year at the time.

India was also eligible to receive loans from ADB. The loan sanctions from ADB were much smaller, under \$1 billion a year. There were over 20 other bilateral development agencies, with the UK's DFID, the Japan International Cooperation Agency (JICA), the United States Agency for International Development (USAID) and Germany's KfW being the larger ones. In all, these four bilateral agencies provided annual development assistance of over \$50 million each. Some of the other agencies had annual budgets for India of under \$10 million a year.

The World Bank was the largest and the loans and grants flowing from it were larger than the sum of all the other agencies put together. The fund-bank division handled all matters related to the World Bank and the IMF.

Sarma puts me in the fund-bank division

The first job assigned to me upon joining the DEA in May 2000 was the ECB division, which dealt with the policy and approvals of ECB inflows in India.

After about three months in the DEA, Secretary E.A.S. Sarma decided to post me to the high-profile and coveted fund-bank division. One possible reason was my seniority in the service. While I was the newest deputy secretary or director in the DEA, I happened to be the senior-most after Snehlata

Srivastava, an officer of the 1982 batch who had joined a couple of weeks before me. She was already in the fund-bank division.

The fund-bank division was quite large and had eight sections. One section, FB-II, dealt with all the institutional and administrative issues between India and the four affiliates of the World Bank Group: the International Bank for Reconstruction and Development (IBRD), International Development Association (IDA), International Finance Corporation (IFC) and the Multilateral Investment Guarantee Agency (MIGA). The IBRD and IDA together were referred to as the World Bank, and all four institutions together as the World Bank Group (WBG). The division FB-I dealt with the IMF.

There were six sectoral sections that dealt with the loan and technical assistance proposals of various sectors. I was made in charge of FB-II and FB-IV, the section dealing with infrastructure, including the power sector and structural adjustment loans. Without doubt, within the fund-bank division, I was entrusted with the most significant parts of it.

As director in charge of the FB-II section, I had the opportunity to prepare for the participation of Indian delegations in the annual and spring meetings of the IMF and the World Bank. I also attended a few of these meetings. Review of the entire India portfolio with the World Bank team was a regular feature of my work. In addition, processing cases to maintain the value of India's capital contribution to the WBG institutions, contributing to the triennial IDA funding rounds, processing important agenda matters for the World Bank board to convey the Government of India's official position to the ED in the Bank (B.P. Singh) and many other matters occupied my attention as director of the FB-II Division.

I continued to hold the charge of FB-II through the calendar years 2000, 2001 and 2002. In early 2003, I requested for a change of section from FB-II to FB-I, as I wanted to learn what happened on the IMF side as well. For about six months, I dealt with the FB-I section. When I demitted charge in the DEA in September 2003, I'd had the benefit of a well-rounded stint and enriching experience that included the entire fund-bank division.

Tedious World Bank loan cycle

The World Bank loan cycle began with the Government of India 'posing' a concept note to the Bank after it received proposals from the states or ministries/departments. If the World Bank found the proposal, in principle, in line with its articles, policy and current lending preferences, the project would enter a long preparation phase. This involved several studies, field visits, interactions with project authorities, rounds of preparation missions and the like.

Once the project was 'prepared', the Bank would formally negotiate the loan. In those days, World Bank loan negotiations took place in Washington, DC, at the Bank's headquarters. The opportunity to travel to Washington for a loan negotiation was a major attraction for most officers concerned with the project. Once negotiated successfully, the World Bank board would approve the project and the additional or joint secretary in charge of the fund-bank would formally sign it into a contract.

The most significant engagement of the DSs or directors in charge of sectoral sections was to go through this cycle of posing concept notes, supervising and participating in the preparation of the projects, negotiating loans and finally monitoring the progress of loan implementation. The DSs or directors headed the negotiating teams as leaders even if the delegation included a state's chief secretary or a Government of India secretary of a ministry or department.

My first negotiation

In early December 2000, I had my first World Bank negotiation, coincidentally for the Rajasthan Power Sector Project.

The negotiations involved poring over numerous documents. The Bank would prepare an extensive set of papers – a public information document (PID) – that would disclose all the essential features of a project for public information, a comprehensive loan document which would set out all the terms and conditions of the loan, a project implementation document which would set out obligations of the project implementing agency in the state, and a host of other papers. After negotiations, the loan document would be signed with the Government of India but the project implementation document with the state concerned. Most of these documents were received in advance before the negotiating party went to Washington, DC, and were scrutinized by the concerned sectoral division in the DEA, Controller of Aid, Accounts and Audit (CAAA), the budget division and the plan finance division. Any issues or unacceptable conditions in the documents would be taken up for final negotiations in Washington, DC.

Loan negotiations were typically scheduled for five days, beginning on a Monday and concluding on Friday. As most documents were pre-negotiated and the typical issues that came up in negotiations had also been reduced to acceptable formulations (for example, the Bank's insistence on an independent auditor auditing project accounts was met by India entrusting the audit to the CAG and the World Bank accepting the CAG as an independent auditor), mostly there were not really any intense or back-breaking negotiations. Any extra time was used to meet the wider World Bank team of experts in the concerned sphere and learn about reforms in other parts of the world.

The negotiations for power sector reforms in Rajasthan went quite smoothly. I questioned a fair number of legal covenants and conditions. The Bank delegation initially resisted, citing this as standard terminology. Vikram Raghavan, the Bank's legal counsel, did have some sharp exchanges with us but finally accommodated most of my concerns and suggestions.

Chequered history of transfer of EAP loans for state projects

In the initial years, the loans and assistance India received from the World Bank and from any bilateral and multilateral partners were retained in the Government of India budget. If assistance was taken for a state-level project or a non-Government of India project, financing was provided as a separate head of assistance from the Government of India budget, completely unlinked to the assistance the Government of India received. At some point in the early 1970s (after the system of plan assistance to the states was streamlined), the Government of India first started passing 25 per cent of external assistance received to the states as additional plan assistance.

In the 1980s, the Government of India started providing 100 per cent of external assistance funds (rupee equivalent of the external assistance received in foreign exchange) to the states. However, transferring the entire amount created a complexity. As external assistance came for different terms (IDA credit used to be provided for 50/35 years, whereas World Bank loans were usually for 20 years) and payment of interest and principal in foreign currency involved depreciation risk, the Government of India designed a 'fool-proof system'.

By considering all types of external assistance (irrespective of whether it was a non-concessional loan, concessional loan or grant) as part of one pot, the Government of India gave the states a simple alternative arrangement on the lines of the terms used for transferring normal plan assistance. This arrangement made all external assistance to go to the states as 70 per cent loan and 30 per cent grant for a 20-year period, five years of moratorium on the principal, irrespective of the original terms with external financing agencies and interest rate same as plan assistance loans. The Government of India serviced the external loans, bore commitment charges and foreign exchange risk.

The arrangement made both the centre and the states unhappy, which finally led to development of a system of back-to-back transfer of loans and grants. I would deal with this and fix it as joint secretary, Department of Expenditure, in 2005.

B.P. Singh recommends negotiations in Delhi

B.P. Singh, a senior retired IAS officer, was India's ED in the World Bank since 1999. He was not taken very seriously by the board and management of the Bank. When he left in July 2002 after completing his three-year tenure, his numerous degrees and awards were read out during the farewell, as traditionally organized by the board. This led Bank President Wolfensohn to quip that he did not know that B.P. Singh was so erudite; otherwise, he would have taken him more seriously. This comment also passed without B.P. Singh offering an appropriate rejoinder and became part of the World Bank records.

After the 9/11 incident, the World Bank considered decentralizing international staff working from its headquarters in Washington, DC. It sounded out the idea with ED offices, specifically that of China and India, which used to have several operations a year. B.P. Singh thought this was a good proposal and wrote to the finance minister to consider it favourably.

We examined the proposal. On both merit and optics, it did not pass muster. The World Bank had, and still has, a residential board. It also had international experts in almost every branch of development financing and reforms, built up especially after the emergence of the Washington Consensus on governance reforms as the major area of transforming governance and development. It was impossible for the Bank to locate all this expertise in country offices. Country offices would mostly be managed by local hires who might not have the requisite international experience and expertise. The Bank could depute one or two experts for negotiations, but it would not provide the benefit of a full suite of experience. As for optics, negotiations in Washington, DC, represented the high point of the life of projects. Negotiations in Delhi would appear a comedown.

Considering all these factors, we proposed that status quo be maintained, which received the approval of the secretary and finance minister. B.P. Singh was duly advised to convey the views of the Government of India to the Bank.

Some years later, the Bank did decentralize negotiations to Delhi and other capitals. This was the settled practice when I later worked as secretary, DEA. Thereafter, loan negotiations became a routine affair with most loans negotiated within two days. The participation of senior secretaries of the state governments and of the Government of India also mostly disappeared.

Annual and spring meetings

India has always been stingy about sending delegations to participate in the annual and spring meetings of the World Bank and the IMF, which occur every year in October and April. The finance minister would usually be accompanied only by the secretary, Economic Affairs; additional secretary, Fund-Bank, and the chief economic advisor. The delegation participated in numerous meetings: annual meetings, the Development Committee meeting, the International Monetary and Financial Committee (IMFC) meeting and many others. There were several bilateral discussions as well, including with the president of the World Bank, the MD of the IMF, the US treasury secretary and other high-ranking officials.

The additional secretary, fund-bank, was the pivot at Washington, DC, to provide talking points and briefs to the finance minister and the secretary, Economic Affairs, for all the meetings. The director, Fund-Bank, who prepared all the material, briefs and talking points, besides contributing to the formal speeches to be delivered by the finance minister (who was on the board of governors of the World Bank and the IMF), was not a part of the delegation. The briefing material was quite extensive and usually exceeded more than 1,000 printed pages.

I realized the pain the additional secretary, Fund-Bank, and the other members, including the finance minister and secretary, Economic Affairs, would go through in participating in such intense meetings. For the spring meetings in April 2001, I prepared a shorter, precise and to-the-point executive folder, which only contained material relating to participation in specific events and meetings. All the background material was separately organized on the basis of the day of the meeting. Only the additional secretary was expected to delve deeper into the background material, if necessary. The introduction of the executive folder was well received and favourably commented upon when the delegation returned.

The 2001 annual meetings took place in Ottawa, Canada, instead of Washington, DC, and in November 2001 (rather than October) because of the 9/11 terrorist attack. Dr Adarsh Kishore included my name in the delegation for Ottawa. The inclusion of director, Fund-Bank, in the delegation was somewhat inevitable because staff support in the offices of the ED and Indian embassy, which was liberally available in Washington, DC, was not available in the same measure in Ottawa. Though the shadow of 9/11 was writ large, the meetings opened my mind to the global system of finance and economic management, especially the financing of development.

Another reason for my inclusion in the delegation for the November 2001 meetings in Ottawa was because Finance Minister Yashwant Sinha was chairing the Development Committee meeting. The WBG Development Committee was a gathering of 24 finance ministers as well as other senior economic or development ministers and central bank governors, representing the entire membership of the World Bank and IMF, on major development issues facing the world.

Constituted in 1976, the committee is chaired by one of its members. Yashwant Sinha was elected its chairman after spring meeting in April2001 and was to vacate the chair after the annual meetings in 2001. I was the point of contact with the secretariat of the Development Committee to finalize Yashwant Sinha's role, speech and interventions when he chaired the meeting.

Sinha acquitted his role quite admirably. It was a pity he did not get a full two-year tenure. In fact, his successor, Trevor Manuel of South Africa, got two tenures of two years each. Still, Yashwant Sinha remains the only Indian finance minister who had the honour of chairing the Development Committee.

I was excluded from the delegation for the meeting in April 2002 by C.M. Vasudev, secretary, Economic Affairs, despite persuasion and protest by Dr Adarsh Kishore. I participated in the annual meetings in October 2002 and spring meetings in April 2003.

$75 for a cup of tea

Jaswant Singh took over as finance minister in July 2002 and Yashwant Sinha moved to the Ministry of External Affairs (MEA). Jaswant Singh concerned himself with broad strategic and policy issues and left details to the officers. However, he was very conscious of being finance minister of the largest democracy in the world, a nation of over 100 crore people. He, therefore, made it a point that he was accorded the best protocol treatment in Washington, DC, at par with a head of state. For the first time, India's finance minister travelled with US government security escorting him. The fund-bank annual meetings had finance ministers of over 150 countries participating in a more down-to-earth, business-like manner. Jaswant Singh wanted to be different – and he was.

The delegation stays in a major five-star hotel in Washington, DC. The finance minister gets a presidential suite. Jaswant Singh was in a massive presidential suite. My job was to provide papers to him for different meetings and answer any questions he might have. During a visit to his suite, I found a butler serving him tea from the pantry. There was no question of Jaswant Singh bothering to make his own tea or coffee with the facility provided in his room. He would not also accept prepared tea delivered to his room. The tea had to be served by a uniformed butler. Every cup of tea cost $75. I carried the contingency money for the delegation. Tea at $75 a cup and a hired Mercedes that cost over $600 a day was quite an expense for me to stomach!

A lunch or breakfast meeting with business delegations was the most common mode of interaction in Washington, DC. Jaswant Singh could either eat or talk; he said he could not do both. In luncheon meetings organized for him, business was transacted first. Lunch was served only after the meeting was over; in most cases, it went waste as almost no one stayed behind after the meeting to eat. There are no free lunches, they say; with Jaswant Singh, there *were* no lunches.

Walkout from loan negotiation

The Allahabad Bypass Project, a $240 million World Bank-funded national highway project, was negotiated in Washington, DC, sometime in August–September 2003, towards the end of my tenure in the DEA. The delegation for the negotiations included secretary, Ministry of Road Transport and Highways (MoRTH) and Santosh Nautiyal, chairman of the National Highways Authority of India (NHAI). Normally, the director or deputy secretary of the ministry concerned was the member but, the secretary, MoRTH, insisted he would go for the negotiations. I was, as per the practice, leader of the delegation as director, DEA.

Under pressure from civil society organizations, the World Bank had enlarged its environmental and social policy commitments for Bank-funded projects. As per the governance system, such policies were approved by the board. The Bank's negotiation team was to ensure that project documents for any loan were made in compliance with the stipulations and requirements of the policies approved by the Bank. However difficult it was for the borrowing country, the Bank's policy had to be respected. The Bank would simply not negotiate if there was any violation of its policy provisions.

The Bank had adopted a new social and environmental policy sometime in 2002 or 2003, and the Allahabad Bypass Project was one of the early projects to be negotiated after it came into force. As India had to accept the policy, as the leader of the team, I had no quarrel with its provisions. As the policy impacted the resettlement and rehabilitation of project-affected persons and had considerable monetary implications, I had studied it thoroughly.

That said, the Bank had been thrown on the back foot by civil society protesters. Even during the annual meetings of 2002 and the spring meetings of 2003, protestors had gathered near the Bank headquarters. For its part, the Bank had appointed environmental and social policy experts (mostly with a civil society background) to doubly ensure that the Bank was working in line with the adopted policies. The experts in question adopted an evangelical approach. The formal policy adopted by the Bank was just a starting point for them and they increasingly started placing many additional conditions for acceptance.

The loan documents for the Allahabad Bypass Project included quite a few covenants and provisions that were, in my judgement, beyond the formal policy of the Bank. During negotiations, I objected to these provisions. The evangelist experts insisted on our acceptance as they contended it was in the interest of the larger civil society. I tried to explain to them that India was prepared to accept every obligation stipulated by the formal policy of the Bank. However, anything beyond its scope was entirely voluntary and we would only consent to what we considered acceptable. This had to be India's decision, not that of the World Bank.

This created a deadlock. At that stage, when I found that the World Bank delegation was not amenable to reason, I requested secretary, MoRTH, and chairman, NHAI, to walk out of the negotiations with me. They had expected the negotiations to be a smooth affair and an opportunity to spend some time in the US. They were clearly surprised. They had imbibed the mindset that as recipients of assistance, India had to accept whatever the Bank said. I assured them that was not the case at all. India was a founding member of the World Bank, a major shareholder. We were taking a loan; it was not a favour. Accepting conditions that went beyond the Bank's policy was where we had to draw a line.

We walked out and went to the ED's office. After some time, one of the World Bank officers came to meet us. I told him we were terminating the negotiations. We had no interest in taking a loan with conditions the Bank had no business to insist upon – either the Bank accept our demand, or the negotiations could be considered closed.

It took the Bank team about two hours to subdue their evangelist experts. They came back to tell us that the conditions India objected to would be removed. We completed the negotiations on our terms. The secretary, MoRTH, and chairman, NHAI, were visibly relieved and proud at the principled stand I had taken and complimented me for having successfully stood my ground.

From borrower to lender

India was also a founder member of the IMF when it was formed in 1945. The country accepted obligations under Article IV, relating to management of foreign exchange, which were mandatory for all members. Being generally deficient in foreign exchange reserves since the 1950s, India borrowed from the IMF, despite its conditions being viewed as harsh and politically unacceptable in most cases.

In 1981, India borrowed about 3.8 billion SDRs (Special Drawing Rights, the accounting currency of IMF), which at the time was the largest IMF loan to any country. India again borrowed from the IMF after the 1991 foreign exchange crisis. However, the fiscal, foreign exchange, trade and other reforms carried out after 1991 changed the situation. India started building up its foreign exchange reserves. By 1994, India had foreign exchange reserves of about $20 billion. In that year, India also accepted obligations under Article VIII of the IMF (relating to freeing current account transactions completely and furnishing information relating to exchange reserves, debt, investment position and the like).

By 2002–03, India was able to accumulate foreign currency reserves in excess of $75 billion. At this stage, the IMF approached India to join as a lender. This was a critical moment, a tipping point. India could bury the ghost of being a borrower by becoming a lender.

All countries contributed hard currency reserves, including gold, to the IMF, which was quantified as reserve tranche position. India also held SDRs, allocated out of the SDR quotas. If it permitted its reserve tranche and SDRs to be lent, India would be able to earn a slightly higher rate of return. There was almost negligible risk of default. The IMF wanted India to join in the loan it was planning for two countries, including Brazil.

The IMF section under my watch examined the proposal. We found it acceptable. The RBI had also recommended this. It required India to make arrangements that were the reverse of what had been done earlier. The RBI held the Government of India's reserve tranche position and SDR balances in the IMF.

The arrangement had accounting implications in terms of the government's borrowings and investments going up. Vijay Singh Chauhan, an officer of the Indian Revenue Service (IRS) working as deputy secretary in the budget division, had some concerns about India's borrowings going up. We sat together and worked out the accounting arrangement so that the investments would be reduced from the borrowing for accounting purposes, which would leave no impact on the fiscal deficit and debt.

In 2002–03, India lent a little more than $600 million to the IMF for lending to other member countries. It was a good feeling to be part of a watershed moment in India's external balances management. The position has continued since then. India never borrowed from the IMF thereafter. India has, on the contrary, been joining the IMF in many lending operations extended towards other countries.

Disclosure of IMF reports

The IMF staff visits India every year to assess economic, financial, budgetary and external policies, as required under Article IV of the IMF Convention. These assessment reports are quite extensive and bring out a lot of information. Until 2002, India did not allow the publication or disclosure of the Article IV staff assessment report. Instead, a short public information notice was issued by the IMF after discussion in the board.

The IMF disclosed staff assessment reports of most other countries. However, because it felt vulnerable about its external account situation, especially foreign exchange reserves and budgetary position in the twentieth century when the country had to resort to IMF loans thrice, India had clamped down on this information being made available in the public domain.

When the IMF delegation submitted its draft Article IV staff assessment report in July 2003, the question of allowing its publication came up for consideration again. The IMF had been mustering support to persuade India to allow publication. B.P. Misra was more open. He asked me to thoroughly scan the draft report and mark the portions that might cause embarrassment or other problems for India.

After a thorough analysis, I highlighted the relevant portions along with perceived reasons (not necessarily mine) why disclosure might be problematic. However, I also cited the experience of disclosing the monthly accounts of the Government of India (a good summary of the *Government of India at a Glance* had been for two to three years prior to 2003) and why the apprehensions against it had turned out to be highly exaggerated. In fact, by 2003, it had become a non-issue.

I recommended that India allow disclosure of the IMF staff report to bring more transparency to the entire process. Wherever we felt the IMF's assessment was inaccurate, slanted or unjustified, we could always ask it to carry the Indian government's counterview in the report.

The IMF started disclosing India's Article IV staff assessment report from 2003.

22

Dabhol Power Plant For $1 and Other Matters

Kshatrapati Shivaji, an IAS officer of the 1986 batch from Maharashtra, was handling the ECB division of the DEA. As he was proceeding to a posting in New York, I was given charge of the division. External commercial borrowings were permissible only from recognized sources. The division, working with RBI, would screen credentials of newer sources of ECB providers to ensure Indian borrowers did not end up borrowing from suspicious and dubious jurisdictions and sources.

When I took charge as director, ECB, it was probably the first time I heard of ECBs.

Indian companies, mostly in the public sector, had limited access to borrow from external lenders in foreign currencies until the government started liberalizing the Indian economy in the 1990s. In 1996, the first significant liberalization was done for the private sector to raise ECBs. Telecommunications, power and railways were permitted to raise ECBs for financing project-related rupee expenditure. The ECB limit for exporters was raised to $15 million. For small and medium-sized enterprises (SMEs), the ECB limit was enhanced to $3 million to meet their working capital requirements. A division of capital markets and ECBs was created in the DEA in 1996–97, with a director-level officer in charge of ECBs. The delegated powers of RBI to sanction ECBs were increased up to $3 million in 1997. The ECB policy and approval of all other ECBs were in the purview of the Government of India and all these matters were dealt with in the ECB division.

The ECB division was involved significantly in the management of external debt. It compiled and published external debt statistics on a quarterly basis. One of the working groups headed by Arvind Virmani, then additional economic advisor in the economic division (who later went to the IMF as ED), examined the advisability of setting up a middle office in the DEA to take over this function from RBI.

It was in the ECB division that I got the opportunity to examine the S.A. Dave report on pension reforms, which led to the NPS, made applicable to government servants in 2004.

I was shifted as director of the fund-bank division, when V. Bhaskar, an officer of the 1981 batch, was deputed to go to the IMF as advisor to then ED, Vijay Kelkar.

'Automatic' ECBs up to $50 million

The most important task I had to deal with immediately upon joining the ECB division was to get a press note finalized to notify a new ECB policy. The new policy had several important changes. The most important was to introduce approval of ECBs up to $50 million on automatic route. For the first time in India, businesspeople would be able to bring ECBs of up to $50 million without government approval. They only needed to file an application with RBI, with the details of the ECB to be brought in. The banks, as authorized dealers in foreign exchange, would allow the ECB based on the declaration filed with RBI.

The policy had been discussed at the highest level and was approved on file by the finance minister. My predecessor K. Shivaji, who later served as India's ED in the ADB, was instrumental in crafting it. The introduction of the 'automatic' route was quite an event for India. The last major liberalization had been to allow ECBs of $3 million for SMEs a few years before.

S.S. Chaturvedi, special secretary in the DEA, asked me to prepare the press note in consultation with K. Shivaji, who was yet to proceed to New York. The draft went back and forth a few times. Chaturvedi wanted to ensure there were no bloopers.

The revised and revamped ECB policy was issued on 14 June 2000. It was my first introduction to and participation in economic policymaking in the country.

Montek shoots down sovereign bond issue again with opposite argument

The value of the rupee fell to 50 a dollar for the first time in 2000. Though India had survived the Asian crisis of 1998 relatively unscathed, the rupee falling below 50 a dollar caused major concern in the corridors of power and RBI.

India had successfully floated the $5 billion Resurgent India bonds in 1998 after the Pokhran nuclear test, following sanctions imposed on it by the US and other countries. The government considered raising another bond/deposit issue to raise dollars to shore up foreign exchange reserves, which was expected to cool down the rupee–dollar exchange rate.

Dr Bhagwati entrusted the task to me on a need-to-know basis and asked me to study files related to earlier issues, including the Resurgent Bonds issued in 1998. This included a file maintained from 1992, dealing with the proposal to issue foreign currency sovereign bonds in the international markets. India, which faced a near-default situation in 1991 and had to pledge its gold with the Bank of England to stave it off, had examined the proposal to issue sovereign bonds twice: once in 1992–93 and again in 1996–97. Economist Montek Singh Ahluwalia had a long tenure in the DEA, which lasted about seven years. The file relating to the issuance of sovereign bonds both times, in 1993 and 1997, was decided at his level, with the file submitted to finance minister for information.

By 1993, India had moved to a market-determined exchange rate system after devaluing the rupee in 1991, pursuing a dual exchange policy for some time and integrating the foreign exchange market into a single rate. The Reserve Bank of India and the government had abandoned the policy of overvaluing the rupee for exchange rate purposes. In fact, by 1993, there was acceptance of the policy of rupee depreciation, which was seen as necessary to promote exports and contain imports.

The floating rate exchange policy had reasonably settled, though foreign exchange reserves had accumulated only to a little under $10 billion by the end of financial year 1992–93. In this scenario, a proposal was floated on file for India to issue dollar-denominated sovereign bonds to raise foreign currency receipts, which could bolster foreign exchange reserves as well. India had floated India Development Bonds in 1990 to raise NRI deposits before the foreign exchange crisis of 1991. The idea to raise sovereign bonds was to get out of the straitjacket of raising deposits from NRIs and paying off-market rates to them.

Montek shot down the idea, arguing that India's foreign exchange reserves were too low and it might be difficult to defend the rupee–dollar exchange rate if these bonds were to be hammered down by some vested interests. His principal argument was foreign exchange being too low to inspire comfort.

By the time the proposal to issue sovereign bonds was put up again, on the same file, in 1996–97, India's foreign exchange reserves had grown to the vicinity of $25–30 billion and had consistently remained at that level for two to three years. The section felt that the situation was now ripe to float the bond issue. However, the file came back with Montek Singh Ahluwalia rejecting the proposal because foreign exchange reserves were quite comfortable, and so there was no need to issue sovereign bonds.

The matter rested there until 2000, when India again felt pressure on its foreign exchange reserves. In 2000, too, the country decided not to issue sovereign bonds. Instead, India raised about $5 billion as India Millennium Deposits, again paying an off-market higher rate of interest on dollar deposits, mostly by rich Indians living abroad, some of whom borrowed at a lower rate of interest from the same bank in which they made deposits in their Indian Millennium Deposits accounts.

The proposal to raise foreign currency denominated sovereign bonds would not surface for next 19 years. In 2019, when I was the economic affairs secretary, we would bring it to the closest to issuance of such bonds. The proposal would be announced in the budget but would not be followed up.

First step towards pension reforms

The Government of India had commissioned a study by an expert committee, headed by Dr S.A. Dave, on old-age pension. The report, submitted by the committee on Old Age Social and Income Security (OASIS) in 2000, came to the Ministry of Finance sometime in August that year. Dr Bhagwati handed over a copy to me to figure out how its recommendations could be best implemented.

The pension liabilities of governments, both central and state, were rising rapidly. India followed a defined benefit pension system for civil servants. Under this system, the pension promised was in the form of a defined benefit (50 per cent of last pay or 50 per cent of the average of the past nine months, and so on). Government servants were not making any contribution from their salaries towards their pensions. The governments were also not setting aside anything towards pension liabilities. Pensions were paid from budgetary provisions just like salaries.

As pension liabilities were in a way not provided for or actuarially assessed, there was no sense of accumulating the burden of liabilities. Instead, governments and pay commissions were happily increasing pension benefits over time. The Dave Committee proposed that the government consider moving to a defined contribution system. Here, employees paid a certain portion of their pay, matched by the government. This contribution, accumulating in the individual retirement account of the employee to be maintained by a central repository authority (CRA), was proposed to be invested by professional fund managers. The committee also proposed the creation of an independent pension regulator, the PFRDA.

There was no active management of pension liabilities in the Government of India. The Department of Personnel had a pension wing that was concerned with matters relating to sanction of pension benefits. The Ministry of Finance was expected to create an institutional arrangement to usher in pension reforms.

After studying the report, I thought we needed to take some necessary first steps. Someone in the Ministry of Finance had to be made responsible for pension reforms. While the ECB division did not have any direct relationship with pensions, I drafted a policy proposal to entrust policy work on pension reforms to the ECB division. That note resulted in the creation of a pension reforms cell in the DEA, as part of the ECB division, which was also renamed the ECB and Pension Reforms Division.

Sometime after I left, the cell was converted into a full-fledged division headed by a director-level officer. These first steps led to the introduction of the NPS in India in 2004. Later, the pension reforms division got transferred to the financial services department, and that is where it remains till date.

Tensions of Enron power plant at Dabhol

The DEA had a power-sector division as well, headed by a full-time director, considering the significant policy changes taking place in the sector, in the late 1990s.

By the time I arrived in the DEA, no director or deputy secretary held charge of only the power division. It was a tagalong charge, which I got. While it handled power-sector projects for all multilateral and bilateral agencies, the World Bank was a focal point, as it had the largest power-sector investment portfolio in the country.

The power division also examined policy issues concerning the sector and programmes managed by the Ministry of Power. A dispute it was engaged in was with Enron over the Dabhol power plant in Maharashtra, where a white elephant had been established as part of what was more commonly referred to as a 'sweetheart deal'. There was a pending arbitration case against the Government of India, as it had issued a counter-guarantee for investment return and foreign debt taken by the Dabhol Power Company (DPC).

Further, the draft Electricity Act was in a phase of intense discussion, with Gajendra Haldea avidly trying to push the draft he had prepared as a consultant to the Ministry of Power when his brother-in-law R. Kumaramangalam was power minister. The draft contained several outstanding measures to liberalize the power sector.

'If I buy a racing car, it has to perform as a racing car'

Sometime in November 2000, the matter of the Enron-promoted Dabhol Power Company (DPC) landed in the DEA. Ajit Kumar had just taken over as secretary. In addition to his principal responsibility of overseeing the ADB division as joint secretary, Ashok Lavasa (who later became expenditure and finance secretary and quit midway during his stint as the election commissioner to join the ADB as a vice-president) was also handling policy issues related to the power division. I was working as director, power, in addition to my principal charge as director, Fund-Bank.

The Maharashtra State Electricity Board (MSEB) had started delaying monthly payments to DPC. As the Government of India had given a counter-guarantee for certain specified payments in the event of certain events occurring and with the Maharashtra government not paying the due amount, the matter caused deep concerns. Enron was a noisy and pushy company, and pressure was soon expected from the Americans about the alleged failure of the Maharashtra government and the MSEB to make payments.

Over the next six months, Ajit Kumar convened three meetings with the Ministry of Power, MSEB, Maharashtra government and other concerned parties. As understanding and information about the state of play in DPC was limited at the centre, Ajit Kumar wanted to understand the actual situation. It was also necessary to make a judgement whether there was any likelihood of the Government of India's guarantees being called.

The tall and eloquent Vinay Bansal, chairman of the MSEB, led the

Maharashtra team. He explained the situation quite well. From the second meeting, he took a very clear line that DPC was in default of its contractual obligations. In a way, he was turning the tables on Enron by stating that the American company might have to pay instead of the Maharashtra government or the MSEB. This surprised the team from the centre. Asked to explain further, Vinay Bansal used the analogy of a racing car. He argued that no one keeps a racing car for personal transport. Racing cars are meant to be used in sporting events. The fact that racing cars can speed up very fast is why champions pay a much higher price for them. Like a racing car, DPC, which used expensive gas as fuel, was contractually required to be ramped up to achieve near 100 per cent capacity within one hour from a 'hot start' (when the plant was not in operation for less than 12 hours) and within three hours from a 'cold start'. Vinay Bansal informed us that, perhaps fortuitously, the MSEB had discovered that DPC could not ramp up to capacity under either hot or cold start conditions.

By the time the third meeting took place in April–May 2001, the MSEB had decided to terminate the power purchase agreement (PPA) with DPC. As the termination of PPA by the MSEB for an event of default by DPC could not lead to the invocation of the Government of India guarantee, Ajit Kumar felt relieved, and the review meetings were discontinued.

Power plant for $1

Kenneth Lay, CEO of Enron, wrote a nasty letter to Prime Minister Atal Bihari Vajpayee. The arrogance in the letter made us all squirm when it reached the DEA sometime in September 2001. In the letter, Lay threatened India with drying up foreign investments and said it would besmirch the country's reputation, as an unreliable party that went back on its contractual obligations. He wanted the Government of India to own complete responsibility for Maharashtra's actions and pay Enron its dues, failing which India would be hauled up in arbitration and investment protection disputes.

Enron went belly up later in the year, having committed accounting fraud of unprecedented proportions, which even led to the passing of tightening regulatory laws – the Sarbanes-Oxley Act, formally named the Public Company Accounting Reform and Investor Protection Act, in particular – and the folding up of a 'Big Five' global accounting firm, Arthur Andersen. While this dissipated the pressure from Enron, the complex structuring of DPC did not ease matters for the Government of India. Enron had taken loans guaranteed by the US official risk insurance agency, Overseas Private Investment Corporation (OPIC), which, in addition, was covered for political insurance risk, to be borne by India. There were two plant providers and contractors – General Electric (GE) and Bechtel – that had equity stakes in DPC. Further, there were quite a few offshore lenders that had partly funded the plant.

Various proposals kept coming in – formally and informally – through 2002 to protect the interest of OPIC as well as the three American equity investors (Enron, GE and Bechtel). Foreign lenders had their ways of presenting their proposals. Besides the Government of India and the Maharashtra government, Indian lenders who had also lent substantial funds to DPC had their own interests.

In July 2002, S. Narayan took over as secretary, DEA. Ashok Lavasa also left upon the completion of his tenure at the centre. Narayan held discussions and conducted negotiations with OPIC and other foreign parties, in which I was not involved. Sometime in early 2003, Sanjeev Misra took over as joint secretary and was given charge of the fund-bank, ADB and power divisions.

After the spring meetings of the Fund-bank in April 2003, Narayan returned and told Sanjeev Misra that there was an in-principle agreement to take over DPC through a trust controlled by the Government of India. Further, all the American equity holders would hand over all their equity stakes to the trust for $1. The Government of India could thereafter make appropriate arrangements to run the plant by any Indian entity and settle the lenders' and OPIC's claims.

The plan implied passing on of all debt and insurance liabilities of DPC to the Government of India!

A day after this hot potato of 'DPC for $1' plan was passed on to him, Sanjeev Misra, exceedingly worried, called me to his room. He called Narayan 'a cobra' and expressed his helplessness to come out of his clutches. He mentioned that Narayan had asked him to initiate a note at Misra's level to propose acceptance of the proposal to take over DPC at $1. Misra said he did not want to present the proposal as desired. Moreover, in his assessment, initiating the note would expose him to unknown future problems.

It was my assessment, too, that the plan for the Government of India to buy DPC for $1 was a hugely costly one and needed to be questioned rather than accepted. I was the director concerned. In the normal course, the file should have been initiated by the section and gone through me and Misra to Secretary Narayan. I offered, if he felt comfortable, to write the note proposing rejection of the offer. I further offered that he could sign the note, as Narayan had asked him to do, or I could put it under my signature as he felt comfortable.

Sanjeev Misra decided to defy Narayan's diktat. I wrote a comprehensive note bringing out all the financial and non-financial implications of such an insidious proposal which the Government of India had no business to even be a party to, let alone accept.

The proposal to buy DPC for $1 did not proceed further. The file did not come back for a long time from Narayan's office. A few days later, Dr Adarsh Kishore was asked to relieve me of the responsibility of the power division. Adarsh Kishore felt sorry about it, though I did not care. I told him that I knew that the note would result in adverse consequences, but I had to answer the call of conscience and duty.

In addition to shunting me out of the power division, Narayan also saw to it that my promotion as joint secretary was not taken up for nine months despite the DEA having four vacancies during this period.

Preparing Dr Kishore for meetings

Dr Kishore established excellent administrative control in the DEA. Like most people who came to the DEA, Dr Kishore was not very familiar with the issues it dealt with. However, he had a very open mind and would mostly start at point A to go to point Z. As I had some familiarity with the financial world, he would call upon me to explain the fundamental principles of capital markets, foreign trade and commerce, and external assistance. These sessions also helped me to get a good grounding in these subjects as I would read up and understand them before going to him. Dr Kishore would prepare thoroughly for every meeting he would participate in.

But I noticed that he had one limitation. As most financial market subjects were not ones he was hugely interested in (compared to his natural interest in political economy, history and interpersonal relationships), he needed to refresh his knowledge of the subject to be discussed in any meeting everytime. Sometimes, I would refer to his memory as being very rich in RAM but poor in storage on hard disk! These repetitive refresher courses were sometimes irritating but seeing him prepare so diligently for all his meetings (whether in Parliament, with ministers, in Fund-bank meetings or elsewhere), I would assist him to the best of my abilities.

Dr Kishore trusted my judgement so much that he used to refer important policy files of other divisions to me, with his signature instructions on a sticky yellow slip, so that I could study them and provide suggestions accordingly. As these files were related to other divisions and I was not expected to write notes under my signatures, I would prepare the note on his behalf, to be signed by him. Most of the times, the note I proposed was signed by him exactly the way it was. I enriched my understanding of the wider policy issues in DEA through this ghostwriting.

Sometimes, Dr Kishore would get quite nervous before a high-profile meeting. In one such meeting, where he was representing the finance minister in the United Nations–Bretton Woods joint dialogue in 2003, he felt he was not able to master the subject despite succinct notes and background material having been provided to him and a briefing having been held in the day. He called me at 2 a.m. in the morning of the day of meeting asking me to come to his room in New York. He had still not gone to sleep and looked visibly upset. He asked me to dictate to him his intervention in the meeting the next day, referring to me as Ved Vyas and himself as Ganesha. He must have barely slept for two hours after we finalized his intervention. Yet, he delivered it with aplomb in his booming voice the next day, which earned him a lot of appreciation.

India shakes off bilateral development aid

Jaswant Singh was quite keen to say goodbye to bilateral development assistance. India had discontinued the Aid India Consortium, held under the aegis of the World Bank, in the 1990s. The country directly dealt with bilateral development agencies thereafter.

In 2003, there were more than 20 such agencies giving aid to India, with many having an India-aid budget of only $10 million to $20 million a year. A good part of such budgets was spent in maintaining their offices and financing their consultants under technical assistance projects. Even these pygmy agencies expected annual discussions with their delegations, with some expecting preparation of medium-term strategies and plans.

After consulting with officials about the actual situation, Jaswant Singh decided this had to end. From 1 July 2003, more than three-fourths of bilateral development agencies were asked to pack up. The new qualifying criterion for staying in India was an annual aid budget of at least $50 million.

Only five bilateral aid countries or agencies remained: USAID, UK's DFID, KfW of Germany, JICA of Japan and possibly France. Jaswant Singh proudly announced that India could take care of itself and that the resources spared could be better utilized by aid agencies in other parts of the world. Outgrowing the Aid India Consortium and saying goodbye to bilateral donors was true evidence of India becoming self-reliant or *aatmanirbhar*.

Over the years, the remaining five agencies have also, by and large, shut shop. The DFID and USAID stopped their aid programme completely (whatever small technical assistance from USAID remained was shut off by President Trump in early 2025). Japan International Cooperation Agency and KfW primarily offered loans, not grants, which continues till date. The French agency continues with a grants programme.

As secretary, DEA, from 2017 to 2019, I would study the finances of JICA. It received no grants from the Japanese government. It raised all its resources from the market. Yet, it made profits year after year. The average rate of interest the Government of India pays on JICA loans is higher than the cost of 20-year bonds, if the Government were to raise the funds in the Japanese market. To me, it made sense to raise bonds in the Japanese market instead of taking loans from JICA. This could have been done if the proposal in Budget 2019–20 to issue foreign currency sovereign bonds had gone through. India continues to take significant loans from JICA.

23

Pulling States Out of the Debt Trap

The financial relationship between the centre and states, also referred to as fiscal federalism, is deep and extensive in India. Besides a share in central taxes, which are constitutionally transferred on the recommendations of finance commissions, the Government of India provided numerous discretionary financing facilities to the states. Loans made up a major part of these discretionary transfers.

By the turn of the century, the states had become hugely indebted to the centre. They were also borrowing indiscriminately from the market, financial institutions and others to broaden their annual plans. As a result, the states found themselves in a deep debt trap.

The Department of Expenditure had two plan expenditure divisions – Plan Finance I (PF-I) and Plan Finance II (PF-II). The PF-I division was also known as states plan division and states finance division. I was posted to the PF-I/state finance division in September 2003.

The PF-I division was responsible for administering discretionary plan schemes called state plan schemes. The biggest of these was normal central assistance (NCA), an untied facility of a substantial size, which was available to the states to spend on programmes as they wished and was typically delivered to the states in the ratio of 70 per cent loan and 30 per cent grant. Over the years, many tied schemes/programmes, administered by administrative ministries concerned – for instance, Jawaharlal Nehru Urban Revival Mission (JNURM) of the Ministry of Urban Development or Accelerated Power Development and Reform Programme (APDRP) of the Ministry of Power – had got added to the discretionary central plan assistance portfolio, and were called additional central assistance (ACA) to distinguish these from NCA. In 2003, as per the practice prevalent, the ACA amount was released by the state plan division, on the recommendations of the administrative ministries/departments.

The PF-I division was the best place to understand and work in federal fiscal finance of India.

Massive deterioration in state finances

India had a very elaborate project and programme-based central financing system at the time of Independence, though such a relationship was not specifically envisaged or provided for in the Constitution. Article 282, which permitted the centre and the states to give a grant for any project or programme of the other fiscal entity, irrespective of whether such a project or programme was outside its domain, was impliedly and indirectly used for funding specific state projects and programmes.

In 1970, this kind of project-by-project funding was stopped, and the system of NCA was instituted to provide untied general-purpose central plan assistance to states to partially finance their projects and programmes. The national and regional expenditure priorities of the Government of India in the states' domain were funded by the central government in the form of a bouquet of CSSs. With these reforms in the 1970s, financing for state-specific projects or providing grants and loans to any state generally stopped.

The central financing of states' plans by NCA and the CSS (also, ACA) gradually expanded significantly and led to a highly undesirable consequence.

A large part of these funds was given to states as loans. The central government had become the banker of the states. Over the years, these loans accumulated massively. The central government had also started a small savings programme. The states collected these savings under numerous central schemes like the postal savings account, national savings certificates, Indira Vikas Patra and public provident fund. The funds collected were passed on to states as small savings loans. Later, these loans were provided through the National Small Savings Fund (NSSF), though that did not change the character of central financing to the states much, except formally.

These plan and small savings loans, further supplemented by some other budgetary loans, such as medium-term loans and WMA, grew so big so as to constitute over 80 per cent of the states' annual borrowings at the turn of the millennium.

In 2003, the states' repayment and interest service obligations were primarily towards the centre. As the country had also passed through a high inflation phase from the 1970s to 2000, the interest service obligations were quite high.

Some states were spending more than 25 per cent of their revenues simply to service interest on loans.

The Pay Commission reward in 1998, implemented retrospectively from 1 January 1996 and made excessively generous by the coalition government at the centre, had made revenue expenditures of states shoot up sharply. The states were paying salaries and pensions through their noses.

All these factors combined to make the financial position of states excessively precarious. They were perennially in the WMA position with RBI (this meant that the states carried effectively negative cash balances with RBI). State after state was slipping into an overdraft with RBI – an acute ways-and-means situation that led to suspension of states' payments by RBI, the banker of the states, if overdraft persisted for more than 10 days. Such suspensions led to what came to be known as the closure of the states' treasuries, which meant that the concerned states could not make any payment of their obligations, including staff salaries.

Many states went into a lockdown/closure of their treasuries for many days in a month. The Assam treasury remained closed for more than 230 days in 2002–03. States had to resort to desperate ways of managing their treasuries. Some states would ensure that they got revenues and other cash transfers from PSUs or other entities on the last day or a day before for coming out of overdraft to pay salaries at the end of the month and then slip back into overdraft.

India's fiscal federalism was stretched to a limit at the time, and the situation was truly desperate. Serious reforms of fiscal federalism were needed to bring it back from the precipice and put it on a sounder keel. While those were the worst of times for India's fiscal federalism, these were also the best of times to work and find solutions.

Central government brings states' debt swap facility

The yield on the central government's 10-year paper (government securities/bonds which are redeemable after 10 years), which exceeded 11 per cent at the turn of the century, had come down to around 7 per cent in 2002–03 (it fell below 6 per cent later in 2003–04) on account of a sharp slowdown in the economy during 1998–2001. This afforded a great opportunity for the Atal Bihari Vajpayee government to do something to set the states' fractured finances right. The PF-I division found that the states had high-cost loans from the centre (including small savings loans) amounting to about ₹1.15 lakh crore, with an average interest rate of over 12 per cent. The Vajpayee government rose to the occasion and allowed the states to prepay these high-cost loans with their newly raised market borrowings at about 7 per cent. The central government allocated additional market borrowings to states to raise cheaper loans to prepay these high-cost loans.

When I joined the department in September 2003, about ₹35,000 crore of these high-cost borrowings had already been prepaid by the states. I continued the good work with gusto. In financial year 2003–04, about ₹45,000 crore of high-cost loans were prepaid. In financial year 2004–05, with liberal sanctioning of additional market borrowings, another ₹45,000 crore of the high-cost Government of India debt was discharged by the states. With some repayments coming in due course, all the high-cost borrowings of about ₹1.15 lakh crore stood extinguished at the end of financial year 2004–05.

In fact, in their enthusiasm to get rid of these high-cost borrowings, some states ended up paying more than their liabilities – this was on account of poor upkeep of loan accounts on both sides. Excess repayments or prepayments were adjusted against the states' other liabilities to the centre.

At a simple savings of 5 per cent interest per annum, the states saved about ₹6,000 crore a year on their outstanding high-cost loans of ₹1.15 lakh core. These loans would have had an average remaining maturity of about 10 years. If one takes a 10-year average impact, the states would have saved about ₹60,000 crore in interest payments to the centre.

Another systemic change for states' borrowings

Article 292 of the Constitution subjected the states' authority to borrow to the approval of the Government of India in case the concerned state was indebted to the centre. The states were born in debt to the central government at the time of Independence, thanks to the practice of the centre providing loans and grants financing to their development projects.

The PF-I division was concerned with the states' finances and borrowings. The borrowings funded their plans. The plans were handled in the expenditure department except for the overall size of central funding to the plans. However, from the very beginning, the authority to grant approval to the states' overall and specific borrowings had rested with the budget division of the DEA.

The debt-swap programme and fiscal reform facility were all being dealt with by PF-I. Even the number of total borrowings to be allowed to each state and loan components was finalized as part of the annual plans by the Planning Commission, which was coordinated in the Ministry of Finance in the PF-I division.

When almost everything connected with the states' borrowings was processed and managed in PF-I, there was no reason for the budget division to be the authority to grant approval for borrowings. I moved a proposal with all the arguments for transferring approvals under Article 292 to the PF division. Turf issues always crop up in such cases. However, D. Swarup, secretary, Expenditure, who had seen the working of the budget division a long time as joint secretary and AS budget, agreed with the logic. Once he recommended it, the DEA agreed. The authority under Article 292 to grant approvals was transferred to the PF-I division. A major systemic reform could take place.

I used this authority very effectively to restructure the centre's lender–borrower relationship with the states after the recommendations of the FC-XII became available. It had recommended that each state enact a fiscal responsibility legislation prescribing, among others, to bring down fiscal deficits to 3 per cent of SGDP by adopting a fiscal consolidation path for reduction of borrowings and guarantees.

I delinked states' borrowings to their plan size to discontinue their incentives to borrow as much as possible to increase their plan sizes, and made their maximum borrowings match the amount of fiscal deficit permitted by the fiscal consolidation path. This institutionalized the regime of states' overall borrowings being linked to acceptable fiscal deficits. We gave the states a big freedom to choose whatever source they wanted to borrow from, as long as their total borrowings remain within their approved overall borrowings. This initiated the system of states borrowing an increasingly larger proportion of their permissible borrowings from the market and reduction and ultimate stopping of loans taken from the NSSF.

I was glad to see the total transformation these basic policy decisions brought in. While in 2002–03, the states availed more than 80 per cent of their borrowings from the central government, a good part of which was from small savings, a few years on, they borrowed more than 80 per cent from the market by issuing state development loan (SDL) securities.

We stop state plan loans

A fundamental conclusion I had drawn after analysing the reasons of the states' acute indebtedness was the autonomous nature of central government loans to the states as part of plan financing and against small savings collections.

I prepared extensive notes for doing away with loan financing from the central government to the states as part of plan funding. The states had to be given the freedom to raise their borrowings subject to control over the overall borrowed amount. The central government had to stop being the financer of the states. D. Swarup, the expenditure secretary, approved all these notes and proposals. A note on discontinuing the plan loans was furnished to the FC-XII. Veteran economist C. Rangarajan, who headed the FC-XII, called me for discussions. He knew much more than me about how plan loans were responsible for the states' heavy indebtedness. The FC-XII recommended, as we had desired, that the central government should not act as an intermediary for future lending and proposed to allow the states to approach the market directly.

The *Action Taken Report* on the FC-XII's recommendations was placed in Parliament along with the budget on 28 February 2005. These were to be implemented from 1 April. Usually, non-tax devolution recommendations of the FCs take many months to get processed, proposals formulated, approved and implemented. My tenure was coming to an end in the last week of May 2005. I was determined to implement these recommendations from 1 April 2005.

The necessary papers were prepared in March 2005 and all required approvals sought. Along with the decision to link the overall size of the states' annual borrowing to the fiscal deficit limit approved as part of their fiscal reform and consolidation roadmap, another order was issued in the first week of April, advising the amounts of NCA to the states for the year 2005–06. The order indicated the amount of NCA for all the states as per the usual formula, divided in a 70:30 ratio. However, the order further said that the central government would only provide the amount indicated as grant in NCA and the states were free to raise the remaining 70 per cent on their own as part of SDL borrowings.

A big, long-standing practice came to an end. The system of providing loans from the centre to the states for their plans stopped for good.

Cleaning up the remaining vestiges

There were two other small loan facilities from the Centre to the states. The central government occasionally provided three- to five-year loans – called medium-term loans – to the states that were not able to service their loan instalments to the centre, or sometimes just to enable these states to meet other needs. This was a purely discretionary facility. It was another way of postponing the recovery of loan and interest from a state that was left with no recourse except to default.

The global liquidity unleashed after 2003 brought good foreign exchange flows to the country. So much so, that the Government of India had to provide RBI a facility to issue Government of India bonds to sequester excessive cash from the system without the government using such funds, but on which the latter paid an interest nonetheless. The surplus liquidity position brought down interest rates in general in India. This enabled the debt-swap facility to be smoothly implemented in the country.

Taking advantage of the situation after 2004, I proposed discontinuation of the budget provision for medium-term loans from the Government of India to the states in the 2005–06 budget. This was accepted. One more vestige of past debt facility from the centre to the states got knocked off.

I also proposed discontinuation of the WMA facility from the centre to the states for the same reasons. However, more seasoned officers at the senior level agreed only to reduce the budgetary provision. We kept a token provision of ₹1,000 crore in the budget estimates of 2005–06. Later, the government did away with WMAs from the centre. In fact, states' cash management improved so much that many states stopped using WMA facility of RBI as well.

DCRF for states

The report of FC-XII came around the end of December 2004. It recommended two relief facilities relating to states' debt.

First, central loans to states contracted till 31 March 2004 and outstanding on 31 March 2005, about ₹1.3 lakh crore, were to be consolidated and rescheduled for a fresh term of 20 years at an interest rate of 7.5 per cent. This consolidation was designed to provide debt relief exceeding ₹20,000 crore in interest payments. Second, a debt write-off scheme, linked to the reduction of revenue deficit of states, was proposed which would allow waiver of repayments due from 2005–06 to 2009–10 on consolidated loans equal to the amount by which the revenue deficit was reduced in a particular year.

These two proposals were two parts of the total outstanding central loans of about ₹1.3 lakh crore, which were to be consolidated, and their repayment were to be waived if the state concerned was able to reduce revenue deficit. For some reason, the FC-XII recommended these as two different facilities.

As per the prescribed process, all schematic recommendations of the finance commissions were turned into specific schemes, with all details, by the expenditure department. The schemes were then approved by the finance minister and issued officially to the states and all concerned for implementation.

While formulating the schemes for the FC-XII proposals, I decided to merge the two separate proposed schemes of debt consolidation and debt waiver into one and proposed the name 'Debt Consolidation and Relief Facility' (DCRF), building on the analogy of Fiscal Reform Facility (FRF) earlier recommended by the FC-XI. This simplified and brought together the consolidated nature of the two-part scheme. The term DCRF did not appear in the FC-XII's recommendations, but its two critical recommendations got implemented through DCRF.

Backed by the states' fiscal responsibility legislations and other reforms undertaken, DCRF proved to be an exceedingly useful facility to bring down the states' indebtedness. Many states started reporting revenue surpluses from 2006–07 and hardly any state breached the fiscal deficit ceiling of 3 per cent, except during the global financial crisis in 2008–2010, when the Government of India permitted the states to borrow an extra 0.5 per cent of their GSDP.

Back-to-back external assistance

The second of the major policy notes I had prepared and sent to the FC-XII related to reforming the system of passing on external aid to states. The prevailing system, as also referred in Chapter 21, transformed every critical term and condition of external assistance received – tenor of loan, nature of grant or loan, repayment schedule, interest rate to be charged from the states and the like – I recommended an alternative system which got dubbed as a 'back-to-back system'. External assistance, under this arrangement, would be transferred to states on original terms (no transformation of the loan or grant nature of the assistance received, the tenor of the loan, rate of interest applicable and so on) with the states servicing the interest and repayments in foreign currency (by providing equal amount in rupees) on the due dates as per the terms and conditions of the original external loan.

The FC-X, headed by J.C. Pant, had, in fact, recommended such a change. However, it had remained unimplemented. My note to the FC-XII brought out this background, the reasons why it was not done, an analysis of what it might mean to the centre and states, and how to implement it.

The FC-XII recommended that external assistance be transferred to the states on the same terms and conditions as attached to such assistance by external funding agencies, thereby making the Government of India a financial intermediary without any gain or loss. This was exactly what we wanted: a true back-to-back system. It further recommended that external assistance passed to the states should be managed through a separate fund in the public account. We also wanted this recommendation to free up the central finances from the artificial jacking up of fiscal deficit, as external assistance routed through the Consolidated Fund of India meant that much addition to the central government's fiscal deficit.

Plan finance followed a very convoluted and wasteful system every time external assistance was to be released to a state. The CAAA, which kept accounts for external assistance, would make a proposal to PF-I, which would literally do nothing except perform some routine checks, including checking up with the concerned multilateral/bilateral division in the DEA, and then agree with the recommendation. I never saw any value added by either the DEA or PF-I in such transfers. After such approval, which would have led to the loss of some time, the matter would go back to the CAAA to submit the final draft of sanction, which PF-I would issue. Thereafter, the CAAA would instruct RBI to transfer funds to the state's account. All this was presumably necessary as the external assistance was transferred on the new Government of India terms.

Again, seizing the moment, I drafted the order, got approval and issued it, institutionalizing the back-to-back system for external assistance with effect from 1 April 2005. The external assistance has been transferred to the states on original terms since then. For IDA credits, states get all the 35 years to repay the loans, including a long moratorium of 10 years. Grants go to them as grants. While states got the benefits of low interest rates and a long repayment period (of course, with a foreign exchange risk), a Chandrababu Naidu would not get a World Bank loan on a 70:30 basis and a DFID grant as grant thereafter.

The other significant part of the FC-XII recommendation relating to the back-to-back system – managing all external assistance outside the Consolidated Fund of India – would not, however, get implemented.

The file I had made, proposing creation of an External Assistance Administration Account in the Public Account of India to route all external assistance and its repayment, was referred to Vivek Mehrotra, joint secretary in the DEA, who was handling bilateral external assistance and administration. The account proposed by us was to be a simple zero-balance account as all external assistance received would have been transferred to the states on the same day and all repayments made by them would have been passed on to the external assistance agency the same day. This arrangement would have eliminated the need to budget any amount in the Government of India budget for this purpose. This would have another advantage of frictionless transfer of external assistance to the states as it would have removed any constraint in transferring the external assistance on account of the budget not being available.

Vivek Mehrotra blocked the proposal. He would not budge from a theoretical position that all loans received by the Government of India had to be taken to the Consolidated Fund of India. These external assistance loans were really the loans of states, and the Government of India was only a receptacle. Such an arrangement had already been institutionalized when small savings were shifted to the NSSF. No reason, argument or even precedent would work with him. The proposal remained unimplemented during my stay and was shelved after I left.

It would take another 13 years more for this part of the recommendation to be implemented in a different way. As secretary, Economic Affairs, in 2018, I used another trick of the trade to make external assistance to the states an automatic pass-through, with no implications for the centre's fiscal deficit and no budgetary constraints in terms of release, by making the transfers to states a minus entry to the receipt of external assistance. This arrangement allows the CAAA to pass on external assistance receipts seamlessly by the system recording it as a minus entry, also eliminating any fiscal deficit implications for the Government of India.

Return of the debt trap?

India's federal fiscal system was a very well designed one at the time of Independence except for two areas that were open to misuse. One, the Constitution made the states' borrowing authority subject to central control.

The condition that it would be the case only if the states had outstanding loans towards the centre was meaningless, as the states were by and large indebted to the centre at the time of Independence. Second, the avenue provided by Article 282 to provide central grants for states' domain of expenditure opened the floodgates of centre's foray into states domain through CSSs.

These two defects in the Constitution virtually made the states subordinate to the centre in fiscal matters. Central loans expanded so much through several modes, as described above, that the states' outstanding debt at the end of millennium was more than 50 per cent towards the centre alone. Likewise, all sorts of grants under a plethora of CSSs subjected the states' fiscal independence to central control and superintendence.

The measures taken by the Vajpayee government (from 2001) largely corrected the imbalance. The good work was continued by the United Progressive Alliance (UPA) as well.

The central government helped states prepay costly pre-1999 loans through the debt-swap scheme. Debt Consolidation and Relief Facility, implemented on the basis of recommendations made by the FC-XII 2005–06 onwards, took care of most other debts. The real difference was made by the decision taken during UPA-I to discontinue plan loans and other loan facilities like medium-term loans. The Government of India did not provide any plan loans to the states after 2005–06.

By the end of 2005–06, the central government stopped being a lender to the states. Gradually, the states came out of the central loans' quagmire. Their debt to GSDP ratio also improved (in the form of being reduced) remarkably.

In 2016, the NDA government did away with the system of plans itself. However, in the wake of the COVID-19 crisis, the central government came up with a facility in financial year 2020–21 to provide about ₹10,000 crore of non interest-bearing loans to the states for capital expenditure, repayable over 50 years. This has re-seeded the pernicious practice of the central government providing loans to states and has the potential to strike at the root of fiscal federalism. After 2021–22, this facility grew significantly. In 2023–24, the central government provided such capital expenditure loans of ₹1.10 trillion. Budget 2025–26 has a provision to raise such loans to ₹1.5 trillion.

States are walking into the trap of central government loans once again.

24

A 'Smiling Assassin'

The largest source of finance for the states, second only in importance after tax devolution, was the NCA for the state plan, delivered as a block untied assistance, for part-funding the plan. Normal central assistance had been institutionalized since the 1970s and was determined under what was known as the Gadgil (later Gadgil–Mukherjee) formula. More than 90 per cent of NCA was formula-driven and delivered to the states as 70 per cent loan for 20 years and 30 per cent grant. For special category states (SCS), NCA went as 90 per cent grant.

The central government had always preferred specific programmes to assist states, which had led to the flow of funds through the CSSs. The compact with the states in 1970 was that CSSs would be limited to one-sixth of NCA, but the CSSs kept expanding much faster. Centrally sponsored schemes were delivered through budgets in the respective administrative ministries and departments. The PF-I did not have much of a role in the CSSs. In fact, as they were considered part of the central plan and primarily processed in the PF-II division.

The PF-I was the fund-releasing authority for several other specific state-plan schemes, which, though like CSSs, were categorized as ACA schemes. Some more proliferation took place with the emergence of purely discretionary financing windows, such as special central assistance (SCA), which were entirely in the hands of the Ministry of Finance – no budget provision was usually made for SCA; whatever was released during the year was taken as supplementary grants at the end of the year.

There was one more discretionary finance window – special plan assistance (SPA), which, though smaller than SCA, was placed at the discretion of the deputy chairman of the Planning Commission.

The total funds released under NCA, ACA, SCA, SPA and so on were quite large (about ₹50,000 crore in 2003–04 out of a total plan budget of about ₹1.25 lakh crore), and the states received it all.

The PF-I also administered the FC grants to the states, which included formulation of detailed schemes based on the basic parameters decided by the FCs, releasing the grants upon satisfaction of eligibility conditions, monitoring the use of funds and making final releases. There were also a few other minor loan facilities, like a WMA facility (the principal ways and means facility was from RBI).

The PF-I had, over the years, become a lifeline for the states.

Most important joint secretary for states

The financial releases to the states amounted to a lot and there was some discretionary element to them as well. No wonder chief ministers and finance ministers of states were frequent visitors to the capital's North Block.

Chief ministers also met the prime minister on most of these visits. They used these occasions to take up other fiscal federal issues, like small savings loans, permissions to borrow from the market, packages for their states, discretionary releases and so on. The PF-I served these meetings. Most visits would be preceded or followed by visits by states' finance secretaries (sometimes chief secretaries) to the office of the joint secretary, PF-I.

As far as the states were concerned, joint secretary, PF-I, was the most important joint secretary in the Government of India. Considering the frequency with which the joint secretary, PF-I, was asked to see the expenditure secretary, finance secretary, finance minister and, occasionally, the prime minister in connection with calls from CMs and FMs, his or her office was located in the 'power corridor' of the Ministry of Finance, where the three secretaries (economic affairs, expenditure and revenue) had their offices.

The joint secretary, PF-I, would generally be a senior joint-secretary-level officer. There were two other joint secretaries in the expenditure department at that time – Sushma Nath, joint secretary, Personnel, was from the 1974 batch and Vivek Ray, joint secretary, PF-II, was from the 1978 batch. Among them, I was from the junior-most batch, of 1983. I joined the division in September 2003 and left on completion of my central deputation tenure in May 2005. Those 20 months provided me with a rich experience of fiscal financial management, especially fiscal federal issues.

In May 2004, UPA-I replaced the NDA government. I spent a full year with the new UPA government and Finance Minister P. Chidambaram. The FC-XII submitted its report in December 2004, which was implemented from April 2005.

Fiscal reform facility had design defects

The FC-XI answered a special reference from the president to prepare a monitoring fiscal reform programme for the states, by recommending a fiscal reform facility (FRF). The FRF, to be funded by withholding 15 per cent of the revenue deficit grants to states (separately recommended) with an equal amount contributed by the central government, was conceptualized to provide incentives of about ₹11,000 crore to the states. Though the FC-XI suggested complex criteria to release these reform-linked incentives to the states, the Government of India adopted a simple criterion: Bring down the ratio of the revenue deficit to total revenue receipts by 5 per cent a year and take the incentive.

This criterion was simple, but its accompanying structure was exceedingly complex. A comprehensive fiscal reform programme was expected, with milestones that were to be agreed upon by the centre and the concerned state. The states were to sign an MoU with the centre to implement the reform programme. Surprisingly, there was no special incentive attached to the implementation of the comprehensive fiscal reform programme. It ended up only as an entry eligibility condition for the release of FRF incentive as the determination and release of incentive amount was only linked to revenue deficit reduction.

There were also quite a few other design defects in the FRF scheme. As the aggregate revenue deficit of all the states was about 25 per cent of their aggregate revenue receipts, the goal of reducing it by 5 per cent a year was adopted. The individual states' ratio, however, ranged from 10 per cent to 90 per cent. There were a few revenue-surplus states as well. When I joined the department, the FRF scheme had been operational for over a year but had not made any meaningful progress in the form of release of incentives.

The release criterion was modified. An additional incentive component was brought in (specially for states that were not undergoing any structural reforms through any multilateral/bilateral programme) to provide additional market borrowings and some grant incentive upon the implementation of reforms.

These changes had a limited impact. The states were dissatisfied with the programme. This was the first major inroad or interference by the central government in the fiscal domain of the states. Not all states received revenue deficit grants. The states from whose revenue deficit grants 15 per cent was set aside, to be released upon the satisfaction of FRF criterion, complained bitterly, as they – mostly the states in the Northeast – had constrained finances, and the withholding of their 15 per cent deficit grant compounded their misery.

This recommendation of FC-XI had a dissent note from the fiscal economist Amaresh Bagchi. His apprehensions about the intrusion of the central government in fiscal affairs of the states had turned out to be true. Very small portion of the FRF could actually be disbursed.

The assumption by the centre, that it was the epitome of fiscal rectitude while the states were naughty children who needed to be directed on the right path by imposing such conditionalities, hit at the roots of fiscal federalism. The FRF was anti-fiscal federalism. The central government had no business being the fiscal master of the states. I was glad the FC-XII discontinued this facility.

Since 2020–21, the central government has linked additional market borrowings and a part of the capital expenditure loans to the states to the satisfaction of a set of reform conditions. Every now and then, the central government is being forced to relax the same. This reminds me of the bad experience with FRF conditionalities.

Dwindling normal central assistance for state plans

In 2003–04, the NCA budget was only ₹20,000 crore of the total central plan assistance to states of about ₹47,500 crore. The formula-driven non-discretionary central assistance to the states' plan had gone down to about 42 per cent of total central assistance. The rest was made up of various forms of ACA schemes. Until 1986, there was no ACA scheme worth the name. The ACA system was introduced to provide some assistance in the wake of the Bhopal gas tragedy that occurred in December 1984.

In 2003–04, however, there was a plethora of CSS masquerading as ACAs. The APDRP with an outlay of ₹3,300 crore, Accelerated Irrigation Benefits Programme (AIBP) with an outlay of ₹2,250 crore, PM Gramodaya Yojana with an outlay of ₹2,400 crore, Rashtriya Sam Vikas Yojana with an outlay of ₹1,000 crore, National Social Assistance Programme with an outlay of ₹650 crore and rural electrification with an outlay of ₹300 crore were just a few of them.

Seventy per cent of NCA was going to the states as loans from the central government. In that sense, it was really not assistance. If one took out the loan element, central grant assistance to the states from NCA for their plans amounted to hardly ₹6,000–7,000 crore in 2003–04.

Normal central assistance did not have any conditionality linked to its release. However, states' plans were approved by the Planning Commission and NCA was provided subject to the condition that the states spend and achieve 100 per cent of the approved plan outlay. They rarely did, as their plans were bloated, more to play to the gallery about the size of the plan approved (every incumbent chief minister wanted to announce that the plan he got approved was the largest ever).

The PF-I used to retain 1 per cent of the total NCA share of every state, to be released upon the submission of a certificate from the CAG that the actual expenditure on plan was more than or equal to the approved plan size. The certificates, however, very rarely came. No state was able to claim the 1 per cent deducted for many years.

There were many reasons for this. There were disputes about whether the approved plan size meant the amount approved as per the original budget estimates or the revised budget estimates. In fact, the central government and most of the state governments did not keep the records and were reconciled to the fact that only 99 per cent was at best to be released and received.

Most states were facing an acute fiscal crisis in 2003–04. Tripura Finance Secretary R.K. Mathur wanted the state's 1 per cent withheld balances to be released. I got the matter examined. These had not been released for about 20 years. We made a concession and decided that the actual expenditure certificate needed to be given was with reference to the revised size of the annual plan. After much paperwork, Tripura's accumulated withheld amount was released. A couple of other states also made similar efforts. By and large, the withheld 1 per cent balances of most states lapsed to the centre.

Expanding ACAs presented a tough administrative challenge

The preference of the central government to provide assistance through specific schemes (which worked as tied assistance for the states as it could be used only for the specific purposes mentioned in the scheme and was subject to norms laid down) and indirect, albeit soft, restriction on limiting CSSs to one-sixth of NCA, led to the corrosion of the concept of NCA. Specific schemes became part of the central assistance to state plans as ACA schemes.

In 2003, major schemes like the JNURM, APDRP and AIBP were part of the Department of Expenditure budget. These schemes were like CSSs, except that they were not made part of the budget of the concerned administrative ministries and, therefore, the financial releases were made by the Ministry of Finance. Typically, for some schemes like AIBP and APDRP, the file on which the release was recommended would come to the PF-I. For others, the administrative sanctions would be issued by the concerned ministries and departments with prior financial sanction clearance from the Department of Expenditure.

One day, I found two contractors in my office. When asked for the purpose of their visit, they informed me that a file had come from the Ministry of Water Resources about funds to be released to Maharashtra for an irrigation project. As the file had not yet reached me, I politely asked them to leave and promised to look into the matter. When the file arrived, I saw that this was about releasing about ₹100 crore for an irrigation project approved under AIBP. Enquiries revealed that AIBP projects had become bottomless pits where contractors chased files for release of funds. The release criteria were tightened and made more progress related. The AIBP scheme was entirely loan-based. There was no grant. Later, when plan loans were discontinued, the central share of loan for AIBP projects was also authorized as additional market borrowings by the state.

The real solution was discontinuation of ACA schemes or in the least administering these as CSS schemes.

Uma Bharati complains

Reformed APDRP offered large dollops of grants to states if they brought down their losses – one rupee of grant for every rupee of loss reduced. The reformed APDRP scheme got ready for implementation just a little while before state governments changed in three states, including Rajasthan and Madhya Pradesh in December 2003.

Madhya Pradesh was the first to make a claim after a new government under the leadership of the voluble and volatile Uma Bharti took over. The NDA government lost power in May 2004. The overlapping period of four months – December 2003 to March 2004 – suddenly saw heightened demands from

Madhya Pradesh as there were BJP-led governments at both the centre and the state. My batchmate Dhiraj Mathur was power secretary in Madhya Pradesh.

The state came up with a claim of around ₹350 crore as incentive money in financial year 2003–04 for performance improvement in financial year 2002–03. An examination of the claim, which had been recommended by the Ministry of Power, revealed the state had transferred certain expenditures (primarily related to pension liabilities) out of the books of electricity utility, claiming lesser liability upon the separation of Chhattisgarh from Madhya Pradesh. Other than this adjustment, there was no reduction in losses. I refused to approve the release of the incentive. Dhiraj made a hue and cry. As I refused to budge, Uma Bharati raised the matter to the level of the PMO. The PMO suggested to Expenditure Secretary D. Swarup to see whether some accommodation could be made for Madhya Pradesh.

Swarup had excellent manner of summarizing matters on government files; he drafted a short speaking note of not more than four to five sentences while proposing a decision to the finance minister or passing a clear order. He checked with me, and I told him all the facts. He convened a meeting in which representatives of the Ministry of Power and Dhiraj Mathur and his team from Madhya Pradesh were present. I stood my ground. After hearing the team from the state with patience, Swarup decided that no incentive could be released under the circumstances and disposed of the file with his order.

No incentive was paid to Madhya Pradesh.

'He is a smiling assassin'

Quite a few states also attempted to dress up the accounts of their electricity boards to claim incentive money. West Bengal was one such state.

West Bengal claimed improvements under seven different heads of expenditure but none of them were from the revenue side in terms of raising tariff. Sanjay Mitra, CMD of the West Bengal Electricity Board (later joint secretary in the PMO, chief secretary, West Bengal, and roads and defence secretary, Government of India) came to discuss the matter. He was quite professional. We agreed that there was genuine loss reduction for only two of the seven items. These two were accepted. He complimented the PF-I for the scrutiny and accepted our determination of the incentive, which was released.

It was somewhat of a different experience in the case of Gujarat. The state government had released about ₹600 crore in state support grant to the Gujarat

Electricity Board (GEB). This naturally brought down GEB losses by an equal amount. On the strength of this manner of loss reduction, ₹600 crore was claimed as incentive. The Ministry of Power, as usual, had forwarded the claim with a recommendation. Vijay Laxmi Joshi, chairperson of GEB, came to see me. I explained the facts to her. She argued that it did not matter who paid the tariff. If the state government paid part of the tariff on behalf of farmers, it must be treated as loss reduction. I refused to accept the argument. She was visibly angry.

Ashok Chawla, a seasoned and respected IAS officer of the Gujarat cadre, was resident commissioner of Gujarat. The state government asked him to get the grant released. He came to see me. Again, I explained the entire matter to him calmly with my usual smile. He had managed Indian Petrochemicals Corporation Ltd (IPCL). He made a request if I could clear. I refused. He understood. He did not insist and left, accepting the inevitability of decision.

Later, he remarked to D.B. Gupta, my batchmate from Rajasthan who was then serving as housing commissioner in Delhi Development Authority (DDA), 'Your batchmate is a smiling assassin!'

Ashok Chawla would become secretary, DEA, later and serve with distinction. His comment reminded me of the comment made many years earlier by Rajasthan union leader Narain Singh Rathore, that it was always difficult to get concessions from officers who kept their cool.

RBI convenes meetings for the centre and states to discuss issues

For the first 50 years of India's independence, there was no institutional arrangement for the centre and the states to discuss centre–state fiscal issues. Constitutionally, the Inter-State Council could have discussed fiscal federal issues, but its structure, agenda and frequency of meetings were such that the fiscal issues were rarely discussed. In fact, the format of the council was quite inappropriate for discussing these issues. It also met very infrequently.

Except a formal pre-budget discussion with the state finance ministers, there was no tradition of discussing the fiscal issues with states. The Ministry of Finance had no CSSs, which provided other ministries the opportunity to have an intense engagement with states.

Reserve Bank of India Deputy Governor Y.V. Reddy (later governor) found a solution. He offered the offices of RBI to convene meetings of the state finance secretaries twice a year. These meetings evolved into an excellent platform to discuss policy as well as the operational issues causing friction. While the secretary, Expenditure, was a principal invitee from the Government of India, a convention developed that the centre would be represented by the joint secretary, PF-I.

I used these meetings to bring the true state of different programmes, facilities, evolving priorities and contentious issues like CSSs to everyone's notice. It felt good to speak for the Government of India as its representative in these meetings. In fact, I found them so instructive that I bunked a part of my stay in Bihar as an election observer during the 2004 parliamentary elections to attend one such meeting. Somebody complained. I received a show-cause notice from the Election Commission. I explained I had done so only to attend the meeting at RBI, which, without the participation of joint secretary, PF-I, would have been meaningless. The Election Commission closed the case.

Government unsuccessfully initiates reforms in CSSs

In early 2004, the Vajpayee government convened a meeting of chief ministers to bring in some reforms. Besides passing a resolution urging states to meter power supply to agriculture and charge a minimum of 50 paise per unit as agriculture power tariff, the meeting also decided to discontinue the practice of the central government transferring CSS funds directly to the state agencies like the Rural Health Mission, the Sarva Siksha Abhiyan Society and so on.

The central ministries and departments had developed a marked preference for transferring CSS funds directly to their agencies, bypassing the states, though the grants were from the centre to the states and the states had to account for their use. At my suggestion, the budget division compiled a statement that provided CSS-wise details of funds directly transferred.

This decision was vehemently contested by ministries like the Ministry of Health, which suspected that the programme rollout would slow down considerably as states would sit on these budgets because of their perennially precarious financial position. We showed them the way the FC grants for local bodies were transferred by mandating timely transfer from the states and subjecting the states to additional interest in case the transfer was not made on time. However, the government rolled back the decision after some time. Much later, in 2013–14, the UPA-II government in its last year would make transfer to the state budget the only method of transfer, which was successfully implemented by the NDA government after 2014.

As there used to be a loan element in some CSSs as well, there were about ₹10,000 crore of outstanding CSS loans towards the states in 2003–04. As we wanted to discontinue all loans to the states, we decided to also include outstanding CSS loans for a waiver under DCRF. The records for CSS loans were kept by the respective ministries and departments, and their records were in horrible conditions.

As a matter of policy, it was decided to discontinue the system of releasing some part CSS funds as loans. Outstanding loans were also made subject to waiver under DCRF.

Dealing with Chidambaram

The FC-XII recommendations involved drafting six comprehensive schemes for implementation, including the guidelines for local body grants and disaster relief. As noted above, we formulated a new scheme of DCRF by combining the two major schemes of debt consolidation and debt waiver that the FC-XII recommended.

Along with four other schemes, DCRF was submitted on file for approval to Finance Minister P. Chidambaram at about 6 p.m. one day. There were meetings that day that lasted until about 8.30 p.m. The next morning, I found the file back on my table with the minister's approval for DCRF and the other schemes submitted. Chidambaram had not only signed the file, he had marked many changes in the guidelines of the scheme, though mostly of a legal editorial nature without touching the basic scheme anywhere. This, however, meant he read through all the 100 pages of the scheme during the night.

He was a tough boss, but his hard work and meticulous nature were outstanding.

Chidambaram would be thorough in all his work, including preparation for parliamentary questions. He would go through all the papers painstakingly, including reading copious Notes for Pad (with detailed reference material and supplemental information for the minister's use to answer supplementary questions that might be asked in Parliament on starred questions, since some starred questions were taken up for discussion during the question hour). It was a nightmarish experience for most joint secretaries to attend briefing sessions on parliamentary questions with Chidambaram. He would raise a random question relating to some material that might be on page x, y or z of the Note for Pad. Without telling the page number, context or reference, he would expect the officer to respond to his query.

I prepared most briefings, including the Note for Pad, on parliamentary questions relating to my division myself. Dr Adarsh Kishore, who had joined as OSD before taking over as expenditure secretary from 1 April 2005 (after Swarup's retirement), would also prepare very hard but left responding to Chidambaram to me. Fortunately, I never embarrassed myself.

I spent about a year with Chidambaram. He was one finance minister who would draft the budget speech on his laptop. A few years later, Sushma Nath, who became expenditure secretary and India's first woman finance secretary, told me that Chidambaram gave me a rare outstanding ACR, which I saw when copies of these ACRs were handed over to the officers concerned later as part of the new government policy.

S.P. Gupta ropes me in on Rajasthan's fiscal affairs

S.P. Gupta, an officer of the 1975 batch, took over as principal secretary, finance, when Vasundhara Raje won the BJP a clear majority for the first time in Rajasthan and became chief minister in December 2003. A rare combination of intellectual brilliance, ability to work hard and present his case most persuasively, S.P. Gupta was a rising star among civil servants of the Rajasthan cadre.

Very early after taking over, he started involving me in the financial matters of Rajasthan. He wanted to do something to repair the badly managed financial affairs of the state. I visited Rajasthan twice to see him and advise him on initiating some reforms. One reform that emerged from these discussions was the decision taken by the state to discontinue providing housing loans and other loans like scooter loans to state government employees. Instead, the state government agreed to provide a specific interest subsidy on housing loans taken by the employees from financial institutions and banks, like HDFC. Thereafter, Rajasthan sold its entire housing loan portfolio to the State Bank of Bikaner and Jaipur after evaluating offers from three to four banks.

I had an inkling that he was preparing me to join him in Rajasthan as finance secretary when I completed my tenure in May 2005.

I organized an international conference sponsored by the World Bank in Jaipur on urban reforms in the last week of March 2004. S.P. Gupta was gracious enough to host a dinner at Nahargarh Fort for the participants. He, too, participated enthusiastically and discussed several areas of financial reforms that evening.

I was shocked to learn that just four days later, he had a massive cardiac arrest and passed away. I visited Jaipur to pay my last respects. Rajasthan and India lost an able administrator of outstanding calibre very young. I am certain he would have become chief secretary or cabinet secretary of India if he had served his full career.

'Teach rather than being taught'

My son Shrey was to appear for his Class 12 examinations in March 2006. My central tenure came to end in May 2005. I took end-of-tenure leave until 30 June 2005. I had applied for a nine-month, in-service course at the Indian Institute of Public Administration (IIPA). I was selected and set to join the IIPA from 1 July 2005. The course would have allowed me to retain my government house in the capital until March 2006, by when Shrey's examination would be done.

Govind Rao, who headed National Institute of Public Finance and Policy (NIPFP), came over in May before I demitted charge. He had interacted with me in many seminars and conferences. He asked me to come over to NIPFP as a part of the faculty. NIPFP had a system of taking on officers and experts as senior consultants. He argued that I should research and teach rather than be taught. It sounded interesting enough. However, this would not have allowed me to retain the government house. There is a provision in the house allotment rules that you can retain a government house for six additional months (over and above the two months you got at the end of deputation) on educational and health grounds. This would have carried us to the end of January, leaving two months' shortfall.

I thought the risk was worth taking. I requested that the IIPA nomination be cancelled. I was relieved from the Government of India on 28 June and reported on duty at the secretariat, Jaipur. I was allowed to go to NIPFP on deputation under a rule that permitted deputation to such institutions. I joined NIPFP on 1 July 2005.

It was an exciting nine-month stint at NIPFP. I worked on a couple of research projects, including the state accounts for the Planning Commission and how to manage back-to-back external loans prudently by creating fiscal reserves for a state government. I could participate in several discussions on fiscal policy issues. The biggest offshoot was the opportunity to work on an

ADB consulting assignment on pension reforms in six states of India, which continued until 2008 and proved to be a rewarding experience. I was also invited to work on health issues in Andhra Pradesh on another consulting project of DFID, UK.

Towards the end of my NIPFP tenure, my family and I experienced two tense months with regards to the housing matter. The Directorate of Housing promptly served me a notice to vacate the house on 31 January. My request for a two-month extension, even at the cost of penal rent, was rejected with a warning that my household goods would be thrown out and house repossessed if I did not vacate immediately. Somehow, me and my family got through this period. On 21 March, after Shrey's examinations were over, I vacated the house, sent my belongings to Jaipur and moved the family to Rajasthan House (the state guest house) for about 10 days. I left Delhi on 31 March, after the completion of my NIPFP tenure, to begin my duties with the Government of Rajasthan.

My first foray into writing

In addition to conducting and writing research reports at NIPFP, I got initiated into writing in newspapers and journals.

Sunil Jain, noted financial journalist and later editor of the *Financial Express*, who died far too soon in May 2021, would see me about state financial issues when I was serving as joint secretary PF-I. He was always thorough and had a lot of searching queries. It was a joy to explain the intricacies, complications and deformities of fiscal federalism and state finances to him and potential pathways out of the mess. He encouraged me to write for the *Business Standard*, where he was working in 2005–06. I wrote a few pieces for *Business Standard* and one for *Economic Times*.

Upon the encouragement of renowned public finance economist Amaresh Bagchi, whose room was next to mine at NIPFP, I wrote a comprehensive piece titled 'Transformation of Central Grants to States'. This was published in *Economic and Political Weekly* in its December 2006 issue after my NIPFP tenure. Bagchi, who became a member of the Centre–State Commission constituted in 2006, grew quite fond of me. After I had moved as finance secretary, Rajasthan, he included me in a task force that he headed on state finances.

25

Detour to Implementing Agriculture Programmes

After completing my 'cooling-off' period in Jaipur (2006–09), I landed up in New Delhi again on central deputation – this time in the Department of Agriculture and Cooperation. After nine years in finance at the centre and the state, I was in the thick of national agriculture policy-making and programme implementation.

The Ministry of Agriculture in the Government of India had three departments in 2009 when I was posted as joint secretaryin the Department of Agriculture and Cooperation (DAC). The Department of Agriculture Research was primarily concerned with the research and development of crops, fruits, vegetables, cotton, animal feed and so on. The Department of Animal Husbandry looked after development programmes for animal husbandry and fisheries. The DAC was responsible for development programmes for crops, fruits, vegetables, fibres and other field crops; it also worked as a regulator of agricultural inputs and the agriculture cooperative system. It had more than 25 divisions with 20 joint secretary-level officers, including seven IAS officers. I was assigned the responsibility of three divisions: the plan division, trade division and Rashtriya Krishi Vikas Yojana (RKVY) division.

The plan division dealt with the formulation of the annual plan, developing schemes for agriculture development, getting them approved through the Planning Commission and preparing the allocation of the annual plan ceiling for the many development programmes that the DAC was implementing. The work of the division mostly concluded with conveying the annual plan allocation for each programme to concerned divisions and the states.

The trade division dealt with agricultural goods and services issues in bilateral and multilateral trade negotiations. While the primary responsibility of trade issues was vested in the Department of Commerce, considering the excessive sensitivities connected with imports and tariffs on agricultural trade, and the fact that more than half of Indian households depended on agriculture for their survival and income, the understanding between the Department of Commerce and the DAC was that the Ministry of Agriculture had to be on board with whatever position India took in international agricultural negotiations. For trade purposes, the DAC looked after matters relating to the Department of Animal Husbandry as well.

The RKVY division was created in 2007 as an umbrella programme that sought to re-engineer the national strategy of delivering agriculture programmes by offering the states primacy in deciding specific agriculture and other connected sectors (referred to as allied sectors) interventions and strategies for its development, with the Government of India assuming the responsibility of providing funds and overall coordination.

The three divisions I was allocated provided me a very wide-angled view of agriculture. The plan division afforded the opportunity to look at the entire bouquet of agriculture development programmes and budget dealt with by the department. The trade division brought international exposure about multilateral organizations like the World Trade Organization (WTO) and agriculturally important countries that were involved in agriculture negotiations. Rashtriya Krishi Vikas Yojana provided an excellent platform to get involved in the entire spectrum of agriculture since agricultural operations and development take place in states, districts and villages.

'Send him back to Rajasthan'

P.K. Basu, an officer of the 1976 batch of Bihar cadre, was one of three additional secretaries in the department. An energetic and enthusiastic go-getter, he handled administration, RKVY and a few other divisions. He had strong likes and dislikes and felt good if his 'smart thinking' was seconded/applauded by officers. He felt somewhat uncomfortable with officers who had an independent bent of mind.

Atanu Purukayastha, my batchmate and a postgraduate in agriculture from the well-known Pantnagar University, had handled RKVY since its inception in 2008. Atanu understood the science and technology of agriculture much better. Basu, however, did not find him to be agile enough and held the opinion that the rollout of RKVY, the most important agriculture programme initiated since the Green Revolution era, was suffering under Atanu's stewardship. He had wanted Atanu to carry out certain changes in the RKVY programme implementation based on the experience of over a year. Atanu had prepared some proposals, but Basu was not happy with them. That perhaps explained the RKVY division being taken away from Atanu and being entrusted to me, though he continued to be a joint secretary in the department.

I found most of the amendments proposed by Atanu quite good. Very soon, I prepared another note recommending most of his proposals and adding a few of mine. Basu was, again, not pleased perhaps as it did not reflect what all he wanted.

The trade division came under J.C. Pati, an IAS officer of Odisha cadre, who had been promoted to additional secretary a few months earlier and had handled the division as a joint secretary before. Agricultural negotiations were taking place in WTO and there was global urgency to complete the negotiations on the draft before WTO. The working rule in the Department of Agriculture was that joint secretary, Trade, would represent the department in these meetings in Geneva if the issues under discussion were of a policy nature. For operational issues, director, Trade (Mamta Shankar, at that time), would go. As a policy round of negotiations was being held in early October, I was nominated on the file, which was routed through Additional Secretary Pati per usual practice. On the eve of my proceeding to Geneva, Basu, who handled the administration division that issued the foreign deputation orders, asked me to come to his chamber. He, for reasons best known to him, felt that director, Trade, should have gone instead. I explained the policy and practice of deputation and still left the matter to him to change the deputation if he wanted to. After a few hours, the file came back with my deputation orders.

Considering Basu's seniority and assertiveness, a common practice had developed in the department – a joint secretary or director was to discuss important matters and references with him before the matter was put on file. I had never followed this practice and did not make it my practice in the DAC as well. There were a few occasions in the first two months when Basu felt my proposal should have been differently framed; a couple of times, he wrote a note to the secretary modifying my proposal, which was fine with me.

About two months into the job, I received a call from Atul Garg, Basu's batchmate from Rajasthan cadre. He enquired whether everything was alright with my posting in Delhi. I confirmed that was the case. He then went to share that Basu had spoken to him and had told him that the DAC had contemplated repatriating me to the cadre, but the proposal had since been shelved. I was a bit surprised as I had not heard of any such development, but I laughed it away.

RKVY: Driver of agriculture development

Green Revolution technology – the use of high-yielding varieties of seeds along with adequate fertilizers, water and plant protection measures – had become the only and highly centralized approach of agriculture development in India since the late 1960s. Central research institutions under the Department of Agriculture Research and Education (DARE) developed newer varieties of seeds and packages of practices. The DAC took these varieties and technologies to the states. Through their vast agricultural set-ups, states demonstrated these in the field of farmers. Agriculture was a state subject, but the centralized interventions of Green Revolution had made agriculture development in the country almost entirely driven by the centre's agriculture development programmes. States had become mere implementing agencies.

This worked for two decades, the 1970s and the 1980s. Indian agriculture, especially irrigated wheat and rice cultivation, was transformed completely in agriculturally advanced states. Then, stasis set in. With no real development of new varieties and no real change in technology packages, the agriculture development programme became routinized. The annual agriculture growth rate settled at a low 3 per cent in the 1990s and the first decade of the twenty-first century. The rate of new investment in agriculture, especially private investment, fell to atrociously low levels. Green Revolution was also seen to be bypassing rainfed areas and the central and eastern parts of the country.

The worried government assessed that the rate of investment in rainfed agriculture had to be stepped up to achieve even the modest ambition of generating a 4 per cent annual growth rate of agriculture GDP. It also reckoned that the states needed to be put in charge to encourage them to allocate more of their plan resources to agriculture to leverage more private-sector investment in agriculture strategies based on what would work in local conditions, in place of a one-size-fits-all national strategy.

This thought gave birth to RKVY in 2007. The National Development Council (NDC) approved it. Prime Minister Manmohan Singh announced this from the ramparts of the Red Fort. The scheme was designed to focus on achieving a 4 per cent rate of agricultural growth by increasing investments in rainfed agriculture through allocating more grants to the states with larger unirrigated agricultural areas. To incentivize the states to allocate more funds for agricultural development, the quantum of central grants given to them was directly linked to an increase in the states' allocation for expenditure on agriculture and allied sectors' development, as compared to the average of the past three years. Finally, the programme envisaged preparation of comprehensive district-level agricultural development programmes to focus on local planning. The central government promised grants of ₹25,000 crore over the Eleventh Five-Year Plan. The states were given complete liberty to choose agriculture and allied sector development projects and programmes. The plans were to be primarily approved by the states in state-level coordination committees (SLCCs) constituted by them and headed by chief secretary. A joint secretary level officer from the DAC participated as a member.

Putting RKVY on its feet

Rashtriya Krishi Vikas Yojana was excellent in intent and design but extremely challenging to implement and monitor.

The states were required to frame district and state agriculture development plans as a starting point. What did an agriculture plan mean? Would a uniform template be used to draw up these plans for all districts? The central government, which was providing the grant, needed a uniform template for capturing details of the projects approved by SLCCs, their allocations and monitor their utilization. The Planning Commission was entrusted with the task of preparing guidelines for the states and district plans. It took some time and RKVY implantation commenced in the first two years – 2007–08 and 2008–09 – virtually without any such plans.

What constituted the states' baseline expenditure on agriculture? Volatile elements like natural disasters or agriculture market interventions led to differential allocation in agriculture budgets from year to year. It was discovered that the allocation for agriculture in 2007–08, the first year of the scheme, was lower than the baseline in quite a few states.

All these led to grant of major ad-hoc relaxations in RKVY guidelines, which facilitated commencement of implementation but made it difficult to know what was happening on the field. The inability to meaningfully understand what was going on and report the progress to the PM, Planning

Commission and other stakeholders was at the centre of Basu's unhappiness with Atanu.

I decided to work on a threefold approach to bring some sense to the situation.

First, we decided to develop a structure of the universe of agricultural interventions the states were undertaking or could undertake, define these as uniformly as possible, and ask the states to input the requisite information and data in a digital programme for the choices they made.

Second, we decided under what heads of accounts would determine the baseline expenditure in terms of a chart of accounts, with the information objectively sourced from the finance and accounts of the states, audited by the CAG. We excluded volatile elements from such baseline calculations.

Third, states were relieved of the requirement of getting their plans, approved by the SLCCs, again approved from the DAC. Reporting in the RKVY information portal was the only requirement they needed to fulfil. Progress in the field was decided to be ensured by extensive field visits by DAC officers.

This streamlining brought some semblance of sense to the operation and implementation of the scheme over the two-and-a-half years I spent in charge. We could put all the states implementation data on the portal. It also enabled cross-checking and referencing. In 2011, all the states could see what each state was doing. With search-and-organize facilities on the portal, discrete activities undertaken by all the states could also be viewed on thematic basis.

The real gains, however, remained limited, though the funds began to be spent more extensively.

In the shadow of Naxalites

Some states did remarkably well. Bihar was one of them. This was partly on account of the good governance restored by the Nitish Kumar government. Agriculture production shot up and Bihar generated excellent growth. Gujarat and Madhya Pradesh also did very well. The southern states of Tamil Nadu and Karnataka introduced many innovations, especially in animal husbandry, nutrient management and mechanization. I visited all these states to see what was going on at the ground level.

Jharkhand and Chhattisgarh were under the shadow of Naxalite activity. Tripura was suffering from an agitation by separatists. I decided to make a week-long visit to Chhattisgarh, going deep in the Bastar zone, to see what was happening there.

I spent two days reviewing state-level progress in Raipur and visiting the Bhilai and Rajnandgaon areas. There were good projects going on to promote vegetable cultivation. Chhattisgarh was also doing well in rice cultivation and had adopted some new technologies like systematic cultivation of rice intensification (SRI).

From Raipur, I travelled to Kanker through Dhamtari. I saw a lot of RKVY work – it was small-ticket work but important in the context of Chhattisgarh. After a night halt in Kanker, I travelled though Kondagaon to reach Jagdalpur by nightfall. There was tension everywhere, but people were going about their business. Small towns like Kondagaon presented some normalcy.

The situation in rural areas was tense. As I was about to begin my interaction at one place at about 4.30 p.m., an official came to tell me there was Naxal activity close by and advised me to rush back. The interaction was cut short to only five minutes and we drove back to the main road for safety. After two more days in Bastar, I travelled through the Jeypore area of Odisha to finally land in Visakhapatnam (Vizag) after spending a night at Srikakulam.

This seven-day visit was enriching. It exposed me to the life of people and agriculture in one of the toughest zones in India.

Europeans reject Indian grapes

We had become a major exporter of table grapes to the EU as India's grapes reached the EU market during March–May when Chilean and Egyptian grapes were not available. India exported over 1.2 lakh tonnes of table grapes in 2009–10, garnering export revenue of over ₹600 crore. About two-thirds of the grapes were exported from Maharashtra. In April 2010, a major EU buyer rejected a consignment of 30 tonnes on the ground that it contained more than permissible residue of a chemical called chlorocholine chloride or CCC (known as lihocin locally). More importers began to reject the grapes, which got held up in Rotterdam and other ports. Indian farmers were staring at a huge loss. The Government of India was faced with a big embarrassment.

The news was a major blow for the DAC. The Agriculture and Processed Food Export Development Agency (APEDA) at the DAC was primarily meant to ensure that India's fruit and processed products exports went smoothly wherever the Departments of Commerce and Agriculture, working together, had got market access for export of such products. Table grapes were among such exportable fruits and had been going to the EU and other countries quite smoothly until the year before.

As I was handling the trade division, it was my responsibility to get to the root of this crisis, work with diplomatic and other channels to get the ban lifted and restore smooth export.

My examination revealed that India had an extensive programme to manage residue levels of about 100 chemicals identified jointly. Chlorocholine chloride was unfortunately not one of these. In fact, it was not considered an insecticide but a plant growth stimulant. While no other country had prescribed residue standards for CCC, the EU had done so about 10 years earlier and had begun enforcing it a year before. Indian authorities and exporters had taken no note of it as it was not in the joint India–EU protocol of monitoring chemical residues in grapes. In the EU, too, no government agency was testing for this chemical. A private lab had done it for a department store in Germany and that report had become the basis for other importers rejecting the consignments.

The EU officially refused to entertain India's request to let the export take place that year even on the promise that the growth chemical would be discontinued from use by Indian farmers from the next year. Diplomatic efforts were mounted. Evidence of lab testing for new consignments for CCC were offered. Consignments with higher CCC were promised to be stopped. The EU finally relented, but it took about 40 days to allow import for the season. Exports suffered by about 50 per cent that year.

Indian farmers, though, did not suffer much as domestic prices held up on account of overall lower production by about 40 per cent. India's agriculture was suffering in general from higher and indiscriminate use of fertilizers, insecticides and other chemicals. The grapes crisis in 2010 taught us some valuable lessons.

Banning onions is not good 'onionomics'

India produced about 15–17 million tonnes of onions at the time. There was an annual durable surplus of over 2 million tonnes. There was no year when onion consumption exceeded onion production. India was a consistent net exporter of onions year after year. There were, however, seasonal variations. Sometimes on account of floods or droughts, the onion crop harvested in September suffered a production loss. While the principal crop of onions, which came sometime in February–March, lasted very well until the onset of monsoons, the fluctuations in the monsoon crop created temporary shortages until the next crop arrived in November–December.

Indian politicians had become very sensitive to onion prices since 1979–80 when Indira Gandhi made onion prices a big election issue contributing to loss of the Janata Party government. Whenever there was a suspected shortage, usually around August–October, prices would shoot up. The government had developed two instruments to deal with the situation: impose a minimum export price, pegged somewhat higher than prevalent international prices to discourage exports of onions; or impose an outright ban. Almost simultaneously, the import of onions was opened as a kneejerk reaction. These measures did not impact annual exports and imports but served the government's political interest in the short run.

Also, consider the case of milk, which is a rich source of protein. Casein, which makes up roughly 80 per cent of the protein present in milk, needs to be extracted in plants especially set up for this purpose. The government had encouraged the establishment of casein extraction plants in the country in the first decade of the twenty-first century and there were about 35 of these across the country in 2010. Milk production also had some cyclical features. Every third year or so, the overall milk supply in the country would reduce.

I dealt with trade issues in the Ministry of Agriculture in the years 2009–12. The government banned the export of onions and casein in 2010–11. Onion exports were banned in December 2010 and casein exports in January 2011. The year 2009–10 was a drought year and the government was put on the back foot in resisting calls for a ban on exports.

My thorough investigation into 'onionomics' brought out very clearly the inadvisability of imposing a ban on onion export. The department was encouraging the development of onion storage. This was stabilizing onion supply through the year. Earlier, farmers had to unload their crops as soon as they were harvested. Now, there was price stability most of the year and farmers were beginning to benefit. The onion price crisis in November–December 2010 was expected to be temporary – for only about two months before the new crop arrived in February–March. Moreover, as onions were not such an essential product, a hike in their prices did not lead to much panic; a reduction in the consumption of onions wasn't viewed as a major loss of nutrition. Yet, political considerations prevailed, and onion export was banned in December.

Casein export was formally handled by the Department of Animal Husbandry though the DAC was also involved. It was also evident that the milk used in casein extraction was a minuscule portion of the total milk produced, and it would not have made much difference to the overall supply of milk in the country. On the other hand, investments made in the nascent casein extraction industry would become non-performing if an export ban were imposed as India's domestic demand for casein was quite low. Yet, the government decided to impose a total ban on export of casein.

India's durable surplus in onion has increased much more since 2010–11. The government also brought about an amendment in the Essential Commodities Act (ECA) in 2020 laying down stringent conditions for imposing limits on storage and export of agricultural commodities. However, the export of onion was banned in October 2020, one month after the amended the ECA came into effect. Onion continues to be a political hot potato. Farmers continue to suffer.

'Dr Amartya Sen Award'

P.K. Basu replaced T. Nanda Kumar as secretary, agriculture, in the beginning of March 2010.

Following our initial rocky beginning, Basu soon reassessed seeing my performance, especially my work for the 2010–11 annual plan. The department had numerous schemes with overlapping interventions. There were many programmes even for the promotion of the same crop. For example, promotion of wheat crop technology was undertaken in a scheme called Macro Management of Agriculture, under which mini-kits of high-yielding varieties of seeds as well as fertilizers were provided. The RKVY interventions selected by the states also had many projects directed towards cultivation of wheat. The government had also come up with a new National Food Security Mission (NFSM), which was basically intended to promote production and productivity of wheat and rice crops. Many other programmes aimed to promote wheat crops. Similarly, for rice, cotton and a few other crops, there were numerous schematic interventions that the DAC's annual plan catered to. I started a wholesale restructuring exercise for more than 60 programmes run by the department. Basu had entrusted me with this exercise.

Soon after Basu took over as agriculture secretary, Prime Minister Manmohan Singh constituted two panels. One was a panel of trade and industry stalwarts tasked to look into agriculture, besides primarily focusing on industry and trade issues. The second was a panel of state chief ministers, primarily for agriculture-related issues. The industry and trade panel formed a subpanel under the chairpersonship of the industrialist Jamshyd Godrej, which also included fellow industrialist Mukesh Ambani and business executive Ajay Banga. The panel of chief ministers constituted three subpanels, one of which was on agriculture production. This panel was led by the Haryana chief minister and included three other chief ministers. One of the subpanels on marketing was headed by Narendra Modi, then chief minister of Gujarat.

Basu entrusted me with the overall coordination of the agriculture-related works of the industry and trade panel and the chief ministers' panel. I was also entrusted with the responsibility of organizing meetings of the chief ministers' subpanel on production, which, among other things, was tasked with a review of the National Agriculture Policy of 2007 as well as the M.S. Swaminathan Report, which had recommended minimum support prices (MSPs) for crops, based on 50 per cent profit over the cost of cultivation. Further, I was asked to coordinate the meetings of the industry and trade panel on agriculture as well.

My responsibilities involved preparing background papers, drafting recommendations, assimilating the sense and directions of the panels during the discussions in the draft reports and recommendations, and making sure that the meetings were held in a timely fashion. I think Basu was pleased with my work in this regard.

Unable to resist the temptation to direct the states, the government introduced several interventions in the 2011–12 budget. A new scheme for focusing on the east – Bringing Green Revolution to Eastern India – was announced. Five other interventions were announced, including the integrated development of 60,000 pulses villages in rainfed areas to grow pulses, which India was short of, in order to meet people's protein requirement, the promotion of oil palm, and the promotion of coarse grains that had newly been rebranded as 'nutri-cereals'. All these interventions were made subcomponents of RKVY. The amorphous RKVY got further complicated in 2011–12. Soon, there was a realization that it needed to be revamped. I was entrusted with the responsibility to restructure RKVY and prepare a blueprint for its revamp.

All this work probably impressed Basu. At one point of time, he decided to confer specific awards on each of the joint secretaries in the department. I was given the 'Dr Amartya Sen Award'. My stay in the DAC validated my long-held view that the responsibility of an officer is to do his job sincerely and diligently, guided by the larger public interest, without worrying about how the boss viewed it.

Cotton politics

India produced much more cotton than our industry processed. The country's annual cotton production was about 300–350 lakh bales (a bale is 170 kg of cotton) whereas industrial consumption was in the range of 230–245 lakh bales per annum in the years 2009–12. Even after accounting for non-industrial consumption of 20–25 lakh bales per annum, there was a clear surplus of 50–75 lakh bales every year. There was usually a global shortage of cotton supply and, therefore, international prices of cotton were generally higher than domestic prices. The Indian cotton-processing industry was inefficient compared to the global industry and wanted raw cotton supplied at lower prices to make up for its cost-inefficiency. This meant that the interests of Indian farmers and the Indian cotton industry diverged, further accentuated politically as most of the cotton-processing industry was in southern India whereas the cotton crop was raised in Maharashtra, Gujarat, Madhya Pradesh and other non-cotton industry states.

The Ministry of Textiles was allocated the subject of cotton, so policy related to cotton exports, in terms of administration, was with it rather than the Ministry of Agriculture. Even the Cotton Corporation of India (CCI), the public-sector outfit in charge of implementing MSP for cotton, was under the administrative control of the Ministry of Textiles. The ministry had created a body called the Cotton Advisory Board (CAB) that, dominated by industry interests, estimated cotton availability and the industry's requirements. By its very DNA, it was designed to drive down estimates of exportable surplus as much as possible. Rita Menon, an officer of Kerala cadre, was textile secretary, and V. Srinivas from Rajasthan cadre the joint secretary concerned. I was the representative of the Ministry of Agriculture on CAB, which acted in concert with joint secretary, textiles.

In 2010–11, the cotton season (October–September) was a good one for farmers. International prices shot up and India was able to export more than 75 lakh bales of cotton. Farmers earned roughly twice of what was the domestic price in most of the cotton year. The industry wanted to restrict cotton exports in the 2011–12 season despite a healthy cotton crop at about 340 lakh bales.

The CAB prepared a 'Cotton Balance Sheet', which included its estimate of cotton crop and industry and non-industry requirements, with the balance being exportable surplus. Its meeting for the cotton year 2011–12 saw a major showdown. Choreographed by Srinivas, the meeting wanted to place exportable estimates at only 15–20 lakh bales. As the cotton crop that comes around October takes two to three months to be converted into usable cotton, the industry always wanted a large opening balance of cotton on 1 October. I was determined not to allow the CAB to excessively underestimate exportable cotton. There was a lot of argument. I made a strong dissent. They prepared draft minutes suiting the domestic cotton industry. I revised it thoroughly. It led to a big dispute between the Ministry of Textiles and Ministry of Agriculture.

The Ministry of Textiles wanted to ban cotton exports immediately after the CAB meeting. Cotton prices had fallen, with the difference between Indian and international prices coming down to under 15–20 per cent. We resisted. Agriculture Minister Sharad Pawar wrote to Prime Minister Manmohan Singh. We consistently took up the matter with the Department of Commerce. Rahul Khullar, the highly knowledgeable and effective commerce secretary, convened quite a few meetings, which Rita Menon and I attended. The PM first tasked the Economic Advisory Committee (EAC) headed by C. Rangarajan, and later a Group of Ministers (GoM) headed by Finance Minister Pranab Mukherjee. We were able to hold off on a ban on cotton export for some time, until the Ministry of Textiles finally succeeded in getting it on 5 March 2012.

The acrimonious cotton saga made Rita Menon and V. Srinivas personally hostile to me. The International Cotton Association held its annual meeting in China in November 2011. I was invited to present a paper on India's cotton production measurement and promotion programmes. All approvals, including a green signal from the Minister of Agriculture, were available. However, Rita Menon wrote to the MEA to not grant political clearance for my visit. The MEA accepted her intervention and denied me permission.

Agriculture negotiations in WTO remained stuck

Agriculture is an extremely touchy subject all over the world. Economically advanced regions like the US and the EU provided enormous domestic subsidy support to their farmers to encourage higher production and export even though agriculture is a very small portion of their economies, both in terms of contribution to GDP and livelihoods. Agriculture is still the mainstay in developing countries, mostly in terms of the proportion of population dependent on it for livelihood as well as its role in dealing with chronic food shortages.

As per Article 20 of WTO's 1995 Agreement on Agriculture, the global ambition was to undertake fundamental reforms to establish 'a fair and market-oriented agriculture trading system' that included 'substantial progressive reductions in support and protection' to agriculture. There was also a commitment that developing countries would be provided with 'special and differential treatment' and would also have 'special safeguard arrangements'.

In line with the mandate of Article 20, agriculture negotiations commenced at the Doha Round in 2001, which was designated as a significant development round. A draft agriculture text was circulated in 2006. In 2009, when I got the responsibility to represent India's agriculture interests in WTO negotiations, there was very little going on. My first deputation to Geneva in October 2009 coincided with some stirring to restart the stalled agriculture negotiations. This provided me a good launching pad to understand the complexity of such negotiations.

India was considered extremely important for agriculture negotiations but was generally viewed as reluctant to make any compromise on what was probably the highest level of protection in agricultural trade. India's MSP system, implemented in the form of procurement by the Food Corporation of India (FCI) and other agencies, resulted in our domestic support commitments breaching the domestic support limits. India had also adopted hard-line positions on special safeguard arrangements and 'special and differential treatment'. Indian negotiators believed our position was completely justified in view of our domestic situation, dependence of so many poor and vulnerable farmers for their livelihood on agriculture and other issues. When the Agreement on Agriculture was negotiated in 1994, India came on board very late after virtually being told to leave the WTO negotiations so that the rest of the world could get on with it.

I attended four to five meetings of the general body of WTO, held during 2009–12, while I was in the agriculture department, to discuss the agriculture text being negotiated. I also participated in discussions on India's trade policy review, which had substantial sections on agriculture. A number of notifications were also required to be issued every year regarding the quantification of India's domestic support for agriculture. I got most of the backlog completed. However, during this period of two-and-a-half years, there was no notable movement on the draft agriculture agreement text.

The breakthrough came much later, in 2013 and 2015. In 2013, in Bali, India secured a commitment (peace clause) that the rest of the world would refrain from challenging India's breaches on domestic support while India agreed to negotiate a permanent solution for public holding for the purpose of food security. In 2015, in Nairobi, there was an agreement to eliminate agriculture export subsidies.

The negotiations on special safeguard and other packages got completely stalled. The global agriculture situation has changed drastically. India has become a major exporter of agricultural commodities. Its MSP programme results in massive amounts of wheat and rice being bought by government agencies. The peace clause protects India. There are no more negotiations over the draft of agriculture agreement. Development round ambition has also been shelved. In fact, the whole WTO mechanism is facing an existential crisis now with its dispute resolution mechanism having become dysfunctional and the trade war started by President Trump.

'Don't go to the cabinet secretariat!'

Sometime in late November 2011, P.K. Basu informed me that the cabinet secretary had spoken to him about transferring my services to cabinet secretariat. He did not want to let me go but would have to defer to the wishes of the cabinet secretary, he said. He wanted me to think about it and let him know.

Rajiv Mehrishi had come to Krishi Bhawan, Government of India, as an additional secretary in the DARE. He had worked as deputy secretary in the Cabinet Secretariat. He found the place lousy and demotivating. When he heard that my services were being requested by the cabinet secretary, he told me categorically, 'Do anything but don't go to the Cabinet Secretariat!'

I have always believed that an officer has no right to get or not get any particular posting and should accept what is given by the government irrespective of personal preference.

I found that the Cabinet Secretariat had very little role to play in the economic management of the country. Its focus was on serving the Cabinet and managing the country's general administration. I reckoned going there was not in my personal interest. Rajiv Mehrishi's assessment was quite convincing as well. I told P.K. Basu that, personally, I would prefer to stay in the Department of Agriculture. However, if the Government wanted me to serve in the Cabinet Secretariat, I would have no objection to doing so.

In end-January 2012, I received my orders for the Cabinet Secretariat. I joined on 1 February.

26

'Officers Do What They Are Told to Do'

The Cabinet Secretariat, located in a wing of the Rashtrapati Bhawan, started as the secretariat to the executive council of the viceroy/governor general, headed by his private secretary. In 1935, the private secretary to the governor general was designated as secretary or clerk to the executive council. The Secretariat evolved and was formally designated the Cabinet Secretariat in 1946.

After Independence, the Cabinet Secretariat became the principal fulcrum of interaction between the ministries and Cabinet. It was headed by the senior-most civil servant, also the highest paid, a notch above other secretaries to the government. Very soon, the Cabinet Secretariat became the arbiter of the Government of India's business and transaction rules.

The Government of India (Allocation of Business) Rules 1961 and the Government of India (Transaction of Business) Rules determine what matters would be handled in which ministry and department, and how the government business would be transacted. These rules determine what each minister gets to do and which decisions require interministerial consultation, which go to the Cabinet, and which matters or files the prime minister can call for.

Jawaharlal Nehru had no principal secretary. He operated directly and through the Cabinet Secretariat. Lal Bahadur Shastri appointed the first principal secretary to prime minister and laid the foundation of the PMO. Retired officers, senior to cabinet secretary in service, began to be appointed as the principal secretaries to the prime minister. With much greater seniority and proximity to the prime minister, principal secretaries started calling shots and steering decision-making in the government, leaving the Cabinet Secretariat to concentrate more on routine work. The Cabinet Secretariat, however, remained pivotal for security-related matters and appointments in government besides being the formal record-keeper of the nation.

Over the years, the Cabinet Secretariat has been entrusted with the job of sorting out inter-ministerial issues and coordinating on many issues. The relative importance of the cabinet secretary and principal secretary also depends upon the personality and gravitas of the officers in these positions at any point of time and the PM's disposition towards them.

Charge of security and intelligence

The Research and Analysis Wing (R&AW), India's foreign intelligence agency, functions as part of the Cabinet Secretariat. All formal papers from the R&AW to the prime minister are routed through the Cabinet Secretariat. The Cabinet Secretariat is also responsible for security, disaster management and protocol issues. These key security functions were handled by a part of the Cabinet Secretariat designated as the Top Secret (TS) Cell.

The Cabinet Secretariat had divided ministries and departments in broad groups of security, social, economic and appointments for the purpose of processing papers relating to the Cabinet and its committees. The issues dealt with by the Committee of Secretaries (COS) specifically constituted for each matter were also classified in these broad groups. A joint secretary was in charge of each of these groups.

On joining the Cabinet Secretariat in February 2012, I was given charge of the security-related departments, including defence, home, external affairs and the Rashtrapati Bhawan. The TS Cell was also placed under my charge. Along with that came the responsibility of retaining some of the most confidential papers of the government in my personal custody and handling matters relating to the R&AW and other intelligence agencies as well as disaster management. It was quite a change from what I had been doing for close to 30 years in government!

I was promoted to additional secretary in July 2013. With that, I also got charge of the Cabinet division responsible for processing papers and keeping minutes of the Cabinet and its committees' meetings. As additional secretary, I attended these meetings. In those days, the cabinet secretary would sit next to the prime minister. The additional secretary sat in the beginning of the row of seats on the left of the prime minister. It provided a good ringside view of the proceedings.

Wrangle over warrant of precedence

The post of principal secretary to the prime minister, which had been in existence for many years, was formally treated as equivalent to the post of secretary to the government. In the formal warrant of precedence, the protocol list in which functionaries, dignitaries and officials are listed according to their rank and office in the Government of India, secretaries to the government were placed in Entry 23, while the cabinet secretary was in Entry 11. Administratively, both positions were equally important; in practice, the principal secretary often enjoyed a higher status than the cabinet secretary.

When Pulok Chatterjee took over as principal secretary to the PM in October 2011, around the time Ajit Seth was made cabinet secretary, a proposal was moved to include the principal secretary to the PM in Entry 11, the same as the cabinet secretary. Tara Dutt, my batchmate from Odisha cadre who handled the TS Cell before me, rightly objected and wrote forcefully on file about the inadvisable and irregular nature of the proposal. The file remained in discussion thereafter. cabinet secretary Ajit Seth handed the file to me for fresh examination.

A careful study of the file and consultation with Tara revealed that the proliferation of commissions, regulatory bodies, tribunals, and constitutional and other bodies had created a massive demand for inclusion in the warrant of precedence. The warrant of precedence was developed by the highly hierarchical British essentially for orderly greeting and seating at formal functions. Over the years, especially for Indian public representatives and officials, inclusion in the warrant of precedence accorded social and political status, and every shade of public representative wanted to be included at the highest level possible. Over many years, the government had issued many orders placing dignitaries in the warrant of precedence. However, the formal warrant of precedence was not amended/updated after the 1980s. The situation was fluid and open to controversy.

I proposed not to prolong the confusion and carry out a one-time exercise to examine all the claims and decide whether to accept them and determine the place at which each accepted proposal should be entered. Pending finalization, I suggested that the proposal relating to principal secretary to the PM should also wait. A few meetings were held but nothing conclusive was achieved. No formal amendment, including to place principal secretary to the PM in Entry

11, was made to the warrant of precedence during my two-year tenure at the Cabinet Secretariat.

Chidambaram upsets the administrative apple cart

The ICS was created by the British primarily to manage district administration and collect land revenues – the most important source of revenue at the time. The Boards of Revenues, established as the highest policy and adjudicating bodies in the states, were the premier revenue institutions. The ICS managed the post of the district officer, which was designated 'collector'. As collectors of revenue, ICS officers were paid handsomely before Independence.

Tax matters require sharp minds, especially because the taxpayers on the other side of the table will do their utmost to protect their interests and pay as little tax as possible, if at all! Therefore, there was complete justification to ensure that India's revenue services, which handle corporate, income and indirect taxes, attracted best talent and were well paid. Unfortunately, after Independence, the country opted for a civil service model that was common for most government services – from policy-making, revenue collection, and managing railway and postal accounts, to managing secretarial posts. Further, the rigidity of civil service structures meant that departmental civil services, such as the IRS, got a much smaller number of higher positions and relatively lower pay scales.

Finance Minister P. Chidambaram took two major initiatives to 'reform' the revenue administration in the country: the preparation of a new Indian Income Tax Code and a new structure of posts in the IRS (the first proposal was for the income tax cadre).

There were several discussions about the new income tax code. However, the proposal did not really move and was finally dropped off the agenda. The government did not want to take a risk with a new code just six months before the general elections.

The proposal for revising the income tax service cadre envisaged the creation of over 25 posts at the grade of secretary to Government of India, in addition to posts of chairperson and members of the Direct Taxes Board. The number of additional posts for the next level were proposed to be increased many times more. To place this in context, no other service had more than five posts at the secretary level, and here was a proposal that would have given the IRS more than 60–70 posts if it was to be implemented in both income tax service cadre and in the customs and excise cadre.

A proposal for cadre revisions has to pass through several layers before it comes to the Cabinet. This proposal was opposed at every level. However, Chidambaram's dogged pursuit of it ensured that it reached the Cabinet for final consideration. The cadre review committee headed by the cabinet secretary had recommended the proposal with severe conditionalities and drastic reduction in the number of the highest level of posts, citing various reasons and precedents.

As soon as the gist of the proposal was presented by the cabinet secretary, Chidambaram took the stage. He argued against accepting any of the changes made by the cadre revision committee and asked the prime minister to approve the original proposal. Ajit Seth, quite unusually, as he rarely spoke in justification of stand taken by cabinet secretariat, tried to explain the rationale of the changes proposed by the cadre review committee. As the prime minister, had been briefed prior to the meeting, he was leaning towards accepting the version of the proposal recommended by the cadre review committee.

However, Chidambaram would have none of it. He literally staked his post on acceptance of the original proposal. He usually made his case with arguments. This time, he took an 'accept it or I leave it' approach. The prime minister soon relented, and the Cabinet approved the proposal. The IRS got about 60–70 secretary-level posts.

This has disbalanced the civil service structure in the country without improving tax collections. We should find a better way to get the right kind of talent to man the revenue services with the right pay and perks rather than upset the basic structure of the civil services.

Rahul Gandhi tears up ordinance on TV

Indian institutions are traditionally given to protecting the interests of elected representatives. Until July 2013, legislators and parliamentarians convicted of 'corrupt practices' and sentenced were allowed to continue as members of legislative bodies, provided their appeal against the judgment was filed and pending. Even in cases where the appellate court had not stayed the judgment, the membership of the convicted legislator continued unaffected merely on his appeal being filed. On 10 July 2013, the Supreme Court ruled against this blatantly abhorrent situation, stating that membership of the legislative house would immediately cease upon conviction unless the appellate court had suspended the sentence.

The UPA-II government, dependent on the support of some parties with convicted (and likely to be convicted) members of Parliament and state legislative councils, brought a cabinet note to promulgate an ordinance in the week of 16–20 September 2013. The note envisaged the restoration of the pre-July 2013 position with a minor tweak: the convicted member would be allowed to retain membership of the House but would lose the right to vote. As a vote count was rarely taken, it meant continuance of membership without any difference.

In the usual briefing at the Cabinet Secretariat on the morning of Tuesday, 24 September, the officers, including I, spoke about the gross inappropriateness of such a proposal. We were told that the political leadership had made up its mind and our job was only to take the proposal to the Cabinet for a decision. At the cabinet meeting, the item was passed without any real discussion. No minister spoke against the proposal. The Cabinet Secretariat sent the proposal to President Pranab Mukherjee the same day for his signature. He took some time. The prime minister flew to the US the next day.

On Friday, 27 September, we were at the Cabinet Secretariat when all the TV channels suddenly switched to a 'breaking news'. Rahul Gandhi, then Congress vice-president, barged into a party press conference where the spokesman was justifying the ordinance. He took the mic, called the ordinance 'nonsense' and tore up a copy of it in front of the cameras. It was a stunning denunciation of the Cabinet and the prime minister. The PM was to meet US President Barack Obama the same day.

The Prime Minister had been humiliated twice in the matter. First, when he was forced to get the ordinance passed in the Cabinet, much against his own feelings and convictions. Manmohan Singh usually maintained a stoic face, but there was a clear tinge of anguish on his face when the Cabinet cleared the ordinance on 24 September. He was humiliated again by a public display of rebellion by Rahul Gandhi who, it seemed, was keen to take the moral high ground.

Another humiliation awaited the PM. An emergency meeting of the Cabinet was called on Sunday, the day he returned to India. As advised, we had kept the proposal of withdrawing the ordinance ready. The Cabinet was in full attendance. There was only one item on the agenda. Law Minister Kapil Sibal spoke for a few seconds. Prime Minister Manmohan Singh acquiesced, saying something to the effect, 'Well, if it has to be done, do it.' The proposal was passed. The ordinance was withdrawn.

The correct thing was done eventually, but by a public humiliation of the Cabinet and the prime minister by his own party's vice-president. It was painful to see a learned, reformist gentleman like PM Manmohan Singh so weakened, reduced to a caricature.

Environment minister keeps PM waiting

In 2013, infrastructure and other large investment projects were experiencing inordinate delays, in many cases owing to pending environmental clearances. That period, which was later characterized as an era of 'policy paralysis' by media and opposition parties, had the government worried. Determined to stem the rot, it created a dedicated Cabinet Committee on Investments. Anil Swarup, energetic and enthusiastic as ever, was put in charge of the secretariat set up to find the root of the problem. He prepared the notes for consideration first in the COS headed by the cabinet secretary, and then by the Cabinet Committee on Investments. I processed the proposals for the COS and then took them to the Cabinet Committee on Investments. Anil Swarup was not allowed to attend the cabinet committee meeting, where I took care of the agenda.

The rot in the Ministry of Environment and Forests (MoEF) was evident. The rules and guidelines to get forest and environment clearances were excessively complex. The process was too slow and procedural, with several stages of consultation and preparation of documents. The committees constituted by the MoEF that examined proposals for clearances were institutionally biased against industrialization and infrastructure creation and their 'no-objections' were riddled with several complex and unimplementable conditions. The woes of investors did not end with getting recommendations from these committees. The final clearances were accorded only by the environment minister, Jayanthi Natarajan, who sat on files for months. The environment secretary's helplessness was apparent – there were over 400 files reportedly pending, waiting for the minister's approval and signature. There were widespread allegations that corrupt practices were the reason for such massive pendency.

It was hoped that the Cabinet Committee on Investments might succeed in nudging the recalcitrant minister to act.

A meeting of the Cabinet Committee on Investments was convened for taking up agenda items relating to important projects where environmental or forest clearance was pending. Jayanthi Natarajan was expected to clear the files before the meeting or explain her reasons for keeping them pending in the meeting. All the members of the Cabinet Committee on Investments were present along with Finance Minister Chidambaram and Prime Minister Manmohan Singh. Jayanthi Natarajan did not arrive on time. The environment secretary was on leave. Additional secretary Hem Pandey, who had joined only a few days earlier, was present and sitting next to me. Though he had tried to prepare for the meeting, he did not deal with all the aspects of the ministry and was unsure what stand the minister would take as he could not see her before the meeting.

The spectacle was bizarre. The Prime Minister was in the chair with the entire cabinet committee present. But the minister concerned was missing. On a cue from the cabinet secretary, the joint secretary, cabinet secretariat, called the minister's staff. A few minutes later, he reported that she was not well and would take some time to come. Somebody from the PMO was sent to call her. Fifteen minutes went by. On the suggestion of Finance Minister Chidambaram, the agenda items were taken up for consideration. Hem Pandey tried to respond to the questions but could not be of much help. I tried to provide some responses. The conclusions were clear. The files were pending with Minister Natarajan unjustifiably. What should the Cabinet Committee on Investments do in this bizarre situation? Pass approval orders without waiting for the minister? Prime Minister decided to wait for some more time.

Jayanthi Natarajan finally came to the meeting about 40 minutes late. She only said that she was still examining the projects and would take some more time. There was no explanation or admission of the delay and no commitment to clear the pending files in a specified timeframe.

The meeting ended with the prime minister advising the minister to try to clear the projects at the earliest. No one needed better evidence to conclude how weak and ineffectual Manmohan Singh had become in his own cabinet.

Kamal Nath takes over allotment of bungalows

In the 1990s, Delhi, the seat of the central government, had a massive mismatch between the housing requirement of its officers and employees and the availability of government houses. The government had reasonably well-defined rules for allotment of houses, which provided for 10 per cent of houses being allotted 'out of turn' at the discretion of the Ministry of Housing and Urban Development, while 90 per cent were to be allotted on the basis of seniority of posting in the government and their relative pay scale, in the group of houses where the applicant was eligible. At the time, the Minister of Housing and Urban Development, Sheila Kaul, had thrown the rules in the dustbin and made a large number of allotments on 'special compassionate grounds', breaching the 10 per cent limit by a wide margin. There were also allegations of extensive corruption, for which she and two of her officers were charge-sheeted later. She was convicted as well.

Public interest litigations (PILs) in courts led to a final judgment by the Supreme Court on the matter. After the judgment, the government reduced the special compassionate quota limited to 5 per cent of each category of houses and framed comprehensive rules to define what compassionate grounds could be used and the order of their priority for using the compassionate quota. This made the quota essentially rule-driven in place of minister's sweet will passing as discretion. Any deviation from the rules of the compassionate quota required prior approval of the Cabinet Committee on Accommodation (CCA). Defence Minister A.K. Antony headed the CCA. Housing and Urban Development Minister Kamal Nath was a member. The Cabinet Secretariat served the CCA, like other cabinet committees.

Kamal Nath did more than what Sheila Kaul had done. He interpreted 5 per cent of total pool of houses as his discretionary compassionate quota, which could be exercised in any one or more categories of government houses. New bungalows (Categories 7 and 8) were recently built in New Moti Bagh. He decided to apply a good part of this total 5 per cent quota entitlement in this one category, which meant the allotment of all Moti Bagh bungalows, besides many other bungalows in Delhi, became his sweet discretion. There was no doubt that this was an illegal interpretation and practice. He took the CCA for granted and made allotments as he wished – to ineligible officers or even an eligible officer only upon approaching him or seeing him in person. Instead of taking prior approval of the CCA, he would keep making allotments for about four to six months, and then ask his officers to send the file for approval of the CCA. Until the time I took over this work, Cabinet Secretariat and the CCA had been obliging the minister without raising any questions.

A file was received from the Ministry of Housing and Urban Development to convene a meeting of the CCA. The proposed agenda was approval of about 50 discretionary allotments made by Kamal Nath. There were no explanations of 'compassionate grounds'. The expectation was that the CCA would meet and rubber-stamp the proposals.

My examination of the file revealed that the proposed agenda was completely ultra vires of the housing allotment rules, and on merit, there was no justification for the CCA to approve the allotments made. I prepared a note and submitted it to cabinet secretary Ajit Seth to bring the entire matter to the prime minister's notice and seek his instructions. Even though he had been a willing party to such post facto approvals in the past, he agreed in principle to take it up with the PM. It took a while for Ajit Seth to discuss the matter. Some time passed by. Kamal Nath's officers started visiting me at the Cabinet Secretariat asking for expeditious convening of the CCA meeting. At one stage, Kamal Nath came on the line himself. I told him politely that the matter was under examination.

After some further goading, Ajit Seth discussed the matter with the prime minister. His oral instructions were to take it up with Defence Minister A.K. Antony, who was the head of the CCA. We went with all our data and files to meet Antony. He listened to us patiently and generally agreed with our view. But, he said, he would not overrule the minister and would approve the proposals in the CCA meeting. However, he permitted us to write the factual position of rules and houses allotted in the notes to the CCA and, if necessary, speak in the meeting to apprise the CCA of the factual situation.

Around the time when this final stage of examination was taking place, a full Cabinet meeting was convened on a Tuesday (the Cabinet usually met on Tuesdays and Fridays). Most of the ministers had arrived and had taken their seats. The prime minister was yet to arrive. We were also seated. Suddenly, Kamal Nath entered the room, shouting, 'Where is Subhash Garg?' I rose and started walking towards him. Ajit Seth asked me to stay where I was. Kamal Nath came closer. Shouting further, he asked why the CCA meeting was not being convened. I told him it was under final examination. He said, 'It is not the officers who run the government. Officers do what they are told to do.' Before I could respond, the prime minister entered the room.

After a few days, the CCA meeting was convened. We put up a detailed note, explaining the factual position, which unequivocally conveyed that the proposed regularizations were against the rules and that the CCA should only approve the proposals before the allotments and not have to do it after they were made. Kamal Nath was present, as was Defence Minister A.K. Antony. There were six other ministers present. Kamal Nath said something to the effect that the allotments were done in the public interest and helped improve occupancy in New Moti Bagh. This was patently wrong. For his part, the chairman merely said that the proposals for allotment from the compassionate quota should be brought before making the allotment and approved the entire agenda. In other words, all the irregular allotments made by Kamal Nath got approved.

Return to Rajasthan

In the November–December 2013 elections, Vasundhara Raje returned to power in Rajasthan with a stunning majority, winning 76 per cent of the total seats in the Assembly. I got a call from her on 10 December. She complained I had not called her in the past two years. After I congratulated her on her performance, she invited me to Rajasthan to take over as principal secretary, Finance. I accepted the call of duty.

Soon after she took over on 14 December, a formal request for repatriation of six officers, including Rajiv Mehrishi, was issued. The Government of India followed the practice of seeking the formal consent of the officers concerned and agreed to relieve Rajiv and me on 20 December. The Rajasthan government issued my posting orders as principal secretary on 21 December.

I had planned a private Christmas vacation in Sri Lanka with my family and our tickets and visas were ready. The trip was cancelled.

I arrived on Monday, 23 December, in Jaipur to resume my responsibilities in the same post and room from where I had been ejected by the Ashok Gehlot government five years earlier.

C.K. Mathew, who, in the meantime, had gone on to become chief secretary, moved to Rajasthan Roadways. Rajiv Mehrishi arrived the next day and took charge of the office of chief secretary.

27

Serving Global Development at the World Bank Group

I have recounted the drama surrounding my appointment as ED in the World Bank by the new government led by PM Modi in Part III. Anjali and I reached Washington, DC, on 31 October to assume my responsibilities as ED with effect from 1 November 2014.

The WBG is an exemplary institution to work in. I was there in two capacities – as a member of the World Bank Board and as head of India's Resident Mission. As a board member, my constituency comprised Bangladesh, Bhutan, India and Sri Lanka, and I worked for the institution of World Bank. As head of India resident mission, I was expected to take care of India's development and financing interests.

WBG and the global development challenge

The IBRD is more commonly known as the World Bank, along with its soft loan affiliate, the IDA. Established in 1945, the IBRD was expected to contribute significantly to reconstruction of the war-ravaged economies of Europe and finance development investments in poorer countries like India. The IDA came into existence later in 1960.

One of the original members of the IBRD and IMF, India had a seat on the executive board of the IBRD right from its inception, which it has retained ever since – initially, as one of the six countries entitled to nominate its director on the Board, and later, elect a director as part of a larger constituency (which also includes Bangladesh, Sri Lanka and Bhutan).

The IBRD was not created to provide charity. It was expected to grow into a financially strong (later described as AAA credit-rated) institution supported by equity contributions (including surpluses recapitalized) and debt resources raised from the financial markets at rates the best sovereign governments got. Such resources were expected to equip the IBRD to lend at rates much lower than what the borrowing sovereign governments could raise from the market on their credit strength. In addition to lower interest rates, the borrowing governments were also expected to get significantly large funding and relatively longer terms – about 15 to 20 years. To protect against defaults, the World Bank lent only to creditworthy sovereign governments.

The IDA was established to provide soft/concessional (mostly zero interest) ultra long-term loans (35 to 50 years) for financing development projects of less creditworthy and non-creditworthy least-developed countries (only a small service charge levied). Assisting India was one of the primary reasons for the establishment of the IDA. India had become the largest borrower from the IBRD in 1958 and, in the 1960s, the IDA provided a big chunk of its credits to India.

The IBRD's annual financing commitments were going down – from the peak of $44 billion in 2010 to $27 billion in 2011, $21 billion in 2012, and only to $15 billion in 2013 before recovering somewhat to $19 billion in 2014. The IDA's commitments also stagnated between $15 billion and $22 billion during this period.

The repayments by the IBRD borrowers were rising. As a result, net disbursements (difference between new disbursements to and repayments by a country) had become quite small. In 2013, net IBRD disbursements were only $6.4 billion.

The IFC was formed to fund private-sector investments and draw private investments in developing countries. Private flow of investments in developing countries was sought to be encouraged by the MIGA, which offered political risk guarantees to investors.

The bouquet of these four institutions – together known as the WBG – came to occupy a centre stage in funding reconstruction and development in the world from its inception to at least the advent of the twenty-first century.

The pioneering development financing work of the WBG was supplemented by the emergence of many regional developmental financial institutions such as the ADB, European Bank for Reconstruction and Development (EBRD), Inter-American Development Bank (IADB), African Development Bank

(AfDB) and the like. Development financing of most countries was dominated by these multilateral institutions. India's external debt was predominantly multilateral and bilateral until the 1990s.

The collapse of communism and exit of governments from the production of goods and services on the one hand, and the rise of technology, creation of global value chains and emergence of financial markets, banks and other investment banking institutions in the private sector on the other, gave a big boost to private investment flows in many forms: FDI, FPI and debt flows in myriad forms. Private financial flows gradually stymied official multilateral and bilateral institutional flows. In the beginning of the second decade of the twenty-first century, aggregate financial flows from multilateral financial institutions made up less than 2 per cent of global financial flows.

It was indeed a big opportunity to serve on the board of these four major institutions of the WBG.

A serving 'young' officer into this responsibility

The IBRD executive board, which also serves as the IDA's board, had 25 members in 2014 when I joined. The IFC and MIGA boards are legally and institutionally separate and separately elected but, in practice, the composition of all three boards – World Bank (IBRD plus IDA), IFC and MIGA – was the same at that time.

The World Bank executive board, like the IMF's board, is a residential board with its office in the main complex of the World Bank in Washington, DC. The ED is assisted by an alternate ED and a staff of senior advisors and advisors. India chose the ED in the World Bank who was assisted by an alternate ED from Bangladesh; two senior advisors of the joint secretary level and two advisors of the deputy secretary or director level, all from India; two staff members from India; one staff member from Bangladesh; and one programme staff hired locally in Washington, DC.

India usually sent very senior officers on this position – usually retired or just about to retire secretary-level officers as ED. Occasionally, a cabinet secretary had also gone as an ED. Many officers from the PMO and DEA had gone to serve as advisors and senior advisors to ED.

I was the first additional-secretary-level officer to go as ED, with six years of service still left before superannuation. As India usually gave a tenure of three years as on this position, I was expected to come back and actively serve the

Government of India in an important economic ministry or in the ministry of finance itself after completing my tenure.

One advisor and one senior advisor had left in September and October 2014 before I joined. Of the remaining senior advisor and advisor, both from the PMO of Manmohan Singh, the advisor completed his term within one month of my arrival. The new Modi government was struggling to find replacements as it believed that everyone serving in the PMO – or in economic ministries like finance – was a favourite of the previous government. I had only one senior advisor for my first nine months in Washington, DC.

I had a job to do. Despite the constraint of resources, I decided to delve deep into my work.

Poverty alleviation is the principal goal of WBG

Robert McNamara, president of the World Bank from 1968 to 1981, first repositioned it as the bank for developing countries and enlarged its scale of financing (reconstruction work post World War II was also over by that time). Its annual commitments rose from $1 billion in 1968 to over $13 billion in 1981. China joined the Bank in 1980. McNamara also made meeting 'basic human needs' and tackling poverty head on as the principal planks of his reorganization of the Bank. Poverty reduction remained its guiding goal thereafter.

In 2013, the World Bank redefined its mission in the form of two more specific goals bringing poverty reduction into sharper focus: ending extreme poverty by reducing the per centage of people living on less than $1.25 a day (in 2005 prices) to 3 per cent by 2020, and promoting shared prosperity by improving the living standards of the bottom 40 per cent of the population in every country. These goals were set in the first year of the presidency of Kim Jim Yong (Jim Kim, hereafter).

Developing countries beginning to be a force to reckon

By the 1980s, the growth of China, India and other emerging market countries; the relative decline of high-income European countries; and the massive expansion of private capital flows had begun altering the relative equation between the 'developed countries' (that were expected to contribute most of the capital of the WBG) and the 'developing countries' (that were primarily the recipients of concessional loans and credits).

Developed countries had started seeing emerging market economies as competitors and were increasingly reluctant to cough up more capital (though they did not want to cede control in terms of shares of votes and directorships). Developing countries, including China, wanted to maximize the flows of resources as much as possible and acquire higher share of directorships and votes. This opposite set of objectives created visible differences and tensions in the WBG.

New challenges of climate change and new preferences for aspects like gender equality came to the forefront of development financing. Developed countries were increasingly interested in pushing these issues with project financing. Agreeing on environmental and social standards had acquired a centre stage in development finance policies. New formulations for procurement, dealing with corruption and other governance issues, and acceptance of health and safety standards were also becoming integral to financing.

Falling interest rates globally after the global financial crisis in 2010 had hit the Bank's income levels. There were shrill calls to increase the capital of both the IBRD and IFC from developing countries, while the advanced countries were in no mood to put in more capital.

At one stage, the developing countries brought a proposal to establish a $100 billion loan facility in the World Bank to finance infrastructure. It was shot down by advanced countries. This move later contributed to establishment of Asian Infrastructure Investment Bank (AIIB) and New Development Bank (NDB) by the borrowing countries of the world bank.

The developed and developing countries were in the process of becoming two warring groups.

G-11 to bring developing countries together

The US, with more than one-sixth of the voting power in the IBRD, de-facto veto power in certain decisions and its nominee as the president, exercised substantial formal and informal authority in the WBG. Between them, the Europeans effectively held more than 10 board seats. Along with Japan and Canada, the developed countries exercised a substantial say in the affairs of the Bank. They met every week to discuss and coordinate strategy on issues and agenda.

Developing countries had about 11 seats in all. They had also formed a group, G-11. However, it met infrequently and was generally not cohesive.

Nasir Mahmood Khosa, an experienced and affable civil servant from Pakistan, chaired the G-11 (by arrangement, the chair shifted every six months) when I joined.

The diverse priorities of G-11 members fragmented it further. Sub-Saharan Africa, mostly the IDA countries dependent on concessional credit and grant support, was the most vulnerable to pressure from developed countries. China, having grown significantly and moved by an intense desire to increase its stake and say in the IBRD but more interested in dealing with developing countries bilaterally, ploughed its furrow selectively. Some Latin American countries, including Mexico, were unabashedly pro US to serve their interest. Consequently, discussions in G-11 used to be quite peripheral, and it rarely issued common position statements. The occasional statements it issued were not taken very seriously by the developed countries or by the management.

However, there were quite a few important issues coming to the fore that required developing countries to act together. G-11 was essentially the borrowers' group, and its interests were quite different, and in some sense opposite, from the interests of developed countries. The new environmental and social framework, procurement framework, need to arrest the declining trend in new loans and commitments, the need to raise the IBRD and IFC capital, and develop new ways to enhance the IDA resources had fundamentally different implications for developing countries.

I underlined the need to upgrade coordination and for a qualitative improvement in G-11's work and profile in the first meeting I attended. Nasir Khosa came over to my office later and requested India to take the lead. We developed a good friendship. After a few months, I took over the G-11 chair and stayed on for about one year (two terms). G-11 transformed into a strong forum during this period and made substantial contribution.

'Renegotiating' India's IDA transition deal

From its modest start in 1960, the IDA has come a long way. For many years now, its new resources to finance development projects have been raised in three-yearly replenishment rounds. In these rounds, developed countries made fresh commitments to enhance the IDA's resources from repayments of earlier credits and investment incomes.

The IDA's seventeenth replenishment held in 2013–14 was to raise resources for the period 2014–17. For India, IDA-17 was of special significance. The IDA, which was primarily established to provide cheaper financial resources for India, discussed and finalized the terms of India's exit (called graduation) from the IDA in that replenishment round.

While the country had achieved impressive reduction in poverty, India was still home to the largest number of poor in any country in the world. More than 25 per cent of the worlds' poor still lived in India. Therefore, the country was keen to stay on in the IDA despite meeting the criteria laid out for moving out of it. The World Bank had developed its poverty alleviation work on the strength of the great experience it had gained in India. The World Bank system was also keen that India remain in the IDA fold in some way. Many other countries held similar views.

A formula was designed to 'transition' India's graduation. India's share of the IDA's total programmed financing was capped at 11 per cent in the sixteenth replenishment. As per the resource allocation formula adopted for the seventeenth replenishment, the country would have received the same 11 per cent assistance if it had not graduated.

One of the ways to smooth India's graduation was to create a new class of 'transition support' for the country. The IDA's replenishing partners agreed that India would receive 'exceptional transitional support' during IDA-17 that was two-thirds of the 11 per cent of IDA-17 resources the country would have received had it not graduated. In hard terms, this amounted to about $1.8 billion of fresh credits over the three-year period of 2014–17.

Indian negotiators made two costly compromises in their eagerness to get this exceptional transitional support.

First, they agreed to the revised financing terms. India, being a 'blend country' (eligible to receive financing from both the IBRD and IDA), paid 0.75 per cent service charge and 1.25 per cent interest in 2014 for IDA credits. Transitional credit terms were set in a complicated manner (an interest rate 100 basis points below the fixed-rate interest for an equivalent IBRD loan plus the service charge of 0.75 per cent). In practice, that meant that the rate of interest of 1.25 per cent was raised to 2.35 per cent from the September 2014 quarter when IDA-17 came into effect – a clear increase of 1.1 per cent. India had never borrowed from the IBRD on a fixed-rate basis, and compared to the prevailing variable rate, the IDA transitional support interest was higher by over 1.6 per cent. The 0.75 per cent service charge remained in addition.

Second, India agreed to an 'accelerated repayment' of earlier taken IDA credits. The country's rescheduled accelerated repayments were more than twice the transition credit flow of $1.8 billion.

The IDA-17 replenishment was done and had become a binding commitment by the time I landed. India had also agreed to become a donor to the IDA, raising its contribution to $200 million. The World Bank Board had approved the package eight months earlier and implementation had started from 1 July 2014.

I was quite shocked when I studied the matter upon reaching Washington, DC.

The DEA team that had negotiated the package was gone. Arun Jaitley had replaced P. Chidambaram as finance minister and Rajiv Mehrishi was the DEA secretary in place of Arvind Mayaram.

I prepared a detailed note and sent it to Rajiv Mehrishi. Tarun Bajaj was the joint secretary handling the World Bank. He tried to justify the terms. After much explanation and a great degree of persuasion, I got the clearance to raise the matter with the World Bank, which I did in the World Bank Board during a loan proposal relating to India. There was great reluctance to revisit anything. I persisted with a detailed note to the management and continuously hammered upon the issue. Finally, after about three months, the Bank agreed to discuss it.

I succeeded in getting the World Bank to offer the option to India to take the loans in either SDRs or single currency (all IDA loans were in SDRs earlier), and either at the earlier agreed IDA-17 transition terms (which we had no intention to go with) or at the standard World Bank variable interest loan terms. This effectively brought down the earlier negotiated rates for India by more than 50 per cent of rates applicable then. Many World Bank staffers told me that it was unprecedented for IDA credit terms to be modified after implementation of replenishment had begun.

For accelerated repayments, nothing could be done for India, as it would have unravelled the size of the IDA-17 replenishment. My exposure of the inequity of accelerated repayments and persistence, however, benefitted Sri Lanka, which was a candidate for graduation in the eighteenth round. Before the eighteenth-round package was finalized, I succeeded in getting the acceleration clause suspended, and so Sri Lanka did not have to make any accelerated payments.

Edgy Shaktikant Das scuppers India's moment

The IDA-18 replenishment package was negotiated in 2016. The final fourth round of negotiations was scheduled to take place in Yogyakarta, Indonesia, in the middle of December 2016. India had played a prominent role in the IDA-18 negotiations. The IDA replenishments are negotiated by high-ranking officials of about 60 donor countries, officially termed IDA deputies.

The joint secretary, World Bank, in the DEA was India's official deputy. I participated in all the three rounds from Washington, DC, as well. I was the de facto Indian deputy for these three rounds. For the final round, I was officially nominated by the Government of India as the head of the Indian delegation.

The eighteenth round of IDA was unique for the World Bank, developing countries, India and the Indian constituency. For the first time, the IDA was being allowed to raise debt from the market. It was offering its loans and credit in any single currency (an off shoot of our renegotiation of India's IDA transition terms), besides SDRs. A private-sector financing window was also being created for the first time.

For India, this round marked a watershed moment. We had decided to forgo some of the limited transition finance facility, taking a high moral ground. India had also committed additional financing resources for IDA replenishment. From being its largest borrower, India was transiting to a pure donor to the IDA.

Sri Lanka was also graduating from the IDA. The acceleration clause had been suspended, and Sri Lanka was not faced with negative IDA fund flow. Bangladesh, another member of the Indian constituency, which had become the largest borrower from the IDA, had performed remarkably well. Its transition was also emerging in sight, two or three replenishments away.

I had played a major role in negotiating this package and was looking forward to making India's final commitments and participate in the adoption of the IDA-18 replenishment report at Yogyakarta.

The matter of the Indus Waters Treaty was moving in parallel from September to November 2016. I will recount this in the next chapter. Like me, Nripendra Misra had initially advised Shaktikanta Das, then secretary, DEA, to stay away from the issue. The trust between Arun Jaitley and Jim Kim had broken down signficantly. Developments on Indus Valley arbitration front had made New Delhi anxious.

Shaktikanta Das thought and proposed to Arun Jaitley to put pressure on Jim Kim by withholding its proposed commitments in the IDA-18 replenishment. All this was happening behind my back. A few days before I was to meet Jim Kim for the Indus Waters arbitration issue, the DEA decided that India would boycott the IDA-18 replenishment session at Yogyakarta. Director Lekhan Thakkar was deputed to represent India not to say anything on behalf of India except conveying the decision of India withdrawing its IDA 18 commitments and to take notes. I was asked not to go to Yogyakarta.

It was a very poor judgement. I told Shaktikanta Das that the IDA-18 deal was done and it was mostly formalization of the deal at Yogyakarta. If India decided not to make a commitment, it would get singled out. There was no way the country could permanently walk off. Sooner or later, India would render the resources it had already officially indicated to the World Bank team. I also told him that this move would act as a further irritant to Jim Kim; there was no way he would allow the IDA-18 replenishment not to conclude. Shaktikanta Das would not agree.

In the first week of December, the Indus Waters Treaty matter was suspended to our satisfaction. I sent a detailed note on the agreement arrived at with the World Bank president. Thereafter, I requested Shaktikanta Das again to restore India's participation in the final round of the IDA-18 replenishment negotiations. He did not agree.

India was represented in Yogyakarta only by Lekhan Thakkar, who sheepishly announced the country's decision not to make its financial commitment to IDA-18. India, which in a way was representing Sri Lanka and Bangladesh as well, did not get any credit for all that was achieved in IDA-18.

Three months later, when the IDA-18 replenishment package was formally discussed and adopted by the World Bank Executive Board, I made the commitment again on behalf of India that should have been made in Yogyakarta.

Our country did everything it had promised to do for IDA-18 and graduated fully and completely from IDA, yet the big moment passed without any recognition and acclaim for India's role.

A 'forward-looking' exercise

My first few months in the job were enough to convince me that the World Bank model was in danger of falling apart. The US and European countries had lost the appetite to inject more capital to grow financing from the WBG. They were more interested in using its financing to push environmental, social and governance agenda as well as other non-financial objectives. The IBRD was funding about $15–20 billion a year, the IDA also in the same range and the IFC about $10 billion a year. The total annual funding was around $50 billion at best. Viewed in the context of India, the World Bank had become a minor player. India's plan expenditure exceeded $600 billion, whereas total gross financing from the WBG amounted to less than $6 billion a year. The FDI annual flow had crossed $50 billion in that year.

The World Bank governors had agreed to conduct a capital review every five years. The next review was due by 2015. A capital review takes more than a year to complete, yet there were no preparations afoot in the last quarter of 2014. The World Bank took some tentative steps in the first quarter of 2015. The trend of discussions confirmed that there was great reluctance on the part of the Americans and the Europeans for a capital review. The Europeans especially felt that any capital review would diminish their hold over the Bank because their share of capital would fall – the directorships of small countries like Belgium, Netherlands, Switzerland and Italy were under threat. The expanding role of emerging market countries, especially China, also threatened their cosy situation.

In a way, the WBG was facing an existential dilemma. What was its role in the emerging world where developing countries were contributing more than 70 per cent of its annual growth, where new multilateral banks like the AIIB and NDB were being established by the borrowing countries themselves, and where private investment flows had totally dwarfed investment resource flows?

The developing countries wanted the WBG to become 'bigger' in terms of its services and lending resources. The developed countries did not want to contribute any more capital and wanted the WBG to become 'better' in terms of its quality of lending. Bigger, better or both became the principal issue, both consciously and subconsciously.

In this state of confusion and with conflicting objectives, the World Bank Board embarked on a 'forward-look' exercise to figure out what kind of WBG its stakeholders wanted by 2030. The Committee on Governance and EDs' Administrative Matters (COGAM) was in charge of capital increase. I was its vice-chairman. We ensured the WBG remained focused on capital increase as well. It was agreed that along with the forward-look exercise, a roadmap for capital increase would be developed and endorsed from the governors in Lima in October 2015.

Capital increase in IBRD and IFC finally takes place in 2018

The stunted lending capacity of the IBRD and IFC was a major cause of worry for developing countries. India shared this view.

In one of the earliest COGAM meetings organized for this purpose in the first half of 2015, I asked for a clear package to raise capital of the IFC. Strangely, the IFC officials stated point-blank that they had adequate capital and did not need any new capital. Evidently, they were not being truthful and echoing the preferred stance of the developed countries.

I persisted. A few meetings down the road, particularly after French economist Philippe Le Houérou joined as CEO in March 2016, the IFC started dropping hints that it needed capital. In a meeting organized around this time, I spoke of the need to infuse $10 billion of capital in the IFC. It had raised capital of only $200 million in the last round in 2010. The mention of $10 billion appeared akin to asking for the moon.

The quantification of the actual capital needed began thereafter. I left the ED position in July 2017. S. Aparna, who replaced me at the Bank, working very closely with me in my capacity as secretary, Economic Affairs, and alternate governor in the World Bank, kept the good work going.

Finally, in April 2018, a capital increase package of $5.5 billion was agreed for the IFC, an unprecedented level of increase.

For the IBRD, a capital increase had been agreed in 2010, which was, however, only sufficient for maintaining lending levels of about $15 billion a year. Increasing demand for lending capacity since 2010 had put the developed countries and the Bank's management on a different path.

The capital adequacy ratio (called equity to loan or ETL ratio) was brought down from close to 36 per cent in 2007 to 23 per cent in 2014. This permitted leverage (borrowed resources) of over four times compared to less than three times earlier. The developed countries proposed it be brought down further to 20 per cent. We had no objection, but it was not yielding much resources.

The IBRD capital increase also followed quite a tortuous path. A roadmap was agreed on in Lima in 2015, which was endorsed by the governors in the annual meeting. This envisaged the completion of all negotiations and finalization of the capital increase package by the next annual meeting in October 2016. Continued pressure from the advanced countries and lack of interest from the US derailed the Lima roadmap.

The capital increase in the IBRD took two forms: a general capital increase (GCI) and a special capital increase (SCI). The GCI divides new capital in the existing ratio of capital held by member countries (barring a small portion that is allocated in the form of an equal number of shares to all members). The SCI envisages the use of a formula taking on board relevant factors, which, with relative weights, results in allocating new capital in a different ratio than the prevailing capital distribution. As the relative share of developing countries in the global GDP and its growth was going up, they, including India, were in favour of higher weights to be assigned to share of GDP. Advanced countries wanted to use their higher contributions to the IDA replenishments as the basis for allocating capital.

The COGAM held several meetings to figure out the share and formula for the SCI. The differences resulted in a virtual stalemate. Finally, US ED Mathew McGuire created a small team, which included me. We thrashed out many issues, though our differences persisted. The US elections in November 2016 saw Donald Trump become president. There were widely shared apprehensions that the capital increase was as good as dead. However, some favourable developments in the US in 2018, including the interest of Ivanka Trump – the daughter of President Trump – towards the World Bank, brought the capital increase back on the table.

Finally, a capital increase of $7.5 billion was agreed to in April 2018.

Saving India from loan-price increase

The advanced countries had adopted the strategy of raising the IBRD loan prices in order to increase the IBRD's surplus as a preferred means of increasing its capital. Developing countries, including India, did not examine these proposals very carefully and mostly focused on the volume of financing. Between 2007 and 2014, the IBRD management succeeded in raising loan prices three times. During my stay in Washington, DC, I tried to find how India had approached this issue during this period but could not find much of a record of India working assiduously to ward off these interest rate increases.

The Bank did numerous calculations and presentations before the board, COGAM and other fora to present scenarios of what options of price increases were available and what each option would yield in terms of additional financing resources for itself.

During my Washington stay, we did a thorough analysis of all these proposals and consistently hammered the point that all those proposals would only yield a meagre increase in resources in comparison to the resources required. We also underlined the IBRD's raison d'être to intermediate not non-concessional but cheaper market resources for reconstruction and development.

Our analysis also showed that the increases made already had brought the IBRD financing rates very close to market rates for good credit developing countries like China and India. We also pointed out the utter senselessness of the proposed pricing policy, which envisaged charging a higher rate of interest for better credit countries and lower rate of interest for lower credit countries.

All these analyses and arguments were convincing, but the developed countries wanted the item to be part of the final capital-increase package when it came to be negotiated in 2018. In the final stages of negotiations, S. Aparna informed us that India's hard stand on no loan-price increase was becoming a deal-breaker. The Bank management also reached out to us. They were prepared to make only a small increase in loan prices and keep India exempt from it as much as possible.

We then worked to ensure that only a higher maturity premium (loan charge linked to maturity of loan; the higher the maturity, the higher the premium) would be built into the loan-price package. There would be no increase in maturity premium for loans up to 10–12 years. We succeeded in getting an IDA transitioning country like India exempt from this increase, at least until 2025. The Bank agreed to our conditions.

Finally, the maturity premium across the entire spectrum was made applicable to only those countries that had a higher per capita income than the graduation cutoff of about $7,000. For lower middle-income countries like India, there was a reduction in existing premium up to a certain maturity and, thereafter, a smaller increase for much longer maturities. India was exempted from any maturity premium until 2030.

I felt vindicated and satisfied when both the capital increases of the IFC and IBRD were approved in the Development Committee meeting in Washington, DC, in April 2018; I was in India's governor's chair as Finance Minister Arun Jaitley could not travel to the US on account of ill-health.

In my formal statement to the Development Committee, pointing out that India had been 'at the forefront of designing and completing the shareholding review of 2015 and also building consensus for the voice reforms in the World Bank Group', I supported 'the proposed joint package of $13 billion paid in capital for IBRD and IFC'.

A contentious ESF

The World Bank decided to replace the practice of theme-specific safeguard policies with a new comprehensive environmental and social framework (ESF).

The first draft was issued sometime in 2014. The Committee on Development Effectiveness (CODE) was in charge of the business of the ESF. There were objections from both sides of the aisle – capital providers and borrowing clients. These issues were noted, and it was decided that the World Bank team would come up with a second draft of the ESF.

A few weeks after I joined, the director in charge of the wing tasked with the formulation of the second draft of the ESF came to see me. This meeting led me to study all the previous papers, India's position, the position of G-11 countries, the advanced countries' position and related literature. India and the developing countries did not want the ESF to impose an impractical and excessive burden on them. While they were supportive of the goal of sustainable development, including fair treatment to workers and project-affected people, they did not want the ESF to become an albatross around their neck and make projects economically unviable and excessively difficult to implement. These were fair concerns.

In June 2015, the second draft of the ESF emerged. It was worse than the first draft. Everything the developing countries wanted was simply ignored. The advanced countries succeeded in introducing additional safeguards and restrictions.

We studied the second draft carefully and raised the subject forcefully in the CODE meeting. The advanced countries were somewhat taken aback at the vehemence of the opposition and the massive changes we wanted in the second draft. The discussions became very intense, and positions started hardening. I issued a statement that was placed in the public domain, quite unusual to the mode of working in the Bank. It highlighted issues of serious concern, such as moving away from national frameworks and enlarging the scope of direct, indirect and cumulative impacts, while carrying out the environmental and social impact assessment; extending labour standards to community and voluntary labour; extending the ESF to third parties such as agents, intermediaries and small suppliers; bringing intangible heritage within the scope of cultural heritage and so on. This statement was also meant to reach out to civil society in advanced countries, which was pushing for these excessive expectations.

The G-11 rallied together this time. Nasir's statement in the CODE was drafted by us and we spoke in one voice. The heat was felt across the leadership of the Bank and the defenders of the ESF draft. The CODE agreed to postpone further consideration on it by six months and hold consultations in all major developing countries. It also agreed that the Bank would prepare a template of issues, taking on board the issues G-11 suggested, which would work as the basis of consultation. The World Bank team was directed to prepare the next draft based on these consultations.

With the help of the DEA, we organized extensive discussions with the concerned ministries and organizations in India, making them responsible for justifying the position we were taking and highlighting the impracticality of what was proposed in the second draft. We went through the presentations prepared prior to the formal consultation workshop. The preparations paid off. India came out strong in the three-day workshop held by the World Bank in India. Hart Schafer, the vice-president leading the ESF consultations, took away several points from India. We also proposed line-by-line changes in the second ESF draft.

The third draft incorporated most of our concerns. Still, there were some issues. We persisted with them. I made a final statement in the executive board meeting, highlighting the remaining issues. The Bank agreed to taking those on board as well, as far as possible. Bilateral consultations between the Bank and my office ensured that most of these were also taken on board.

The ESF was approved by the World Bank Board in August 2016 after more than 15 months of the second draft, with the agreement of the developing countries. It was also agreed that the ESF would be field-tested and detailed guidelines developed (in consultation with borrowing countries) over a period of two years, before it formally came into force in 2018.

Transfer of surplus from IBRD and IFC to IDA

The IDA was designed to be funded from donors' contributions and the repayments of credits by borrowers. In the first decade of the twenty-first century, the IBRD and IFC started transferring a part of their profits to the IDA, which began its third source of replenishment. The IBRD and IFC surpluses formed part of their capital on which their lending capacity depended; transfer of surplus dented their combined lending capacity. Transfers to the IDA had acquired a kind of untouchable nature as this was projected as a measure to help poor countries.

It made no sense in terms of funding borrowers. The IBRD was able to leverage its capital at least five times by borrowing from the market. Therefore, a dollar of capital in the IBRD funded $6 of loans to IBRD borrowers. When this got transferred to the IDA, that dollar funded only $1 of credits or grants, as the IDA did not leverage its capital. There was also an acute shortage of funding for middle-income countries like India that were borrowers from the IBRD. In the IDA, this formed a small part of their overall resources.

Convinced this was a bad policy, I began raising the matter in board committee meetings. Soon, other directors took it up. Russian ED Andrei Lushin became a major critic of the system of transfers. The IBRD and IFC management defended the system. The directors of developed countries, who were the main contributors to the IDA, opposed our intervention as they saw that the gap that the stoppage of surplus transfer would create would fall to them to fill.

The storm created by Andrei and me forced the management to bring up the policy of surplus transfer to IDA for a comprehensive discussion in 2016. In this meeting in November 2018, we insisted on complete elimination of transfers. Though we lost the vote, our principled and sound stand forced the board to recalibrate the surplus transfer system by linking it to the income levels of the IBRD. This led to a downward revision of the surplus transfer committed under the IDA-17 replenishment period.

The IFC later realized the loss of opportunity to its business and profitability that had been caused by making these transfers to the IDA. It brought the matter before the board in 2017 to suspend the IDA transfers, which I happily supported.

The capital increase package of 2018 retained income-linked transfers of the IBRD surplus to the IDA with considerable income exempted from transfer. The IFC surplus transfer was permanently suspended.

28

Bringing Indus Waters Arbitration Back from the Brink

Presidents of the World Bank used to be larger-than-life figures, at least for developing countries. While the World Bank's financial resources had become a small proportion of the overall development financing of a country like India, its president was still treated akin to a head of state and his visit to the country was much sought after.

The new World Bank Board that assumed office on 1 November 2015 had its first full session on 2 November, chaired by President Jim Kim, a US citizen of South Korean origin and a medical doctor by profession. More than half the members changed in every two-year cycle of board elections. There was no custom of individual meetings of EDs with the president for a courtesy call. However, for significant countries like India, a precedent had developed of the president scheduling a review session with the new ED to go over the country project portfolio and other policy issues. This interaction with me was fixed for some time in the last week of November 2014.

The inaugural session of the seventh edition of Vibrant Gujarat was to take place in Ahmedabad on 11 January 2015. This was the first edition of the global investor summit that Narendra Modi was scheduled to address as prime minister. The Gujarat government was keen (as was Prime Minister Modi) that World Bank President Jim Kim attend the inaugural session.

Around the middle of November, I received, in the diplomatic bag, an invitation addressed to President Jim Kim from the Gujarat chief minister. There was also a follow up from the Indian embassy and PMO to deliver the invitation personally to him and ensure his attendance.

I sought an urgent appointment to see Jim Kim personally. His office checked on the dates and a few more details but did not confirm my appointment. I found this grossly inappropriate. In my judgement, the EDs should be able to walk into the chamber of the World Bank president when they needed to. I wrote a slightly harsh mail to Yvonne Tsikata, his chief of staff. She came rushing to see me and promised a meeting with the president soon but sounded unsure about his participation in the event.

I was puzzled. Jim Kim was a big admirer of Prime Minister Modi. He had gone to listen to his speech at New York's Madison Square Garden in September 2014 and sat in the audience. He looked forward to sharing a platform with Prime Minister Modi. Why, then, was he signalling his reluctance to attend Vibrant Gujarat?

Yvonne and some others helped me get some answers.

The inaugural event of Vibrant Gujarat was scheduled for a Sunday. It appeared President Kim was always determined to be in Washington, DC, on Sundays, ostensibly to attend church. Therefore, he had developed a practice of not travelling on weekends. Further, the president reportedly was generally reluctant to travel by commercial airliners and going to Gujarat meant some changeovers as well. In short, he was reluctant because of the inconvenience of travelling in a commercial jet and on a weekend.

A few days later, I did meet Jim Kim one on one. I told him Prime Minister Modi personally wanted him there. He broke tradition and travelled to Ahmedabad. He reached late in the night of 10–11 January, attended the inaugural session for about two hours, spoke for five minutes, praised the leadership of Prime Minister Narendra Modi and returned to Washington, DC. This was the shortest-ever visit of a World Bank president to India.

Jim Kim complains about me to Arun Jaitley

The World Bank Board had developed some working rules for efficient disposal of the agenda in board meetings. EDs were expected to speak for not more than four minutes on an agenda item. If they had more to say, they had the facility to issue a statement in writing and put it on the board's exclusive electronic system before the meeting. Almost every ED either issued a statement in writing or read a prepared text in the four-minute window. The electronic clocks in the boardroom started ticking the moment someone was given the floor by the presiding officer.

I found the business of reading from the text redundant. If something was to be stated in writing, it might as well be circulated as a statement before the meeting. In my judgement, the window of speaking orally in the board was given to emphasize critical points that most find worthy of hearing. Therefore, right from the beginning, I adopted the practice of speaking extempore in board meeting within my allotted four minutes. Of course, speaking without written notes required a thorough study of the agenda papers (which were usually very well prepared but long, running into about 100 pages on an average), selection of key points and delivering the same within the four-minute window. I usually highlighted important points and completed my address in less than or on dot of clock touching end of four minutes. This practice made me stand out.

For the World Bank management, this practice presented a bit of a challenge. First, they did not know what exactly I would say and, therefore, found it difficult to prepare in advance. Second, they had a really short time to prepare a response (the practice was that the management would respond to all important points after the EDs had spoken and before the item was approved). The most important meetings, annual regional review meetings and meetings to discuss the agenda for annual and spring meetings were chaired by the president, with the rest being chaired by managing directors and sometimes even a vice-president.

By his own admission, Jim Kim wanted to do everything to please India and Prime Minister Modi. However, he had initiated a poor administrative restructuring of the organization and had become quite unpopular with the World Bank staff. He did not have a real grip on issues of development finance as well. He was always looking for ways to promote himself. His efforts to cultivate Prime Minister Modi were also essentially intended to raise his own global stature. In reality, there was nothing that could be taken as hard evidence of his favouring India.

I examined all the proposals coming before the board objectively from the point of view of India, the developing countries and the system of global development finance. Whenever I found that the proposals did not serve these three interests well, I would speak frankly and forcefully in board meetings. Sometimes, this meant taking positions that were contrary to what Jim Kim stood for or wanted approved. Initially, he acknowledged my points and tried to find some ways to accommodate them. However, an increasing number of such interactions created doubts in his mind about the reasons of my critical stands. Unknown to me, he probably concluded from my interventions that Prime Minister Modi might be unhappy with him about something.

The IMF and World Bank organized every third of their annual meetings outside Washington, DC. The 2015 annual meetings were in Lima, Peru. Normally, the Indian finance minister and the World Bank president met during every annual and spring meetings, their delegations in tow. In Lima, the president's secretariat wanted a one-on-one meeting on the sidelines with Finance Minister Arun Jaitley. This was agreed to in view of the special nature of commitments in off-Washington, DC, meetings.

After the meeting, while going down the escalator, Arun Jaitley asked me what the issue with Jim Kim was. He informed me that the World Bank president had complained about my attitude and approach in board meetings, which he found quite aggressive. Jim Kim wanted to check with him, as Jaitley told me, whether Prime Minister Modi or Arun Jaitley were upset with him for something. That said, Arun Jaitley had clearly formed his own opinion about the man and, half in jest, asked me to give him a little more respect.

India's trust deficit with Jim Kim

Jim Kim's five-year tenure as World Bank president was due to end in June 2017. The process of selecting a new president is set in motion only about two to three months in advance by the board of directors, the appointing authority of the president. Jim Kim, who was considered close to Hillary Clinton and the Democrat US government, was not sure what would happen in 2017 as the US presidential elections were due in November 2016. Thus, he wanted his election to be completed in 2016 itself.

The World Bank had reviewed and finalized new rules for selection of the president in 2012. This changed the unwritten understanding that the World Bank president would always be a US citizen. The new rules provided for an open and transparent selection process, making a qualified citizen of any member country eligible to contest for the position, and when it came to the crunch, the American candidate was expected to be backed by the majority vote. In 2012, three candidates were shortlisted and interviewed by the Board. The Barack Obama administration had decided to back Jim Kim. The American sponsorship finally tilted the balance in his favour. To choreograph his reappointment one year ahead, Jim Kim wanted public endorsement of his candidacy by India and Germany before the selection process was set in motion. He visited India in the last week of June 2016 and met Prime Minister Modi.

Being a doctor, Jim Kim had developed a theory that the best development investment was in infants under a year old as brain development for life is virtually decided during this one-year period. If not cared for at that time, he believed, children grew stunted. Despite India's extensive child nutrition and development programme, the statistics reflected poorly on malnutrition and stunting among India's children. Jim Kim worked on financing innovations for 'bringing billions of dollars' to invest in India's children. He thought he would be able to impress Prime Minister Modi with this pitch and, in return, seek his agreement to endorse his reelection as World Bank president.

Narendra Modi and the Indian establishment, however, were quite sensitive about expressions like 'stunting' and were not keen to support Jim Kim's candidacy so proactively, although they did not mind him getting a second term. Jim Kim did not find a receptive ear to his proposal. He could only get an assurance that India would support his re-election.

The World Bank Board initiated the election process in August 2016. Jim Kim emerged as the only candidate. When the board interviewed him. I asked him some tough questions. After the formal process was over, Jim Kim's re-election was announced in a board meeting. The ever-obliging dean of the board, Mirza Hasan (ED from constituency including Kuwait where he came from), proposed a glowing tribute to his leadership. The proposed statement had some factual errors as well. I wanted the statement amended, which was done. India was also a stickler to the rule book in the entire run up to the reselection. We did not issue any public statement supporting Jim Kim's candidacy until the election process was over. Such a public statement was not permissible according to the rules, though quite a few other countries violated this code of conduct.

Jim Kim's doubts about India's support for him deepened further. Once, when he mentioned to me that India did not support his re-election. I assured him that India was always supportive of his re-election, as was indicated to him by Prime Minister Modi in June 2016. We were just playing by the rule book.

India changes stance on EODB ranking

India's complex and labyrinthine processes ensured that it was placed in the bottom quadrant of countries in the World Bank's ease of doing business (EODB) rankings. Instead of fixing the processes and costs, until 2014, India used to question the ranking, its methodology and its very objectives.

On the sidelines of one of the G-20 meetings, Jim Kim suggested to Prime Minister Modi that India should work with the World Bank to bring its EODB ranking to the top 50. The prime minister liked the idea and set in motion a process fundamentally altering India's approach towards EODB.

Ease of doing business rankings are based on numerous process-oriented simplifications, not any big-ticket reforms. There were 11–12 broad heads (starting a new business, granting electricity permit, registering a document and so on). Under each of these heads, on a three-way matrix – number of processes, time taken and cost of completing the process – there are hundreds of small reforms in deeply entrenched processes and procedures. At one point of time, the Department of Industrial Policy and Promotion (DIPP), later Department of Promotion of Industry and Internal Trade (DPIIT) identified about 400 small-ticket procedural reforms that India was required to make to get close to the top 50 ranking. These procedural reforms were spread over many ministries and departments and autonomous organizations, such as municipalities, both at the centre and in the states.

Another handicap was that procedural reforms on paper did not mean much. The process of verification involved World Bank surveyors talking to users of these services and their real-life assessment of changes having come into effect. Bringing such a slow change required a monumental effort. Investments are not attracted by ease of doing business alone. They are influenced by many other factors, most significantly whether foreign investors see an opportunity to make profits, with the financial impact of lack of ease of doing business being built as part of the cost of doing business.

The World Bank provided a preview of its report to the ED's offices, which we duly forwarded to the DEA and DIPP. Countries were invited to file their objections/additional evidence if they objected to the scores assigned. A delegation from the DIPP landed up in Washington, DC, after the draft 2016 EODB report (released in 2015) was provided by the World Bank. They wanted the new orders issued by the Government of India to be reflected in EODB ranking for India. The Bank's rules allowed only changes effected before June 2015 to be taken on record, that too if the change had been experienced by users. What the delegation had brought amounted to really nothing.

After a discussion, we asked the Bank to send its survey team to India for conducting verification of the effect of changes made. It agreed. With that began the practice of the Bank sending its survey team every time the draft report was released. Ease of doing business became a primary agenda for the

Government of India as well as the ED's office. Ramesh Abhishek, secretary, DIPP, enthusiastically and painstakingly worked on this for the next couple of years. India succeeded in improving its EODB rank from 142 in 2014 to 63 in 2020.

The EODB rankings came under a cloud in 2021 and were discontinued thereafter.

Projects in disputed territories

Territorial disputes between neighbouring countries are common across the world. When member countries of the World Bank wanted to take up projects in any disputed territories held by them, it was almost always opposed by the member country that claimed the area to be its own, though it may not physically hold it. Passions ran high in both the concerned countries whenever such projects came up for a World Bank funding.

The Bank had evolved a policy and a process to deal with such projects in disputed territories, which centred on two key elements. First, the Bank sought the other member's views and concurrence, reserving the right to take such projects to the Board for approval in case of an objection by the other member, if the project served necessary development objectives. Second, the Bank invariably attached a disclaimer to the effect that its financing of the project was in no way an endorsement of the disputed territory belonging to any party to the dispute. The Bank also used a map where the disputed territory was shown in dotted lines and not as part of internationally accepted borders.

India has territorial disputes with its neighbours, Pakistan and China. Two projects in Jammu and Kashmir (J&K) and Pakistan-occupied Kashmir (PoK) came up for approval during my time at the World Bank.

The IFC proposed to invest $50 million directly in the Gulpur hydro project in PoK, which was a subsidiary of Korea South East Power Co. Ltd (KOSEP) to construct, operate and maintain. This project had earlier been proposed as part of eight power projects to be funded by the World Bank and IFC in 2013, with a good part of the funding coming from China as well. Mukesh Prasad, my predecessor, had welcomed the investment in the power-starved area. The MEA had cleared it.

When the IFC wanted to bring the Gulpur project for board consideration in 2015, it approached India's ED's office for pre-board consultation considering the usual sensitivities. When asked to provide its views by us though the DEA, the MEA conveyed its completely changed stance from 2013, reflecting the preference of the new Modi government. It wanted the ED's office to ensure that the World Bank or IFC did not fund this project. This stand was untenable both in terms of the World Bank's policy and India having previously endorsed the project. No amount of explanation seemed to convince the MEA, with the DEA virtually reduced to a messenger. I tried to explain that even if India was to go back on its earlier support and object to or vote against the proposal, IFC proposal would go through the Board. Yet, the MEA anad DEA made India's ED's office issue a statement in the board, objecting to the IFC investment. India was the sole dissenter. The investment was approved. We did not gain even brownie points.

Floods in Jhelum and its tributary Tawi in 2014 caused devastation on both sides of the line of control (LoC) in J&K. India wanted the World Bank to fund a reconstruction and recovery project in the area it governs while Pakistan wanted the same in its controlled territory. India did not want the Pakistani project to be funded as it contended that Pakistan was holding Indian territory illegally. The Bank wanted to fund both projects. The PMO had come onboard with the idea that both projects might be funded. Pakistan calls the portion of J&K it holds Azad Jammu and Kashmir (AJK). This is a term unacceptable to India, and the country would, under no circumstance, allow its use in any World Bank document. Nasir Khosa and I sat together to find a solution with the World Bank team. Finally, we decided not to use any territorial names in both projects. The entire project was named the Jhelum and Tawi Flood Recovery Project, an unusual precedent for the World Bank where the name of the country or province or state concerned was not used. This 250-million-dollar project was approved on 2 June 2015. It had a slow implementation. As I finish writing this book, the project is still active and under implementation, with the likely closing date of 31 August 2026.

I believe India's approach of not fine-tuning its stance in line with World Bank policies has harmed its own interests more than serving it. Sometime in 2010 (when Pulok Chatterjee was ED), India wanted to take up a multi-state development project, which included Arunachal Pradesh, funded by both the ADB and World Bank. China objected, citing its claims on Arunachal. As per the Bank's policy, even if China objected, the project could have been funded by the World Bank as its development objectives were well-formulated. India could have mobilized a majority vote in its favour in the World Bank. However, China put pressure on Japan and other members in the ADB, and India could have lost the vote there. Instead of postponing the project under the ADB and taking the approval of the World Bank project first, defeating China, India buckled under. The country made a statement of its own accord to the effect that India would not take up any World Bank/ADB-funded development project in Arunachal Pradesh and instead fund the same itself. India has not been able to take up any multilateral-funded project in Arunachal Pradesh for last 15 years.

Kishanganga hydroelectric power plant dispute

The Indus Waters Treaty was brokered by the World Bank in 1960. Under its provisions, India could construct run of the water (not resulting into consumption or storage of water) hydroelectric power projects on three western rivers – Indus, Jhelum and Chenab (including on their tributaries) – the waters of which were otherwise almost exclusively allocated to Pakistan, subject, of course, to the detailed provisions and conditions laid down in the treaty. India was constructing a hydroelectric power plant on the Kishanganga River, a tributary of the Jhelum, in J&K. The project involved permissible non-consumptive use of water with an inter-river basin transfer.

Pakistan did not like this as it felt that the Kishanganga power plant stored more water than was permissible under the treaty, apart from a few other reasons. It was also unhappy about another hydroelectric power plant, Ratle, being built on the Chenab in Kishtwar district of J&K.

At one stage, unlike the Ratle dispute that wasn't taken to the International Court of Justice (ICJ), Pakistan had taken the Kishanganga dispute to it, which had ruled that India had the right to construct the Kishanganga power project. The ICJ also gave certain directions regarding the water storage in the dam being constructed for temporary holding of water. India redesigned the Kishanganga project, taking into account the ICJ's rulings and observations, and began construction again sometime in 2015.

The Indus Waters Treaty had elaborate provisions to deal with issues between India and Pakistan classified into three categories – 'questions', 'differences' and 'disputes'. It had created an Indus Water Commission, comprising one commissioner each from both countries. The commission was envisaged as the principal forum to crystalize and sort out questions and differences. The treaty provided for a formal dispute resolution mechanism as well. The types of 'differences' were enumerated in great detail in an annexure to the treaty; if the commission could not resolve them, these differences were to be referred to a 'neutral expert' appointed by the two parties, failing which the World Bank would step in. For 'disputes', the treaty envisaged the creation of a court of arbitration. An elaborate process was laid down to constitute the seven-member court of arbitration, with two arbitrators appointed by each of the parties and three remaining arbitrators/umpires under a detailed procedure. These three non-partisan umpires comprised a highly qualified engineer, one person well-versed in international law and one person qualified by status and reputation to be the chairman of the court of arbitration. In the event of the three non-partisan umpires not being appointed by the process laid down, the legal expert was to be appointed by the chief justice of one of three listed supreme courts and the qualified engineer by one of three listed international institutions of repute, selected by way of lottery. The chairman of the court of arbitration was to be appointed by the president of the World Bank.

Pakistan asks for arbitration

Pakistan decided to ask for the constitution of a court of arbitration for the Kishanganga power plant. It sent a one-month notice as required by the treaty to India stating the nature of the dispute, the nature of relief sought and the names of its two arbitrators. Dissatisfied by India's response, it made a request to the World Bank to set up a court of arbitration in August 2018.

India, using the provisions relating to 'differences' to be enquired into by a 'neutral expert', gave notice to Pakistan to agree to appoint a neutral expert. When Pakistan disputed the appointment of the same, India reached out to the World Bank to appoint one in the matter.

Prima facie, the World Bank had no locus standi to decide whether the matter was a difference or dispute, but the principal issue before it – whether to appoint a neutral expert or set up a court of arbitration – hinged on its determination of its nature – a difference or a dispute?

As with any dispute involving India and Pakistan, passions started running high on both sides of the border. Dignitaries at the highest level were involved. S. Jaishankar, who was the ambassador when I joined, had moved from Washington, DC, a few months earlier to take up the post of foreign secretary. He was replaced by Arun Kumar Singh as ambassador. Taranjit Singh Sandhu, who later became India's ambassador to the US, was deputy chief of mission at the time.

MEA almost loses the plot

The Indus Waters Treaty is quite complex. While the Indus commissioners were appointed by the Ministry of Water Resources, which also managed the water-related operations of the system, the administration, political and diplomatic aspects of the treaty were handled by the MEA. While the ED, World Bank, is the principal agency for the Government of India to deal with the World Bank, the MEA preferred and decided to deal directly with the World Bank for matters related to the treaty.

Taranjit Sandhu was designated India's point person for the 2016 Kishanganga dispute. On the advice of Jaishankar, Nripendra Misra, principal secretary to the prime minister, told me to keep off the matter and attend meetings between the Taranjit Sandhu-led MEA delegation and the World Bank delegation just for the sake of form and courtesy. I knew this would not carry the MEA too far, as they did not understand the World Bank dramatis personae and work processes, I abided by the directions but decided to study the subject thoroughly and keep myself in the loop to be fully ready if and as and when the occasion arose.

Mary Leroy, the World Bank's legal counsellor, primarily handled the matter. She was of a view that it was not for the World Bank to go into the nature of the issue – whether it was a difference or a dispute, whether a neutral expert was better suited or a court of arbitration be appointed. She was successful in persuading Jim Kim that the World Bank was best advised not to get into the merits of the matter at all; it only had a procedural role to appoint a neutral expert or court of arbitration, and the choice between the two options should be determined by ascertaining which of the two requests had come earlier.

Taranjit Sandhu held two meetings with the Bank team besides running an elaborate correspondence and speaking on telephone. I was present in one of them for listening only. The Bank also organized a discussion with the Pakistani and Indian teams, which I also attended. There was a flurry of correspondence, which was duly delivered by my office to the right person in the World Bank as requested by the MEA. My office and I extended all due assistance to the MEA and ambassador's office promptly.

By the middle of November, the MEA team was getting nervous. It was not able to nudge the World Bank team in the direction it wanted, i.e., to appoint a neutral expert and began to sense that the Bank was tilting towards Pakistan.

Jaishankar asks me to step in

Around this time, Jaishankar visited Washington, DC. He invited me for a discussion. In the discussions, I told him about Mary Leroy's personality, orientation and leanings. I also told him that the formal process of setting up a court of arbitration had been set in motion by the World Bank as Mary Leroy had successfully convinced the president that the Bank's job was to only appoint and Pakistan's request for the appointment of a court of arbitration had been determined to have reached first.

Jaishankar probably knew most of it. He asked me to do something to retrieve the situation. Thereafter, he established a direct WhatsApp connection with me.

I got into the act quickly.

The World Bank, in fact, had moved far ahead in the process of appointment of the court of arbitration. The US Supreme Court had nominated an 'international law expert'. The Royal Society of Engineers in the UK had appointed a 'highly qualified engineer'. The only person left to be appointed was the eminent person who would also act as chairperson of the court of arbitration. The proposal for this appointment had reached President Jim Kim's office.

I sought a meeting with Jim Kim to discuss the matter. I was given an appointment two days later. I informed Jaishankar. He said he was sending Gopal Bagley, who was handling the matter as a joint secretary in the MEA, with a brief. I told him I would go through the brief, but it would be a meeting between me and the World Bank president.

Travelling non-stop for 20 hours, Gopal Bagley turned up the morning of my meeting with President Jim Kim. I went through the brief. There was not much that was new. Bagley wanted to control the discussions with the president within the four walls of the brief he carried and wanted to join the meeting.

I refused point blank. He did not like it, but I stayed firm. I took a copy of the brief with me and went to meet Jim Kim without Gopal Bagley.

Jim Kim steps back from the brink

As I expected, Jim Kim was on the horns of a dilemma. He did not want to annoy India and Prime Minister Modi, but the papers before him had left him with no option but to appoint chairperson of the tribunal which Pakistan wanted.

I told him that the true nature of the dispute was technical, for which only a technical expert needed to be appointed. I also pointed out that the World Bank had its own technical experts who could be appointed and that any other expert chosen by the World Bank was acceptable to India. The treaty provided that if the technical expert believed it was not a difference enumerated in the treaty annex, the court of arbitration could be appointed thereafter.

I drilled the fear of God in him that if a fair opportunity was not given to India, he would not only lose the country's confidence but probably set in motion a process that may turn out to be far more dangerous, including India walking out of the Indus Treaty.

President Jim Kim understood the gravity of the situation. He offered to temporarily stop the process of appointing a chairperson for the court of tribunal and instead to task a technical person (not a formal neutral expert in terms of treaty) instead to assess the real situation and report to him.

This was enough to help us and the Bank to step away from the brink. I accepted the offer.

I returned to my office where Gopal Bagley was anxiously waiting. I called up Jaishankar to inform him that the World Bank was not appointing a chairperson for the moment, which meant that the court of arbitration was not being constituted. I briefed him about the other decisions taken as well.

He was pleasantly surprised and asked me to send everything to him in writing for record, which I did promptly by sending an email with a copy of Shaktikant Das.

The process of appointment of court of arbitration, temporarily stopped that day, persisted for long, for India's good.

A former American ED, Ian Solomon, was appointed by the World Bank president's envoy to examine the matter. Thereafter, the matter went into a different trajectory, which suited India. Ian kept discussing the matter and visited India and Pakistan. He was more sympathetic to India's views.

Prime Minister Narendra Modi inaugurated the Kishanganga project in 2018. The same year, the World Bank informed Pakistan formally that it was not proceeding with the appointment of a court of arbitration.

Pakistan took up the matter again. A World Bank press release, issued on 17 October 2022, informed that Prof. Sen Murphy had been appointed as chairman of the court of arbitration for the Kishenganga and Ratle hydroelectric power plants. The World Bank also appointed a neutral expert, Michel Lino. This is precisely the 'solution' that the World Bank wanted to apply in 2018, and India was most opposed to it. India has boycotted this court of arbitration. In July 2023, the Murphy tribunal determined that it had competence to decide the arbitration. In May 2024, the tribunal visited Neelam-Jhelum Hydro-Electric Plant in J&K region administered by Pakistan. In July 2024, the tribunal concluded hearing for the first phase. There has been no further press release by the Court of Tribunal by the time I have finished writing this book.

Following terrorist attack on Indian tourists in Pahalgam on 22 April, India decided to hold the Indus Waters Treaty 'in abeyance with immediate effect' on 24 April 2025.

Pitching for a managing director from India

The World Bank had two managing director positions under the president when I joined. Economist Sri Mulyani Indrawati, who went on to become the finance minister of Indonesia, was MD and chief operating officer (COO). The position of the second MD and chief financial officer was occupied by a French professional, Bertrand Badré. There were two positions of the same level in the IFC and MIGA. Chinese professional Jin-Yong Cai headed the IFC and Japanese national Keiko Honda headed the MIGA. When Jin-Yong Cai left the IFC and was replaced by a French professional in November 2015, the World Bank created a third position of MD (in charge of administration and other associated functions) to accommodate China. In the World Bank's history of over 70 years, India had only one of its nationals – Gautam Kaji – serve as MD, in the mid-1990s.

When Bertrand Badré was made to leave the World Bank by Jim Kim (quite unfairly) in late 2015, I sounded the finance minister and PMO about pitching an Indian for this position. The follow-up from India was not very enthusiastic, and Joaquim Levy, former finance minister of Brazil, got the job. However, by the time the next opportunity arose, when Mulyani Indrawati left to join as finance minister of Indonesia in July 2016, the issue of appointing an Indian national had gained good traction. Both the prime minister and finance minister had flagged the idea to President Jim Kim, who had committed to give it a serious shot.

Our search for an outstanding professional – the preference was for a woman – ended in Arundhati Bhattacharya, who was serving, on an extended tenure, as chairperson of SBI. Her name was officially proposed by the Government of India, and we started lobbying for her in the World Bank. I reached out to her and helped her prepare for the job. Bhattacharya made good progress. She was one of the two final shortlisted candidates, the other being Kristalina Georgieva, a Bulgarian national with extensive experience of working in international organizations, including the World Bank at vice-president level.

Arundhati Bhattacharya was interviewed by President Jim Kim at length. Though she turned in an impressive performance, the superior credentials of Kristalina Georgieva in operational roles worked in her favour. Jim Kim spoke to me personally before he took Kristalina Georgieva's appointment to the executive board for formal confirmation. He was somewhat apologetic that he could not keep to his word. In his opinion, Bhattacharya was outstanding for the MD and CFO's job; however, for the MD and COO's job, Georgieva was heads and shoulders above. I accepted the decision and spoke in the board supporting his choice; I also reminded the president to appoint an Indian professional the next time. Arundhati Bhattacharya also took the matter in her stride.

The next opportunity came when I had moved to New Delhi as secretary, economic affairs. Joachim Levy left the Bank in 2018. With Kristalina Georgieva, appointed as chief executive officer, and President Jim Kim having committed to appoint an Indian national this time, we proposed T.V. Somanathan, later finance secretary and cabinet secretary, Government of India, who had also worked at the World Bank in the finance wing. There was, however, considerable resistance from insider professionals of World Bank who had served in positions senior to him. To keep its word, the World Bank cancelled the entire process and tasked its headhunting agency to propose a fresh shortlist. This time around, Anshula Kant, who was also working in SBI as finance director, made the cut. She is serving in the senior management of the World Bank as managing director and chief financial officer even as I give finishing touches to this book.

Bidding farewell to the World Bank

After a three-month extension, Shaktikanta Das retired on 31 May 2017 from the position of secretary, Economic Affairs. My tenure in the World Bank was until 31 October 2017. There were some indications from finance minister Arun Jaitley that I might be asked to move to the Ministry of Finance though no specific position was indicated. The charge of secretary, Economic Affairs, was given to the secretary, Ministry of Corporate Affairs. I received my orders for appointment as secretary economic affairs on 22 June 2017 while I was in a G-11 meeting. It took me some time to wind up. I left Washington, DC, on 10 July to join new assignment on 12 July 2017.

The World Bank president usually presides over the board meeting to bid farewell to a departing ED. By the time I finalized my programme to leave Washington DC, the president's availability suiting my timetable proved difficult. Chief Executive Officer Kristalina Georgieva, who had become a friend after her arrival 10 months earlier, presided over the meeting. Jim Kim bid me farewell from his room one day.

At my farewell, Kristalina Georgieva spoke eloquently about my contributions to the World Bank. I spoke extempore as usual, this time for about 15 minutes. I explained that my practice to speak extempore without notes on the subjects that came before the board or committee was in fact a tribute to the excellent work of the Bank staff and management in putting together document packages. I not only enjoyed reading and learning from them but tested my own abilities to absorb and present the gist of the concerned agenda in my four-minute interventions.

My 32-month tenure in Washington, DC, at the World Bank truly gave me a world of experience in global development finance architecture and the state of global development finance.

29

'You Are Arun Jaitley and Piyush Goyal for Me'

I returned to India and assumed the responsibility of secretary, Economic Affairs, on 12 July 2017. A secretary to the government is responsible for managing and administering the programmes, policies, legislations, rules and institutions allocated to the department. A secretary also works with the minister and the government in formulating new policies and programmes and getting them approved in accordance with procedures.

Anjali closed her chartered accountancy firm before I assumed my responsibilities. I am no Caeser, yet in our opinion, a Government of India secretary's wife should also be above suspicion.

My book, *We Also Make Policy,* published in 2023, deals with policy and other institutional matters and issues, which I was party to during my stay in the Ministry of Finance and Ministry of Power from July 2017 to October 2019. It is the administrative part which requires a steely resolve. In this book, I have described the matters which, to my mind, required initiative and a certain steeliness. Some episodes and events in this book overlap with *We Also Make Policy*. I have tried to, however, highlight the steely aspect more prominently here. Some events are exclusively covered in this book.

PM's grudging confidence

Prime Minister Narendra Modi understandably had greater faith and confidence in officers working with him in India and facing its challenges. In his very first meeting with me, he mentioned the cosy job I had in the World Bank and advised me that it was time to get into the rough and tumble of work in India.

He also did not have a very favourable view of foreign-educated and foreign-trained economists, officers and other professionals, classically captured in his taunt of 'Harvard v/s Hard Work'.

The PM also mentioned two priorities to me. First, his keenness to promote digital payments, and second, shifting to a calendar-year budget in place of the April–March format.

I initiated action on merit for both the directions. A comprehensive examination and assessment of the pros and cons shifting to a calendar year format led us to conclude that there were more cons than pros to it. I decided to seek orders not to pursue this proposal.

I made a presentation before Finance Minister Arun Jaitley first. He also did not find the rationale of changing the financial year strong enough. On his advice to take the PMO in confidence, I informed senior PMO officials about the conclusions we had reached and offered to make a presentation before the PM. The presentation was never scheduled. As there was no follow-up from the PMO thereafter, we assumed that the urgency of the matter was lost for good.

The matter died a slow death. In reply to an unstarred question asked in the Lok Sabha on 15 July 2019 on the subject, I authorized a reply that confirmed that the government had made no such decision, effectively communicating that the government did not intend to proceed further with the matter. That was the formal end of it.

The other matter – promotion of digital payments – was not majorly with the DEA. The subject was assigned to the Ministry of Electronics and Information Technology (MEITy). Reforms in the Payment and Settlement Act, 2007, including creating the institution of an independent payment regulator, was, however, within our scope of work.

We worked hard on it, developed a new Payment and Settlement Bill, 2017, which provided for modernization of India's payment landscape and system with new payment infrastructure institutions, equal treatment to fintech, and an independent payment regulator outside RBI. The bank first agreed and signed the report. Later, it developed second thoughts and wanted to dilute the report. We did not agree to RBI's changed views. It issued an unprecedented dissent note after signing the report and published it on its website. The Payment and Settlement Bill, 2017, and proposal for creation of an independent payment regulator died with that.

'You are Arun Jaitley and Piyush Goyal for me'

In March and April 2018, many ATMs ran dry, inconveniencing people. The problem was quite acute in certain states like Telangana, Andhra Pradesh, Karnataka and Madhya Pradesh, though most states felt some shortage of supply. Opposition parties, media commentators and many others blamed the government for mismanagement. The government was rightly worried.

Prime Minister Modi was also concerned. In the first week of April, the prime minister spoke to me and wanted me to make sure that people did not suffer, and normalcy was restored as soon as possible. He said to me, 'Subhashji, you are Arun Jaitley and Piyush Goyal for me at this moment. Make sure the currency situation gets resolved immediately.' It was quite reassuring to see the PM place so much confidence in me.

I explained the situation as it stood and assured him that the shortage of currency notes in ATMs in some states would be completely over in three to five weeks and that we would soon build surplus stocks to ensure India did not face a shortage again.

We took a series of steps. In a press conference, I explained the basics of currency-note printing and management. I also explained the seasonality factors, unusual demand for currency that year and some temporary distributional problems.

I informed the media about the ramping up of production of ₹500 notes from ₹500 crore a day in March to ₹2,500 crore a day and a total increase in currency supply of over ₹75,000 crore a month from then on. These statements were carried in all news channels and newspapers. I think they reassured the public considerably.

We managed to meet a record increase in currency circulation of about ₹80,000 crore in April. As anticipated, additional net demand fell to about ₹25,000 crore in May and to less than ₹15,000 crore in June 2018. In July 2018, the currency in circulation contracted by about ₹30,000 crore. The currency shortage, which some people dramatized as a crisis, had blown over by the end of April 2018.

Managed to roll-out the electoral bonds scheme

The electoral bonds announcement was made on 1 February 2017 in the budget speech, delivered by Finance Minister Arun Jaitley. The RBI Act had been amended to allow issuance of electoral bonds through the banking system. The scheme to roll it out had been under discussion for over five months when I landed in the DEA in July 2017.

The finance minister took more than half an hour to explain to me the background, rationale and broad features of the electoral bonds in the very first meeting when I called on him after taking over. Nripendra Misra indicated that this was priority number one at that time.

There was widespread opposition to the bonds – both internally in the DEA and outside the Ministry of Finance. The RBI bureaucracy had found the electoral bonds akin to bearer bonds, susceptible to use as currency and money laundering and was quite uncomfortable with it. The DEA's budget division shared this view. The Election Commission considered the scheme a non-transparent way of funding political parties and had shot off a letter to the Ministry of Law expressing concerns about the bonds, including being used by shell companies.

My long meeting with Arun Jaitley convinced me that the electoral bond scheme was not a perfect answer for India's poor state of policy and affairs for electoral funding, but it was certainly better than the existing situation, which were heavily based on cash donations and actually routed political donations through a maze of shell companies. I decided to push the scheme through.

It took me some time to bring RBI officers on board and neutralize the Election Commission's objections at the official level. With this, I got the in-principle approval of the electoral bond scheme in a meeting chaired by the prime minister. Broad features of the scheme included making political parties that had received more than 1 per cent of total votes cast in the last election, nationally or in a state, eligible to receive donations through electoral bonds. The scheme envisaged four quarterly bond sale windows with one additional window in the year of Lok Sabha elections. The bonds were to be issued as physical bonds and by the scheduled banks authorized by the government.

On the advice of Finance Minister Arun Jaitley, I met the full Election Commission and succeeded in extinguishing their active hostility. Despite Election Commissioner O.P. Rawat's objections, the commission did not raise any concerns publicly thereafter until a petition was filed in the Supreme Court by the Communist Party of India (CPI) in 2018.

Strangely, RBI Governor Urjit Patel, for reasons best known to him, decided to play spoilsport and wrote to the government at that almost last stage, questioning the issuance of bonds by anybody or a bank other than RBI. He also wanted RBI to be solely authorized to issue the bonds, that too in digital mode instead of as physical bonds. Considerable correspondence took place between RBI and the government thereafter on the issue. Finally, Urjit Patel relented and conveyed his agreement silently by recording in the RBI's committee – Committee of Central Board (CCB) – minutes: 'If the Government decides to issue electoral bonds in script through SBI, the Bank (RBI) should let it be.'

After some more wrestling with the Ministry of Law, finally, the electoral bonds became a reality. SBI sold the first tranche of electoral bonds from 1 March 2018. There were challenges in Supreme Court, however, the electoral bonds tranches kept getting issued as Supreme Court did not stay the scheme. A total of 30 tranches of electoral bonds were issued, with political parties receiving about ₹16,518 crores in political donations until the Supreme Court declared the scheme unconstitutional and stopped its issuance through its judgment in February 2024.

Not only did the Supreme Court stopped the electoral bond scheme, it also unravelled its guarantee of non-disclosure of the fact of who donated to which political party by directing SBI to furnish the details of parties that a purchased electoral bonds and the political party that encashed the same. SBI, which first denied that it had these details, sheepishly surrendered and provided all these connecting details, sourced from the records it maintained clandestinely without government authorization, using a secret alphanumeric code invisibly printed inside each electoral bond for the purpose of ensuring that the electoral bonds were not faked. As per Supreme Court directions, the Election Commission published all these details on its website. With that, all the confidential details of who donated how much to which political parties came out in the open.

The electoral bond scheme was not the most transparent and most ethically correct scheme. But it certainly was a serious effort to bring as much transparency and ethical conduct as possible in the circumstances and ensure flow of sizeable funds to political parties the use of which was completely transparent and accounted for. The electoral bond scheme had achieved another near impossible objective to routing corporate donations to all political parties with the BJP receiving only around 55 per cent of the total electoral bond funds. With the electoral bond scheme gone, the companies sharply reduced their political donations in Lok Sabha 2024 and assembly elections following thereafter.

The non-existing 'best' bested the 'doable good'.

IL&FS board thrown out

One Friday in the middle of September 2018, Hari Sankaran, the powerful MD of infrastructure conglomerate IL&FS, called and, in sum, told me that the IL&FS was facing a temporary though enormous liquidity problem. It needed the government's support to nudge LIC or SBI to lend it ₹10,000 crore for some time against its assets. He tried to convince me that the IL&FS was perfectly solvent with assets exceeding ₹1.2 lakh crore and total debt of less than ₹80,000 crore. He also said they were shortly raising equity.

I was not prepared to accept what Hari Sankaran said at face value. I called him two days later and along with the CFO of IL&FS, went over the accounts and numbers to assess the solvency and liquidity situation based on their documents and all available financial details. In the meantime, the matter had reached Nripendra Misra. He was told that IL&FS was about to collapse, and 'India's Lehman Moment' was round the corner.

The meeting with Hari Shankaran and his CFO convinced me that the liquidity hole was much bigger, many assets were phony, and the liabilities were materially understated. In the meeting in the PMO, I proposed that the government needed to throw out the IL&FS board and appoint in its place a professionals' board along the lines of what was done in the case of Satyam. While there were some discordant voices and diversionary attempts, the government decided, within the next couple of days, to supersede the IL&FS board.

With this principal decision, we moved quickly to take the next necessary steps to execute the plan. Uday Kotak was identified as the man of the moment to chair the IL&FS board. He agreed to take on the responsibility. Prime Minister Modi gave his go-ahead. The DEA provided the rationale of public interest to justify superseding of the board. The National Company Law Tribunal (NCLT) ordered the IL&FS board's immediate suspension.

The PMO appointed a committee under my chairmanship, with the secretary of the Ministry of Corporate Affairs (MCA), Injeti Srinivas; the secretary of the Department of Financial Services, Rajeev Kumar; and the PMO joint secretary, Brajendra Navneet, as members to set the policy and take major operational decisions for full resolution of IL&FS and its hundreds of subsidiaries and associate companies. Considering the sensitivity of the situation and the formal authority vested in the IL&FS board and the NCLT in the matter, the committee operated informally to deal with strategic issues.

Quite a few meetings took place over the next two months. Many policy and strategic issues were discussed and thrashed out. Infrastructure Leasing & Financial Services was put successfully on course, which would ultimately lead to the resolution of about one-half of its liabilities.

I ceased to take active interest thereafter and the MCA spearheaded the process. There were many slips, and still after seven years, IL&FS has not carried out complete resolution. Many IL&FS entities still continue to operate as its part. As per the press release put out by IL&FS, the group had resolved debt of ₹45,281 crores as of 21 March 2025 out of the total debt of ₹99,355 crores.

Six airports privatized

In 2015, after the NDA government had settled down, it wanted to promote further concessioning/privatization of airports. The Ministry of Civil Aviation (MoCA) and the AAI adopted a very timid operations and maintenance (O&M) model and got it approved in a review meeting chaired by Prime Minister Modi. This model only envisaged handing over the non-aeronautical revenues in the terminal building to the concessionaire, with the AAI remaining in charge of both the air side (all airport operations facilities like runaways, ferrying of passengers, etc.) and the city-side (development of land and buildings outside the terminal building exits). It did not attract any interest and was floundering when I joined the department.

Nripendra Misra convened many meetings to nudge the MoCA towards a more ambitious airport privatization and monetization plan. I was invited to some of these meetings in later stages. The MoCA, however, did not seem to budge. In a meeting sometime in the middle of October 2018, where Amitabh Kant, secretary, NITI Aayog; R.N. Choubey, secretary, MoCA; Guruprasad Mohapatra, AAI chairman; Sujoy Bose, CEO, National Investment and Infrastructure Fund (NIIF); and I were present, besides officials from the PMO, Nripendra Misra finally lost his patience. Cursing Choubey that no real initiative had been taken for long and despite many meetings chaired by him, which had been 'utterly useless', Misra announced that he was closing the matter of privatization of airports then and there. He said he would not ask for any progress report in the matter from then on and left the room in a huff.

This was shocking and everyone was clueless about future course of action. After a few minutes of uneasy silence in the room, to retrieve the situation, I spoke to Kant, Choubey and Mohapatra and suggested that we must work out the key features of a real PPP concession and complete the monetization deal before the general elections process, scheduled to start in March 2019.

Somehow, we got going. Possibly shaken by Nripendra Misra's outburst, Secretary Choubey also dropped his inhibitions. In the same room from which Nripendra Misra had walked out about half an hour before, we thrashed out the key features of real privatization of six airports on a PPP concession basis: 50 years of concession against 30 years in the case of Delhi International Airport Limited (DIAL) and Mumbai International Airport Limited (MIAL) carried out in 2006; complete freedom for land development on the city-side; and increasing the bidders' pool by enlarging eligibility to anyone with experience of maintaining a major real-estate infrastructure facility (hotel, mall and so on). We decided to shoot for six airports at one go and not restrict any bidder to a specific number of airports. If the bid was the highest for all six, someone could take all six airports, we agreed.

I informed Nripendra Misra about the consensus we had reached after the meeting and the ambitious process we were going to commence soon. He was sceptical but allowed me to go ahead.

Things moved pretty fast thereafter. R.N. Choubey rose to the occasion and got all the paperwork done in two weeks, using his existing consultant for the O&M project. In an unprecedented manner, the Public Private Partnership Appraisal Committee (PPPAC), which I chaired, approved all matters despite vehement opposition by my own joint secretary, DEA, who also happened to be member-secretary of the PPPAC and NITI Aayog representative. Many path-breaking decisions were taken in that meeting improving on the decisions taken in the PMO meeting, including offering a termination value based on a formula when the assets would be taken over after 50 years, making a decisive break from the past.

The MoCA and AAI completed the entire process – setting reserve prices, issuing tenders, receiving and examining them, and evaluating bids – in a record time of less than 90 days. When the financial bids were opened on 25 February, the highest bids for all the airports exceeded four to five times the reserve price decided by us. Adani's bids were the highest for all six airports. National Investment and Infrastructure Fund had also bid quite aggressively and was only marginally behind Adani in the case of three airports. The incumbent airport operator GMR's bids were low, only a little higher than reserve prices in most cases.

The MoCA and AAI put the cabinet note quickly to award the six airports to Adani on file on 28 February. We had pulled off the impossible. The out-of-box solutions – giving airports away for 50 years in one go, allowing development of all city-side land freely by the concessionaire, a simple but sound system of revenue share, expanding the pool of bidders and so on – generated a tremendous response, both in terms of competitiveness of participation (35 bids were received) and the bids offered (four–five times of the reserve price and full reimbursement of capital investment made by the AAI).

The integrity of the bidding process was unquestionable (no one has questioned that in any court until now). Yet, the government did not award it before the elections as the PMO developed some doubts about awarding all the airports to Adani companies. After the elections, in July 2019, the MoCA moved the proposal for the Cabinet to approve the award of three airports – Ahmedabad, Lucknow and Mangalore – to Adani. I was still in the DEA when the Cabinet considered and approved this proposal on 3 July. The government took much more time for the remaining three. The concession agreements for Jaipur, Guwahati and Thiruvananthapuram airports were finally signed on 19 January 2021, about two years after the finalization of the bids.

Unfortunately, thereafter, the process of airport privatization got stalled. Despite a lot of noise and statements, the government could not issue bids for the monetization of even a single airport. This is certainly disappointing, as the monetization of six airports was the only major successful monetization by the Modi government, besides being enormously financially successful.

There was a nagging doubt in the minds of many people that Adani would manage to get the terms of airport concessions modified later in such a way that the airport deal became highly profitable for him. He did try once after COVID-19 to get an additional fee levied on passengers for use of these airports. He, however, did not succeed. While Adanis have been operating these six airports for four–six years now, the financial and contractual integrity of the concession we designed have remained unaltered.

Getting NIIF off the ground

In July 2015, the government decided to set up NIIF, an alternative investment fund (AIF), as India's sovereign wealth fund (SWF) to principally provide equity support for infrastructure projects. The government committed to ₹20,000 crore (about $3 billion) initially to take a 49 per cent stake in NIIF to build a corpus of about \$6 billion. National Investment and Infrastructure Fund was set up as a Category-II AIF with a trust structure with its assets to be managed by NIIF Ltd, registered under the Companies Act.

National Investment and Infrastructure Fund was yet to get its first investor when I took over as secretary, DEA, and chairperson, NIIF. Working with CEO Sujay Bose and a team from IDBI Capital, all the requisite documentation and policies were completed. We finalized the fund structure creating three funds: a Master Fund, a Strategic Opportunities Fund and a Fund of Funds. The NIIF Trust was created as a combined entity of three separate trusts, one for each fund.

The size of the Master Fund was kept at \$2.1 billion with the government contributing about ₹7,000 crore (equivalent to \$1 billion) from the committed corpus of ₹20,000 crore. It was decided that the government would retain a 49 per cent stake in the investment manager, NIIF Ltd, and give other investors in the Master Fund the opportunity to hold a majority stake in the investment manager. We designed the basic structure that, of that 51 per cent, major foreign investors, primarily SWFs and pension funds, would hold a 49 per cent stake with the remaining 2 per cent offered to the domestic financial institutions.

I wrote to the heads of Indian financial institutions. ICICI Bank, HDFC, Kotak Mahindra Bank and Axis Bank responded enthusiastically. The 2 per cent stake was split between these four institutions. Abu Dhabi Investment Authority (ADIA) was the first foreign-domiciled SWF to commit to investing in the Master Fund. In October 2017, we made the first close of NIIF with Mubadala, another Abu Dhabi SWF, making an investment of \$300 million. With Temasek committing \$100 million, the second close of the Master Fund was completed in September 2018. With Australian Super and Ontario Teachers' Pension Fund each committing \$250 million each, the third close was completed in August 2019 (the transaction was fully structured but was formalized after I left DEA in July 2019). With this, about \$900 million of the targeted \$1.1 billion was in the kitty. Finally, with two more closes in December 2019 and December 2020, NIIF closed the Master Fund at \$2.34 billion.

We also targeted multilateral institutions like the ABS, NDB and AIIB to invest in the Strategic Opportunities Fund. The AIIB was the first to respond with a proposal to invest \$200 million. The Strategic Opportunities Fund made its first strategic acquisition in July 2019, when it bought an infrastructure debt non-banking finance company (NBFC), IDFC Infrastructure Finance Ltd, to create an infrastructure debt financing platform. After the AIIB, the ADB and NDB also made investments in the Strategic Opportunities Fund. I could facilitate NIIF's Fund of Funds's investment in a renewable energy fund, the Green Growth Fund, jointly established by NIIF and the UK Treasury. National Investment and Infrastructure Fund made its first investment in January 2018, when it partnered with DP World to create an investment platform for ports, terminals, transportation and logistics in India, named Hindustan Infralog Ltd.

Despite excellent progress, the pace of investment disappointed the PMO. Nripendra Misra raised this with me a couple of times. Once, sometime in July 2018, he told me the government was contemplating appointing Haseeb Drabu, former J&K finance minister, as chairman of NIIF. I told him that the PMO could go ahead if it thought he could push faster execution of NIIF but again explained what it required to set up an SWF like NIIF and how important it was that the team be allowed to make all investment decisions, as they had to earn enough returns to satisfy the foreign investors. National Investment and Infrastructure Fund was not a public-sector bank. The PMO did not proceed with the replacement. I continued to be chairman of NIIF until I left the DEA in July 2019.

Resolved stamp duty imbroglio

A state of anarchy prevailed in the country with respect to levying stamp duty on transfer of shares and debentures. There was a voluminous draft law under preparation for handling stamp duty rates and several other matters. Very soon after joining, I made two decisions: first, to separate the proposals relating to stamp duty on transfer of shares and debentures; and second, the DEA would do all the work to handle this part. The Department of Revenue resisted at first but finally agreed.

The subject was complex and required deep analysis and discussion. A deeper diagnosis of the problem threw up the solution. We concluded that rates of stamp duty to be applied would need to be uniform across all the states. A single instrument or document in the entire chain of transaction would have to be selected and declared as the only instrument on which duty would be payable. A single agency would need to collect the stamp duty and distribute it among the states. Therefore, it appeared logical and sensible that a single rate of duty would be applied on a single instrument and collected by a single agency.

These basic reforms in the stamp duty system for transfer of shares and debentures presented the opportunity to resolve some other issues as well. It was felt that stamp duty should be levied and collected from buyers, as it is one transaction and one document. In case of initial allotment, the duty would be paid by the issuer, not the buyer. For the options also, a single point was identified. For a fair distribution of stamp duty collections among states, duty collected by the trading institution should be distributed based on where the buyer or allottee resided. A few iterations of a fair rate of stamp duty led to a structure that was estimated to double the total collection of stamp duty.

Once we had a good solution, we went ahead and prepared the draft amendment law. The draft Indian Stamp Act (Amendment) Bill, 2017, got ready quickly. We wanted to introduce it in the winter session of Parliament in December 2017. Due to revenue Secretary Hasmukh Adhia's insistence on consulting the states, we missed the winter session. We completed consultations in time for the Budget 2018–19 session. Yet, another precautionary decision from the PMO to refer it to the cabinet secretary led to that session being missed too. We completed these discussions as well. The Ministry of Law then raised some constitutional questions, which were also answered though at the time of the interim budget 2019–20 in January 2019, the Ministry of Law still had doubts.

Sometime in January 2019, I mentioned to Piyush Goyal that amendments in stamp duty provisions were extremely necessary for the smooth functioning of the stock and debt markets. I also told him that we had done everything we could, but the Ministry of Law was holding up the matter on some minor issue of constitutionality. I proposed that we take up the stamp duty amendment bill as part of the Finance Bill along with the interim budget.

Piyush Goyal, who understands the stock markets well, agreed and promised to speak to the law minister if necessary. This gave us the authority to bring it in the Finance Bill. Conventionally, almost no legislative business is transacted through the Finance Bill when the budget is interim. However, we dug up a few precedents. Ajay Bhushan Pandey, the new revenue secretary, had no strong views on the matter and agreed. Piyush Goyal cleared it on file. The matter again landed up with the Ministry of Law.

The Ministry of Law rejected the proposal at least three times on file in three days. Every day mattered. The capital markets division and I kept up the pressure. Finally, possibly tired of endless examination and, in my judgement, internally accepting that the DEA was on stronger ground, the Ministry of Law relented and approved it on file. The Amendments to the Indian Stamp Act, 1899, became Part I of Chapter IV – Miscellaneous of the Finance Act, 2019.

The Finance Bill 2019 was passed by Parliament and received the assent of the president on 21 February 2019 and published in the official gazette on that day.

We wanted to operationalize the new system quickly by making the law and rules applicable from 1 April 2019. The general elections were declared in March 2019. Arun Jaitley had been seriously ill. The rules could not be approved in April–May while the elections were on.

Nirmala Sitharaman took over as finance minister at the end of May 2019. We submitted the rules for her approval in June. She did not think the matter was that urgent. The file remained pending in her office until I demitted office on 24 July.

The Indian Stamp (Collection of Stamp Duty through Stock Exchanges, Clearing Corporations and Depositories) Rules, 2019, were finally notified on 10 December 2019. After postponing the implementation of rules twice, on 30 June 2020, the government issued a comprehensive press note headlined: 'Implementation of Amendments in the Indian Stamp Act, 1899, and Rules made from 1 July 2020 for Rationalized Collection Mechanism of Stamp Duty across India with respect to Securities Market Instruments'.[1] Finally, the system of collection of stamp duty on capital market instruments through stock exchanges was implemented in the country. Ever since then, the system is working highly satisfactorily.

Unified regulator for international finance city

India had wanted to set up an international finance city for quite some time. The Mistry Committee appointed in 2005 had recommended setting up an international finance city in Mumbai, with an ambitious finance reform agenda, in place of an international finance centre which the government's terms of reference had asked for. No action was taken on it.

After Prime Minister Narendra Modi assumed power in 2014, the centre of gravity shifted to Gujarat. The government decided, in April 2015, to set up the international financial services centre (IFSC) at the Gujarat International Finance Tech-city (GIFT) in Gandhinagar, established earlier in 2008 when Narendra Modi was chief minister of Gujarat. Soon after, the process of transferring financial functions to IFSC started with the GIFT authorities playing the role of facilitators. It seemed necessary to establish a unified regulator for the financial services transacted in IFSC as all financial services, savings, loans, equity, bonds, insurance and so on are tightly regulated by powerful regulators like RBI, Securities and Exchange Board of India (SEBI) and IRDA.

The capital markets division in the DEA, responsible for the subject, had entrusted the task for formulating the law for establishing the unified regulator to the Indira Gandhi Institute of Development Research (IGIDR), Mumbai. GIFT city authorities were at their wits' end, struggling with the regulators so that the financial services providers could set up shop in IFSC. The IGIDR was taking its own time and it had its own woolly ideas about the unified regulator. This was the state of affairs when I entered the department.

A thorough review, in a series of meetings, with the capital markets division (Shashank Saksena first and Anand Mohan Bajaj next) suggested that there were serious pitfalls in the structure of the unified regulator proposed in the IGIDR draft. I thought of a simpler structure, which identified specific financial products, services and institutions for transfer to the IFSC, and conferred exclusive regulatory authority on the envisaged IFSC authority thereon, excluding the sector regulators like RBI, SEBI and others. I thought such a practical structure would work best and avoid frictions caused by overlapping authority. The IGIDR structure was based more on principles than any specified structure.

As the IGIDR was not quite willing to redraft the proposed unified authority bill – the International Financial Services Centres Authority Bill – in line with our requirement, I decided to dispense with their services. The DEA assumed full responsibility of the Bill. We finalized the draft and were satisfied with it. After obtaining the approval of the finance minister, we circulated it to the law ministry and other concerned ministries. The consultation process was completed quickly. The Cabinet happily approved the bill without any changes.

The International Financial Services Centres Authority (IFSCA) Bill, 2019, was introduced in Rajya Sabha by Piyush Goyal, acting finance minister, on 12 February 2019, as we did not want the bill to lapse with the Lok Sabha elections round the corner. The bill was referred to the standing committee on 22 February. Because the budget had to be passed, the bill could not be taken up in the budget session in July–August 2019. I left the finance ministry on 24 July. The standing committee report also came much after the elections.

The bill was taken up for consideration in Parliament in November 2019, almost in the same form in which we had drafted it, and was passed in December. The IFScA, 2019, was published in *The Gazette of India* on 19 December 2019. India had the unified regulator for the IFSC.

Ensuring sovereign wealth funds stay in

The FPI regulations treat investment by a foreign portfolio investor owning more than 10 per cent of the issued equity of a company as FDI. If more than one investors are part of a group, the 10 per cent limit is applied on the entire group. Sovereign wealth funds like ADIA and Mubadala, ultimately owned by the Government of Abu Dhabi or the sheikhs ruling the emirate, though operationally independent, were treated by SEBI as part of one foreign portfolio investor group. Abu Dhabi Investment Authority considered itself operationally independent from other sovereign funds of Abu Dabhi and wanted it be treated as such without being clubbed with other Abu Dhabi funds. SEBI's regulation on clubbing their investment limit with other SWFs of UAE irritated them.

The government had exempted Singapore SWFs a few years earlier from this restriction, following a bilateral treaty with Singapore. The ADIA wanted either Singapore treatment or SEBI not treating them as one group. They flagged this issue with me and in every meeting that the prime minister or finance minister chaired with UAE delegations. India's UAE ambassador was also following this up on a regular basis.

Continuous follow up with Tyagi and SEBI resulted in some movement. SEBI issued a circular, after agreement with the DEA, making certain clarifications regarding the clubbing of investment limits of foreign governments/foreign government-related entities. These clarifications treated the sovereign funds established by provincial governments distinct from the ones established by federal government and other provincial governments. This measure provided relief to Canadian and Australian funds, but not to ADIA.

SEBI refused to make any further accommodation. I had to find a different solution. Finally, I decided that a permanent solution for such situations was for the government to assume the power to declare, by way of a notification under FPI rules, specific countries whose entities would be treated as separate entities and not part of a group.

We incorporated this rule in the draft Foreign Exchange Management (Non-Debt) Rules, exercising government's powers under the Foreign Exchange Management Act (FEMA). These rules were finally notified in October 2019. The ADIA and other Abu Dhabi investment vehicles were thereafter exempted from the clubbing provision, ending their long wait.

These rules, issued for the first time by the Government of India (this was earlier handled by RBI), streamlined the entire regime of FPIs investment in shares and other non-debt instruments.

No RBI auto-debit facility for solar projects

In the middle of May 2018, a proposal landed up from the Ministry of Power and MNRE (common Minister), asking for the Finance Ministry's direction to RBI to make an auto-debit to state government's account in case its power distribution companies (DISCOMs) failed to make payment to the Solar Energy Corporation of India (SECI) for the power supplied. While the proposal had also asked for a similar arrangement for the Power Finance Corporation (PFC) and the REC, it was particularly important for the SECI, as it was developing a model to auction solar power generation capacities to enable implementation of the PM's announcement of 175 gigawatts (GW) renewable power capacity in India by 2022, including 100 GW of solar power.

The SECI model of promoting solar power generation in India is based on three key components: First, the SECI bids out solar power generation capacity (some bids included additional facilities like manufacturing of solar cells/ modules). Second, SECI enters into a power purchase agreement (PPA) with the winning bidder to buy the power generated from the awarded projects and pay for the same. Third, SECI concludes a power sale agreement (PSA) with the state DISCOMs for the quantity the state agrees to buy. While this model assures the bidders some comfort as the SECI is owned by the Government of India, the assurance is not as strong as the payment by RBI through auto-debiting a state government account in case the state DISCOMs fail to make the payments.

I was aware of the problems that such an auto-debit facility for the bonds of state power utilities and finance corporations in the late 1990s had led to. The Government of India had stopped providing auto-debit facility for securing payments of any entity other than the state government in 2002. The DEA opposed the proposal. After a good deal of wrangling, the proposal was dropped.

In the absence of the auto-debt mechanism, the MNRE and SECI had to go with a watered-down power payment security mechanism (PSM) which included the creation of a PSM fund of ₹1,500 crore and a letter of credit (LC) from DISCOMs. The Government of India did not contribute anything to the envisaged fund which remained largely on paper.

Over the years, some state DISCOMs started delaying payment of power purchased through SECI. SECI's 2023–24 Balance Sheet speaks about Rs.

62.61 crore of trade receivables due for more than six months, including Rs. 16.84 crore for more than three years.

As the implicit guarantee cover and PSM got effectively blown away and payments got delayed, the power generators started losing interest. The SECI auctions started getting very low or no bids (some offered high rates, factoring in cost of delayed payments, which found no off-taker later). Most foreign pension and other ventures funds which had provided finance for solar auctions also lost interest and began selling their investments.

SECI's solar capacity awards ran into rough weather and suffered. As per SECI website, SECI's award of solar power generation capacities (cumulative), after progressing rapidly in the three-year period of 2017–18 to 2020–21 (from 4.05 GW in 2017–18 to 32.69 GW in 2020–21), simply stagnated thereafter. In 2021–22, it merely rose to 35.68 GW. In 2022–23, not a single gigawatt was awarded. In 2023–24, it grew to 40.18 GW. In this three-year period (from 2020–21 till 2023–24), the solar power generation capacity awarded by the SECI grew only by 7.49 GW (against as much as 28.64 GW during 2017–18 till 2020–21).

Most of the capacity awarded by SECI after 2019–20 remained largely on paper. The DISCOMs refused to buy the power awarded by the SECI. As I complete this book, it is reported that as much as 10 GW of solar power awarded by the SECI has no buyer.

The SECI got into other problems as well. The manufacturing-cum-power-generation auction of 8 GW, which Adani and Azure power won, had a much higher price tag than the prevalent price. The DISCOMs refused to play ball and enter into PSAs with SECI. That is what led to Adani and Azure power, purchased by SECI, remaining unsold for long. The SECI had to climb down and revise the price discovered in its auction (though still higher than market). The SECI also had to re-engineer the contract for enabling purchase of power by Andhra Pradesh and four other states, persuaded allegedly by Adanis using corrupt practices, and for transferring the capacity surrendered by Azure power in favour of Adanis.

In 2024–25, the SECI model and India's grid power generation ambitions seemed to be failing. The whole mess, however, needed somebody's head.

The services of R.P. Gupta, an efficient and assertive Gujarat cadre retired IAS officer, were terminated abruptly on 9 May xxxx, barely a month ahead of his contract coming to an end in normal course. R.P. Gupta was at the helm of the SECI post-retirement for about two years. He did everything, even that which was not permissible under the tender conditions, to force the surrender of power by Azure Power and reallocate the same to Adanis. Under his watch, SECI did not initiate any investigation into the alleged corruption by Adanis.

That, perhaps, was not enough to save him. Utter failure of the SECI to award new solar capacities to move towards the big ambitious goal of generating 470 GW of renewable power by 2030 (the 2022 target had been missed) and ensure that awarded capacities were taken by the DISCOMs has perhaps been aided at this door.

The refusal of the Finance Ministry to provide RBI's auto debit facility has had its impact. It empowered the state power agencies not to buy the high-cost power. It, in a way, saved the states. Solar power generation has to be placed on a firm foundation instead of any artificial financial prop like auto-debits to state government accounts with RBI.

30

'Stay Away from the PM KISAN Scheme'

There were many satisfying moments for achieving something outstanding (some recounted in the previous chapter). There were also many issues where I could not get through something that I wanted to do in public interest. In some cases, however, I could prevent undesirable damage that could have been caused by moves that were not really sound or in public interest. I recount some of these matters in this chapter.

Investigating fake notes that never were

A confidential demi-official (DO) letter from Nripendra Misra landed up on my table sometime in April–May 2018. He wanted me to audit all the paper purchased and used for printing currency notes over the last 10 years. There was no explicit purpose mentioned for undertaking this massive exercise.

When I spoke to him to find out, he was not very forthcoming. It appeared that there was some suspicion in the mind of the PMO that the previous government had used the currency note printing presses to print notes over and above what were officially accounted for to use the same for political funding.

As this was an order and indeed a sensitive matter, I decided to undertake a detailed audit. In consultation with government's note printing company, the Security Printing and Minting Corporation of India Ltd (SPMCIL), I designed a broad worksheet to capture all the currency printing paper purchased over the past 10 years in square metres, all the currency notes printed during this period, the paper consumption which these printed notes accounted for by taking their dimensions into consideration and all the resultant and accounted for wastages. I gathered the international norms of wastages to benchmark wastages accounted for by note printing presses.

It was a Herculean exercise and took a couple of months. Collecting records of all notes printed over 10 years, counting the paper lengths by converting the tons into normative lengths, converting the currency notes printed into square metres, and then working out the proportion of paper used in printing the notes accounted for and the resultant wastage. The SPMCIL officers did this thankless job.

The results were worked out and tabulated. There was slightly higher wastage (though nothing alarming) than the international norms, but it was quite close to the Indian experience and the long-term trend.

I went through all these calculations and got the SPMCIL management to send the report along with all the details officially concluding that there was no unexplained wastage. I thereafter forwarded it to the PMO with my covering note that I did not find anything particularly suspicious in the printing of notes over that period of 10 years.

The PMO perhaps was still not satisfied. I received another DO confidential communication from Nripendra Misra informing that it had been decided to constitute an expert committee headed by an external professional. I found it uncalled for and decided to meet him to persuade him not to embark on that wild goose chase.

He was insistent. I said that the government might appoint an expert committee but under no circumstances would I find it acceptable that an outside professional be allowed to go into the highly sensitive and confidential currency printing presses. He agreed to this. The PMO decided to appoint Bibek Debroy as head of the committee, a decision that was taken just prior to the Lok Sabha elections of 2019.

The Debroy Committee did not start its work until the time I left the Department in July 2019. Nothing has been placed by the government in public domain about the work done and conclusions reached by the Debroy Committee.

States are not the centre's subordinates

The FCs make recommendations on standard terms specified in the Constitution – distribution of union taxes between the union and the states, principles for governing grants-in-aid of the revenue states get from the union, and measures needed to augment the states' resources for supplementing resources of panchayats and municipalities as stipulated in the Constitution. The Constitution permits the president/government to refer any other matter to FCs under the one broadly-worded and open term – 'any other matter', referred to the FC by the president in the interest of sound finance. This allows the government to propose additional terms of reference (ToRs) for the FCs.

We finalized the draft ToRs, making three departures from the past. One, that the latest census population data (Census 2011) would be used by the FC-XV. Second, to task the FC to recommend the share of taxes for union territories (UTs) with legislature. Third, to consider doing away with the system of revenue deficit grants. After the approval by the finance minister, the ToRs were sent to the PMO for further consideration along with a draft cabinet note for approval.

I was on tour of Singapore with the finance minister when Prashant Goyal, joint secretary, Budget, called, sounding exasperated. Prashant said that the file had come back from the PMO with a note proposing an almost complete recasting of the proposed ToRs and adding many new ToRs.

A closer analysis revealed three types of suggestions. There were some suggestions that emanated from the impression that GST was a losing proposition for the central government (states were assured of a 14 per cent annual increase, with the centre expected to bear all risks of future rate reductions or bad economic performance). Another set of suggestions emanated from the desire to integrate the states' expenditures with national objectives and priorities. Finally, with the underlying assumption that the states were spendthrift, there were suggestions to control their borrowings and expenditures.

While it was apparent that the changes were perhaps suggested with honest intention to improve fiscal management, the basic thrust of the communication went far beyond the fundamental architecture of India's fiscal federal system and the constitutional provisions. The FC was the instrument to transfer a share of central taxes to states without any conditions attached to the transfers, whereas the additions virtually treated states as subordinate entities that needed to be disciplined and integrated into national development decision making.

We prepared a detailed point-by-point commentary on all the suggestions received from the PMO, stating what they meant, their nature in terms of the FC's constitutional mandate and work and how best to build them into the draft ToRs we had prepared, for those suggestions that we found worth incorporating.

A round of discussions took place with Dr P.K. Mishra, additional principal secretary to the prime minister, with the PMO joint secretary, Brajendra Navneet joining in. For many suggestions tasking states to do this or that, I finally proposed a single integrated solution. Taking a cue from the fiscal reform and debt consolidation and relief facilities, which were designed to incentivize states based on predetermined measurable performance indicators, when I worked as joint secretary, Expenditure, I suggested that the government create a ToR that provided incentives to the states for 'good behaviour'. This idea appeared to strike the right balance between an expectation of good behaviour from the states without impinging on their freedom to incur expenditures on the heads and priorities they wanted. Good behaviour, for those states that choose to willingly participate in this endeavour, I proposed, would be rewarded with additional grants from the centre as per the scheme recommended by the FC-XV, which was expected to be an honest arbiter between the centre and states.

All such expectations – efforts made by states to expand the tax net under GST, eliminating losses in the power sector, adoption of DBT system for fiscal transfers, progress in adoption of EODB and progress made in sanitation, among others – were identified as areas for the FC-XV to 'consider proposing measurable performance-based incentives for states, at appropriate level of government' as a term of reference (ToR) given to the FC.[2]

The most elusive suggestion – about controlling the states' populist expenditure, particularly what is unleashed before elections – was also bundled with this performance-based reward ToR. I proposed inclusion of a sub-ToR to reward the states that could control populist expenditure. This device also passed muster.

The ToRs of the FC-XV were unusual but fair. We were able to ensure that there was no ostensible bias against the states or any attempt to treat them as subordinate entities. The Cabinet approved the ToRs. After the president's approval, the ToRs, along with the constitution of the FC-XV, were released on 2 December 2017.

Later, the PMO forced issue of another additional ToR with an intention to nudge the FC-XV to recommend creation of a 'non-lapsable fund' for defence expenditure. I could only manage to use a language for the ToR, which did not mandate XV to necessarily do it. The FC was asked to 'examine whether a separate mechanism for funding of defence and internal security ought to be set up and if so, how such a mechanism could be operationalized'.

With these ToRs, even the ever-obliging FC-XV chairperson N.K. Singh could not make any recommendations which were heavily tilted towards the central government.

FRDI bill was withdrawn

The global financial crisis in 2008 had led global policy makers and the financial community to find solutions for major problems – 'too big to fail' banks, uncertainties in the shadow or non-banking sector, risks to deposits of savers in financial institutions, and so on. There was also a general consensus that central banks like RBI, which were primarily the regulators of the banking system besides being the monetary authority, were not the best institutions to deal with the incipient sickness and collapse of banks and other financial institutions. It was considered appropriate to create new resolution institutions in the financial sector as the normal bankruptcy institutions for non-financial sector companies also did not serve the purpose.

India conceived and drafted the Financial Resolution and Deposit Insurance Bill, 2017 (FRDI Bill, 2017), proposing a financial resolution corporation to deal with bankruptcy in financial sector including banks, non-banks, insurance companies and so on; categorization of systematically important financial institutions (SIFIs); and repeal of deposit insurance and credit guarantee corporation to be merged with the Resolution Corporation.

The FRDI Bill, 2017, was drafted in the DEA during the time Shaktikanta Das was secretary, economic affairs. It was almost ready when I joined in July 2017. Only some final touches remained. After understanding the purpose and the instrumentality of the bill, I got it wrapped up and took the necessary approvals. The Cabinet approved and the FRDI Bill, 2017, was introduced in the Lok Sabha on 10 August 2017. It was referred to a joint committee of Parliament for examination and a report. Bhupendra Yadav, MP, headed the joint committee. Several meetings of the joint committee took place. There were some reservations from the Reserve Bank, but the joint committee was progressing towards finalization of its report.

Unfortunately, a large outcry emanated from certain interests relating to the 'bail-in' provisions of the FRDI Bill, intended to play on the fears of bank depositors and trying to create panic amongst them. These interests argued that their deposits would be taken away by the government, like their cash was taken away by demonetization.

This was obviously wrong and hugely exaggerated. The bill provided, in certain limited circumstances, for deposits to be used for resolution/restructuring of the liabilities of a weak financial institution. While there was no likelihood at all of the public-sector banks – and even major private-sector banks – ever using this provision, the campaign launched by these interests could create a sentiment that this provision was like a 'demonetization of deposits' and that the deposits in banks would no longer remain safe.

The PMO suddenly developed cold feet. I, along with officers in the DEA, tried to explain why it was advisable in certain situations – for example, where the deposits had been mobilized at much higher interest than the market rate, with depositors taking undue risk – to make them also suffer. Discussions went on for some weeks. Yet, the PMO, most particularly Nripendra Misra, could not overcome their fears.

The FRDI Bill, 2017, was finally withdrawn in August 2018.

India has still not developed a strong resolution regime for the financial sector. In a crisis in the non-banking sector, for example, IL&FS, the government decided to replace the board. Reserve Bank of India was later conferred the authority to act as the resolution authority for the NBFCs. There were rumours in 2020 that the government was contemplating bringing the FRDI Bill again. The government issued a press note officially in July 2020 denying that it had taken any decision to reintroduce the FRDI Bill.

K. Subramanian selected as CEA despite not being number 1

The selection committee headed by Bimal Jalan, former governor of RBI, C. Chandarmouli, then secretary, DOP, and me, secretary, DEA, interviewed Krishnamoorthy Subramaniam for CEA's job in 2018. The Committee did not find him adequately qualified for the job. No other candidate from those who applied, including Poonam Gupta, who has recently been appointed deputy governor of the RBI, were meeting the requirement.

In the given circumstances, the Committee suggested expanding the zone of consideration by the government reaching out and inviting other reputed economists and finance sector experts. Of the five economists and experts invited, one expressed unwillingness to take up the job. Anant Nageswaran, who is currently the CEA as I complete the book in July 2025, was found to be the most suitable.

The Committee placed Nageswaran at number one and included Subramaniam (from the original applicants) at number two, more for the form's sake.

Nageswaran, at that time, was a citizen of Singapore, but was working as dean of IFMR school in Chennai. We scrutinized the rules which permitted a foreign national to be appointed as CEA. As Nageswaran was a person of Indian origin and had almost always worked almost on India, the DEA processed his case for appointment as CEA. We were quite convinced that Nageswaran would be appointed CEA by the appointment committee of cabinet (ACC).

To our complete surprise, K. Subramaniam's orders were received for being appointed as CEA. Obviously, K. Subramaniam had worked through the system, convincing the PMO that he was the right choice. In the Cabinet Meeting held on 1 February in the Parliament House for approving the interim budget, Prime Minister Modi personally introduced K. Subramaniam to the Cabinet.

For six months, the time I spent with him as CEA, I found him highly ambitious and opportunistic (always working to push him in the eyes and ears of the powers that be) but quite superficial in macro-economic matters, besides being impulsive. I did not allow his half-baked ideas much space in economic policy making during that period. We drifted apart. By the time the regular budget was presented in July 2019, he had become quite antagonistic. It did not matter to me though.

I stopped interacting with him once I moved first to the power ministry, and later, out of the government, by taking voluntary retirement. However, our paths did cross occasionally in some media interactions. He apparently did not do a great job as CEA. For some reasons which I am not aware of, his term as CEA was not extended in 2021, though it has been a norm for almost all CEAs who preceded and succeeded him. From his public appearances at that time, however, it was clear that there must have been some disenchantment with him. Nageswaran was appointed CEA in his place, three years after our recommendation.

In a year's time, however, Subramaniam managed to repair his relationship with the government and bounced back as India's ED in the IMF. He spent about two and half years at IMF. During this period, Subramaniam appeared in countless interactions on business channels and other media, speaking on economic, financial and budgetary issues relating to the Government of India. He was always highlighting how great the Modi government was, and the great future the Modi government was building for India. His book, *India @100: Envisioning Tomorrow's Economic Powerhouse*, is also a paean of how great the Modi government's policies are, built around four pillars, and how India is racing ahead to be a $55 trillion economy by 2047. I have not seen any ED in IMF or World Bank spending so much time in India on India.

In an unprecedented move, the Government of India, on 30 April 2025, 'terminated' services of ED K. Subramaniam in IMF 'with immediate effect'. He was not given any time to wind up his establishment in IMF. To the best of my knowledge, this kind of termination has never happened in India's 80 years history of appointing EDs in the World Bank and IMF. Why did the Government of India have to act in such a hurry? Why did the Government terminate his services, amounting to a dismissal?

The Government of India did not mention any specific reason in the termination order. The extraordinariness of its nature and the unambiguous message the government was sending was in its wording. Services 'terminated' with 'immediate effect' said it all.

The most proximate reason seems to be an unprecedented purchase order for his book, placed by the Union Bank of India in December 2024. The Bank purchased 2 lakh copies of his book, paying an advance of ₹7.5 crore to the publisher Rupa Publications.[3] No such order has perhaps been placed in India's publishing history. This had become a scandal, though nothing came in public domain despite the general manager who ordered the mass-purchase of Subramaniam's books being placed under suspension in December/January.

There seems to be something beyond the book scandal. It seems that the Union Bank of India's book purchase matter reached IMF's Ethics Committee, which examines the case of misconduct on the part of EDs. There could have also been use/misuse of IMF's funds in paying for his visits to India for the promotion of his book. In addition, there was reportedly a case of the use/misuse of IMF's confidential data in an unauthorized manner to promote India Viksit Bharat story and/or his book.

The sense of the Committee not selecting him as CEA was right. Its disregard led to such a big embarrassment for India.

Sidelined on PM KISAN

The farmers' situation was worsening. In 2018–19, food inflation turned out to be only 0.7 per cent as against general inflation of 3.4 per cent. Lower food inflation translated into lower price realization for farmers. Instead of moving towards doubling, their income was declining. Farmers were in distress. Some states like Telangana and Odisha had implemented schemes to provide additional cash benefits to farmers. The Department of Agriculture started developing an income support scheme sometime in December, which was going to have a big impact on government finances. I had earlier proposed the replacement of the subsidized fertilizer scheme with an income transfer scheme, which Nripendra Misra found politically disastrous. Perhaps knowing my mind in matter, I was not involved by the PMO in the scheme formulated by the Department of Agriculture.

Agriculture receives vast amounts of subsidy – fertilizer, seeds, electricity, water and so on – and still most farmers remain poor. Some more cash support was not going to make a fundamental difference to their economic status. I, therefore, worked on an alternative income support scheme.

Computations revealed that governments were spending over ₹3 lakh crore on farm subsidies and support. For the net cropped area of 140 million hectares in India, this worked out to a little over ₹20,000 per hectare. There was so much expenditure, though most farmers in the country did not earn ₹20,000 profit from a hectare of agricultural land. I, therefore, felt the government could provide ₹20,000 per hectare to every farmer and discontinue fertilizer and other input subsidies.

I reached out to the finance minister and made a presentation before him, proposing a basic reform: replace all input subsidies and eliminate the MSP system to bring in a blockbuster income support scheme for farmers. I argued that besides improving the financial lot of farmers, this would also engender freedom from agriculture and enable farmers to move into higher, value-added skills. Arun Jaitley found my proposals worthy of consideration. Aware of the political economy and delicateness of the time (the general elections were only a few months away), he asked me to make my presentation before Nripendra Misra and, if he agreed, before the prime minister.

Nripendra Misra looked at the presentation and asked me to stay away completely from any discussion on the farmers' income support scheme. He said I would be given the paragraphs on the scheme to include in the budget speech, which I was expected to incorporate without any modifications.

True to what he said, the interim budget presented by Piyush Goyal on 1 February 2019 not only announced the farmers' income support scheme but made it applicable for the outgoing financial year 2018–19 to make it possible to deliver one instalment before the close of the financial year and more importantly before the model code of conduct came into force in early March 2019. The government took upon itself additional financial expenditure exceeding ₹60,000 crore a year.

The scheme, thought to be a short-term measure, has become a permanent feature, making the central government spend ₹60,000–65,000 crore a year on 10–11 crore farmers a year at the rate of ₹6,000 per farm family. Many states also top up this. PM KISAN exceeds total other budget of the Department of Agriculture and Farmers Welfare. Recently, demands have been raised to increase the amount of ₹6,000 per farm family. It may not be long before the government concedes to this.

'Let us not waste money on BSNL and MTNL'

The secretary, DEA, is a member of the Telecom Commission (later renamed Digital Communications Commission or DCC). Sometime in December–January 2018–19, the Department of Telecommunications (DoT), which services the DCC, brought a proposal of a revival package for BSNL (including MTNL) for DCC to consider and recommend to the government. I questioned the proposal and essentially killed it by unambiguously noting that there was no rationale for the government to spend money on and even to revive BSNL. The DoT Secretary Aruna Sundararajan tried to plead their case. Other members were sympathetic to BSNL but did not strongly support it. At the end, it was officially noted in the minutes that BSNL would have to rework their proposals.

A few days later, Aruna Sundararajan told me that the BSNL revival proposal was discussed in the PMO, and she had been asked to move a cabinet note on the matter. She wanted the proposal to be approved by DCC first. I reiterated that there was no rationale in the proposal, and if she brought it up before DCC, I would reiterate my position. She dropped the idea of taking the proposal to DCC and instead circulated the draft cabinet note for the proposal to be taken directly to the Cabinet.

In a discussion with Nripendra Misra at that time, I brought up the subject of the revival package for BSNL and MTNL. I said it amounted to throwing a lot of good money after bad. It made no sense for BSNL to establish 4G networks after other companies had already covered the entire country with it. I further said that BSNL was fast losing consumers, and it was unlikely that any consumers would shift to it from other operators. It would also be grossly unfair and a market distorting if BSNL and MTNL were given 4G licence and spectrum for free when others had paid hefty amounts for them.

For some reason, Nripendra Misra was completely convinced that there were strategic reasons (not explained to me) for BSNL and MTNL to continue to exist. We clearly had strong differences on the matter. He did not agree with my position at all and did not care if government funds were invested for that losing cause. Then, I said I should have at least the freedom to record my views on file. He said I was free to do so. He further asserted: whether I liked it or not, the government would approve the revival package for BSNL and MTNL.

When the draft cabinet note was received, I recorded a comprehensive note highlighting the sheer waste of fiscal resources the proposal would lead to. I also noted that BSNL and MTNL had not been successful in acquiring technologies and equipment in the past, and they probably would not be able to do so this time round too, and so there might not even be any operational revival. I recommended that the proposal not be approved by the Cabinet. The finance minister Arun Jaitley approved my note. This possibly led to the proposal not being discussed by the Cabinet before the general elections. After the elections, the matter was again received in the DEA for views and approval of the new finance minister, Nirmala Sitharaman. She also approved the DEA's comments. The proposal was not approved until I was in the Ministry of Finance.

Eventually, a first revival package of ₹69,000 crore was approved in October 2019. Another revival package of ₹1.7 lakh crore was approved in 2022. A third revival package of ₹89,048 crore was approved on 9 June 2023. Despite three packages totalling over ₹3.3 lakh crore, BSNL (MTNL was operationally merged into BSNL) continued to lose market share and incur large annual losses. Their 4G network has still not become a country wide reality. In December 2024, share of BSNL in wireless/mobile subscribers fell below 8 per cent (7.99 per cent). MTNL had become a defunct player with a share of 0.09 per cent. BSNL reported losses of ₹8,166 crore for the year 2023–24. BSNL and MTNL are being kept alive nominally, wasting lakhs of crores of precious fiscal resources. What a waste!

Foreign currency sovereign bonds failed to take off

In 2018, India was facing rough weather on the foreign exchange front consequent to oil prices rising from early 2018. Foreign portfolio investments withdrew over $15 billion in 2018–19. The rupee was under pressure, depreciating to below 74 a dollar. India's foreign exchange reserves declined to less than $400 billion in October 2018.

Piyush Goyal, who was the acting finance minister at that time, started building pressure to bring in an NRI deposit scheme on the lines of what India had done in 2013. I was opposed to the proposal of issuing such NRI bonds because such bonds and deposits cost India about 1.5–2 per cent in extra interest. The 2018 crisis passed. Neither the NRI deposit scheme was approved nor the sovereign bonds. We did negotiate a $75 billion dollar/rupee swap deal with Japan.

We started preparing to take up the sovereign bond issuance programme in foreign currency nonetheless and list these bonds abroad someday. I had also thought of making this a part of the reforms programme post the 2019 elections. We engaged an international investment bank (without paying them any fee and, also making no commitment to use their services in case the bonds are issued) to advise us on the sovereign credit rating and get information on the international sovereign bond markets. The subject of sovereign bonds was formally taken up in a March 2019 meeting with RBI to finalize the borrowing calendar for the first half of 2019–20. Considering the post-2019 election scenario and my not-so-conducive equation with Nirmala Sitharaman, I had put the programme on the backburner for Budget 2019–20 and did not include it in the first draft budget speech of finance minister.

CEA Subramaniam, in one of the budget strategy meetings with Finance Minister Nirmala Sitharaman, surprisingly and suddenly proposed that India should raise sovereign bonds in external markets to boost investments in Indian economy and advanced good arguments. After Subramaniam finished his pitch, I enumerated the benefits of such a move but also apprised the finance minister about the less-than-enthusiastic support from RBI and active opposition by certain sections of the RSS and BJP. I also underlined the need for her to take it up politically within and outside the BJP to enable the proposal to sail through. While Nirmala Sitharaman viewed me with a little lack of trust, she found Krishnamurthy Subramaniam completely reliable. She lapped up the idea and said that issuing sovereign bonds would be a good move. She assured us that she would deal with the political implications.

I drafted a paragraph and included it in the next draft of the budget speech. The proposed paragraph was read aloud in two meetings with the PM. Piyush Goyal was present in one of these meetings. The final draft of the budget speech was also scrutinized thoroughly in the PMO and by the finance minister. The sovereign bond's part survived all this scrutiny. Finally, Nirmala Sitharaman made the announcement in her budget speech in Parliament on 5 July 2019, at paragraph 103.

This announcement attracted a lot of attention in the media. The market welcomed it. Yields on government bonds went down by about 12 basis points that day. This was one of the major questions directed to me in the post-budget media interactions. I provided more clarity and defended the move. Two groups of people – former RBI top brass, including Raghuram Rajan and Rakesh Mohan, and affiliates of the RSS, including the Swadeshi Jagran Manch – questioned the move. In the days to follow, the debate intensified as opposition from these quarters kept increasing.

I left the Ministry of Finance on 25 July 2019. A part of the media attributed my transfer to the proposal of issuing sovereign bonds. That was not correct. I believed in the merits of the proposal, but I was not its real author in Budget 2019–20.

Finance Minister defended the proposal in one of media interactions. There was no official roll back. However, the proposal was not followed through. The government did not make any issue of sovereign foreign currency bonds in the financial year 2019–20. Neither has it been done so far. Instead, the government continued with the policy of permitting foreigners to make investment in rupee securities of the Government of India. To make such rupee investments easier, the government and RBI came up with a fully accessible route (FAR) mechanism removing some restrictions on foreigners' purchase of the rupee securities. Later, Indian sovereign rupee bonds were included in two global bond indices – JP Morgan's Emerging Market Bond Index (EMBI) and FTSE Emerging Markets Government Bond Index (EMGBI). Inclusion in these indices were expected to result in significant inflow in India's government bonds. This, however, did not turn out to be the case.

31

'Has the Government Approved Your Dissent Note?'

In this chapter, let me take a tour of the contentious matters with other ministries/departments and the institutions like RBI and SEBI I worked with during this period. I did take a principled stand, succeeding sometimes; not succeeding in others. Finance Minister Nirmala Sitharaman's attitude in case of economic capital framework issue with RBI significantly contributed to my decision to seek voluntary retirement as well, as I felt that working in such circumstances was not quite conducive and productive.

'Royalty terrorism' stopped in its tracks

In November–December 2018, the DIPP circulated a draft cabinet note, proposing a cap on royalty payments to foreign technology and other intellectual property service providers. The DIPP was concerned with rising royalty payments, especially in the IT sector, where some firms were paying as much as 80–90 per cent of revenues as royalty payments. Its proposal was to go back to the pre-2009 regime and place royalty limits of 4 per cent on technology transfers and 2 per cent on the use of intellectual property (without technology transfer).

It was a horrifying proposal, as it would undo reforms carried out over the last 25 years and revert to the licence-control mindset. It amounted to substituting the government's judgement for the commercial judgement of the two parties involved: the technology supplier and the technology recipient. There were many other problems: forcing companies to come to the government whenever they wanted to pay higher royalty, getting into the quagmire of what constituted total sales and what constituted royalty payments, and so on. We opposed the proposal strongly, dubbing it 'royalty terrorism'. Finance Minister Arun Jaitley endorsed this view.

The DIPP's proposals and views on the royalty issue were shared by the PMO. After it received the DEA's comments, the PMO convened a meeting chaired by Nripendra Misra. All departments of the Ministry of Finance, as well as Chief Economic Advisor Arvind Subramanian, were present. Ramesh Abhishek, secretary, DIPP, argued his case passionately. Arvind and I stood our ground and argued that there was no justification to bring back the old subjective and restrictive regime and micromanage businesses.

Heated discussions ensued. Ramesh Abhishek accused the DEA of talking in contradictory terms – while the DEA opposed the DIPP proposal strongly, calling it royalty terrorism, at the same time, SEBI, under the DEA, was formulating regulations to put a cap on royalty payments without shareholders' specific approval.

I was not fully aware of this SEBI move. Some quick SMSing to SEBI Chairperson Ajay Tyagi and a Google search helped me gather facts. I explained the difference – while the DIPP had proposed a ban on royalty payment, SEBI's proposal was only intended to improve corporate governance by making the company management seek approval of shareholders in case of royalty payments over a specified limit.

The wider sense of the meeting was quite clear – don't go back and don't adopt restrictive and prescriptive policies.

The DIPP proposal was shelved after this meeting.

SEBI's move to make it necessary to seek a majority of minority approval (approval by a majority of non-promoter shareholders), in case the company intended to pay more than 2 per cent of sales as royalty, was also revised, and a 5 per cent limit, as recommended by the Kotak Committee on corporate governance, was finally implemented.

No company opposed this dispensation, and the system is working well as hardly any company pays more than 5 per cent royalty. One or two who does have taken shareholders' approval.

Data-localization measures continued

Through a notification issued in April 2018, RBI ordered all payment-related data to be stored only in India. The MEITy formulated a Personal Data

Protection Bill, based on a draft proposed in July 2018 by the Justice Srikrishna Committee, which also provided for localization of certain types of sensitive and critical data.

India's IT law did not mandate local storage of any data, including financial and payment data. Therefore, RBI had no jurisdiction to regulate data storage. However, RBI, using some not-so-clear authority under the Payment and Settlement Act, ordered all payment system providers to ensure that the entire data relating to the payment systems that they operated were stored in a system only in India.

This unilateral and not-so-legally strong measure created a huge ruckus. Foreign payment and financial systems operators got together under the aegis of the US India Business Council (USIBC) and US India Strategic Partnership Forum (USISPF) and started making representations to everyone, including to RBI and the DEA. After studying their representations and hearing them out, I found some force in their arguments. I also felt that instead of enhancing the security of transactions (which requires card companies to have access to all worldwide transaction data), the RBI move would possibly compromise it (as card companies would not be able to use Indian data on their global servers).

I convened a meeting of the concerned, including the MEITy and RBI. The RBI ED tried, unconvincingly, to defend their decision. After a long meeting, I tried to thrash out a compromise – while all the payment data would be stored in India as RBI wanted, a mirror copy of the data could be kept in foreign data storages (as that would allow foreign companies to use this data for security purposes). Reserve Bank of India refused to budge, however. I raised the issue at the finance minister's level as well as the PMO. The PMO and Department of Financial Services (DFS) were more sympathetic to RBI's 'nationalist' (Indians only to use Indian data) move. The RBI policy stayed.

We had many serious issues with the Personal Data Protection Bill as well. In our view, it was concerned only with the privacy aspect of data and ignored the bill's business and financial implications. The categorization of almost all financial data as critical data, which required an informed consent of the data principal every time it was to be used and imposed enormous obligations on the data fiduciaries, appeared also to be leading to a situation where the data, on which the digital economy runs, were virtually getting locked up. There were many provisions relating to data localization as well.

I convened a meeting with the secretary and other officers of the MEITy, who appeared to be working with good conscience and intent. However, they seemed to be missing the likely impact of the bill on the economy, business and social lives of people. We provided comprehensive and critical comments, asking for a balance between business and financial transactions and privacy concerns. There were serious concerns raised by the industry and financial systems as well. There were discussions in the PMO and elsewhere. The PMO also realized that the bill possibly reflected major overreach. It was not approved by the Cabinet before the budget session in February–March 2019, nor until I left the Ministry of Finance in July 2019.

The bill was finally introduced in the Lok Sabha in December 2019 and was referred to the Joint Committee of Parliament. The committee submitted its report in 2021, making the bill worse by expanding proposed protections to non-personal data as well. The government did not find the Committee's draft workable. It was finally withdrawn that year. Later, Parliament passed Digital Personal Data Protection Act (DPDA) 2023, a much more balanced and simpler law. This Act, however, is still to be enforced as I complete the book.

AGR on transfer of telecom spectrum

In 2015, the government had permitted trading of access spectrum by telecom service providers (holders of spectrum were allowed to sell the unused spectrum to other telecom operators). Detailed guidelines provide that the arrears of unpaid spectrum charges would have to be paid before spectrum trading was allowed by the government. In addition, a 1 per cent transfer fee and future spectrum charges would have to be paid by the operator acquiring the transferred or traded spectrum.

The operator transferring the spectrum was to receive a one-time payment as consideration for transferring his rights. There was apparently no specific provision in the trading guidelines about the adjusted gross revenue (AGR) – the revenue share payable to the government out of the revenue generated by the operator's use of the spectrum – payable on the sale value of the traded spectrum. One day, a file of the telecom department landed up on my desk in the DEA.

A quick perusal suggested that a wing of the telecom department was of the view that the sale proceeds received by the seller of the spectrum was also 'revenue' for the purpose of the AGR and the seller (or, on their behalf, the buyer) of the spectrum was required to pay 8 per cent AGR charges thereon. The other wing of the department held a contrary opinion and treated the spectrum sale proceeds as capital receipt and not a revenue receipt and therefore was of the view that no AGR was leviable on it. The telecom department had sent the matter to the law department, which, possibly playing safe in view of the past controversies including 2G case, had concurred with the view that AGR was payable on these receipts.

Aruna Sundararajan, secretary, DoT, perhaps considered 8 per cent AGR on capital receipts during trading of the spectrum as inappropriate but was not prepared to overrule it, especially after the law department had endorsed it. She, therefore, conveniently marked the file to the DEA for its advice and view. Strictly speaking, the DEA had no say in the matter. However, as the issue had stalled restructuring in the telecom industry, where numerous spectrum holders were sitting on unutilized spectrum assets while others were short of the spectrum, I decided to examine the issue and offer the DEA's advice if it helped move matters faster.

Unfortunately, I had my back to the wall in the DEA as well. The joint secretary, Infrastructure, otherwise a gutsy officer, came to me and spoke about the unfairness of the proposal to recover 8 per cent AGR on transferred price of traded spectrum. On file, however, he supported the opinion of the law department. Thinking that the joint secretary, Budget, might be more even-handed, I marked the file for his view. On file, he also ended up agreeing with the joint secretary, Infrastructure.

I had so many incorrect but contrary opinions to wade through. Nonetheless, I recorded a note bringing out the facts of the case and the utter lack of justification for recovering AGR payable only on revenue receipts from the capital receipts on sale of spectrum, which were not revenue by any definition. I also brought out the likelihood of the seller suffering large capital loss on the spectrum even without being burdened with AGR levy. I made a very specific proposal at the end of the note proposing to provide the DEA's clear advice that the AGR levy was not payable on capital receipts on sale of spectrum.

I had hoped that Finance Minister Arun Jaitley's brilliant legal mind would approve the clear advice I had recorded. The file came back with him agreeing with the opinion of joint secretary, Infrastructure. The finance minister, I am sure, knew the implications for the telecom industry, which was passing through its worst period in 2018–19. Yet he chose to play it completely safe.

Penalty against Airtel and Vodafone

In June 2019, in a meeting of DCC, the telecom department brought up a proposal to impose a penalty of ₹3,050 crore on two telecom operators – Airtel and Vodafone – for not providing a point of interconnection to Reliance Jio.

It was a curious case. It was alleged that these two operators had not provided good quality interconnection to Reliance Jio when it had launched its maiden services in 2015. The two operators had disputed this and had argued that the kind of interconnection service Jio wanted was to be provided only to a new operator so that it could be enabled to make a pilot launch of its services. In their view, Reliance Jio was launching services of a fully grown competitor and, therefore, they could not be penalized for not providing the interconnections asked for. The penalties were proposed under some regulations regarding the failure of an operator to maintain the specified quality of service.

The matter was referred to the Telecom Regulatory Authority of India (TRAI) in 2016. The quality of service in question was that of Reliance Jio. The rules envisaged penalizing the operator whose services were not up to the quality standards. Instead of penalizing Reliance Jio, the TRAI held the other two operators responsible as they had failed to provide adequate and good quality interconnection facilities resulting into poor services. TRAI recommended a penalty of ₹3,050 crore on the two operators, Airtel and Vodafone.

Closer examination of the matter in the Telecom Commission meeting revealed its bizarre nature. It seemed that the telecom secretary was under pressure to get it approved in the meeting and she had probably spoken to the CEO, NITI Aayog and the IT secretary beforehand. In the discussion that followed, the member, Services, from the telecom department shed his inhibition and expressed his views about the unjustness of the proposal. I had not fully gone through the matter. In that meeting, we agreed to an in-principle decision to impose penalty for poor service but asked the matter be referred again to the TRAI for revising the quantum of penalty.

The Telecom Commission had another meeting on 24 July 2019, which incidentally turned out to be my last working day in the Ministry of Finance. Transfer orders came in late evening. During the day, I attended the Telecom Commission meeting where the ₹3,050 crore penalty came up again. The TRAI had quickly returned the matter and reiterated its view. That day, we had a more detailed discussion. I had also studied it. I made my position clear that the penalty was not at all justified and that this was being placed on the wrong parties. The position of the members remained pretty much the same. I insisted that the views of both the member, Services, and mine be recorded in the discussion part and the decision be recorded as passed by five votes to two. The minutes did not come to me as I demitted my charge the next day.

The Economic Times carried the news about deliberations in the Telecom Commission about the issue and also stated that this particular item was passed with a majority vote.

It seems it was difficult for the department to make a clean case on the file for the minister's approval post the split decision recorded in minutes. After some time, the secretary and the minister also changed. Another newspaper story in October 2021 said that the DoT issued notices imposing a penalty of ₹2,000 crore on Airtel and ₹1,050 crore on Vodafone. The operators went to the Telecom Department Settlement Appellate Tribunal (TDSAT), which made certain observations about the status of Reliance Jio in the case, against which Reliance Jio went to the Supreme Court, where the case still seems to be pending.

It seems the DoT is still to recover the penalties.

Action against Viral Acharya

On 26 October 2018, the deputy governor of RBI, Viral Acharya, delivered his (in)famous 'wrath of the markets' speech. Viral Acharya's theme of the day was the trampling of central banking institutions by governments and its consequences. He quoted the case of Martin Redrado, Argentina's former central bank chief. In his speech, Viral Acharya left no one in doubt that India, in 2018, was facing a similar situation as Argentina had a few years ago. He specifically outlined the 'attempts' of the Government of India to raid the reserves of RBI. Concluding his speech with fire and brimstone, Viral Acharya issued an indirect warning to the Government of India: 'Governments that do not respect central bank independence will sooner or later incur the wrath of financial markets, ignite economic fire, and come to rue the day they undermined an important regulatory institution; their wiser counterparts who invest in central bank independence will enjoy lower costs of borrowing, the love of international investors and longer lifespans.'[4] No sooner than he finished, the provocative parts of his speech were making headlines in the media and trending as 'breaking news'.

Viral Acharya used data from the sovereign bond markets of Argentina to make the point that bonds were sold off, and yields and credit default swap rates rose massively, when the governor of the central bank resigned in the wake of the government's interference. No one in the country, perhaps, cared to look at this data. We, however, decided to check the facts. The conclusions drawn by Viral Acharya about credit default swap rates going up by 25 per cent turned out to be patently false. This raised the question: Did Viral Acharya use wrong data knowingly or unknowingly? Further, if he knew the data to be false, did he deliberately use it to create a storm or put the Government of India in a bad light?

Based on these findings, the matter was discussed with Finance Minister Arun Jaitley. He appreciated the seriousness of the charge. With his concurrence, a file was prepared, laying down the facts of the case and containing a proposal asking Viral Acharya for an explanation for why he used false data deliberately. The file remained in the custody of Arun Jaitley. Its locus after Nirmala Sitharaman took over is not known. Until I left in July 2019, it did not come back with or without approval. In July, Viral Acharya voluntarily left RBI.

Not in the race for RBI governor

Quite unexpectedly, RBI Governor Urjit Patel resigned on 10 December 2018. And he did so in a most unusual manner. He put his resignation letter on the RBI website without sending it to the government as required under the rules and established procedure and simply went home. He said he was stepping down due to 'personal reasons'; attributed considerable accomplishments of the bank during his tenure to its staff, officers and management; expressed his gratitude to his colleagues and directors of RBI Central Bank, but made no mention of the government, the PM and the finance minister.

I called Arun Jaitley who confirmed that he had no prior knowledge of the resignation but said he intended to accept it and not ask for any reconsideration. Within an hour or so, the finance minister issued a statement, accepting the resignation, noting his deep appreciation for the services rendered by Dr Urjit Patel to India. The PM offered a laudatory tribute to him on 10 December. He tweeted noting that Dr Urjit Patel steered the banking system from chaos to order and ensured discipline. I tried to call Urjit Patel that day. He did not pick up the phone. Prime Minister Modi publicly stated in January 2019 that Urjit Patel had discussed his intention to resign some months back with him.

The central government appoints the governor of RBI. As Dr Urjit Patel had 'vacated' his office, the government needed to select the next governor without losing any time as the office of governor could not be left unattended. As I was holding the charge of secretary, DFS, because Rajiv Kumar, secretary, DFS, which is the administrative department for RBI, was on leave, I received a call from the Cabinet Secretariat to come at 8 p.m. the same evening to participate in a meeting of the search-cum-selection committee. When I got there, I found Rajiv Kumar in attendance. This intrigued me. When I asked him why he was there, he cryptically responded, in half jest, that both of us were possibly being considered for the post. Both of us were in the meeting when it commenced business.

As the meeting progressed, at one stage, macroeconomist Dr Rathin Roy, who was at the meeting as an expert member, proposed that I should be considered for the job as he felt I fit the bill the best. Whether it was a choreographed move or a spontaneous suggestion, I have never asked Dr Roy about it. The cabinet secretary immediately asked me to go to his chamber and wait. As soon as I got up and neared the exit to the committee room, he asked me to stop. He mentioned that he thought I had a lot of service left and might not be interested in the job at this stage. He wanted me to indicate my preference, nonetheless. Standing at the end of the table, just near the exit, I told him that as I had about two years of service left, from a personal point of view, I did not think it was an appropriate time for me to go to RBI. However, as RBI was in a difficult situation, I would be willing to go if the government needed my services.

The meeting ended after 45 minutes. The committee decided to make a panel of three IAS officers for the job. I was part of the panel with Shaktikanta Das, former secretary, DEA, and Ajay Tyagi, chairman, SEBI. I was told that Shaktikanta Das and I were the two serious contenders. The next day, on 11 December, the selection process progressed. I had no role to play. I was told later that Prime Minister Modi was not in favour of my leaving the government at that juncture. Shaktikanta Das was appointed governor of RBI on 12 December 2018.

Getting RBI's reserves

Sharing of surplus generated in RBI had been a tug of war between the government and RBI since the early 2000s. Reserve Bank of India wanted to retain as much of the surplus as it could. The government wanted almost the entire surplus to be transferred to it to shore up the budget. Based on recommendations of the Malegam Committee, RBI transferred 100 per cent of surplus for four years until 2016–17. Raghuram Rajan initiated the processes to redefine the capital requirement of RBI. An economic capital framework (ECF) was crafted which was finally approved, without the government's concurrence, when Urjit Patel had just taken over.

The ECF formula was applied for the first time for distribution of surplus for the financial year 2016–17. This came up in my first meeting of the RBI board, that too, as a 'Table Item', circulated only in the meeting, leaving me without the benefit of having it examined in the DEA. The bank proposed retention of ₹13,400 crore out of the surplus of ₹44,200 crore. I could not have agreed to it, though I did not understand all the facts presented first time in that meeting and knew very little of the background. I tried to get 100 per cent of the surplus transferred to the Government of India as in previous four years. There was no support for this view in the board as all of them had participated in the framing of the ECF. In the situation, I asked for my two points to be recorded in the minutes: (i) transfer of ₹30,600 crores to be treated as provisional, and if the calculations as per the Malegam formula suggested that transferable surplus was higher than the total surplus of ₹44,200 crore, the retained amount of ₹13,600 crore to be also transferred to government; and (ii) the ECF to be discussed with the government and whatever was agreed to there to be adopted as the ECF. The board agreed to record my observations in the minutes. In the minutes which I received, my observations were not recorded. It took a lot of effort in subsequent meetings to get them included.

There were considerable interactions, discussions, arguments and disagreements on the ECF matter in the following year. I was quite convinced of its unfairness. However, there was little support from the PMO for many months. Finally, sometime in August 2018, we could convince the prime minister to take it up with the recalcitrant Urjit Patel. In a meeting, the prime minister gave Urjit Patel a piece of his mind, equating his stand to a snake sitting over wealth in its burrow: '*Aap, saamp ki tarah kundli markar kyon baithe ho?*' This helped move matters a little.

After a lot of drama and issuance of formal consultation notices under Section 7 of the RBI Act, finally the RBI board agreed to constitute an expert committee in November 2018. Terms of reference and the composition of the expert committee were agreed to by the government and RBI. The committee was headed by Bimal Jalan, former governor of RBI; and included Dr Rakesh Mohan, former deputy governor of RBI, two RBI board members, Sudhir Mankad and Bharat Doshi; N.S. Vishwanathan, deputy governor, RBI; and me, secretary, Economic Affairs.

There were strong disagreements within the committee. I presented and vehemently put forth the government's views that RBI needed little to no cash reserves and only much smaller valuation reserves. Most committee members wanted to ensure that as little surplus as possible was transferred from RBI to government.

When it was clear that my proposals would not go through, I decided to write a a comprehensive dissent note, explaining why in my judgement the majority opinion of the committee was not right one and what the right solution, in my judgement, was.

My inflexible stand contributed, amongst other, to my transfer on 24 July 2019. My dissent note was taken out of the committee proceedings and report. Reserve Bank of India transferred about ₹1.76 lakh crore for the financial year 2018–19, more than 100 per cent of the surplus that year by taking out about ₹60,000 crore of valuation reserves, acknowledging that these were no longer required. For the next three years as well, by artificially converting valuation gains into profits, RBI transferred more than 100 per cent of its normal surplus.

'Did the government approve your dissent note?'

My differences with other expert committee members had become quite crystallized and irreconcilable by the fifth meeting held on 24 April 2019. There were four major irreconcilable areas of difference. Seeing no possibility of the others accepting what I thought was the reasonable and correct stand, I told the chairman and the committee members that I would write a comprehensive dissent note.

I brought the entire matter to the notice of the finance minister and the PMO after the fifth meeting on 24 April and explained in person to the principal secretary the serious implications of what the majority committee members were going to recommend. I requested that the issues were serious enough to warrant the personal attention of the PM even though he was in the midst of Lok Sabha election campaign. The principal secretary agreed with me on the seriousness of the matter.

I wrote a comprehensive dissent note, running into about 20 pages, with point-by-point arguments and evidence of why the recommendations of the other four members were wrong on the four major issues I had identified, and detailed the right course of action. I used emphatic language to make my points.

In the sixth meeting held on 13 May, I formally placed my dissent note before the committee. The RBI secretariat incorporated my dissent note as an appendix to the main report. The dissent note was also discussed in the next meeting held on 12 June. The draft report of the committee, including my dissent note, made for interesting reading. It exposed the fallacy and weakness of the recommendations which the majority wanted to push.

I mentioned the matter briefly to Nirmala Sitharaman on 1 June, after she had taken over as finance minister. On 3 June, I submitted a file and the entire set of documents on the ECF matter, a copy of the majority report and my dissent note. I mentioned it to her to approve my proposals. She promised to look into the matter soon. I accompanied her for the G-20 finance ministers' meeting in Fukuoka, Japan, during 7–9 June 2019. During this visit, I briefed her extensively about the matter, the issues involved, the reasons for the serious differences of opinion and the implications of the majority's recommendations for the government. She seemed to appreciate the enormity of the issues involved and promised to take it up with the RBI governor upon her return.

Something happened in the three days after we came back from Japan. I don't know what it was, who briefed her and with what intent. She called me to her room in North Block on 10 June. Changing her stance completely, without questioning the contents of the dissent note, she asked me whether I had the government's permission to write such a note. I again explained the entire sequence of events, including the fact that the dissent note had been furnished to the PMO, who had agreed with it broadly, and that I had sought the intervention of the PM to take the matter up with RBI to protect the legitimate interest of the government.

As the discussion progressed, she got visibly disturbed and told me I had no authority or business to file a dissent note. I told her it would not be in the interest of the government if this viewpoint was not reflected in the report. I also told her that dissent notes are not a novelty in committees in which government and RBI participated. I suggested that she intervene with RBI to develop a consensus. When she appeared uninterested in either taking the matter up with the bank to find a consensus solution or permit me to include the dissent note as a member of the committee, I told her I would need her written instructions on the file, which was already with her office. I did not receive them.

No listing of equity in foreign exchanges

In the domestic finance sphere, the most important function assigned to the DEA relates to the capital markets. India's securities market regulator, SEBI, has developed into a formidable organization over the years. The DEA is not only the administrative department but also retains considerable authority under the Security Contract & Regulation Act (SCRA) and has authority to issue policy directions to SEBI. The DEA is also represented in the SEBI board by the secretary, DEA, or the joint secretary in charge of capital markets.

The government formulated a new set of rules to facilitate the issue of DR outside India and notified a new scheme, the Depository Receipts (DR) Scheme, 2014, to come into effect from 15 December 2014. The scheme also provided for direct listing of equity shares in foreign exchanges. SEBI was required to issue guidelines under the 2014 Scheme to implement it, but it did not do so. The DR Scheme was in limbo when I joined in 2017.

A meeting of all concerned revealed that the principal roadblock was SEBI's insistence to get the KYC details of all the holders, including final foreign beneficiaries of the DRs/equity shares, on the lines of domestic holders of securities. International stock exchanges, particularly in the US, went by what is called 'omnibus holding' of securities, where foreign depositories did not need to hold details of individual subscribers and holders of securities. It took many meetings for SEBI to accept the omnibus structure for all Financial Action Task Force (FATF)-compliant jurisdictions.

SEBI then latched on to a rule in the Prevention of Money-Laundering (Maintenance of Records) rules, 2005, and wanted these rules to be amended to the effect that there was no statutory obligation on SEBI to collect details of the final beneficial holders under the omnibus securities holding schemes of the permissible jurisdiction. It took another six months to persuade the Department of Revenue to agree to amend the Prevention of Money Laundering Act (PMLA) rules. Finally, in March 2019, we agreed to a draft of the amendment that the Department of Revenue would make. The notification incorporating the gist of the agreed language arrived in March 2019 and was finally issued in September 2019 after I had left the department. The depository receipts scheme and direct equity listing are still not operational.

Making SEBI part with surplus

SEBI collects three kinds of revenues: (i) fees and income for registering and servicing market intermediaries, (ii) income from fines and penalties imposed for offences and infractions under the Act, and (iii) proceeds of disgorgement and other receipts levied for insider trading and other stock-market malpractices.

All grants, fees and regulatory service charges are retained by SEBI and not credited to government account. SEBI levied fees and charges for its services at rates that were far higher than its expenditure requirement. It was quite liberal in incurring capital expenditure and establishing investor education institutions. Still, SEBI could not utilize its annual revenues. Consequently, it had a balance of over ₹4,000 crore in the corpus fund at the end of financial year 2018–19. It used to earn an annual surplus of over ₹400 crore.

I felt that there was no justification in SEBI retaining revenue much beyond its current and future needs. We, therefore, drafted amendments in SEBI law to allow it to retain 25 per cent of its annual surplus (obviously computed after accounting for all its expenditures) and further subject to not exceeding two years' expenditure requirement. The surplus to this extent was to be retained in SEBI's reserve fund.

These proposals were presented to finance minister Nirmala Sitharaman for consideration and approval for inclusion in the Finance Bill 2019. Ajay Tyagi had serious reservations. He met the finance minister and argued against this expropriation by government. He gave a public statement to this effect as well.

For a change, Nirmala Sitharaman agreed with me and approved the proposal. Part IX of the Finance Act amended the SEBI Act to provide for capital expenditure to be approved by the SEBI Board and the central government. It created a reserve fund on the lines I proposed.

32

'You Are Not in Tune with the Government's Thinking'

Prime Minister Narendra Modi and Finance Ministers Arun Jaitley, Piyush Goyal and Nirmala Sitaraman were my political bosses during my time in the DEA. Nripendra Misra, principal secretary to the PM; Dr P.K. Mishra, additional principal secretary to PM, and cabinet secretary P.K. Sinha were my administrative bosses during this period.

Of these, there were no serious issues with Dr P.K. Mishra and P.K. Sinha during these two years. There were serious differences with Piyush Goyal on policy issues, which I have recounted in the book *We Also Make Policy*. As he was not a full-fledged finance minister, these issues did not lead to any serious interpersonal problems.

Nripendra Misra was the real administrative decision-maker in most of the policy issues I was concerned with. Despite his initial impressions of me being an upstart, he developed enormous confidence in me as my innings progressed. He involved me in many matters that were not of direct concern to me. He would consult me and take my opinion into consideration on serious and contentious issues in the Ministry of Finance. He would also use me to troubleshoot many times. In the last six to nine months, however, there were more issues on which he felt that my approach and stand were inappropriate. As he is not one to hold himself back, he would expressly tick me off and criticize me. Sometimes, he would exclude me from the decision-making process. Here I am recounting the matters where the going really became tough, sometimes a bit unpleasant, contributing to my leaving the government finally.

The most serious differences arose with Nirmala Sitharaman. In this chapter, I recount some of these not mentioned elsewhere in this book. The prime minister also started cooling off towards me in my last few months in the service.

'Why did you do it?'

The coin and currency division processed cases for issue of commemorative coins with portraits of eminent persons in line with the department's order issued in 2017.

The government wanted commemorative coins to be issued on the birth centenary of Rajmata Vijaya Raje Scindia. The proposal was received in the department sometime in 2017–18. The birth centenary probably fell in 2020.

The examination of proposal when it was received for the first time revealed that it was not in accordance with the departmental guidelines as the commemorative coins were issued for only those individuals who had attained excellence in public life, in areas such as science, literature, arts, including performing arts, or had made exceptional intellectual contributions. The rules made it very clear that commemorative coins were not to be issued for politicians. This first examination had concluded that Vijaya Raje Scindia was not eligible as her contribution in public life were political and not in any of the five areas mentioned in the guidelines. The proposal was not approved.

Perhaps because of the Lok Sabha elections in 2019, there was a political decision to issue the commemorative coin in Vijaya Raje Scindia's name. The message was conveyed to me by Nripendra Misra. The examination this time by the coin and currency division was not rigorous in terms of guidelines (possibly, they had also received an appropriate message). The division and joint secretary Prashant Goyal recommended that the commemorative coins be issued in her name.

I found the proposal on file inappropriate for two reasons. First, the very fact that the guidelines as they stood allowed commemorative coins to be issued for people with a record of excellence as scientists and in literature, arts and other intellectual domains, which Vijaya Raje Scindia did not satisfy, and therefore the proposal was violative of government policy. Second, I sensed that if this was done for her, it would open the floodgates for issuing commemorative coins for other politicians as well.

I wrote my note on the file opposing the proposal and sent for appropriate orders to Arun Jaitley. Before perhaps it reached the table of the finance minister, Nripendra Misra called, and in an irritated tone asked me why I had done this despite the PMO backing the proposal. I told him my reasons.

Finance Minister Arun Jaitley overruled me. The proposal went to the PMO for the PM's approval (all proposals for commemorative coins were finally approved by the PM), who approved it. The Prime Minister released the special commemorative coin of ₹100 denomination to mark the completion of birth centenary celebrations of Rajmata Vijaya Raje Scindia on 12 October 2020.

'Don't ever go to the PM over my head'

The amended Fiscal Responsibility and Budget Management (FRBM) Act required the government to bring down fiscal deficit to 3 per cent by 2020–21. To continue with the glide path, we proposed the fiscal deficit to be retained at 3.3 per cent in the revised estimates of 2018–19 and fixed it at 3.1 per cent for financial year 2019–20 so as to peg it at 3.0 per cent in the year 2020–21, as envisaged in the FRBM Act. I had initially proposed attaining 3 per cent in financial year 2019–20 itself, one year ahead of the target. Finance Minister Arun Jaitley thought differently and suggested it be kept at 3.2 or 3.1 per cent for 2019–20. We settled for 3.1 per cent.

Suddenly, one day, Expenditure Secretary Ajay Jha advised Arvind Srivastava, joint secretary, Budget – who has been recently appointed as the revenue secretary, Government of India – to keep the fiscal deficit at 3.4 per cent for financial year 2018-19 and 3.3 per cent for 2019–20. He told Srivastava this was what the PMO (Nripendra Misra) wanted. I found this quite strange. First, it was conveyed in such a roundabout way (why was I not told directly?) and, second, deviating fiscal deficit by 0.1 per cent in the revised estimates made no sense; it was small money but would convey a bad message to the markets about the government not being able to stick to its deficit estimates.

Arun Jaitley had left for the US by that time. I conveyed it to him. I also took the matter up with P.K. Mishra in the PMO. He, too, found the change baffling. It seemed Nripendra Misra had spoken to the PM about it and indicated that some slippage on the fiscal deficit was necessary on account of the envisaged new PM KISAN scheme (one instalment of ₹2,000 to 10 crore farmers was roughly equal to 0.1 per cent of India's GDP). P.K. Misra agreed that I should meet the PM and explain the fiscal numbers to him. He also set up my meeting with the PM.

Prime Minister Modi heard me out and was completely clear. He wanted one instalment of PM KISAN to be accommodated. But he also agreed that it would be better if the fiscal deficit could be maintained at the budgeted level. However, he wanted Arun Jaitley to be fully on board and advised me to take his views. I did that the next morning. Arun Jaitley agreed, and I told the budget division to retain the fiscal deficit at 3.3 per cent for revised estimates for 2018–19 and 3.2 per cent for 2019–20.

That evening was reserved for the presentation of the draft budget speech to the PM. All the secretaries of the Ministry of Finance were waiting in the adjoining room before the meeting. Suddenly, Nripendra Misra walked in. At his furious worst, he asked me whether I had met the PM to discuss the fiscal deficit issue. After I confirmed that I had done so, he blew up. Quoting statistics from the UPA era when the fiscal deficit had ballooned after the global financial crisis, he questioned the very logic of the fiscal consolidation path and the Ministry of Finance's fixation with low fiscal deficits. He bluntly said I had no business going over his head to discuss the matter directly with the PM. I listened to him without demur, only saying I was simply following the call of duty.

I made the presentation before Prime Minister Modi, which went reasonably well. The subject of deviating from the fiscal deficit did not come up in the discussion. Nripendra Misra also did not raise it. I took that to mean that we would stick to 3.3 per cent for the revised estimates, as agreed by Finance Minister Arun Jaitley.

After the meeting, the expenditure secretary stayed back and waited till the taxation-related discussions (in the next meeting in which I and he were not invited) were over. Apparently, once the meeting was over, he checked what to do about the fiscal deficit with Nripendra Misra. Nripendra Misra told him (as he conveyed to me the next day) that the fiscal deficit would stay as he had originally wanted – 3.4 per cent for the revised estimates for 2018–19 and 3.3 per cent for the budgeted estimates for 2019–20. Ajay Jha also conveyed the PMO's decision to Arun Jaitley, who reluctantly agreed. The final printed fiscal deficit numbers in the budget were what Nripendra Misra had decided.

'You are not in tune with the thinking of the government'

Some additional matters besides the two cited above made Nripendra Misra become somewhat stiff towards me, though most of our normal interactions continued unaffected. He was perhaps a little bit bottled up as well. The lid finally came off in the matter of the second recapitalization of banks proposed to be done by way of providing funds in the second supplementary grants for 2018–19.

I had told Nripendra Misra in several meetings that the recapitalization programme was excessively large, and instead of spending so much money like that, we needed to design it better. Secretary, DFS, Rajiv Kumar, however, was pushing for it with little care for fiscal implication and stability. For my part, it was important to keep the size of recapitalization as small as possible to not excessively burden the fiscal resources of the government.

The principal secretary took a view on the funds to be provided as recapitalization bonds for PSBs and conveyed it to Rajiv Kumar. Kumar went on leave for his daughter's wedding, and I was assigned the charge of DFS as well.

The DFS put the file in line with what the principal secretary had indicated. After studying the entire matter, I recorded a long note, pointing out how the DFS prescription and its ask were not in the government's best interests. I also suggested an alternative formulation. With that, I submitted the file to finance minister Arun Jaitley.

The finance minister perhaps mentioned my file note to Nripendra Misra. He was livid. He called me. For the first time, I was clearly told: 'The prime minister is unhappy with you. The finance minister is unhappy with you. Subhash, you are not in tune with the thinking of the government.'

The finance minister recorded a long note overturning my recommendations and approving the DFS formulation.

Stiff and unwelcoming in the G-20

I left to attend the finance deputies' meeting in Japan late evening on 4 June, reached Tokyo in the morning of 5 June and proceeded to Fukuyama via Shinkansen high-speed (bullet) rail, reaching in the evening. The hardest part of the work the finance deputies do is to negotiate the communique of the finance ministers' meeting. We wanted numerous changes in the first draft presented by the Japanese presidency. Every change was hard fought. On 6 June, the first day, the negotiations went on until 11 p.m. The next day was even more strenuous and finally closed only at 3.30 a.m. on the morning of 8 June.

The finance minister arrived on the evening of 7 June with her first briefing scheduled for 8 p.m. As the communique negotiations were going on, I suggested that Aparna Bhatia, G-20 advisor, brief her or we could alternatively have the briefing at 8.30 a.m. on 8 June. She decided to have the briefing on 8 June. At 8.30 a.m. on 8 June, after a short nap, I went to brief her along with two other officers. Mustering all my energy and fighting the sleep deficit, I began briefing her on the issues, beginning with the taxation seminar, which she was to participate in at 11.30a.m. After about 15–20 minutes, she abruptly asked us to leave as she wanted to prepare in her own way.

We had prepared sharply focused interventions for her for the four sessions in which she was to speak at the G-20 finance ministers' meeting. In the meeting, she chose to go by the written interventions we had given her and delivered them without any changes. During the coffee break that followed, I complimented her for speaking very effectively in the meeting. Her reaction surprised me. 'I hope I did not disappoint you,' she said. Her tone was sarcastic. My suspicion that she was carrying biases against me were confirmed but I chose to ignore it.

There is a tradition of issuing a press release every day during G-20 meetings, highlighting the finance ministers' interventions and matters raised in the G-20 and bilateral meetings. I had carefully edited and expanded the draft press release for the first day. At about 7.30 p.m. on 8 June, we handed the draft press release to Nirmala Sitharaman's private secretary, Vipul Bansal. We were informed that she wanted to edit it further. She decided to summon a director-level officer after dinner to help her finalize it. He later related the sequence of events to us. First, she expressed her unhappiness at the draft. Then, she started writing alternative formulations for some portions. Subsequently, she rejected all the alternatives she had formulated. Thereafter, she dictated some paragraphs to the director but later deemed them not good enough. Finally, after about an hour and a half, she more or less cleared the draft we had provided her and returned it for release.

'Don't think I can't violate you!'

On 11 June 2019, Finance Minister Nirmala Sitharaman was to chair the first of the pre-budget consultation meetings in North Block with agriculture experts and representatives. Following tradition, I went to her chamber to accompany her to the conference room but was told to proceed directly and that she would join us there. As there was limited time available for consultations, we began listening to the experts as she was running late. She came in about an hour late. She looked rather stiff when talking to me, with an unsmiling, grim face. I requested the principal speakers to highlight their suggestions again in brief, which they did.

The meeting was moving towards closure. She discussed a few suggestions with the participants. When I was making my concluding remarks, I mentioned that all their suggestions had been duly noted. To assure the participants that the government valued their suggestions, I underlined that while we could not discuss the merits of their proposals in the meeting, all their views and suggestions would be put up for the consideration of the finance minister for appropriate orders, after due examination.

I don't think I said anything objectionable. However, she reacted sternly when I finished my closing remarks, saying, 'I will abide by what the finance secretary says, especially a finance secretary who is much older than me in the finance ministry, and not discuss the suggestions.' Her remarks were certainly not in order, but I said nothing. That said, she did not close the meeting.

One secretary and another expert, believing that the finance minister was interested in their ideas, initiated a discussion on two more issues. I remained quiet during this discussion. While listening to them and interacting with them, she suddenly snapped at me, saying: 'What do you think, I cannot violate you? I would.' It was very clear that she was deeply frustrated with me over something. I remained quiet.

I went to her room to clear the air before the next meeting in the afternoon. She was livid. I offered to reshape the process of consultation as it pleased her. I also apologized if anything I had done had caused any misunderstanding. She was relentless. She said I treated her like a *bachchi* (child). At one stage, she said that I had gone to various people and 'bitched' about her, which was false. She also threatened to bring the entire matter to the notice of the prime minister.

Strangely, despite her diatribe, she maintained that the pre-budget consultations must be conducted in the way I wanted. She said she would not even open her mouth in the consultation meetings thereafter. I don't know what had got into her. It was clear, though, that there was a serious problem and that our functional relationship had broken down.

The budget was drawing very close. With a cooler head, I decided to ignore everything that had taken place and carry on ensuring the budget preparations went off smoothly.

Budget speech proved to be a rocky exercise

I had started working on the draft of the budget speech very early in the month of June and informed the minister that I would deliver the first draft to her latest by 24 June, before I left on the night of 25 June as part of the PM's delegation for the G-20 leaders' meeting in Japan. Despite the stressful conditions, worsened by the virtual snapping of communications between us, I drafted the budget speech and handed it over to the finance minister on 24 June. I requested her to work on my inputs and send me the first version of her draft as soon as possible. I had made all the arrangements to receive her version of the speech and update it while attending the G-20 meeting.

I did not receive her comments while I was away. I worked to further improve the draft I had submitted to her on 24 June on the flight back on the PM's plane from Japan on 29 June. I delivered the revised version of the first draft to her on 30 June, again underlining the absolute urgency for her to work on it and finalize it so that the same could be shared with the PMO.

In budget-making, the PMO plays an important and intensive role. It vets every paragraph that goes in the budget speech. The presentation before the PM was scheduled on 2 July to finalize the basic thrust of the budget speech. Very strangely, on the forenoon of 2 July, Nirmala Sitharaman delivered her version of the draft speech directly to the PMO, without providing me a copy. When I asked her for a copy, she said the speech as sent by her was by and large what I had given her and that she had only added a few paragraphs.

This created an unprecedented situation. I was responsible for finalizing the speech and seeing it through to print without any glitches. Further, I was also primarily responsible for presenting and defending the speech in the PMO. Still, I did not have a draft of it which my finance minister had finalized.

Normally, the budget speech is read by the secretary, Economic Affairs, in a meeting chaired by the prime minister. Here, I didn't even have a copy of the speech! Anyway, I reached the PM's residence for the meeting. At the meeting, Brajendra Navneet, joint secretary in the PMO, read from the physical copy of the draft budget speech sent by the finance minister. I only had my draft version.

She had included 10–12 new paragraphs, dropped a few and left the bulk of the draft speech untouched. Over the next three hours or so, Prime Minister Modi went through the draft, accepted only a few of her additions and asked for a lot of re-orientation of emphasis and priorities.

When the meeting finished past 9.30 p.m., I was worried how to carry forward the process and come up with a revised draft that the PM wanted read-out before him the next day, 3 July. The budget was to be presented on 5 July. I asked her how to handle the matter after the meeting finished. 'I will hand over all the papers, including my draft, to you and you have to get this done tomorrow,' she responded. I could see a disaster waiting to happen. I told her this was not the best way and that she would have to guide the process to complete the draft. I suggested we meet at 8 a.m. in her office in North Block and work together to complete the revisions. She agreed. I informed the concerned staff to be available in her office at 8 a.m.

I was in the office with staff at 8 a.m. on 3 July. She did not turn up. In fact, her personal staff did not even open her office at 8 a.m. When I called her at home, I was informed that she had been working from very early in the morning on the draft and would reach the office only at 9.30 a.m.

After she arrived, I worked with her from 9.30 a.m. to about 4 p.m. to put together the revised draft – she did a lot of work on it too. There were many loose ends, some paragraphs were missing, and some paragraphs needed to be dropped, pruned or tightened. I worked to improve it as much as I could until 6 pm.

The second reading of the draft speech to the PM took place at 6.30 p.m. This round again went on until 9.30 p.m. Prime Minister Modi was still not satisfied and offered a lot of new leads to work on. However, realizing the gravity of the situation with almost no time left with the budget team and the finance minister, he indicated that he did not need to see the further revised version, saying he would listen to the budget speech in Parliament on 5 July.

We worked together on 4 July and prepared a near-final draft by 4 p.m. At this stage, I was quite relieved that a good part of my original budget proposals, relating to capital market reforms, PPP, opening up the economy to FDI and FPI, containing the fiscal deficit, and announcement of new initiatives like sovereign bonds in foreign currencies, all intended to push investment in infrastructure and manufacturing in India, had survived almost unscathed.

The finance minister's contribution was mainly political and social messaging. After sharing it with the PMO and undergoing two more iterations, I was happy that the budget speech could go for printing at about 9 p.m. It was delivered in Parliament on 5 July and was largely well received.

The last straw for me

Principal secretary to the PM Nripendra Misra was very keen that a financial package be announced for NBFCs. This package was to include two kinds of measures: first, giving further regulatory and resolution jurisdiction over

NBFCs to RBI, and second, announcing a special window to provide them liquidity support.

Secretary, DFS, Rajiv Kumar proposed a package of amendments in the RBI Act, including conferring regulatory and resolution jurisdiction to RBI, to be included in the Finance Bill. I was opposed to vesting resolution authority in RBI. I favoured creating a resolution mechanism on the lines of the FRDI Bill. Besides this principal issue, I found certain weaknesses in the package, including the unintentional insertion of a bail-in clause and excessive penalty provisions.

During my absence from Delhi to attend the G-20 meeting, the draft amendments proposed by the DFS got approved and vetted by the legislative department. I wrote a letter to the secretary, DFS, on 30 June, asking for three changes to be made in the material that he had got approved for the Finance Bill. He agreed with two of these proposed changes but disagreed with not conferring resolution authority on RBI. He routed the file through me, recording his views on my letter. I recorded my reasons for not conferring this authority on RBI and submitted the file to the finance minister.

Finance Minister Nirmala Sitharaman found it difficult to clear any file on which differing views were recorded. She wanted every file to be completely clean before she signed. In my short time with her, I could not find a single file where she recorded her views or decided to take a stand. She would either sign it, return it unsigned or keep it pending.

In view of the urgency to finalize the Finance Bill, she called Rajiv Kumar and me on the morning of 2 July for a discussion. I explained my reasons. I did not think she understood the difference between regulation and resolution, but she seemed persuaded to agree with my opinion. She asked me to record some background and additional reasons for my line of suggestion and resubmit the file. I did so. Rajiv was not happy. He brought up the matter again in the speech-reading session with the PM. There, Nripendra Misra supported Rajiv. The finance minister only commented that I had recorded a long note opposing Rajiv's proposal. The PM said that the view expressed by Nripendra Misra and Rajiv Kumar was to be accepted.

The next day, the file was returned to my office from the finance minister's office with the oral instruction: 'FS knows what is to be done.' I sent the file to secretary, DFS, who submitted the same back, noting on a fresh page that the proposal of the DFS might be approved. I signed it and sent it to the finance minister in view of the specific decision taken the previous day. However,

Nirmala Sitharaman had different ideas. She would not sign the file with the earlier notes still in it. Her office conveyed this clearly to Rajiv. Rajiv told me the note sheets recorded earlier would have to be taken out, destroyed and replaced with new note sheets with same dates and numbers. Though I had never allowed such a thing in my life, I acquiesced only to ensure that the budget process could go through.

But I decided that I would not to be party to something like this ever again. It was the moment I made up my mind to quit the IAS.

Epilogue

I had begun mulling over voluntary retirement in the first week of July. I made up my mind around 12 July after I concluded that it would be dysfunctional for the finance minister and me to continue working together in the finance ministry. Upon some more reflection, I felt it would perhaps be better to work outside government, as part of the larger civil society, to understand and contribute to the goal of building a $10 trillion Indian economy.

I had some discussions with Anjali and made up my mind fixing 31 October 2019 as the date on which I would take voluntary retirement from the IAS.

I received a call on 18 July from Dr P.K. Mishra to come over for a chat. We had an excellent relationship, and I would have gone to him to broach the subject of my voluntary retirement anyway. Interestingly, he too had the subject of my transfer from the finance ministry on his mind. This is what he said more or less:

'Subhash, you are a brilliant, hardworking, competent and very committed officer, but you would need to be shifted from the finance ministry. The finance minister has met the prime minister a few times and has continuously complained against you. We cannot change the finance minister. Therefore, you will have to make way. We are thinking of shifting you to the ministry of power. You can choose any other department or autonomous organization if you want.'

I had known this was coming and was ready with my response. I thanked him for sounding me out on the transfer and offering me my choice of posting. I then told Dr Mishra I had already contemplated the matter and, after considerable thought, had decided that I would take voluntary retirement from 31 October. I also told him that I was thinking about setting up a foundation (I discussed the formation of a foundation with Nishith Desai later in August–September) to work for policy and other reforms required for India to usher in the $10 trillion economy.

Dr Mishra, an extremely nice and supportive person, was quite surprised and worried. He felt that such a move would not be viewed favourably by the government as it would be equated with the departures of Arvind Panagariya and Arvind Subramanian showing the government in a bad light. He asked me to reconsider.

I reiterated my resolve and requested that my decision be brought to the kind notice of Prime Minister Modi. I also mentioned that I was working on 100 major policy and structural reforms that were needed to put India in the $10 trillion economy orbit, which I would like to present before the PM. I also underlined that I would always be positive and constructive and would be happy to work with the PM as it was my considered opinion that if anyone could propel India into this orbit, it was Prime Minister Narendra Modi.

Dr Mishra promised he would discuss the matter with the prime minister reiterating that I should also reconsider it.

Filed for voluntary retirement

I drafted my application for voluntary retirement on my office computer on Saturday, 20 July, and dated it 29 July with a view to submit it a couple of days before 31 July. I wanted to give the required notice of three months. This would make my retirement effective from 31 October, exactly a year before my normal date of superannuation.

I had expected my transfer orders to be issued around 30 or 31 July. I had also expected a response on what the prime minister thought about it. A little unexpectedly, my transfer orders to the ministry of power were issued on 24 July at around 8.15 p.m., when I was participating in the finance group secretaries' meeting in the DFS conference room. I did not hear about what the PM thought about it. I assumed, if the subject was indeed discussed between Dr Mishra and PM, that PM was fine with my voluntary retirement.

I came straight to my office in North Block. I changed the date of the VRS application from 29 July to 24 July and printed three copies.

I signed a copy for the Government of Rajasthan, as it was that government, which was, under the rules, competent to accept my voluntary retirement application, and addressed it to Chief Secretary, Rajasthan, D.B. Gupta, my batchmate. Another copy was addressed to the DoPT secretary, Government of India, for information. I signed the last copy as my office copy.

Handing over these two applications to K. Abdulla Syed, my principal private secretary (PPS), for taking necessary action in the morning, I left for home. I had taken a photo of my office copy on my phone.

On my way home, I spoke to D.B. Gupta to inform him so that he wouldn't be unduly surprised when the letter reached him the next day. He was very understanding. I wasn't unduly ruffled and had my normal sound sleep.

Taking leave of Nirmala Sitharaman

On the morning of 25 July, the day after I signed my voluntary retirement application, I went to the finance minister's chamber to attend the meeting of secretaries she would hold every day. After two other secretaries had briefed her on the important issues at hand, I sought leave to speak.

I informed her of my decision to take voluntary retirement. I told her that I wanted to be relieved right away. I also informed her that the power secretary needed a day to clear his office etc., and that Atanu Chakraborty, who was designated my successor at the DEA, wanted to take over only the next day. Therefore, it had been agreed that I would hand over charge in the morning of 26 July. I added that my application for voluntary retirement had reached the Rajasthan government, my cadre-controlling authority, and the DoPT in the morning. I then thanked her for Budget 2019–20 and wished her well.

She did not comment or speak. Her expression said it all – 'good riddance'.

The meeting ended and I left the room of the finance minister, where I had attended numerous meetings and discussions in the preceding two years. This was my last time in that room.

With the burden of maintaining such a tough relationship over, I was completely at ease. I had a 'farewell' session with the senior officers of the DEA in the afternoon of 25 July in a very relaxed setting, though some of them were tense, possibly thinking of their future in the department.

That day, almost every officer and staff member in the DEA came to meet and wish me. Many senior officers from the sister departments of revenue and expenditure also came. There was literally a flood of people for some time in the afternoon.

Around 4.30 p.m., I asked Atanu Chakraborty to take charge as I did not want to come back the next morning. He agreed. We signed the charge handover papers. I bid goodbye to North Block on the evening of 25 July 2019, never to return.

A transitory stay in the Ministry of Power

While the expiry date was very prominently printed for my innings in the Ministry of Power, I worked for those three months as though it was a full-length normal posting. Here, I will just recount one episode and my departure from the service.

There was considerable difference between mine and the minister R.K. Singh's worldview of the government's role in the power sector, in particular the relationship of the government with the PSUs.

I would record my views frankly and, in my judgement, persuasively on the files. R.K. Singh, a career bureaucrat, loved to impose his writ on the decision. He tried to write long notes giving reasons why he disagreed with my proposal and what his orders were. That was fine except that I would resubmit many of these files with additional facts and arguments to request reconsideration.

Very soon, the minister got irritated with me. In two weekly meetings, which he would convene to take stock of the progress and implementation of his previous orders, he cryptically said that officers of my batch had been his 'probationers'. I refused to take any hints and continued to work in my way.

Sometime in late August, a note came from the minister ordering that, as the routine and administrative files needed to be quickly disposed of, they must be put up directly to him by divisional heads (special secretary/additional secretary/joint secretary). He further ordered that secretary, Power, be bothered only with policy matters. This order was a bit mischievous and funny as no file stopped with me for more than a few hours, and nothing remained pending in my office at the end of the day.

This bizarre order sought to turn the conventional role of minister and secretary on its head. It is the minister who should be concerned only with policy matters, leaving all administrative and day-to-day matters to the secretary. This was what Finance Minister Arun Jaitley did with considerable success. This was what the transaction of business rules envisaged.

To ensure the order did not create any unnecessary confusion in the ministry, I wrote out a detailed note in hand on the same file that came from the minister's office. I referred to the business rules, the real division of work and responsibility between the minister and secretary, and the kinds of problems such an order could create in the discharge of the secretary's responsibilities as the chief accounting authority of the ministry in ensuring expenditures undertaken in accordance with the rules of procurement, answering Parliament questions and giving evidence before parliamentary committees as the administrative head of the department.

In the end, I noted that the administration wing might examine the minister's order keeping in consideration my observations and put up a revised allocation of business in the ministry. I specifically directed that the file be routed through me for final orders of the minister. S.K.G. Rahate, additional secretary, later Secretary Justice, Government of India, in charge of the administration wing at that time, came rushing. He was quite indignant. I told him to examine the matter very objectively and put it up on file as soon as possible.

I didn't think the administration division had the intellectual gravitas to propose anything different in the matter. The officers must have shown my notes to the minister and expressed their helplessness in implementing his orders. I did not hear about that file thereafter. Nor did the minister mention it again.

Farewell to the IAS

At 5 p.m. on 31 October 2019, after serving in the IAS for a little over 36 years and one year before my date of superannuation, I bid farewell to the service at the Shram Shakti Bhawan, where the Ministry of Power is housed.

The officers gathered in the conference hall, and we chitchatted for half an hour. It was a light-hearted farewell. Some of them asked for my advice. I am reluctant to offer advice or exhortation, as I believe everyone must find his/her own solutions, yet, on that day, I suggested to them to pursue the bold and challenging path to completely transform the power sector in India by privatizing the entire sector, particularly the distribution segment. I knew it was too difficult an undertaking, especially with a government that talked about privatization of central public sector enterprises (CPSEs) but had no conviction and a minister who was totally steeped in the socialist mindset and saw the public sector as an essential instrument to achieve political goals. Still, civil servants must continue to work for the right policies and to serve the public interest to the best of their abilities.

The minister was not at the Shram Shakti Bhawan. I did not bother to make a farewell call on him. The officers came down to the gate and I bid goodbye to the Ministry of Power, Shram Shakti Bhawan, the Government of India and the IAS.

A very satisfying 'vanprastha'

I released a farewell note on my X and LinkedIn accounts once I reached home. It recounted the great time I had in the service despite many out-of-turn transfers and sometimes being relegated to unwanted positions. I also laid out my vision for India's economic future and how I would try to play a role in it. The note is available on my X account @Subhashgarg1960 and my Facebook and LinkedIn accounts. There was enormous response from the people from all walks of life.

A few days later, I released my take on the 100 most pressing reforms India needed to build a $10 trillion economy, which I had presented to Prime Minister Modi in early August 2019. This is also available on my blog page subhashchandragarg.blogspot.in as well as my X and LinkedIn handles.

When I completed one year after leaving the IAS, when my cooling-off period was over – the rules prohibit officers from taking commercial employment for the first year after superannuation – I posted a blog that recounted why I left the IAS and how meaningful and satisfying my post-service life was. This post, too, received a tremendous response.

However, I realized that setting up of a think tank was not a great idea. There was too much non-intellectual effort involved in that, including asking for financial support, hiring staff to do research and manage the same. Instead, I found that all the world's knowledge has indeed come to everyone's study through the Internet, search engines and artificial intelligence. I began to feel that acquiring and creating knowledge did not really need a think tank.

I began reading a lot and writing books and opinion editorials regularly.

In the last six years, I have been able to publish seven books, including the one in your hand, on three broad themes. The first focusses on realization of my love for India's ambition of building a $10 trillion economy by mid-2030s. My first book, *The $10 Trillion Dream: The State of Indian Economy and Economic Reforms,* was published in February 2022. In order to make a periodic assessment about the progress (or lack of it) towards that goal, I wrote *The $10 Trillion Dream Dented: The State of Indian Economy and Economic Reforms in Modi 2.0 (2019–2024),* which was published in October 2024. The book presented an unbiased and critical assessment of the functioning and results of the Modi government in its second term.

I started an annual series of books on budgets in 2023, with *Subhash Chandra Garg's Explanation and Commentary on Budget 2023–24* published in April 2023, and *Subhash Chandra Garg's Explanation and Commentary on Budget 2024–25* published after the interim budget 2024–25 in August 2024 and *Subhash Chandra Garg's Explanation and Commentary on Budget 2025–26* published in March 2025 after presentation of Budget 2025–26.

The book *We Also Make Policy: An Insider's Account of How the Ministry of Finance Works* focussed on my policy-making years in the government, spent in the ministries of finance and power. It was received quite well. My fabulous journey continues with this book, *No, Minister: Navigating Power, Politics and Bureaucracy with a Steely Resolve,* in your hands, which also focusses on the public service challenges that IAS officers face in their lives and the opportunity the society offers to them to find right and innovative solutions to solve people's and nation's problems.

I have been writing weekly opinion pieces on topical policy subjects which are published in *Deccan Herald*, *The Quint*, *Moneycontrol*, *Business Today*, *Outlook* and many others. I would have written over 200 opinion pieces by now.

For me, the post-IAS period is like a *vanprastha ashram* of a complete and fulsome life – a life devoted to learning and creating knowledge. I am truly in a state of *anand.*

Notes

1. Ministry of Finance, 'Implementation of Amendments in the Indian Stamp Act, 1899 and Rules Made from 1st July, 2020 for Rationalized Collection Mechanism of Stamp Duty across India with Respect to Securities Market Instruments', *Press Information Bureau*, 30 June 2006, https://www.pib.gov.in/PressReleasePage.aspx?PRID=1635399.
2. XV Finance Commission, *Finance Commission in Covid Times: Report for 2021–26*, https://fincomindia.nic.in/asset/doc/commission-reports/XVFC-Complete-Report-1.pdf.
3. Vyas, Hitesh, and Ritu Sarin. 'Ex-CEA Book: Union Bank Admits Lapses; Publisher Got over Rs 3 Crore', *The Indian Express*, 7 May 2025, indianexpress.com/article/india/ex-cea-book-union-bank-admits-lapses-publisher-got-over-rs-3-crore-9986833/..
4. Acharya, Viral V., 'On the Importance of Independent Regulatory Institutions: The Case of the Central Bank', A. D. Shroff Memorial Lecture, Mumbai, 26 October 2018, https://www.bis.org/review/r181030a.pdf.

Acknowledgements

Genes are primary determinants of one's physical and mental health and abilities. I thank my parents Sita Ram Garg and Satyawati Devi for passing on the genes and neurons that have conferred my good health and an alert, productive and sensitive mind.

Your siblings ensure that you grow up happily and with intellectual curiosity. I was quite fortunate in having a brilliant and can-do bunch of siblings. Satyendra, who joined the IPS and finally hung his boots as director general of police, Andaman and Nicobar Islands; Sudesh, who joined the IRS but quit it after 20 years as the departmental work was not exciting enough for his energy and intelligence; and Bharat, who, after completing his CA, has been managing the global finances first and investments later of India's multinational Motherson Group, have all done exceedingly well in their lives. My sister Sharda also played her innings and completed her service as a labour officer in Rajasthan. My youngest brother Avdhesh, whose birth I have referred to in Chapter 1 during the Emergency in 1975, unfortunately died young in 2003. I am thankful to all my four siblings for their support and companionship.

I have always been lucky to have good friends, some of whom helped me enormously in my most difficult childhood days when I did not sometimes have funds to deposit college fees, pay for my books and minimum expenditures to go to Jaipur for appearing in ICWA/IAS examinations. Some of my friends in the little group that formed in Ajmer to improve our spoken English also helped massively. I thank Sunil Saxena, Digvijay Mantri and Om Prakash Dadhich in particular.

During my service in the IAS, I was fortunate to work with many stalwarts – Priyadarshi Thakur, C.S. Rajan, Rajiv Mehrishi, Adarsh Kishore, M.L. Mehta, Dr E.A.S. Sarma, Dr P.K. Mishra and Nripendra Misra, to name a few. There were others who facilitated my journey in service with their kindness – S.D. Srivastava, for one. I thank all of them from the bottom of my heart.

I had five lucky breaks which altered the course of my service life. S.D. Srivastava saw to it that I was posted as additional collector, Development, and project director, DRDA, Jaipur. Dr E.A.S. Sarma was instrumental in getting me into the DEA. Vasundhara Raje Scindia and Rajiv Mehrishi entrusted me with the responsibility of principal secretary, Finance, in Rajasthan at the youngest possible age. Prime Minister Narendra Modi and Dr P.K. Mishra catapulted me to the World Bank as ED. Finally, Prime Minister Modi and Dr Mishra gave me the final big break when I was posted as secretary, Economic Affairs. I am thankful to all of them as without these unique forks in my path, my career in the IAS would not have been that eventful.

I also had five postings where either I did not have enough work to spend my office hours productively or there were dissatisfactions and problems, making the raison d'être of those postings meaningless. These were: CEO, Rajfed soybeans project, Kota; IG (R&S), Ajmer; director, SIPF, Jaipur; registrar, University of Rajasthan, Jaipur; and finally, joint and (later) additional secretary, Cabinet Secretariat, Delhi. I used the spare time available to study accounts, finance and economics of government functioning, which served me very well. I experimented with innovative and out-of-the-box solutions for the problems in these dysfunctional places, which almost invariably gave very promising results. The best of my learnings and innovations came from these postings. I thank all the powers that be who placed me in these positions, probably to ease me out or punish me, but which turned out to be excellent rewards for me.

I have been able to live a productive, healthy and happy life mostly because of the love, affection and care of my wife and soulmate Anjali. No thanks can be enough to acknowledge the value of the contribution she has made in my life. My two sons Shrey and Dhruv have grown to be excellent professionals and working with multinational corporations abroad. Dhruv read a good part of this book as well and offered many constructive suggestions. Shrey married Urvashi, and Dhruv Bhoomika, both of whom are women of great mind and substance. Much of *anand* in my life is due to this formidable foursome of Shrey-Urvashi and Dhruv-Bhoomika.

My trials and travails in the IAS have come into the public view thanks to the initiative taken by Swati Chopra who persuaded me to share this manuscript with her and Juggernaut. She has improved the structure and story of the book to make so eminently readable and relatable. Padmini and Rhea combed through the manuscript so meticulously that I honestly believe that there are no errors in it; neither is possibly a sentence that could have been framed better. My most sincere thanks to Chiki, Swati, Padmini and Rhea.

The central conclusion of my life in the IAS is that one must only be guided by the consideration of public interest. The conflict between a political executive's personal interests and overall public interest can be best resolved by the civil servant offering the political executive options and alternatives which serves the public interest well while also taking care of the executive's political interests. In situations where a politician is interested in serving only their political or personal interests at the cost of public interest, it is the duty of the civil servant to put his/her foot down and make sure that public interest is not compromised. That is the real steel in the IAS.

Subhash Chandra Garg
New Delhi, 13 July 2025